THE DYNAMICS OF POLITICAL COMMUNICATION

What impact do news and political advertising have on us? How do candidates use media to persuade us as voters? Are we informed adequately about political issues? Do 21st century political communications measure up to democratic ideals? *The Dynamics of Political Communication: Media and Politics in a Digital Age* explores these issues and guides us through current political communication theories and beliefs.

Author Richard M. Perloff details the fluid landscape of political communication and offers us an engaging introduction to the field and a thorough tour of the discipline. He examines essential concepts in this arena, such as agenda-setting, agenda-building, framing, political socialization, and issues of bias that are part of campaign news. Designed to provide an understanding and appreciation of the principles involved in political communication along with methods of research and hypothesis-testing, each chapter includes materials that challenge us by encouraging reflection on controversial matters and providing links to online examples of real-life political communication. The text's companion website provides expanded resources for students as well as materials for instructors to use in the classroom.

The Dynamics of Political Communication immerses readers in contemporary events through its coverage of online campaigning, effects of negative advertising, issues of gender bias in campaign politics, and image-management strategies in the 2012 campaign. It will prepare you to survey the current political landscape with a more critical eye, and encourage a greater understanding of the challenges and occurrences presented in this constantly evolving field.

Richard M. Perloff, Professor of Communication at Cleveland State University, has written a scholarly book on political communication, published in 1998, and a persuasion textbook, now in its fifth edition. He is well-known for his scholarship on the third-person effect and the role perceptions of media effects play in public opinion. A Fellow of the Midwest Association of Public Opinion Research, Perloff has been on the faculty at Cleveland State University since 1979 and served as director of the School of Communication from 2004 to 2011. He is an inveterate follower of political communication, reading the news each day in a coffee shop following a morning swim.

THE DYNAMICS OF POLITICAL COMMUNICATION

Media and Politics in a Digital Age

Richard M. Perloff

Routledge
Taylor & Francis Group

NEW YORK AND LONDON

Acquisitions Editor: Linda Bathgate
Development Editor: Mary Altman
Assistant Editor: Chad Hollingsworth
Editorial Assistant: Julia Sammaritano
Senior Production Editor: Gail Newton
Copyeditor: Judith Oppenheimer
Proofreader: Julene Knox
Typesetter: Keystroke
Indexer: Penelope Kent

First published 2014
by Routledge
711 Third Avenue, New York, NY 10017

and by Routledge
2 Park Square, Milton Park, Abingdon, Oxon OX14 4RN

Routledge is an imprint of the Taylor & Francis Group, an informa business

© 2014 Taylor & Francis

Library of Congress Cataloging-in-Publication Data
Perloff, Richard M.
    The dynamics of political communication : media and politics in a
    digital age / Richard M. Perloff, Cleveland State University.
        pages cm.
    Includes bibliographical references and index.
    1. Communication in politics—United States. 2. Mass media—
    Political aspects. 3. Digital media—Political aspects.
    4. Political campaigns—United States. 5. United States—Politics
    and government. I. Title.
    JA85.2.U6P467 2014
    320.01'4—dc23   2013019944

ISBN: 978-0-415-53183-2 (hbk)
ISBN: 978-0-415-53184-9 (pbk)
ISBN: 978-0-203-11531-2 (ebk)

Typeset in Times
by Keystroke, Station Road, Codsall, Wolverhampton

Printed and bound in the United States of America by Sheridan Books, Inc. (a Sheridan Group Company).

To my father, Robert Perloff (1921–2013)

Contents in Brief

PART THREE: COMMUNICATION AND THE ELECTION CAMPAIGN   233

Contents

Acknowledgments

As always, a book owes debts to many people. I am grateful for the contributions provided by a number of thoughtful individuals. First, I thank the reviewers who gave instructive feedback on the prospectus and different sections of the book. You pointed me in directions I had not thought of, suggested helpful research directions, and offered excellent ideas on issues to pursue more deeply. Second, I appreciate the insightful ideas and support of Routledge editor Mary Altman and senior editor Linda Bathgate, whose counsel is always supportive. I am also appreciative of the excellent work that Jonathan Herzberger did in developing a student-friendly companion website for the book. Thanks are also due to Gail Newton for her excellent, patient work with the details of manuscript editing.

Sharon Muskin, who has worked steadily and expertly on my previous books, was superb, locating terrific pictures and skillfully weaving them into the manuscript, while providing state-of-the-art technical assistance.

Colleagues generously responded to email messages and attachments with grace and supportive comments. Thanks to Lee Becker, Erik Bucy, Ann Crigler, Jim Dearing, Robert M. Entman, William "Chip" Eveland, J. Michael Hogan, Lance Holbert, Dennis W. Johnson, Jeffrey P. Jones, Jerry Kosicki, Anup Kumar, Kurt Lang, Paul V. Lavrakas, Joel Lieske, Jack McLeod, Bruce Newman, Markus Prior, Dietram Scheufele, Dhavan V. Shah, Natalie (Talia) Jomini Stroud, Michael W. Traugott, David Tewksbury, and Ellen A. Wartella.

Thanks also to inlaws Jerry and Selma Krevans, for coupling in many warm conversations an abiding enthusiasm for politics with wary skepticism of political actors. As always, I thank my father, for introducing me years ago to the political world outside our heads, to call on Walter Lippmann, and the important role ethics should play in public life. I thank my mother anew for the gift of learning she imparted, and the insatiable, never-to-be-quenched desire to acquire and integrate knowledge.

I appreciate the philosophical insights offered by my son, Michael, whose knowledge of virtue ethics helped inspire me to think more philosophically; conversations with my daughter, Cathy, whose political and journalistic courage know few bounds; and my wife, Julie, for her continued support of my writing projects.

Preface

Is there anything we don't know about the media and politics? Is there any view that has not been shown on television, shared on the Internet, or described in a book? Politics is a colorful, throbbing sport in America, bringing to mind presidential elections, red, white, and blue balloons unleashed from ceilings of majestic convention halls, the ubiquitous, understated presence of Barack Obama, raucous commentary of Rush Limbaugh, unabashed liberal anchors at MSBNC, the gaggle of reporters with smartphones, cameras, and gawky microphones trailing politicians across the planet, millions of election tweets, and YouTube political ads with endless parodies. The images that cross one's mind when political media are broached are seemingly endless. Now that's a big topic, people say when you disclose you are writing a book on media and politics, and of course they're right. Where do you begin? What do you emphasize? What do you leave out? What's your angle?

One thing I knew at the get-go: I did not want to begin with a scholarly lecture or stern warning about our ill-fated system, or by trotting out staid concepts. Something different that could pull in diverse readers, who varied in their political interest and knowledge levels, seemed appropriate. Something that could entice readers, excite them just a little and stimulate intellectual debate seemed a good way to launch a book on the colorful world of political media. Telling the story of Bill Clinton's sexual dalliance with Monica Lewinsky, coupled with the incendiary political battles over presidential privacy and impeachment, would titillate even the most jaundiced readers. I ordered lots of books and read as many as I could. But the more I read of Clinton in 1998, the more I realized this was old-hat, more an exception than the rule of politics, and perhaps not so relevant to an era of 21st century media. I gave some thought to telling the story of Barack Obama's amazing rise—his biracial beginning, experience as a community organizer, and discovery of his political voice—but felt this had been written and told so many times it would not intrigue many readers.

Then I read that Sarah Palin was touring historical sites on the Eastern seaboard, contemplating a potential presidential run, and seemed to have misspoken about Paul Revere's famous ride. The non-stop controversy over her comments, display of journalists going gaga over Palin's bus tour, and ceaseless buzz on the Internet seemed to be a little different, off the beaten track, and emblematic of the ways media and politics entwine in our era. Although I was never a fan of Palin, I admired her rise from a one-time sportscaster to governor to vice presidential nominee and was impressed by her ability to serve as a role model to millions of working women. A motif for the first chapter emerged.

Of course, Palin-as-exemplar of political communication was not enough to launch a scholarly textbook. As a starry-eyed undergraduate philosophy major, I had acquired some knowledge of several philosophical precepts and sometimes turned to those which I could still remember to shed light on knotty issues. Perhaps by introducing normative ideals of "what could and should be," I could offer a perspective with which to view the present. By offering guiding ideals on how political communication *should* work, I could hopefully sketch out a more optimistic vision to readers. Normative philosophy also provides a series of benchmarks to evaluate contemporary political communication, while also suggesting ways to improve the mottled, politically problematic present. It formed a foundation for Chapter 1.

One of the aims of this book is to introduce readers to political communication. Oddly, the many good books on political communication do not dwell much on this issue. What is political communication? How do you define the concept? Try it some time. If you ever have attempted to comprehensively define a complicated concept, you know how gnawing this can be. Struggling to define this term, I sought to differentiate political communication from propaganda and persuasion, and wrestled with intended versus unintended effects. I provided a definition in the second chapter, while also setting forth the distinguishing characteristics of political communication, notable features of communicating politically in a digital age, and some of the quandaries and contradictions of contemporary political media.

Another aim of the book is to richly describe the field of political communication. Academic textbooks frequently chart the history of a field of study, introducing readers to historical developments in, say, biology, sociology, or child psychology. It seemed to me that a political communication book should do the same, explaining the historical origins of political communication, beginning with Walter Lippmann's path-breaking work, propaganda analyses of the 1930s, the classic studies that every political communication graduate student knows well, twists and turns in the field, and the methods that help us find answers to theoretically driven hypotheses. I want students to appreciate that political communication is a bona fide interdisciplinary field that has a rich intellectual history with zestful debates about ideas. I hope readers will appreciate that political communication scholars coin concepts, develop theories, test hypotheses, and employ a host of social scientific methods to advance knowledge.

Political communication is a cross-disciplinary area. This makes it interesting and multifaceted. An important goal of the book is to introduce readers to the different arenas of the field and the ways that politics is communicated in elite, electoral, and everyday settings. This is fascinating stuff, overlaid with moral and ethical questions. I want readers to appreciate the concept of citizenship in a media age, how people acquire political attitudes through political socialization, and classic scholarship on agenda-setting, agenda-building, framing, and determinants of political news. I want students to understand the dynamics of presidential campaigns; the role of news, advertising, and debates; the increasing part played by social media; changing contours during different elections; and the controversial effects of that time-honored constant: money. I want them to appreciate that political media effects are complex, and just because people assume that media influence voters in decisive ways does not mean that they do. I hope students and instructors will question the effects of political media, viewing popular notions like news bias with a critical eye, and thoughtfully examining controversial issues, such as whether news is a watchdog or lapdog, if social media bolster or hinder democratic aims, and the benefits of negative advertising. My approach is not always to offer answers, but to raise Socratic questions. A theme is the quote by Pascal that underlines the "Reflections" boxes that appear throughout the book: "A man does not show his greatness by being at one extremity, but rather by touching both at once."

At the same time, I stand four-square (not in terms of the social networking website for cell phones, though I like the device!) behind certain general themes: Politics is not inherently manipulative or corrupt, but a critical part of a democratic society that, if used properly, can produce major improvements in people's lives. Journalism—news and investigative reports—while frequently misunderstood, acts as a critical safeguard against government corruption and can illuminate how politics works. Election campaigns are wonderful American inventions that put candidates before the people and force them to argue openly for policy ideas. Our politics, though colorful and adrenalin-filled, is imperfect and flawed, corroded by an excess of money. Communication has always shaped electoral politics (attesting to the importance of studying history), but today communication is a centerpiece, the place where politics happens, with different groups vying to control the agenda, seize the dominant frame, and influence policy, using a wealth of media—mass, electronic, and increasingly social and hand-held. Finally, the future of political communication—in America and abroad, for political media effects operate across electoral contexts—is there for the defining and shaping, with readers of this book hopefully seizing on a couple of concepts, threading them with their own experiences, and harnessing them creatively, taking the study or practice of political communication in flamboyantly new directions.

COMPANION WEBSITE ICON

 When you see this icon in the text, go to the book's companion website (**www.routledge.com/cw/perloff**). You will find links to related material for expanding the discussion, including political ads, speeches, and polls, as well as related webpages. The companion website also provides flashcards for reinforcing key terms and their definitions.

PART ONE

Foundations

1

The Panoply
of Political
Communication

Sarah Palin jaunted from city to city along the Eastern seaboard as speculation mounted that she might—just might—announce her candidacy for the 2012 Republican presidential nomination. It was spring, 2011, more than a year before the 2012 presidential election, but Palin and her entourage were in high gear. She had just launched her "One Nation" bus tour of American historical landmarks, and Palin was a study in political motion. Here she was, roaring through Washington, D.C. on the back of a Harley-Davidson, clad in a black leather jacket, thundering into town in time for the annual Memorial Day weekend motorcycle ride from the Pentagon to the Vietnam Veterans Memorial. Palin, the former governor of Alaska and 2008 Republican vice presidential candidate, was accompanied, as always, by a gaggle of reporters, photographers, bloggers, and other members of the mainstream media elite who hung on her every word, parsing, dicing, analyzing, and frequently critiquing what she said or they heard her say. There she was in historic Boston, speaking in that aw-shucks, small-town, good-ol' American twang that endeared her to supporters but angered opponents to the point of apoplexy. Standing in the home of Paul Revere, she spontaneously offered up a description of Revere's storied ride, speaking casually with a lilt in her voice:

> He who warned the British that they weren't going to be taking away our arms, by ringin' those bells and making sure as he's riding his horse through town to send those warning shots and bells that we were going to be secure and we were going to be free.

Fox News anchor Chris Wallace quickly seized the opportunity to pounce on her mistake. "You realize," he told her during the course of a television interview, "that you messed up about Paul Revere." And, in many ways, she had. She said Revere had warned the British. Yet as any school child who had recited the fabled Longfellow poem, "Paul

Revere's Ride," knew, Revere sallied from town to town to warn *the American colonists* that the British Army was advancing and poised to attack! According to Palin, Revere also wanted to make sure that the British did not seize the colonists' weapons and trespass on their freedom. To many observers, she had transformed Revere into a Second Amendment pro-gun zealot more than a decade before the U.S. Constitution had enshrined the right to bear arms.

Yet, in the TV interview with the ever-combative Wallace, Palin stuck to her story, maintaining that Revere *had* warned the British, ringing bells to let them know they had no right to take away American arms. As it turned out, there *was* a kernel of truth to her account. The British were traveling to Concord, Massachusetts to seize guns that colonists had stockpiled, and Revere did warn the British that colonial troops awaited them. But Revere issued his warning when he had been captured by British soldiers, and as a ploy to divert them from locating patriots Sam Adams and John Hancock (Fischer, 1994).

Yet truth was less important than the way Palin's comments played out on the political communication landscape. No sooner had she suggested that Revere had rung bells and sent up warning shots than their 21st century technological equivalents thundered across the land. Newspapers and network newscasts leapt onto the story. It became fodder on radio talk shows. Nowhere was the controversy more vitriolic than on the Internet, where it fueled pro- and anti-Palin blogs, countless tweets, YouTube videos, and numerous comments critical and in support of Palin. Some users called Palin names, but others defended her. "Is she drunk or just a total idiot?" one anti-Palin partisan wrote. A pro-Palin activist remarked that "these smug liberals in the media make the same kind of slip of the tongue as Palin. They knew what she meant. But they just had to jump on it. And the press wonders why people trust them less and less."

The fusillade became particularly intense on Wikipedia. The online encyclopedia's article on Revere registered half a million page views during the 10-day period that followed her remarks (Cohen, 2011). Palin's supporters added sentences to the Revere Wikipedia page that bolstered her account of his storied ride. The traffic became so heavy—with so many users inserting their views—that Wikipedia padlocked the site to prevent further changes.

The Palin episode is a rousing example of contemporary political communication in action—the inextricable relationship between media and politics; the predilection of the press to focus endlessly on an intriguing, but basically trivial, gaffe; and the ways that symbolic constructions of events can light up the Internet. And, for better or worse, it illustrates the ways that a political leader with strong convictions and a divisive message, burnished by celebrity wattage, can dominate the media landscape. The protagonist in the drama was Sarah Palin, whose rise in American politics speaks volumes about the art of 21st century political communication. Let's follow her saga for just a little longer, as it helps to set the stage for the discussions that follow.

PALIN AND POLITICAL MEDIA

Sarah Palin catapulted to national attention back in August, 2008 when Republican presidential nominee John McCain named her as his vice presidential candidate. McCain, behind in the polls, believed that he needed a vice presidential jolt to electrify the public and jump-start his campaign. Palin, the 44-year-old governor of Alaska with impeccable conservative credentials and an uplifting life story, seemed just the medicine the campaign needed. She was a beauty queen who married her high school sweetheart and bore five children: a son soon to depart for military duty in Iraq, three daughters, and an infant with Down syndrome (see http://www.sarahpac.com/).

Intrigued by politics, she ran for city council in the small town of Wasilla, Alaska, won and was twice elected mayor. In 2006 she was elected Alaska's first female governor, where she took on the oil producers, successfully fought for an oil tax, and helped the state build a $12 billion surplus (Green, 2011). She was her own woman: pro-life, pro-gun, and anti-stem-cell research.

What's more, she proved to be a compelling political orator, wowing the Republican national convention with a devastating combination of charm, clever attack lines, and rhetorical zingers, epitomized by an adlib that drew a hearty laugh from the partisan crowd: "You know, [what] they say [is] the difference between a hockey mom and a pit bull? Lipstick!" Her speech, with its down-home style and folksy rhetoric, was a stunning success, helping to boost McCain's poll numbers with key demographic groups (Spiker, 2011).

Political communication had played an instrumental role in enhancing her image. But it would soon dim her luster and trigger a series of problems that would dog her during the 2008 campaign and the years that followed. First, she revealed that her 18-year-old daughter, Bristol, was pregnant out of wedlock. This produced a firestorm of press coverage. Stories about her family began to take center stage. They became something of a Rorschach that tapped into different values. Conservatives respected Palin's defense of her daughter's decision to bear the child, admired her courage in raising a child with Down syndrome, and appreciated the religious values that guided her life. Liberals disagreed with her views on abortion and found it hypocritical that Palin, who supported abstinence-only education, had raised a daughter who had engaged in pre-marital sex.

Even after she and McCain lost to Obama–Biden in 2008, Palin continued to command substantial air time on television news. Infatuated by her star quality and intrigued by the possibility she might become a presidential contender sooner or later, the news media covered her comings and goings, even when they bordered on the trivial. Her attendance or non-attendance at political events overshadowed whatever actually occurred at the events themselves (Draper, 2010).

Ultimately, she, and her daughter, branched out from the news to the sports and entertainment media (see Figure 1.1). Building on the long tradition of politicians appearing on entertainment television to advance their political prospects, Palin took it one step further. She didn't just appear on a prime-time variety show like Richard Nixon or play her saxophone on late-night TV like Bill Clinton. She launched her own reality TV program, unabashedly called *Sarah Palin's Alaska*, complete with a theme song and a marquee listing of main actors and actresses (her husband and children, listed by first name only because, hey, everyone knew who they were, right?). Not to be outdone, her daughter Bristol became a contestant on *Dancing with the Stars* and advanced to the final round, provoking a series of controversial reactions, with supporters suggesting that she received audience votes because of her sunny optimism and cynics complaining that conservative Tea Party activists had flooded phone lines and sent thousands of text messages.

Figure 1.1 Sarah Palin, schmoozing with the public, showcases the inextricable relationship between media and politics, and the ways media, entertainment, and politics entwine in contemporary life.

Getty Images

Predictably, she made it onto *Family Guy*, somewhat amusingly or disrespectfully (as always with Palin, depending on your point of view). In one episode, the awkward, not-so-smart character on the show, Chris, went on a date with a character, Ellen, who has Down syndrome. "So what do your parents do?" Chris asked. "My dad's an accountant, and my mom is the former governor of Alaska," Ellen deadpanned.

Palin called the comment "another kick in the gut." Her daughter Bristol said the writers were "heartless jerks" who lacked compassion. You could understand the Palins' reaction. On the other hand, we're talking here about Seth MacFarlane, the show's creator who lives to lampoon. The actress who played Ellen has Down syndrome and complained that Palin lacked a sense of humor. Others suggested that in America, political figures and their families are appropriate targets for sarcasm, and that consuming sarcasm is as American as eating, say, baked Alaska.

Palin's "will she or won't she?" exploration of a presidential bid ended a year before the November, 2012 election when she announced, with much fanfare, that she would not run for president in 2012. Although she claimed that her decision stemmed from concern about the impact a presidential campaign would exert on her family, reporters suspected there were other important determinants, such as stiff competition from candidates already in the race, difficulty of starting a campaign late in the game without any infrastructure, and Palin's obvious satisfaction with her success as an author and a star on reality television (Shear & Zeleny, 2011). Alas, stars in the political universe rise and fall, and ultimately lose their luster. Palin proved to be no exception. In January, 2013 Fox News announced that it had decided not to renew her $1 million annual contract as a commentator, perhaps because she no longer offered a relevant or novel political perspective. But all was not forgotten. "Sarah, where are you?" asked one of her more than 3 million Facebook fans, no doubt hoping to catch one more installment of Palin's distinctive homespun brand of political conservatism.

Love or hate her, Sarah Palin is an American original. Her saga is a Rorschach on American politics, writ large. It showcases the rise of a self-made political woman, speaking her mind and displaying the courage of her convictions. Her narrative stirringly displayed a female vice presidential candidate who broke ground by embracing her femininity, while also espousing muscular Republican positions. On a broader level, the Palin saga illustrates a thriving media system that questions authority, as well as a public that enjoys following its leaders in the media and participating vicariously in their family extravaganzas.

The Palin saga also raises troubling questions. We have a leader, at one time a potential president, who preferred to deliberately deliver divisive messages rather than to engage the electorate by offering a blueprint for political change. A parade of journalists and colorful assortment of bloggers and entertainment reporters followed Palin slavishly, giving her statements considerable air time. Her stories frequently crowded out news of politically consequential events.

Welcome to 21st century American politics, an arena in which media, technology, and the symbols of communication occupy center stage. Nowadays, politics is almost entirely mediated, or Facebooked or Twittered, or whatever social media term you want to place in the past tense. Can you think of a political figure—candidate, elected official, or president—whom you have seen or spoken with in-person? For many, the answer is no. Isn't what you know, believe, and feel about politicians based on what you have gleaned from the multitude of media? That is one point on which conservatives, liberals, radicals, and even rabid conspiracy theorists agree. The media, broadly defined, are the place in which politics happens, "the center of gravity for the conduct of politics" (Jones, 2010, p. 23). As communication scholars remind us, "politics is carried out today in a multimedia environment that operates 24/7 and includes online and traditional media supplemented by entertainment shows as well as more typical venues such as news and political talk programs" (Kosicki, McLeod, & McLeod, 2011, p. 550).

Social media have assumed a particularly important role. Reporters measure deadlines by minutes, not hours, and they tweet updates on campaign strategic developments frequently throughout the day. Political advertising air wars no longer occur merely on television, but on YouTube, where candidates swiftly post attack ads and humorous responses. Striving to reach young adults, who are never without cell phones and frequently in touch with social media sites, candidates insinuate themselves into the edgy conversations on Facebook, Twitter, and Tumblr.

Nowadays we cannot talk about politics without invoking media, and we cannot understand contemporary media without appreciating the role they play in the political system. This book introduces you to the processes, effects, pros, cons, and vexing conundrums of contemporary political communication. Political communication is the study of how politics is communicated, the role played by language and symbols, and the impact that political messages exert on citizens, political leaders, and the larger political system.

A CONTEMPORARY APPROACH

This textbook will help you appreciate what may seem like a distant realm: how media convey the high-adrenalin, ego-driven, and ideologically polarized world of contemporary politics. The book is designed to introduce students to the many facets of political communication and the divergent perspectives on contemporary politics and media.

The text looks at the world of political media through different lenses than the ones we ordinarily apply to the political universe. We are accustomed to viewing politics through our own beliefs and attitudes. This book takes a step back and applies the vistas supplied by social science theories, research, and political philosophy. Our aim is to understand the processes of political communication, mediated communication effects on citizens and elections, and broader philosophical issues, such as whether the news serves democracy, if political persuasion dupes more than it delivers helpful information, and whether citizens are adequately informed. We want to criticize political communication when it fails to achieve democratic ideals and celebrate it when it spurs citizens to work collectively to change the status quo.

But let's get something straight at the get-go. When you talk about politics, many people's eyes glaze over. They think about gridlock in Washington and how Congress can't accomplish anything. Or maybe they think about Jon Stewart, Stephen Colbert, or Seth MacFarlane's *Family Guy*, and they crack a smile. In either case, they don't think politics has much to do with them. One of the themes of this book is they're wrong. Politics and political communication affect you, whether you like it or not. If you are digging deeper in your pockets or your purse to pay for college, politics affected you. Your university decided to raise your tuition because they're not getting as much money from the state on account of the fact that the state is getting less money from the federal government as a result of the national recession and all the problems caused by aftershocks of the financial crisis of 2008 that you don't understand but maybe now think you should read up on a little.

If you are nearly done with college and breathe a sigh of relief because you will still be covered on your parents' health insurance until you are 26, politics affected you. Obama's health care legislation enacted that provision, and the health care law was bitterly contested, nothing if not political. Or if you are finishing college, but are piping mad that the government is going to charge you a penalty if you choose not to buy health insurance when you are 27, then politics affected you. And if a friend recently returned from a stint in Afghanistan, where he told you the harrowing story of how a buddy died when a roadside bomb exploded near his vehicle, politics has affected you. Two U.S. presidents ordered troops to Afghanistan to fight terrorists that they believed threaten the security of the United States. You may staunchly agree with their assessment. Or you may believe the benefits were not worth the human sacrifice. In either case, international events led you to develop a political attitude.

Perhaps you are someone who has strong attitudes on issues like these. Maybe you care a lot about politics. Perhaps you feel our politics is too negative, the news ceaselessly consumed by the pratfalls of politicians rather than emphasizing the positives of politics. Alternatively, maybe you believe that people go into politics with altruistic goals and elected officials work hard to help citizens navigate a bureaucratic system. Or perhaps you're struck by how removed political communicators—both pundits and politicians—are from everyday life.

Opinions are the oxygen of democracy, and they are to be celebrated and appreciated. But—there is always a "but" when we talk about politics!—we also want to know if opinions like those above are based on fact and the degree to which they represent a reasoned evaluation of political communication.

To answer these questions and determine whether our political communication measures up to our ideals, we must begin by asking what we want the system to accomplish. We must examine what constitutes an ideal democratic system and the role communication ought to play in democratic politics. People frequently criticize the role political media play in democratic societies, but how can we come to terms with their criticisms without a working concept of democracy or a notion of the role communication *should* play in the process of self-government? To adequately appreciate contemporary political communication, one must begin first with ideals. We need to grapple with great thinkers' visions of how democracy should operate. To do this, we need to turn the clock back, and not just a little, but way back, to the time of ancient Greece, and then proceed chronologically to explore core visions of the democratic state.

Theoretical accounts that prescribe or suggest what ought to be are called **normative models**. The next sections of the chapter review normative precepts of classical Greek Democracy, liberal democracy, and the deliberative democratic approach. Guided by these philosophical perspectives, I subsequently outline four shortcomings of our contemporary media-centered democracy, along with a more general defense of democratic government. The final section of the chapter presents a roadmap of the chapters that follow.

WHAT DO YOU THINK?

People sometimes assume that politics is removed from everyday life. They assume it is something that "they"—the Washington, D.C. media and politicians—do. But this is not necessarily so. Which political issues do you care about and which ones have influenced your life? What do you think about the role the media play in politics? Are you a fan of media or more of a critic?

NORMATIVE THEORIES OF DEMOCRACY

Classical Direct Democracy

Athenian democracy was distinctive, unique in its time. It also has articulated key principles that have guided subsequent democratic theories and underpin contemporary democratic governments.

In ancient Greece, citizens ruled. In the 5th century B.C., an assembly with a quorum of 6,000 Athenians met over 40 times each year, discussing, debating, and making policy on taxes, foreign alliances, and declaration of war. Politics was the centerpiece of the polis or city-state. The classic democratic model embraced liberty and enshrined *equality*, emphasizing that each citizen was guaranteed the opportunity of "ruling *and* being ruled in turn" (Held, 2006, p. 17). The Greek model presumed that individuals directly participated in many everyday legislative and judicial activities. In the Greeks' direct democratic model, citizens were expected to participate in politics. The statesman Pericles put it bluntly. "We do not say that a man who takes no interest in politics is a man who minds his own business; we say that he has no business here at all" (cf. Held 2006, p. 14).

Imagine a politician who uttered those words today. She or he would be called an elitist (as well as a sexist), and would be parodied on YouTube. But, for the ancient Greeks, political participation was endemic to citizenship. The philosopher Aristotle endorsed this view, arguing that human beings were political animals. But he did not mean that people were political in the sense we sometimes use the term today—networking and conniving to gain advantage over others. Aristotle believed that the good life consisted of participation with others on common tasks and deliberating in public to determine just outcomes for the larger community.

Rhetoric (what we now call persuasion) played a central role in Greek society. Intense discussions preceded policy decisions, such as whether to invade a foreign land (Finley, 1973). According to Aristotle, the capacity to formulate reasoned arguments about justice and injustice predisposed people to form political communities where such issues could be discussed and solved (see Figure 1.2). Communication presumably helped to constitute a political community, defining and shaping the community's identity.

Although civics books traditionally sing the praises of Greek democracy, it has short-comings and nuanced complexities. The Athenian model enshrined equality, but allowed only male citizens over the age of 20 to participate in politics. Slaves outnumbered free male citizens, but they were precluded from participation. Women had few civic rights and no political rights whatsoever. To paraphrase Orwell (1946), all Athenians were (in theory) equal, but male Athenians were much more equal than others.

Liberal Democracy

There is not one model of **liberal democracy**, but many. The models have been articulated by some of the most famous theorists of democracy, including John Locke, John Stuart Mill, and James Madison. Liberal democratic concepts, which emphasize individual rights and representative government, are the ones that are popularly associated with democracy. However, liberal democracy theorists do not use the term "liberal" in the sense we use it today, as when we refer to liberal Democrats. Theoretically, the term corresponds more closely to "libertarian," emphasizing a system of democracy that preserves individual liberties and disdains government intervention.

Figure 1.2 The Greek philosopher Aristotle championed political communication, arguing that the good life involves active participation with others on common political tasks.

Shutterstock/Panos Karas

Liberal democratic theories evolved in the 17th and 18th centuries as people grew frustrated with the power of absolutist rulers and the many ways that European monarchies stifled individual freedom. Democratic government emerged as a way to protect individuals from oppressive use of political power. Liberal perspectives on democracy emphasize *the natural rights of individuals*—their right to life, liberty, property, and pursuit of happiness, to combine the writings of Locke and Thomas Jefferson. This was exciting and important stuff, the notion that individuals had inalienable rights that government could not sever. Liberal democratic approaches emphasized that an individual should be allowed to follow his (much later, her) own drummer in matters of speech, press, religion, and economics. People needed a sphere of life where despotic monarchs could not intervene. Thus, liberal theories embraced the *private sphere*: for example, private enterprise and private property.

But there was a problem. If people had inalienable rights, what role should government play? How could the need for order, preserved by government, be reconciled with individuals' rights? How could *might* be reconciled with *rights* (e.g., Held, 2006)? These are a quintessential questions, still relevant today, and the first liberal democrats developed a series of creative ideas. Noting that society had become too large and cumbersome for all to participate, they recognized that the Athenian notion of direct democracy was impractical for mass society. They advocated representative government, in which citizens elected others to stand in for them and represent their viewpoints on matters of policy. Elections provided a way to ensure that individuals determined government policy, making "public officials the servants rather than the masters of the citizenry" (Katz, 1997, p. 63).

Communication plays a key role in liberal democratic models. With its emphasis on the private market, liberal democracy theorists view politics as a marketplace of ideas, in which a variety of media products—good and bad, accurate and inaccurate—compete for audience attention. Just as different products compete in the economic market, political ideas collide in the intellectual marketplace. In the end, some philosophers argued, truth will win out. Censorship is problematic and unnecessary. John Stuart Mill pinpointed the problems with media censorship, famously noting that "if the opinion is right, [people] are deprived of the opportunity of exchanging error for truth: if wrong, they lose, what is almost as great a benefit, the clearer perception and livelier impression of truth, produced by its collision with error" (Mill, 1859/2009, p. 20).

Liberal democracy advocates call for a free, competitive press, in which a thousand flowers—roses and daisies, but also weeds and underbrush—bloom. In the 19th century, theorists embraced the penny press, newspapers that cost a penny and were filled with crime stories, as well as partisan papers that took political positions. Libertarian scholars of the 21st century similarly argue that society needs a no-holds-barred free press, one that includes mainstream media; public, educational television; cable television shows, which endlessly cover sexual indiscretions of celebrity politicians; blogs; and partisan websites. Noting that "people are able and willing to put aside their social biases," liberal theorists emphasize that "the best way to guarantee truth in the public sphere is free, open, and unchecked debate in which both error and truth have equal access" (Christians et al., 2009, p. 49).

Deliberative Democracy

Deliberative democracy theorists, the newest intellectual kids on the democracy block, take issue with liberal democratic theory. What could be wrong with liberal democracy, you may ask? How can one argue with freedom, liberty, and competition among ideas in the political marketplace? Deliberative democracy advocates look at liberal democracy through a different set of lenses, noting that the marketplace metaphor diminishes the deeper role that politics ought to play in the lives of its citizens. Voters are not mere *consumers* choosing among different political brands, but *citizens* whose thoughtful participation in politics serves as the foundation for democratic government. Politics, they emphasize, should not focus simply on protecting the *rights* of individuals, but on discovering ways to enhance the collective *good* of society. They urge "an imaginative rethinking of democracy offering a new kind of participation, one that not only gives citizens more power, but also allows them more opportunities to exercise this power thoughtfully" (Held, 2006, p. 235).

Deliberative democracy theories parallel other contemporary perspectives that emphasize the importance of the public sphere, as opposed to the private sector, and call for more citizen participation in politics (Barber, 1984; Habermas, 1996). Deliberative democrats, like other critics, maintain that we need to take democracy back from moneyed interests and elite institutions. More power to the people, they say, but let's make sure that people reflect thoughtfully on how they want this power to be used. Lamenting the *quality* of contemporary democracy, deliberative democracy theorists argue that our politics needs a cognitive revamping. A vigorous democracy requires that citizens: (a) engage in broad, reflective consideration of political issues; (b) take into account a variety of perspectives that extend beyond their own material self-interest; and (c) articulate sound arguments that can be competently justified in group settings and will ultimately influence public policy (Cohen, 1998; Gastil, 2008; Guttman & Thompson, 1996; Offe & Preuss, 1991).

To deliberative democrats, the platitudes of liberal democracy—liberty and equality—are nice, but without reflective thinking, our politics is nothing more than a loud cacophony of selfish interests competing futilely on the public stage. Deliberation advocates argue that we need more civil and respectful public dialogues, such as community forums that can help set agendas and shape municipal policy. They urge that journalists cut back on horse race reporting that focuses on election polls and consultants' strategies. Instead, deliberation proponents argue that journalists should embrace **public journalism**, which emphasizes ways that reporters can reconnect with the larger communities in which they work, elevating the concerns of the public over those of political elites (Rosen & Merritt, 1994).

When it comes to the Internet, deliberative democrats applaud websites like patch.com that offer citizens opportunities to discuss community problems. They embrace e-democracy programs, such as online public forums and collective dialogues on blogs, like DailyKos on the Left and RedStateDiaries on the Right, in which online members contribute ideas, others respond, and people can revise ideas in light of the thread of discussion (Perlmutter, 2008). In their attitudes toward communication and other topics, deliberative democrats hark back to the classical theorists of ancient Greece, arguing that a good life is lived in the context of a vibrant civic community that embraces citizenship (Finley, 1983).

Pulling the Democratic Strands Together

Each of the three perspectives celebrates democracy, focusing on different elements (see Table 1.1).

By braiding the different strands of these approaches, we can appreciate the core characteristics of democratic government. **Democracy** has five primary characteristics: (1) the right of all adult citizens to vote and run for office; (2) free, fair elections that involve competition between more than one political party; (3) individual liberty and freedom of expression, including for those who oppose the party in power; (4) a civil society characterized by the right to form associations, such as parties and interest groups, that attempt to shape the agenda and influence public policy; and (5) to the extent possible in a large complex society, opportunities for reasoned public deliberation on major national issues (Coleman & Blumler, 2009; Dahl, 1989).

POLITICAL COMMUNICATION: A CRITICAL APPROACH

Each of the three philosophical approaches to democracy assigns an important role to communication. To the ancient Greeks, vigorous debate and the formulation of cogent rhetorical arguments were core elements of direct democracy. In the view of liberal

Table 1.1 Three Normative Perspectives on Democracy.

Classical Greek Direct Democracy	Liberal Democracy	Deliberative Democracy
Principles		
Direct citizen participation	Natural rights of individuals	Reasoned public deliberation about issues
Equality	Representative government	Civil discourse
Citizen obligation to society	Private marketplace of ideas	Collective dialogue that influences policy
Communication emphasis		
Well-crafted rhetorical arguments	Free expression, no-holds-barred press	Forums/articles that encourage deliberation
Shortcoming		
Impractical in mass society	Treats citizenship as a private commodity rather than public good	Preachy and dismissive of decisions not based on pure deliberation

democracy advocates, free and open access to diverse media is the best way to guarantee truth and advocate different political ideas. For deliberative democrats, thoughtful reasoned dialogue builds the civic culture and "commitment to citizenship" that sustains democratic life (Christians et al., 2009, p. 102). Theorists of all three approaches would agree that you cannot have a vibrant democracy without thriving communication. "Free communication among the people," as James Madison noted, is an essential part of democratic self-government, the "only effectual guardian of every other right" (Sunstein, 2002, p. 155). The converse is also true, as Madison observed. A democracy that fails to provide critical information to its citizens, he suggested, "is but a prologue to a farce or a tragedy; or, perhaps both."

So, political communication is an important ingredient in a functioning democracy. Let's switch gears now, moving from normative theory to the descriptive facts on the ground. This raises the question of how political reality measures up to democratic ideals. In the view of many contemporary critics, it does not measure up well. Critics identify four key shortcomings in contemporary American democracy that represent departures from normative ideals.

1. *Citizens are neither able nor motivated to partake in politics.* Philosophers from Plato onward have lamented that individuals lack the cognitive competence and motivation to partake in democratic government. Such is the case in America today.

   "Vast numbers of Americans are ignorant," one scholar observed, and "not merely of the specialized details of government . . . but of the most elementary political facts—information so basic as to challenge the central tenet of democratic government itself" (see Delli Carpini & Keeter, 1996, p. 23). There is evidence to corroborate this claim. Just over a third of the public could accurately identify a right guaranteed by the First Amendment to the Constitution. Yet two-thirds could name a TV judge on *American Idol* (Breyer, 2010)! Americans are more ignorant of international affairs than are citizens in other industrialized western democracies (Iyengar & Hahn, 2011).

   The competence problem is compounded by a motivational deficit. Just over half of Americans vote in high-profile national elections, compared to three-fourths of their counterparts in Britain and Germany. Voter turnout in the United States is near the bottom of all democratic societies (Martinez, 2010). How can one place the United States among the pantheon of the world's democracies when its voters know so little and participate so infrequently?

2. *The media are neither free nor diverse.* Contrary to liberal democratic ethos, there is not a purely free and unfettered marketplace of political ideas. The media are

controlled by the rich and powerful. Five global companies own the majority of newspapers, magazines, motion picture studios, and broadcast stations in the U.S. (Bagdikian, 2004; Parenti, 2011). The Internet, critics point out, is dominated by multinational corporations, such as Google, Microsoft, and Time Warner.

Moreover, media content is distressingly similar in different regions of the country. Consider a culinary analogy: If you travel across the country and want to have dinner, you find a sadly similar set of choices. The Applebee's menu is the same in Augusta, in the Northeast, as it is in Anaheim in the West. Denny's serves the same food and doles out basically identical menus in Maine and California. The diet for news is equally homogenous, no matter where you happen to be: poll-driven election stories in newspapers, celebrity celebrations in magazines, and short political snippets on television. Not only is the content remarkably similar in different locales, critics point out, but there are preciously few instances in which print, broadcast, or Internet outlets offer stories that challenge the powers-that-be.

3. *Politics is awash in greenbacks.* Contrary to democratic ideals, all citizens do not have equal access to the political process. Those with more money—millionaires and billionaires—exert an outsized effect on politics. In 2012, immensely wealthy Americans, political action committees, and other groups sank a record $6 billion into the presidential election, an amount likely to be topped in 2016. As a result of a controversial 2010 Supreme Court decision, spending by independent political groups has grown exponentially over the past several years. Major donations are frequently kept secret and donations are slipped through tax-exempt groups that can hide the names of donors who doled out the cash. This runs counter to democratic norms of transparency.

4. *Contrary to deliberative democratic ideals, media coverage of politics is simplistic and superficial, and negative.* Political journalist Joe Klein (2006) spoke for many Americans when he lamented that "I am fed up with the insulting welter of sterilized, speechifying insipid photo ops, and idiotic advertising that passes for public discourse these days" (p. 13). Other critics lament that the media focus more on scandals and candidates' personalities than on serious political arguments, offering air time to battering arguments between liberals and conservatives on cable TV talk shows (see Figure 1.3).

Add to this the loud, one-sided views on talk radio and the Internet, visceral attack ads, and candidates who are quick to exploit public fears to get elected.

Political manipulation and angry, cacophonous talk may exert dispiriting effects on voters. As one political leader observed, "the public, and particularly young people,

Figure 1.3 In the daily ideological battles on political talk shows, commentators passionately advocate for their positions, while giving short shrift to the opposition. Here, Fox News talk show host Sean Hannity speaks with a conservative compatriot, former Speaker of the House and 2012 presidential candidate Newt Gingrich. Are these high-octane programs good for democracy? Libertarian theorists and deliberative democrats offer different perspectives.

Getty Images

now have less faith than ever in . . . democracy. We who constitute the 'political class' conduct politics in a way that turns off our voters, readers, listeners and viewers . . . Too many people believe that government is something that is done to them" (Coleman & Blumler, 2009, p. 1).

Perspectives

Concerned by these problems, critics argue that American politics is in jeopardy. They maintain that our system is in crisis. The arguments are cogent and the issues that critics raise are disturbing.

Is there another point of view? In fact, you can raise questions about each of the criticisms. A theme of this book is that multiple perspectives on problems shed light on complex issues. Thus, in response to the first lamentation about citizens' lack of knowledge, one might ask whether voters can forget some of the civics they learned in high school, yet still be capable of evaluating the fitness of politicians for public office. Second, if America's media system is dominated by only a few companies and content so homogenous, how come new blogs keep popping up that challenge the powers-that-be? Third, regarding money in politics, one might invoke First Amendment freedoms to argue that political groups should be free to spend as much as they wish in elections. And contrary to deliberative democrats, who decry political marketing and simplistic persuasive appeals, can't you defend these by arguing that persuasive appeals help voters keep abreast of candidates' issue positions (see Reflections box). And aren't there plenty of examples of political leaders, from Reagan to Obama, who have harnessed masterful rhetoric to impel citizens to action?

REFLECTIONS: CAMPAIGN SOUND AND FURY

A man does not show his greatness by being at one extremity, but rather by touching both at once.—Pascal

This epigram emphasizes the importance of appreciating multiple points of view. It celebrates the beauty of approaching issues from divergent perspectives, emphasizing that one gains wisdom by viewing issues from many different sides. This approach underlines the Reflection boxes that appear here and in the chapters that follow. Each box poses a contemporary problem, frequently offering a pro and a con. It invites students to reflect on the complexities, focusing on the virtues and shortcomings of each perspective or broad issue. Here we go:

Let's say it is presidential election season, and you turn on the television or flick on your computer. Here is what you will glimpse: the latest report on the poll numbers; a reporter breathlessly discussing the neck-and-neck race to the finish line between the candidates for the highest office in the land; one candidate's consultant lamenting the onslaught of negative advertising in the "air wars," while a strategist for the rival candidate proudly explains how her side has outmaneuvered the opposition by mounting an unbeatable, high-tech "ground game."

Continued

You would think it was Super Bowl Sunday. But it's not. It is the way our media communicate about the presidential election in the United States of America.

The media rarely offer civil, thoughtful dialogue on contemporary political issues (e.g., Sobieraj & Berry, 2011). This critique of contemporary politics is persuasive and familiar. Politics is dominated by a strategic, superficial focus on who is ahead and searing attack ads. It lamentably lacks a discussion of broad issues facing the country. But the system has its defenders.

Defenders point out that campaigns are not designed to educate. Their purpose is to offer a forum where candidates compete, advocate for their side, and make their case to the electorate. Candidates hire pollsters to discover how they are perceived by voters; they use this information to build winning coalitions. They aggressively advocate for what they believe and try to persuade voters to accept their political positions. Reporters are supposed to cover the ins and outs of the political race. Citizens make their best judgment, and when the election is over, the winner implements new policies.

In addition, negative back-and-forth cable commentary gets a lot of bad press. But viewed differently, what is wrong with it? Don't we want a democracy where people harbor strong views? We have tough problems and they evoke strong sentiments. Commentators speak passionately in favor of or against particular views. Doesn't passion indicate that people care? Doesn't a battle of liberal and conservative ideas advance the cause of democracy by allowing divergent perspectives to gain a hearing, with the most articulate position ultimately gaining ascendancy? Or does it increase cynicism, elevate argument, and place elocution over education?

What do you think?

Who is right? Who's wrong? The answers are neither easy nor simple. Some of the problems that face the U.S. are endemic to democracy. Democracy is an imperfect form of government. It depends on citizens to make decisions, and citizens have pet peeves and biases. It relies on elected officials to put aside self-interest and work for the common good, but politicians are ambitious. Democracy depends on different parts of government to work together, but the Constitution disperses power among different branches of government, impeding efforts to find common solutions (see Box 1.1). Democratic society depends on media to relay critical facts and opinions, but in a capitalist and partisan society, the media can be influenced by the lure of profit and partisans who speak with the loudest voices.

BOX 1.1 HOW WE GOT HERE

During the steamy summer of 1787, the framers of the American Constitution labored over language and debated principles in Philadelphia. There was much curiosity about what these men of reputation and privilege had accomplished behind closed doors. A large crowd formed, gathering outside the building where they met. One of those milling about the crowd cornered Benjamin Franklin as he left the meeting, asking Franklin, "What have you given us?"

"A republic, if you can keep it," he groused.

I love his quote. It gives me goose bumps every time I read it. *A republic, if you can keep it.* Franklin was making two important points. First, he emphasized that the new United States of America was not a direct democracy, where each citizen participated directly in political affairs. The delegates who drafted the Constitution recognized that the country was too large to permit citizens to partake in each decision (as had occurred to some degree in ancient Athens). In addition, the Founding Fathers did not want a direct democracy. They did not trust the masses, fearing they would be overtaken by their passions and let emotion interfere with reason. However, although the new government did not give citizens direct rule, it was democratic in that it enshrined popular consent. As a **republic**, it enabled citizens to choose the individuals who would represent them.

The second noteworthy aspect of Franklin's comment was his emphasis on duty. He was at pains to suggest that everyone had an obligation to work for the public good and do their civic utmost to ensure that a political experiment over which much blood had been shed could survive.

Meeting in Philadelphia in the hot summer of 1787, the delegates at the Constitutional Convention accomplished a great deal. They created "a wholly new written constitution, creating a true national government unlike any that had existed before. That document is today the world's oldest written national constitution" (Wilson & Dilulio, 2001, p. 24).

The Constitution had strengths and shortcomings. A strength was the Bill of Rights, a gift and American invention. The Bill of Rights, the first 10 Amendments

Continued

to the Constitution, includes freedom of religion, speech, press, and assembly (the First Amendment); right to bear arms (the now-controversial Second Amendment); no unreasonable searches or seizures (Fourth Amendment); prohibition against a person testifying against himself or herself (Fifth Amendment); and right to a speedy, public impartial trial with defense counsel (Sixth Amendment).

A shortcoming was race. Although slavery continued apace in the new United States, subjugating one people to the whims and powers of another, the Constitution said nothing about this. Its silence was deafening. In fact, the Constitution sanctioned slavery, determining apportionment of seats in the new House of Representatives by counting all free persons and three-fifths of "all other persons," namely slaves. Many of the signers of the Declaration and Constitution owned slaves, yet they did nothing to halt its continuance.

There were other noteworthy aspects of the founding legal document. Concerned that power could be vested in one group and that a majority of citizens would selfishly act to the detriment of others, the framers decided that safeguards were needed. Of course, as Madison famously said, "if men were angels, no government would be necessary." But men (and women) were not angels. Thus, "ambition must be made to counteract ambition," he observed.

The framers insisted on **separation of powers**, whereby power is constitutionally shared by three branches of government: the executive (e.g., president), legislative (Congress) and judicial (Supreme Court). This involves the elegantly articulated checks and balances among the three branches. For example, Congress can act as a check on the president by refusing to approve a bill the president favors. The president can serve as a check on Congress by refusing to sign—or vetoing—a bill it has passed. The Supreme Court can perform a check on the president by declaring the president's actions to be unconstitutional and it can check Congress by ruling that a law is unconstitutional (Wilson & Dilulio, 2001).

The strength of checks and balances is that they restrain one branch of government and allow powers to be dispersed among a pluralism of groups. A drawback is gridlock: each branch checks the other and nothing gets accomplished. This is a problem we face today. Congress and the White House can't agree on how to reform entitlements like Social Security or Medicare, and nothing gets done.

Nevertheless, the Constitution remains a vital document, providing legal guidance on social dilemmas, some of which the framers anticipated, many others raising questions they could have never expected. Whatever its flaws, it offers the nation a civilized, frequently elegant, way to reconcile conflict.

Yet for all its flaws, democracy remains, as Winston Churchill famously said, the worst form of government, except for all the others. Democracy's advocates make its case by noting that democracy grants all citizens an inherent, equal right to self-determination, is more likely than other forms of government to maximize the collective good, and offers people opportunities to fulfill their human potential by working for the public good (Delli Carpini & Keeter, 1996).

Consider this seemingly unrelated, but actually salient, example: Over the course of the thousands of years the world has existed, a famine has *never* occurred in a democracy (Sen, 1981). Noting that famines do not inevitably result from a scarcity of food, but have their roots in social and economic decisions, political philosopher Cass Sunstein (2001) explains that "when there is a democratic system with free speech and a free press, the government faces a great deal of pressure to ensure that people generally have access to food" (p. 90). In an undemocratic system, governments are more corrupt and lack an incentive to allocate resources equitably. Democracy is justified both by its intrinsic good and by the outcomes it produces.

Political theorist Michael Mandelbaum (2007) reminds us that democracy has "a good name, the best of any form of government" (p. xi). Democracy earns its esteemed status, he notes, by crystallizing "the relationship between two entities: the government and the people it governs" (p. 104). Communication plays a central role here by connecting the leaders who govern with the people they govern. How this happens, how effectively it works, and how well it comports with democratic ideals are grist for the chapters that follow.

WHAT DO YOU THINK?

Do you believe that the mainstream media—and social networking—do more good or more harm in contemporary politics? What might be some of their positive and negative influences? Taking it one step further, try your hand at this more difficult issue: How might advocates of classical direct democracy, liberal democracy, and deliberative democracy view the increasing role played by social media in contemporary politics?

PLAN AND GOALS OF THIS BOOK

The text explores political communication, describing what it is, how it works, and why it exerts the impact it does. It looks at the "should" questions as well, examining whether political communication content and effects are good or bad for the political system, and just what is meant by the terms, "good and bad." There is a great deal of discussion of these issues in contemporary life, at water coolers, Starbucks, on the ubiquitous media, and in the tell-all Internet. Some people (especially those who follow Fox News) claim that news contains a left-liberal bias; others (the ones who like MSNBC) claim that it props up the conservative Establishment, and still others argue that news is fairly fair. Some critics argue that political campaigns sell candidates like advertisers sell soap. Other scholars point to the ways that online technology manipulates voter sentiments. Still others passionately defend political campaigns, arguing that they allow proponents of different policy positions to make their case to the electorate.

The text examines these issues, introducing students to an array of theories, research findings, and broad perspectives. You may find that you fiercely disagree with what some activists advocate and staunchly agree with what others contend. You may find that you are ambivalent, seeing both sides of the coin. You may find yourself rethinking some of your assumptions about political communication in light of what you read. The book is designed to increase your understanding of the super-charged, volatile, sometimes-unfathomable realm of political communication. It intends to help you appreciate what political communication is, why it works as it does, and the impact of the media and the Internet on politics. The book will introduce you to contemporary academic perspectives on political communication, attempting to deepen your under-standing of why politics is communicated as it is, how this differs from the historical past, what is problematic about today's communication, and which aspects are worthy of emulation. Technology, which plays an ever-increasing role in contemporary politics, is discussed throughout the book, with applications described in many chapters. It is important to appreciate that technological changes evolve over time and can be under-stood by appreciating the context in which they occur (Wolfsfeld, Segev, & Sheafer, 2013).

The book is organized into three sections. The first section explores the foundations of political communication. This chapter introduced the topic and described guiding philosophical concepts. Chapter 2 describes the main features of political commu-nication, focusing on the distinctive characteristics of contemporary political media. Chapter 3 explores the colorful history of the political communication discipline, ways it has changed over the years, and abiding concepts and methods that are harnessed to study political media effects.

The fourth and fifth chapters explore citizenship in a media age. Chapter 4 examines an issue central to democracy—citizens' knowledge of politics and understanding of government. The chapter describes what Americans know and don't know about politics, as well as the role contemporary media play in imparting political information. Chapter 5 examines political socialization, focusing on the processes by which a nation inculcates democratic values and political attitudes in its citizens. Media content—both news and satire—plays a key role in forming beliefs about politics.

The second part of the book focuses on political news, examining major theories of news effects and content. Chapters 6, 7, and 8 offer in-depth discussions of three key perspectives: agenda-setting, agenda-building and framing. You may have heard the phrase "the media set the agenda" or "that's how they're *framing* that problem." These three chapters take you deep into these domains, shedding light on concepts, processes, and effects of news, as well as the role news plays in policymaking. Chapters 9 and 10 follow up the discussion of news effects by unpacking the news, examining the many factors that shape political news. Is news biased? Does news reflect reality? Is political news a watchdog or lapdog? The chapters explore these issues in depth, offering answers that may surprise you.

The third part of the book focuses on a centerpiece of American democracy: the presidential election campaign. Chapters in Part Three explore the role communication plays in election campaigns, with a focus on the presidential election. Chapter 11 takes a foray through American political campaign history, examining how campaigns have changed over the past two centuries. The chapter describes the main features of today's media-centric campaign, the central role image management plays, and pivotal influences of online technology-based campaigning. Chapter 12 describes the key players and forces in election campaigns. Chapter 13 focuses on the presidential nomination process, examining the central role news plays in the 18-month-long presidential election campaign, from the multitude of events that occur before the primaries, through primaries and caucuses to the nomination conventions. You will read about the nomination journeys traveled by Bill Clinton, Hillary Clinton, Barack Obama, Mitt Romney, Rudy Giuliani, and a host of dedicated, ambitious also-rans.

The next three chapters examine the persuasive impact of campaigns on voters and the political system. Chapter 14 looks at persuasion front-and-center, reviewing theories of political persuasion and how candidates use communication to change voter sentiments. Chapter 15 gives a full-court press to the always controversial issue of political advertising. The chapter describes the influences of advertising in presidential campaigns, pros and cons of negative ads, and the ethical quandaries that surround political advertising. Chapter 16 discusses the history and impact of presidential debates, offering a balance sheet on a promising, but imperfect, campaign format. A postscript at the end of this chapter brings these issues together, broaching the problems of contemporary campaigns, but also spotlighting some surprising areas where American politics still glistens.

CONCLUSIONS

This chapter began by calling on the story of Sarah Palin, who rose from Alaskan obscurity to become a major player in the political scene. Palin provides a rousing example of contemporary political communication: the inextricable linkage between media and politics, the seamless relationship between news and entertainment, and ways that the public projects its own meanings on what happens in the world of politics.

People have many opinions about politics, which is as it should be in a democracy. In order to assess the quality of these opinions—to separate out the philosophical wheat from the chaff—normative philosophies of democracy were reviewed. Truth be told, there is not one theory of democracy, but many, with each offering different perspectives on the proper role of citizens, government, and communication.

The classical Greek model emphasized direct citizen participation in politics and citizens' obligation to contribute to the common good of the community. Liberal democratic theories stress individual liberty, politics as a marketplace of ideas, in which truth emerges in its collision with falsehood, and a feisty no-holds-barred press that challenges government. The deliberative democratic model, arguing that the liberal marketplace metaphor diminishes the deeper role politics ought to play in public life, highlights the importance of thoughtful consideration of political ideas and communications that try to encourage collective deliberation on community problems.

In practice, democratic societies, such as the United States, do not measure up to these normative ideals. American democracy is fraught with paradoxes, and shortcomings. Critics argue that in the U.S., citizens are neither able nor motivated to participate in politics, media are neither free nor ideologically diverse, politics is awash in money, and political discourse is simplistic and superficial, hardly a paragon of deliberative thought. Critics see the contemporary democratic glass as half empty, but defenders of the U.S. system view it as more than half full, doing more good than harm. They emphasize that the system offers multiple opportunities for citizen participation, encourages candidates from diverse cultural and economic backgrounds to hold public office, and, through a vital system of mass communications, offers a way to hold leaders accountable for their mistakes.

Scholars with different political perspectives agree that, for all its inherent shortcomings, democracy remains the best form of government that humans have developed. Communication plays a critical role by connecting leaders with the citizens they govern. How this happens, how effectively it works, and how well it comports with democratic ideals are the focus of the chapters that follow. So get ready for a ride through the dynamic, active, zany, troubled, but vital, world of political communication; hold on to your hat, and prepare to consider a multitude of new ideas and even some bumpy jostling of cherished political assumptions. You may end up reviewing, recalibrating, or even reconsidering some of your beliefs.

CHAPTER

2

What Is Political Communication?

What comes to mind when someone mentions *politics*? Wheeling and dealing? Candidates posing for the camera, offering up slimy, smarmy smiles? Talk shows on Fox or MSNBC where the guests talk soberly about "the problems in Washington" and everybody disagrees with everyone else? Merciless parodies of politicians by Jon Stewart and Stephen Colbert? Endless tweets, blogs, and chatter on the Internet about why Republicans or Democrats are really stupid? Spin?

Does that cover it?

Notice I didn't say anything positive. That's because for most people, the word *politics* evokes sighs, recriminations, and even disgust. "It's just words," voters tell pollsters, when asked to describe their views of politics. One voter lamented that politics involves "such a control of government by the wealthy that whatever happens, it's not working for all the people; it's working for a few of the people" (Greenberg, 2011, p. 6). We say "it's just politics" when we want to deride the actions of elected representatives. However, political scientist Samuel Popkin says "that's the saddest phrase in America, as if 'just politics' means that there was no stake" (cf. Morin, 1996, pp. 7–8).

Consider this: One of the greatest presidents of the United States was "one of the most astute professional politicians the country has produced" (Blumenthal, 2012, p. 34). Abraham Lincoln cut deals, gave political favors, and applied canny strategic skills to persuade Congressmen to approve the Thirteenth Amendment which abolished slavery from the U.S. Constitution. When one Congressional representative indicated he would support the amendment, the president rewarded him by appointing him minister to Denmark. Lincoln recognized that "great change required a thousand small political acts" (Blumenthal, 2012, p. 35). The Stephen Spielberg movie *Lincoln* celebrates

Lincoln's moral and political achievements in persuading Congress to pass the Thirteenth Amendment (see Figure 2.1).

Politics calls up negative associations, but it can be harnessed for good, as well as pernicious, outcomes. Without politics, landmark legislation on the minimum wage, Medicare, tax reform and health care would never have been enacted. On the other hand, political logrolling and favor-giving helps explain why Congress failed to enact stringent gun control legislation in the wake of the Newtown massacre. Political scientists view politics as the science of deciding who gets what, when, and why (Lasswell, 1936). More complexly, **politics** is "a process whereby a group of people, whose opinions or interests are initially divergent, reach collective decisions which are generally regarded as binding on the group, and enforced as common policy" (Miller, 1987, p. 390). Politics is endemic to democracy.

A couple of centuries ago you could explain American politics without talking much about the media. In the 19th century, political party bosses ran the show. A coercive quid pro quo frequently operated: Bosses gave jobs to new immigrant voters and in exchange immigrants gratefully voted the party line. Chomping cigars and spewing smoke into the political air, party leaders played a key role in selecting party nominees. That has changed. The road to the White House winds through CNN, Fox, and *The New York Times*, while at the same time snaking through Twitter, Facebook, and countless blogs.

Figure 2.1 Abraham Lincoln showcased the ways politics could be harnessed for morally positive ends. He used the tools of political persuasion to convince Congress to pass the Thirteenth Amendment, which abolished slavery.

iStockphoto

We use the term political communication rather than more popular terms, like political media or media and politics, because communication captures the broader, symbolic process by which people transmit and interpret messages and confer meaning on the universe in which power is wielded. This chapter presents a broad-based introduction to political communication. It describes the main features of political communication, discussing the different components and offering examples.

DEFINING POLITICAL COMMUNICATION

What is political communication? Scholars have advanced a number of helpful definitions, and the present view builds on contemporary perspectives (e.g., Denton & Kuypers, 2008; McNair, 1995; Smith, 1990). **Political communication** is the process by which language and symbols, employed by leaders, media, or citizens, exert intended or unintended effects on the political cognitions, attitudes, or behaviors of individuals or on outcomes that bear on the public policy of a nation, state, or community. There are several aspects of the definition.

First, the definition emphasizes that political communication is a process. It does not occur with the flick of a wrist, or flipping of a lever. A president can propose a particular initiative, but to turn an idea into a credible bill and a bill into a law, the chief executive must persuade Congress, which involves multiple influence attempts on legislators, mediated by countless communiqués with the public. A journalistic exposé of corporate malfeasance that produces a policy change does not magically exert an impact. Instead, it unleashes a variety of forces, including changes in public opinion, which, through poll results, influence policymakers, who, themselves, must consider the most effective and politically advantageous ways of altering policy.

Second, political communication calls centrally on words and symbols. Political communication can be viewed as "the practice of using language to move people to think and act in ways that they might not otherwise think and act" (Ball, 2011, p. 42). Leaders harness the power of language—colorful phrases, apt metaphors, syntax, and rhythm—to mold attitudes and move citizens. Presidents, from Franklin Delano Roosevelt to Ronald Reagan and Barack Obama have aroused the imagination of Americans, using speech to captivate, language to mobilize, and metaphors to galvanize support for their policies. FDR's "the only thing we have to fear is fear itself," words heard as families huddled together listening to radio sets during the cold, despairing days of the 1930s Depression, offered up hope and optimism, activating the collective confidence of a country. Ronald Reagan spoke tender words to the nation's school children after they watched, in tearful disbelief, as the space shuttle *Challenger* exploded during take-off in January, 1986. "The future doesn't belong to the fainthearted. It belongs to the brave. The *Challenger* crew was pulling us into the future, and we'll continue to follow them," Reagan said, harnessing the best of presidential rhetoric to help a grieving nation cope with tragedy, using words to soothe and language to transform grief into hope for the future.

Barack Obama aroused passions with his eloquent rhetoric. Speaking at the 2004 Democratic convention, four years before he ran for president, Obama used a series of verbal parallelisms as he called on a benevolent rhetoric of unification, warning "those who are preparing to divide us" that "there's not a liberal America and a conservative

America; there's the United States of America. There's not a Black America and White America and Latino America and Asian America; there's the United States of America."

The language of political communication is laden with symbols. A **symbol** is a form of language in which one entity represents an idea or concept, conveying rich psychological and cultural meaning. Symbols include words like justice, freedom, and equality, and non-verbal signs like the flag or a religious cross. In America, elected officials frequently invoke the American flag, the Founding Fathers, Lincoln, Jefferson, freedom, liberty, and equality. (And let's not forget the Tea Party, the colonial protest-inspired name for a conservative political party.)

Political communication involves the transfer of symbolic meanings, the communication of highly charged emotional words that can arouse, agitate, and disgust. Words convey different meanings to different groups. To conservatives, freedom conjures up immigrants' dreams of owning a business in the USA or practicing religion as they see fit. To liberals and minorities, freedom calls to mind the opportunity to display one's own creed publicly without fear of prejudice. It also conveys empowerment, the way a previously victimized group can throw off the shackles of oppression, openly expressing its own cherished values. Political messages inevitably call up different meanings to different groups, an inevitable source of friction and conflict in democratic societies.

Third, there are three main players in political communication. The first is the broad group of leaders and influence agents. These are the "**elites**" of politics, who include elected officials, as well as the plethora of Washington, D.C. opinion leaders spanning members of the president's Cabinet, policy experts, and chieftains in the vast government bureaucracy.

The next player or players are the media. This increasingly diverse group includes the conventional news media, bloggers, people armed with a cell phone camera and an attitude who call themselves citizen-journalists, partisan promulgators of websites, and the gaggle of political entertainment hosts and comedians.

The centerpiece of political communication is the citizenry. Citizens are a cacophonous combination of the politically engaged and opinionated, along with the indifferent and woefully ignorant. The citizenry includes those who actively partake in civic groups— for example, pro-Life and pro-Choice; evangelical Christian and unabashedly atheist; Wall Street investors and blue collar unions, as well as pro- and anti-fur, vegan, and virulently pro-red-meat.

Fourth, political communication effects can be intended or unintended. A presidential speech is intended to influence, and a flurry of favorable emails and text messages received at the White House after the speech are examples of intended effects. A negative political advertisement is designed to cause voters to evaluate the targeted candidate more unfavorably, and declines in the attacked candidate's poll ratings illustrate an intended communication effect. But not all political communication effects are intended by the communicator.

In some instances, communicators do not deliberately set out to change an individual's attitudes. When a sexual scandal breathlessly discussed in the news media stirs people up and leads them to tell pollsters they believe the offending politician should resign, the news has exerted an impact, but not one that the news media intended. Journalists are not interested in changing people's attitudes toward the political figure so much as they are hoping to expose an aspect of a politician's behavior that the public official would rather you not see. Reporters believe that it is their professional responsibility to offer a critical perspective on the men and women who wield great power. Their other motives are more personal and self-interested: to grab the big headline, gain the byline or on-air credit, or, in the case of network executives, broadcast a story that attracts viewers and boosts ratings. But their goal is not to *persuade* the public to change its attitude in a partisan direction.

In still other cases, a story covered on television or streamed across the Internet can exert an impact that was neither intended nor anticipated. During the height of the 2012 campaign, a secretly recorded video of remarks Mitt Romney made at a fundraiser surfaced. Romney's comments that 47 percent of Americans do not pay income taxes, "believe that they are victims," and do not take "personal responsibility" for their lives sparked controversy and reduced his credibility with voters. Neither the mainstream media that covered the story (nor Romney, of course) intended to transmit a message that would taint Romney's image. But in the 24/7, no-holds-barred media environment, communications like these can exert a slew of effects that few anticipated.

In America, political communication casts a wide net. Political communication includes messages to influence, such as presidential speeches, campaign debates, and public campaigns designed to influence attitudes on topics ranging from health care to partial-birth abortion. This includes stealth campaigns, designed to influence attitudes by calling on the armamentarium of contemporary political marketing research (Manheim, 2011). A variety of political action committees, funded by billionaires, developed attack ads in the 2012 presidential campaign that eluded a paper trail. Donations were passed through tax-exempt advocacy groups that could legally shield the names of the donors who signed the checks (Confessore & Luo, 2012). The public did not know who funded the campaign, violating an ethos of transparency.

Political communication also encompasses news, relayed on television and via the Internet. It also includes Rush Limbaugh, Homer Simpson, *Family Guy*'s Peter Griffin,

South Park's Stan Marsh, Michael Moore, political talk radio, YouTube videos, Facebook posts, and other media content that touches on what people think and feel about politics (e.g., Davis & Owen, 1998). Political communication involves more than media. It includes old-fashioned dinner table political arguments, trying to persuade a friend to join a campus protest, and knocking on doors on wintry mornings to gather signatures for a state-wide petition.

WHAT DO YOU THINK?

What are examples of political messages that are intended to persuade, ones that are intended to entertain or communicate information, and ones that blur the line? In particular, where does news fall? Do you think the news media deliberately try to influence political attitudes? Or are they trying to inform? Do you see differences among different news genres, like newspaper news, cable TV opinion shows, and blogs?

A fifth aspect of political communication is that effects occur on a variety of levels. What makes political communication so significant is its breadth. Political media exert influence on the **micro level**, affecting individuals' thoughts, candidate assessments, feelings, attitudes, and behavior. The first 2012 presidential debate, in which Obama seemed lethargic, exerted a micro-level impact if it led an undecided voter to rethink her support for Obama. Political communication also works on the **macro level**, exerting broad-based effects on public opinion, institutional change or retrenchment, political activism, and public policy. For example, *The Washington Post*'s groundbreaking coverage of President Nixon's unethical actions during the Watergate scandal of the early 1970s led to macro-level institutional changes, such as the appointment of a special prosecutor and a series of Senate hearings, which ultimately paved the way for Nixon's resignation.

Even broader macro-level effects occur on the cultural level. Scholar Michael Schudson (1995) notes that "the news constructs a symbolic world that has a kind of priority, a certification of legitimate importance . . . When the media offer the public an item of news, they confer upon it public legitimacy. They bring it into a common public forum where it can be discussed by a general audience" (pp. 33, 19).

CONTEMPORARY POLITICAL COMMUNICATION

As we have seen, political communication involves more than just the words, "political" and "communication." Delving deeper, scholars conclude that there are five core features of today's political communication.

Political Communication Involves Three Key Players: Leaders, Media, and the Public

There are different perspectives on which of these groups exerts the greatest impact. Scholars argue that under different circumstances, leaders, media, and the public have the strongest influence.

One view is that elite leaders exert a preeminent impact on opinions and policy. After the tragedy of September 11, the nation looked to the president, as it often does in national crises. Addressing a joint session of Congress and the nation on September 20, 2001, George W. Bush gave a moving speech, in which he spoke of "a country awakened to danger and called to defend freedom" and articulated the threats the nation faced from terrorist groups, while taking pains to show respect for Muslims in America and throughout the world. Through his rhetoric and actions, Bush rallied the country around a new and unsettling war on terror.

More than a year later, the same president was under siege, accused of using the communicative powers of his office to launch an unnecessary war on Iraq. As two scholars noted, critics advanced "the serious and plausible suggestion that the Bush administration 'manipulated' the country into war [with Iraq] through a variety of techniques: controlled leaks to the press, exploitation of jingoistic sentiment, cherry-picking of vital intelligence, persecution or ostracism of war critics, and a campaign of image management and stagecraft designed to reinforce the government's daily message at the expense of a full public dialogue on the question of war" (Le Cheminant & Parrish, 2011, p. 2).

Not all political observers would agree with this evaluation of Bush's actions. But there is little doubt that he aggressively used political language, news management, and public appearances to advance his view that the Iraq war was essential to protect U.S. security. In this way, Bush showed how a political leader can use communicative powers to dominate the national agenda.

A second view places the onus on media. It emphasizes that the media—both news and entertainment—exert a preeminent effect on the conduct of politics. This viewpoint notes that the news media's choice of issues, and the way they frame the news, can influence leaders and the public. For example, some observers argue that the news media—frequently called the press—paved the way for Barack Obama's nomination back in 2008. Obama was attractive and charismatic, qualities that can captivate a television audience. He was initially an underdog. The press likes to push underdogs who challenge the status quo. As he started to gain in the polls and win primaries, he gained political ground, creating a bandwagon effect, producing even more favorable press coverage (Patterson, 1993). Obama also received substantially more positive press coverage than his opponent for the Democratic nomination, Hillary Clinton. Some scholars maintained that the press gave Obama better coverage because he powered together an unstoppable political juggernaut that captivated so many young voters, while others pointed to suggestive evidence of press bias on the part of journalists (Falk, 2010). In either case, the favorable press coverage netted him momentum, a key commodity in primary campaigns that helps to propel candidates to victory.

A third viewpoint argues that the public calls the shots. In order to get elected and reelected, leaders have to be responsive to their constituents, implementing polices that the average voter supports (Hurley & Hill, 2010). For example, in the 2012 election, the state of the economy, with the unrelentingly high unemployment rate, was the most important issue to the public. The media made this a preeminent part of its coverage. It formed the centerpiece of Republican attacks against Obama and provided the backdrop of Obama's strategy of blaming Republicans for blocking his legislative proposals to improve the nation's economy. The electorate—or voting public—helped push the issue to the front-and-center for both candidates and media.

In most political contexts, all three influence agents—elites, media, and public—interact in complex ways. The drama of political communication involves a trifecta: leaders, media, and citizens symbolically jousting among themselves and framing problems in different ways. The key, of course, is power: Leaders invoke language, symbols, and the trappings of their offices to gain and maintain power. Media relay, interpret, challenge, or reinforce the use of power. Citizens, some more than others, the richer and better-connected more than the poorer and less-educated, become involved in the political process, wielding modern communications to advocate for causes and candidates, sometimes wisely, other times foolishly.

WHAT DO YOU THINK?

In your view, which of the three players of political communication—political leaders, media, and citizens—exerts the largest impact on American politics? Think of an example of when each influence agent had a particularly strong impact.

Politics Is Played on a Media Platform

"American politics is almost exclusively a mediated experience," political communication scholar Shanto Iyengar (2004) notes. "The role of the citizen has evolved from occasional foot soldier and activist to spectator" (p. 254).

Jesper Strömbäck and Lynda L. Kaid (2008) take a complementary view, noting that the mass media *mediate* between citizens on the one hand and the institutions of government on the other. But the media are not neutral, bland mediators. They apply their own judgments and rules, in this way transforming politics (Mazzoleni & Schulz, 1999). In the United States, as well as other western democracies, media have become such a centerpiece of governing that politicians adapt their behavior to the media's criteria of newsworthiness. Journalists and a gaggle of political media entertainers determine who gains access to the electorate. As a result, candidates are exquisitely

Figure 2.2 Journalists press President Barack Obama for comments, using an array of modern technologies. The media are the centerpiece of modern politics. They are where politics happens, the access points for both leaders and the public. Politicians must adapt their styles to fit the styles of political journalists, commentators and online bloggers who shape the information that reaches the public.

Getty Images

conscious of styles and messages that make for good television and flamboyant YouTube videos (Mazzoleni & Schulz, 1999; see Figure 2.2).

But even this view understates the role communication plays in contemporary politics. Not only do media intercede between politicians and public; they are the playing field on which politics occurs. Jeffrey P. Jones (2010) thoughtfully points out that:

> Media are our primary points of access to politics . . . and the place for political encounters that precede, shape, and at times determine further bodily participation (if it is to happen at all). Furthermore, those encounters occur through a panoply of media forms (books, magazines, newspapers, newsletters, billboards and advertisements, direct mail, radio, film, emails, websites, blogs, social networking sites, and, of course, cable and network television) and across numerous fictional and nonfictional genres . . . Such encounters do much more than provide "information" about political ideas, issues, events, or players. They constitute our mental maps of the political and social world outside our direct experience.
>
> (p. 23)

Notice that Jones refers to a variety of media in discussing political communication effects. The media are plural. Pundits typically refer to the media as an all-powerful singular term, invoking the powerful aura of other monolithic entities like the Vatican or the Establishment. They utter the phrase in a dry, stentorian tone: *The Media*; or they speak it derisively, as when they talk about The Liberal (or Capitalist) Media. In fact, there are many media—for example, national print media, local newspapers, talk radio, television networks, and an array of politically diverse blogs (see the political blog directory at http://www.etalkinghead.com/directory).

Genres like blogs, websites, and political television talk shows on cable TV are full of opinion. They are not designed to offer an impartial rendition of the day's events. Some blogs and opinionated commentaries are really insightful, offering thoughtful opinions about politics. In other cases, online writers are ideological provocateurs, hurling invectives, revealing salacious information to discredit opponents, and combining "a relatively new form of weaponized journalism, politicking and public policy into a potent mix" (Rutenberg, 2013, p. 4).

In today's day and age, it can be difficult to differentiate between opinionated news outlets and genres that transmit straight news. Yet many television, radio, and newspaper news organizations, while imperfect, typically attempt to offer a reasonable facsimile of the world. Journalists and news media gatekeepers select and transmit news stories; their decisions are guided by a host of professional, organizational, and economic factors. To paraphrase the late publisher of *The New York Times*, Arthur O. Sulzberger, you're not buying news when you buy a newspaper. "You're buying judgment" (Haberman, 2012). This is an important point. When you get political information from Facebook posts, blogs, or snippets from Yahoo! News, you can't be sure about the objectivity or fairness of what you have read. The information is up-to-date, but it may be partisan or untrue. News that is gathered by a reputable news organization is filtered through the lenses of professional journalists; the best political reporting is not only accurate, but also provides a broader perspective that illuminates the political world.

Technology Is a Centerpiece of Political Communication

Although technology has always played a role in politics, it wields more influence today than ever before. There is a greater volume of political information, more instant communication between leaders and followers, and more opportunities for voters to exert control over the message (Johnson, 2011).

The technological revolution has had two major influences. It has vastly increased the supply of information, with conventional media, websites galore, blogs, and politically oriented social media posts offering a plethora of facts and opinions about politics. Technology has also greatly expanded choices, with a wealth of sources and channels available to people (Bennett & Iyengar, 2008).

The days when television networks dominated the political campaign are gone—they're history. Nowadays, candidates have a major presence on social networking sites. During the 2012 campaign, Obama turned to the social news site Reddit to shore up support among young voters. "Hi, I'm Barack Obama, president of the United States. Ask me anything," he said, using the informal argot of social media.

Campaign attack ads are immediately posted on YouTube, attracting millions of hits. Twitter has fast become the province of both the political intelligentsia and the populace. During the 2011 crisis over the raising of the national debt ceiling, Obama asked citizens to tweet their representatives to encourage legislators to support a bipartisan compromise. Palin says she regularly tweets; it's the way she rolls, she boasts (Draper, 2010). Within about the first seven minutes of the first 2012 presidential debate, negative reviews of President Obama's performance from political professionals and journalists flooded onto Twitter, causing an Obama campaign manager to declare "We are getting bombed on Twitter" (Nagourney et al., 2012, p. P1).

In the same fashion, contemporary technologies have made it easier for citizens to communicate with leaders. With close to 50 percent of Americans reporting they get most of their news from the Internet, there is little question that the Internet has increased opportunities for access between voters and their elected representatives (The Economist, 2011).

Political information that would be formerly kept inside the recesses of government is now public, porous, and (for better and sometimes for worse) out there for citizens to peruse. Thus, WikiLeaks, a non-profit organization dedicated to releasing classified documents, revealed classified information on the conduct of war and foreign diplomacy, obtained from news leaks and whistleblowers. Did this enhance the public's right to know or impede the ability of diplomats to conduct sensitive conversations in private? These are complicated issues, to be discussed later in this book.

There are other cases in which information that years ago would have been kept behind closed doors slips into public view. As mentioned earlier, the secretly recorded video of Romney's remarks that 47 percent of Americans do not take "personal responsibility" for their lives surfaced during the campaign, sparking controversy. Years ago, these remarks would never have been publicized. But today anything said anywhere can be used against a candidate, a development that raises important issues for political communication (see Reflections box).

REFLECTIONS: THE ONLINE GENIE IS OUT OF THE BOTTLE

Conducting a campaign only through television? How hopelessly 20th century! Citizens expressing anger at a news organization by jamming the phone lines? How quaint!

You can no more take online technologies out of political communication than you can take smartphones from holiday shopping or eliminate phone apps of store locations from Black Friday. New technologies unleash a multitude of changes, some positive, negative, and others more ambiguous (see, e.g., views on technology and political communication expressed at http://observer.com/2009/06/the-impact-of-technology-on-political-communication/).

Without question, the Internet and social media have allowed citizens to communicate with leaders more rapidly and efficiently than ever before. They also have facilitated communication from elected officials to constituents, and among elites, media, and citizens. As a result, political information that formerly would

Continued

have been inaccessible is now public, available for citizens and reporters to examine and discuss. All this is good.

But increased interactivity has had a number of troubling effects as well.

A liberal congressman, Anthony Weiner, sent lewd photos, including ones that displayed him in his underpants, to women he met over the Internet. He resigned in disgrace when the sordid tale became public. Did the Internet play a helpful role? It facilitated the resignation of a public official who had engaged in creepy behaviors, hardly befitting a member of Congress. Or did the Internet instead bring to the surface information that was none of the public's business to begin with?

General David Petraeus, a celebrated military leader and director of the CIA, became enmeshed in a truth-is-stranger-than-fiction scandal that could have never occurred in an earlier era. Petraeus resigned his CIA post in November, 2012 after acknowledging he had an extramarital affair with his biographer, Paula Broadwell. Petraeus and Broadwell had shared sexually explicit emails. Broadwell then sent a series of harassing emails to a Tampa socialite, Jill Kelley, whom she seems to have viewed as a romantic rival for Petraeus's attention. And *then* Kelley contacted a friend who worked at the FBI, and the FBI began to investigate, leading to the discovery of the email path. Although romantic jealousy that unravels political careers has occurred through time immemorial, the Petraeus scandal might never have unfolded had it not been for the existence of smoking-gun emails that nailed Petraeus and Broadwell. What's more, the willingness of the FBI to launch an investigation that involved adultery—and not a national security breach that concerned revelation of classified information—raised serious privacy concerns.

The diffusion of interactive media has unleashed many changes, changing politics, altering political communication, and redefining the lines between public and private communications. What do you think of these changes? Should Representative Weiner have resigned? Should Petraeus have quit? More generally, how do you size up the effects interactive media have had on public life? Which are positive? Which are negative? Now that the technological genie is out of the bottle, how do you assess its impact?

Politics, for better or worse, is played out on a mediated, technological stage. But what are media? **Media** are technologies that intercede between the communicator and message recipient, filtering the message through the selection of words, images, and formats. Newspapers, magazines, and television make up conventional, sometimes called mainstream, media. They convey a message to the audience, ignoring, selecting, shaping, and framing information based on a host of factors. Is the Internet media? It is a question frequently asked, but one that is difficult to crisply answer.

The Internet is not a medium per se, but a series of interlocking digital networks that convey information that has been interpreted and mediated by traditional media like newspapers and television, as well as other outlets, like blogs and websites. The Internet is a technological platform that facilitates direct interaction between the communicator and message receivers (e.g., Sundar & Bellur, 2011). It includes sites maintained by the mainstream media, as well as online news organizations, blogs and partisan fare. And then there are social media—for example, the ubiquitous Twitter and Facebook. Some observers say that all these new technologies constitute the new middlemen. Rather than simply facilitating mediation, whereby media come between sources and receivers, they produce "disintermediation" (Pariser, 2011), whereby people circumvent media and communicate directly with leaders.

The Internet (and social media) yanked power from the news media and gave it to people, enabling ordinary people to participate more actively in public dialogue. This is all to the good when it connects citizens with leaders in civilized dialogues or allows people to communicate about politics with others via Facebook and Twitter. The Internet's role in communication is more freighted and controversial when partisans launch vicious, prejudiced invectives against public officials or other users with whom they disagree, shielded by the privacy of a PC in a living room or a cell phone in a coffeehouse.

Political Communication Has Gone Global

To be sure, people communicate about politics in all societies, whether democratic or autocratic, technologically primitive or advanced. What is noteworthy is the ways that the growth of information technologies and acceptance of U.S.-style marketing strategies have diffused across the globe. They have led to remarkable similarities in political campaign strategies and the public's experience of elections in different countries. Western democracies now share an emphasis on personalized, candidate-focused campaigns, reliance on political consultants, and tailoring of everyday activities to fit the requirements of news media and social networking technologies (Swanson & Mancini, 1996). For example, Europe's politicians include a cadre of stylish, physically attractive communicators who make pleasant impressions on television. This contrasts with the more oafish (though commanding) leaders of the past. (One wonders how the verbally gifted, but physically rotund, Winston Churchill, would have fared if he had delivered his World War II "we will never surrender" speech on television.)

Yet even in countries where democratic tendencies are overshadowed by state-sponsored coercion, mediated politics exerts an outsized impact. In Russia, opinion polling plays an integral role in governing. So does television. Vladimir Putin shored up his campaign for the Russian presidency by appearing on television in scuba gear, diving for ancient artifacts, looking very much the macho leader (Barry, 2011a).

Perhaps the most noteworthy aspect of the globalization of political communication technology is that any individual with the technical knowledge to create a Facebook page or distribute an image on YouTube can influence politics. The most dramatic example occurred in 2011 in Cairo, Egypt, or, more precisely, in cyberspace, when a Google executive, Wael Ghonim, became frustrated with his country's abusive autocracy. Harnessing his marketing skills, he created a Facebook group that attracted hundreds of thousands of Facebook users, helping them to channel their frustration into a series of protests that toppled the Egyptian government in the winter of 2011 (Kirkpatrick & Sanger, 2011). "If you want to free a society, just give people Internet access," Ghonim said (Wright, 2011, p. 27).

But let's be careful here. Technology has always been heralded as the second coming, but its effects are laced with complexity. Social networking undoubtedly played a role in the 2011 Egyptian rebellion, but whether it created new dissidents, simply preached to the choir, or primarily reacted to, rather than precipitated, the protests remains unclear (e.g., Wolfsfeld, Segev, & Sheafer, 2013). Moreover, the technology-driven rebellion failed to uproot the powerful elite networks that dominated Egypt for decades. More than a year after the revolt, Egypt's new rulers reinstituted martial law, its Supreme Court dissolved Parliament, and the Egyptian president assumed sweeping new powers, precipitating a revolt in 2013. Technology, harnessed by governments in Iran and China, can be used to repress, as well as create, political protest (Morozov, 2011).

Technology can also facilitate global conversations that never could have occurred in earlier times. This can be beneficial when the conversations bring people together or catalyze ideas. But when the two parties that converse are at loggerheads or at war, technology reinforces and exacerbates tensions. In November, 2012, after Israel killed the military leader of its enemy, Hamas, the extremist Islamic group that rules the Gaza strip (an action that provoked Hamas's launching of missiles into the heart of Israel), an Israeli Twitter feed transmitted vivid rhetorical arguments to defend its action. The posts displayed images of missiles falling in the direction of the Statue of Liberty and the Eiffel Tower, with the caption: "What would you do? Share this if you agree that

Israel has the right to self-defense." Israel's military postings reached Hamas's military division, which aggressively responded that, "Our blessed hands will reach your leaders and soldiers wherever they are," adding that "you opened hell gates on yourselves" (Cohen, 2012, p. A18). Alas, social networking cannot solve intractable problems; it only offers a new place where arguments and biased perceptions occur.

Political Communication Can Be a Force of Good and Evil

Like all weapons of influence, political communication can be harnessed for positive and negative purposes. Charisma can move people to compassion and hope, as those who heard speeches by Martin Luther King, Robert F. Kennedy, Ronald Reagan, and Nelson Mandela would readily attest. It can also malevolently access the spectral figments of human prejudice, playing on dark fantasies of gloom. Speeches of Hitler in the 1930s and Osama bin Laden in our own century exemplify the hideous uses of charisma.

Issues get murky. Manipulation can be morally odious when it exploits citizens' emotions, but a positive force when it moves individuals to band together for the collective good. Favor-giving and quid pro quos raise eyebrows when used by wealthy lobbyists currying influence with legislators. But they may be morally justified when implemented by political leaders seeking sweeping ethical changes, as when Lincoln openly traded favors with Congressmen to pass the iconic Thirteenth Amendment banning slavery. In a similar fashion, negative advertising can dispirit citizens, yet offer challengers opportunities to unseat incumbents.

The Internet can be empowering and offer mechanisms for ordinary people to make their voices known. For example, in January, 2012, social media flexed its viral muscle as people deluged Twitter, Tumblr, and Facebook to protest a decision by America's leading breast cancer advocacy group to end most of its financing of Planned Parenthood. A day after the protest was widely reported, the organization reversed its decision and restored its partnership with Planned Parenthood. At the same time, social media and the Internet have their down sides, offering an outlet for vicious sexist posts against female candidates like Sarah Palin and Hillary Clinton, and racist drivel directed at the nation's first Black president.

THEMES AND QUESTIONS

Questions are as important as answers in academic disciplines, and political communication is a crowning case in point. There are not necessarily easy or simple answers to these questions, but the pursuit of answers can be intellectually instructive.

Here are some questions to contemplate:

1. Can there be true democracy in the United States when the public is uninvolved in most political decisions? Have we become, as Robert M. Entman (1989) dolefully put it, "a democracy without citizens," in which elites use media to manipulate voters? Or have citizens found new pathways for participation, including the multitude of social media that permit instant communication between voters and candidates?
2. Is the Internet bane or boon? Has it (along with modern media) become a hothouse of political vitriol, filled with nasty, uncivil rhetoric? Or has it facilitated improvements in our nation's political discourse? And if so, where and why?
3. Is too much emphasis placed on politicians' appearances, their personal qualities, and posturing for the camera? Or is image-making necessary in an age of mediated presidential politics? Does leadership in a media age consist of an effective mastery of images? Where do we draw the line between style and substance?
4. Do presidential election campaigns stimulate political thinking, offering up opportunities for voters to rethink the tried-and-true political ideas? Or instead are they win-at-all-costs ventures, in which each side pulls out all stops to mobilize supporters and propel its side to the polls?
5. Can news produce an informed, critical citizenry if it props up the powers-that-be? Or does news challenge the power structure, providing a check on political chicanery?
6. Do the political communication shortcomings we face today reflect a contemporary crisis or are they endemic to democracy?

CONCLUSIONS

What comes to mind when someone mentions *politics*? In all likelihood, the term conjures up negative images. This is partly because politicians do pull dirty tricks, but also because Americans harbor a long-standing distrust of political leaders and the news media frequently highlight the seamy side of public life. Yet politics is an essential part of democracy. There cannot be democracy without politics. Truth be told, politics can produce positive changes and lead to improvements in people's lives. Politics involves deciding who gets which resources and why. It is the process whereby individuals who initially disagree reach decisions that are regarded as binding on society as a whole. Political communication is defined as the process by which language and symbols, employed by leaders, media, or citizens, exert intended or unintended effects on the political cognitions, attitudes, or behavior of individuals or on outcomes that bear on the public policy of a nation, state, or community.

Contemporary political communication has five core characteristics. First, it involves an interplay of strategic or symbolic influence among three key players: leaders, media, and public. Second, politics is enacted on a media and Internet stage. Importantly, the media have become such a centerpiece of governing that political leaders adapt their behavior to fit the media's criteria of newsworthiness. Third, technology plays an ever-increasing role in the process by which politics is communicated. Fourth, thanks to the development of information technologies and harnessing of U.S.-style political marketing techniques, political communication, negative advertising, and partisan uses of social media have gone global. Fifth, like all forms of communication, political communication can be employed with beneficent and malicious intentions and with positive and negative outcomes.

Normative theories of democracy place a premium on political communication. It is the cornerstone of a democratic society. But does it work effectively? Or is it more problematic than salutary? And how can it be improved? There are no easy answers to these questions. But the multitude of perspectives brought to bear in answering them can enlighten and educate.

3 The Study of Political Communication

If you had to guess, when would you say that American scholars began writing about the effects of political communication?

a) *In the late 1980s, when* The Simpsons *began satirizing adult authorities.*
b) *During the 1920s, amid concerns about new 20th century media.*
c) *In the 1960s, in the wake of John F. Kennedy's glib mastery of television.*
d) *In the early 1800s, when mass circulation newspapers began to attract large audiences.*

It's not a trick question, but read the choices carefully. What did you pick?

You might think critical, scholarly concerns began in the 1800s. But in those days there were no scholars of mass communication, and few attributed powerful effects to the daily press. True, Kennedy's adroit use of television, especially in the presidential debates, was much discussed. And, yes, *The Simpsons* was an iconic television program that spawned imitators and led researchers to speculate about the role it played in political socialization. But scholarly concerns about political media effects began in earnest in the 1920s, in the wake of criticism of a U.S. communication campaign to mobilize support for America's participation in World War I and the development of a powerful mass media.

Thus, although the study of political communication is popularly believed to have begun with television, it actually dates back nearly a century. It was Walter Lippmann, the American journalist writing in the 1920s, who eloquently and influentially described the ability of the media to mold the images people carried in their heads about a distant world that was "out of reach, out of sight [and] out of mind." This chapter describes the journey Lippmann helped to launch, chronicling the history of political communication research, with its many currents, waves, and oscillating changes. The chapter introduces the fundamental concepts and methods that have guided the field, continuities and changes in academic thinking about political communication over the past century, and the surprising conflicts that make the history of political communication so animating. This is a scholar's chapter, one that will help you appreciate the academic underpinnings of the ideas discussed in this book.

The history of mass communication research is not a placid story of academic scholars gathering facts and dutifully placing each morsel of information into the vessel of knowledge. On the contrary, it is more like a maritime expedition, with competing explorers, armed with different maps and diving equipment. One group amasses findings, only to have these notions questioned by another group of explorers, who, guided by their own maps, probe a different portion of the ocean's depths, uncovering new facts and theories of what constitutes the underlying structure of the sea. All too often we think of the history of an academic discipline as a monotonous description of how naïve thinkers developed ideas that were overturned by their more intelligent, savvy, and contemporary disciples. But this understates the excitement of intellectual discovery. By reviewing the twists and turns in the history of political communication research and describing some of the personal aspects of the scholarly journey, I hope to engage readers, helping them appreciate the intellectually vigorous issues that animate scholars.

The chapter is organized chronologically. The first portion reviews the early classic scholarship, and the second section looks critically at the early research, particularly its implications for today. The third portion focuses in depth on social science, explaining the social scientific dimensions of political communication and major empirical methods.

EARLY HISTORY OF POLITICAL COMMUNICATION SCHOLARSHIP

Lippmann's Insights

Ideas were combusting and crystallizing at a furious pace. The old guard was under siege.

Across Europe and the United States, a new, darker explanation of human behavior was afoot. In France Gustave Le Bon (1896) gravely warned of the irrational power of a new force in society: the crowd, a barbaric mass, in which emotion overtook reason, placing civilization in jeopardy. Prophetically forecasting the powers of 20th century media, French scholar Gabriel Tarde argued that modern newspapers could "set off a million tongues," transporting thoughts across vast distances and molding ideas. In a similar fashion, German sociologist Ferdinand Tonnies warned that the newspaper was packaging information like "grocers' goods," marketing and manufacturing public opinion, shaping public sentiments in powerful ways (Ewen, 1996). In America, the sociologist Robert Park echoed these views, expressing pessimism about the power of reason to conquer public opinion formed by a manipulation of catchphrases. Sigmund Freud synthesized these disparate sentiments, arguing that the conformist crowd behavior which Le Bon and others had described had its underlying roots in the unconscious, psychodynamic forces of the individual.

Figure 3.1 Walter Lippmann, the journalist and scholar who helped pioneer scholarship on political communication. Lippmann argued that in a political world few experienced directly, media symbols and interpretations influenced public attitudes and opinions.

Getty Images

Enter Walter Lippmann. Lippmann synthesized these ideas with his knowledge of the prevailing political practices of the time. Graduating from Harvard in 1910, in a class that included the poet T.S. Eliot and radical reporter John Reed (immortalized by Warren Beatty in the movie *Reds* many years later), Lippmann served as founding editor of *The New Republic*, the avant-garde political magazine of the 20th century. He also wrote books that earned the praise of a U.S. president and Supreme Court justice (Steel, 1999; see Figure 3.1).

Lippmann had worked in Europe during World War I, at the behest of the administration of President Woodrow Wilson, frankly trying to harness the powers of **propaganda**—the word *du jour*—to assist the U.S. war effort. But after the terrible war, which, in the memorable words of a British foreign secretary, had darkened the lamps of Europe (Tuchman, 1962), Lippmann began to lament the powers of government to spin and control information in the service of war-time victory. During World War I the White House took extraordinary steps to manufacture support for the war effort. President Woodrow Wilson appointed publicist George Creel to direct the Committee on Public Information (CPI). The CPI disseminated 100 million pamphlets and posters, sent countless educational materials to schools, and plastered war posters on streetcars and trains. In 1917 Congress passed the Espionage Act, which permitted the government to fine or imprison people who intentionally made false statements with the intent of interfering with military operations. The CPI raised the specter of government control of information, producing a firestorm of controversy.

You could argue that Creel had done the nation a service: by convincing the public of the necessity of war, he had unleashed American power during a time when the nation's military might was needed to save the people of Europe. Or you could contend that Creel's effort was deceptive and manipulative, and, when taken in concert with Wilson's application of political censorship, represented a foreboding development in American history. Viewing these issues a century later, one is struck by the continuity between then and now. The same questions were raised in other manipulative mass information campaigns, such as those waged during the Vietnam War, the 1990–91 Persian Gulf conflict, and the controversial 2003 War in Iraq.

Back to Lippmann in the 1920s. After the war, Lippmann became disillusioned by the ways that Creel had used the powers of persuasion and coercion to influence the mass public. He rejected classic liberal democracy concepts, such as the power of rational thought or the ability of the press to relay accurate information. Instead, he concluded that people were prone to psychologically distort information and engage in stereo-typing. "We do not first see, and then define, we define first and then see," he said. But there was more. Unlike earlier eras, where individuals lived in small towns and had direct experience with issues of their communities, in the modern world, people were compelled to make decisions about complex problems that they could not directly experience. Living in a world that was "out of reach, out of sight, out of mind," Lippmann (1922) poetically penned, people had to rely on governments and the press for accurate information (p. 18). But—and here was the modern wrinkle—governments could effectively manipulate symbols to *manufacture* consent. The press did not convey deeper truths, Lippmann concluded. Instead, it simply transmitted events, even forcing attention on selected issues.

Writing at the end of the 20th century, Stuart Ewen (1996) observed that "one cannot avoid being struck by Lippmann's clairvoyance; the extent to which his analysis of symbols—how they may be employed to sway the public—sounds uncomfortably familiar" (p. 158). Prior to Lippmann and others writing during this period, there was little appreciation of the ways that media images could mold public sentiments. Moreover, Lippmann grasped that the media would necessarily assume a large role in shaping public opinion in a world where individuals had to rely on indirect experience to make sense of politics.

ABCs of Propaganda

The United States was changing, and perceptive observers took note. Chronicling the ways government could exploit mass media, political scientist Harold Lasswell (1927), following in Lippmann's footsteps, described the power communications could exert on the mass soul. Lasswell and others used the term "propaganda" to describe these effects, although today these might be referred to as persuasion or social influence.

In the 1930s, a group formed an Institute of Propaganda that assembled a list of the "ABC's of propaganda" that included *testimonial*, the ability of a communication to call on the views of a credible spokesperson; *bandwagon*, the persuasive influence exerted by the perception that large numbers of people supported a cause; and *transfer*, the powerful impact that a message could exert if it was associated with a popular image or symbol. The organizers of the Institute feared that these techniques could be used widely and for pernicious purposes. (Readers might find it interesting to review the classic strategies at http://www.propagandacritic.com/.)

As it turned out, scholars working in the Institute of Propaganda during the 1930s accurately forecast the future. A decade later, the world witnessed the exploitation of mass propaganda for more heinous objectives. In addition to brute coercion, Hitler's Nazi Party harnessed mass communication—rhetoric, speech-making, and movies—to seduce the people of a once-democratic country, Germany, to adopt a horrific policy of world domination.

The Institute of Propaganda dissolved in the early 1940s. The term propaganda, with its sweeping, heavy, and negative connotations, gave way to less pejorative terms like persuasion and information control. But the questions the Institute raised would continue to occupy students of political persuasion. For example: Should governments in democratic countries manipulate the tools of mass communication? How could the tension between democratic values and elites' ability to manipulate public sentiments be satisfactorily resolved? Could the growing mass media offer citizens the information they needed to make informed judgments?

These questions would be put on hold for a time as the field of political communication research took a different direction. It took in a more concrete, pragmatically American path. Intrigued by the effects of radio, researchers examined the social effects of a new medium that conveyed content that ran the gamut from speeches featuring the melodious voice of President Franklin Delano Roosevelt to the dramatization of H.G. Wells's *The War of the Worlds*, a science fiction story that described the invasion of Earth by Martians (see http://www.transparencynow.com/welles.htm). In contrast to some of the early propaganda theorists, the new researchers adopted a decidedly empirical approach, one that underscored the complexity of media effects of programs like the now-famous *War of the Worlds* telecast. Although the program amazingly led some Americans to believe that Martians were invading our planet, its impact was contingent on a host of psychological factors (Cantril, Gaudet, & Herzog, 1940; McDonald, 2004). The radio studies suggested that media effects might just be more complicated than some scholars originally believed, a conclusion that would also find resonance in a pioneering study of political communication in Ohio during a presidential election.

THE PENDULUM SWINGS

Sandusky, Ohio is a quaint city on Lake Erie's shores. It is more than 400 miles from Washington, D.C. and New York City, the teeming centers of elite influence that housed the powerful purveyors of mass communications. In 1940, Sandusky was a small, quiescent Midwestern community that bore an intriguing characteristic: in every presidential election of the 20th century, it had closely reflected national voting patterns. For this reason it attracted the interest of three political scientists, eager to explore the role communication played in people's voting decisions.

Paul Lazarsfeld and two colleagues from Columbia University made the trip to Sandusky, embarking on a study of the 1940 election that pitted President Franklin D. Roosevelt, a popular incumbent and a Democrat, against Wendell Wilkie, a corporate lawyer and dark horse Republican candidate. Roosevelt won handily, which was not exactly a surprise. But the results that Lazarsfeld, Berelson, and Gaudet (1944) obtained must have been something of a whopper, a balloon-bursting surprise to those who believed in the power of the political communication media. In a scientific study of Sandusky (or, more generally, Erie County, Ohio) residents' uses of newspapers and radio, their conversations with others, and voting, the researchers reported clear and dramatic effects. They found that media exerted modest influences, clarifying attitudes about the candidates and strengthening the voting intentions of those who felt strongly about the election. But they converted only a handful of voters to the other side.

It was not mass media that sent the researchers scurrying to their typewriters. Instead, it was interpersonal communications, or face-to-face conversations. Certain individuals served as **opinion leaders** for others, influencing followers' political views. Ideas seemed to flow from radio and newspapers to these influential leaders; the opinion leaders then scooped them up, distilled them and conveyed them to the less involved, less active members of the electorate. The researchers dubbed this the **two-step flow**. Thus, media did not impact on the mass audience directly, as the propaganda theorists feared. Instead, their influence was itself mediated—watered down, perhaps, but certainly tempered—by these influential leaders.

The model looked like this:

Media → Opinion Leaders → Voting Public

It seemed as if the much-ballyhooed media were not all they had been cracked to be. Instead, they were just another factor in the persuasion mix and not nearly as important as interpersonal communication (see also Berelson, Lazarsfeld, & McPhee, 1954 and a useful web review of classic research at http://www.outofthequestion.org/Media-Research-of-the-1940s/Trends.aspx).

Influence in Illinois

The Erie County, Ohio study propelled Lazarsfeld's career. Born in Austria, Lazarsfeld had obtained a Ph.D. in applied mathematics from the University of Vienna. With the political situation in his native Austria disintegrating in the wake of World War II, Lazarsfeld emigrated to the United States and took up a position as a faculty member in sociology at Columbia University. Lazarsfeld was a complex man: a brilliant researcher, but also something of an operator, a bustling entrepreneur to some, a savvy manipulator to others (Morrison, 2006; Simonson, 2006; see also Gitlin, 1978). Building on the now-internationally famous findings in the Erie County voting study, he sought to explore new venues, hoping to study the new opinion leader notion as a sociologist while, doffing his entrepreneurial cap, seeking to attract new streams of money to the university's Bureau of Applied Social Research. He convinced Macfadden Publications, the publisher of American magazines, to underwrite a study of consumer decision-making in the small, but representative, community of Decatur, Illinois.

Lazarsfeld, for his part, needed money to conduct an in-depth, statistical study of the role communication played in Decatur women's decisions about marketing, fashion, movie-going, and public affairs. He enlisted his graduate student, Elihu Katz, who went on to become a major political communication scholar. Their survey (Katz & Lazarsfeld, 1955) became a milestone in communication research, one of the most cited studies in the social sciences (Lang & Lang, 2006). It made Katz and Lazarsfeld an internationally famous communication dyad. When talking about personal influence, you couldn't say one name without mentioning the other, usually in the same breath. For our purposes, their legendary study's main contributions were that it: (a) pioneered a precise scientific technique to examine the flow of influence; (b) suggested that mass media played second fiddle to interpersonal influence; and (c) demonstrated that context mattered (serving as a leader in the area of fashion did not mean one was a leader in public affairs).

You might say that a half-century before Mark Zuckerberg created Facebook, Katz and Lazarsfeld found that social networks matter, affecting people's consumer and political decisions. What's more, you could not understand the effects of media without taking into account people's social environments and interpersonal friendships. To those researchers who believed that the media audience was an undifferentiated mass of clay shaped by an all-powerful mass media, Katz and Lazarsfeld sounded a caution, emphasizing that the audience was composed of social networks of opinion leaders and their peers, with interpersonal leaders exerting a persuasive impact on acquaintances and followers (see also Box 3.1).

BOX 3.1 AN OPINION LEADER RIDES INTO TOWN

A young boy ran to tell the famous opinion leader that there would be "hell to pay tomorrow." As the day wore on, the opinion leader became more concerned that the enemy was to going to launch its attack and arrest the gutsy dissidents. He decided enough was enough, so he mounted his horse, rode from Boston to Lexington, knocking on doors, and letting his compatriots know that the enemy was preparing to attack. People reacted. They rang bells. They sounded alarms.

At the same time as the famous opinion leader set forth to diffuse information (as we would say today), another communicator embarked on the same mission, taking a different route, and conveying the identical information as the first horseman. But the two had very different effects on the communication flow. The famous opinion leader was, of course, Paul Revere (see Figure 3.2). He rode 13 miles in two hours, letting colonists know that the British were coming. Spurred by Revere's warning, the colonists sounded alarms, spiriting a group of men to take up arms.

The not-so-famous communicator was William Dawes. Although he carried the same information, he did not have the same effect. People did not sound alarms or talk feverishly. Townspeople did not hear the news until later. Dawes had failed to warn colonists in advance.

Why did Revere succeed and Dawes fail? The answer, according to writer Malcolm Gladwell (2000), yields insights on opinion leadership that parallel findings in Katz and Lazarsfeld's study. Gladwell, calling on historical research, explains that, unlike Dawes, Revere was a "connector." He was gregarious. He drank regularly at pubs. He played an active role in a local Masonic Lodge. He knew a lot of people in Boston. When epidemics struck New England, Revere was

Continued

Figure 3.2 A statue of the famous patriot, Paul Revere, in Boston's North End neighborhood, near Old North Church. Revere was an early American opinion leader who plied his communication skills to influence colonial patriots during his fateful ride through the streets of Boston and Lexington. Revere illustrates the time-honored richness and robust application of the opinion leader concept.

Getty Images

selected health officer of Boston, and Suffolk County coroner. He was a networker, a man who matriculated to the center of ongoing events. Revere, to call on the name of a popular professional networking site, was "linked in."

On the night of his fateful ride, Revere knew just the doors to knock on and who led the local militia. Dawes did not. While Revere commanded credibility among the colonists, Dawes, though clearly a patriot, was but "an ordinary man" (Gladwell, 2000, p. 59).

Thus, the concept of opinion leadership is rich in meaning. Opinion leaders date back many years, and their personal influence can help propel change. Revere's case tells us that sometimes the people with the most ability to influence others are those who are socially connected to the larger community.

Joseph Klapper Makes His Statement

So, Joseph Klapper wanted to know, when all is said and done: What *are* the effects of mass media and political communication? Working with Lazarsfeld, his dissertation adviser, Klapper thought it was high time that someone wrote up a summary statement about this new field of communication research. Now that there had been a considerable number of studies of mass media effects and a new decade—the 1960s—was set to begin, it seemed a propitious moment to put together a book that summarized knowledge of media effects.

Following the tradition blazed by Katz and Lazarsfeld, Klapper (1960) concluded that media influences on society were small to modest. People had acquired strong preexisting attitudes before they came to media. They were members of reference groups, like the family, religious organizations, and labor unions. These groups generally exerted a stronger impact on attitudes than did mass media. The media were not the sole or primary agent that influenced political attitudes and behavior. Instead, Klapper emphasized, media worked together with social environmental factors, contributing to or reinforcing the effects these other agents exerted. This became known as the **limited effects model**.

Klapper acknowledged that mass media could strengthen attitudes. But, to Klapper, they did not have the immense effects that many observers seemed to attribute to them. People were not a "tabula rasa" on which media could imprint their message. They brought preexisting group identifications (such as religion) and attitudes (such as liberalism or conservatism) to their encounter with media. These biases helped to determine how individuals reacted to political media fare and the effects that media exerted. For Klapper, the media did not exert the massive impact that so many seemed to assume.

A NEW PERSPECTIVE

Suddenly, things changed.

During the decade in which Klapper published a book describing minimal media effects, something very different was occurring in the supposedly minimally important mass media. The very different phenomenon was television news. It swept the country by storm, expanding to a half-hour, capturing viewers, and captivating audiences with vivid, sometimes visceral, and frequently contradictory images. Televised pictures and sounds bombarded Americans in the 1960s. There was a handsome John F. Kennedy challenging the jowl-faced, sweaty Richard Nixon in the first 1960 presidential debate;

Southern police clubbing impassioned Black protesters; gut-wrenching scenes of American soldiers battling enemy troops in the rice paddies of Vietnam; angry, long-haired, scruffy college students holding signs, circling around campus buildings, protesting, denouncing a president, or strumming guitars, singing blissfully of a non-violent future. These images, TV's ubiquity, and the media's presumptive effects clashed with Klapper's thesis that the media were of little consequence. Intuitively, it seemed, broadcast news exerted a strong impact on Americans' political attitudes, even if no one had yet documented the effects empirically (Lang & Lang, 2006).

There was also this quandary, frequently bandied about: If media were so ineffective, why did advertisers spend so much on commercials for cars like the hot new Mustang? Why were they spending money to promote candidates like Richard Nixon in 1968, whose blatant marketing spawned a book called *The Selling of the President* (McGinniss, 1969) and perhaps a movie, *The Candidate*, with the actor Robert Redford depicting an empty-headed politician who had been sold by vapid TV images? True, the paradox of advertisers spending lavishly on a supposedly ineffective media did not scientifically prove that media advertising had effects, but the question could not be ignored.

A New Set of Questions

"There has to be a problem, this just can't be right, the media obviously have an impact, the limited effects view must be wrong." Ruminations like these no doubt settled in a growing number of researchers' minds as the stormy 1960s ended. Political communication researchers began to take another look at the research that purported to show minimal effects. Among those exploring this issue was Jack M. McLeod, a mass communication researcher at the University of Wisconsin.

In 1975, McLeod, Lee B. Becker (who had worked with McLeod as a doctoral student at Wisconsin and was currently a young assistant professor at Syracuse University), and the researcher Maxwell McCombs came upon an intriguing discovery. They pored over Lazarsfeld's Erie County study, with Becker taking the lead in scrutinizing the charts that broke down the sample on the basis of both partisanship and exposure to media that favored Republican and Democratic candidates. Becker and his colleagues came up with a serendipitous but exciting discovery: Lazarsfeld and his colleagues had unwittingly understated the media's effects (Becker, McCombs, & McLeod, 1975). Upon closer analysis, it turned out that nearly half of Republicans with exposure to predominantly *Democratic* media actually voted for the *Democrat*, President Franklin D. Roosevelt. A similar pattern emerged for Democrats: Democratic voters who had exposure to primarily *Republican* newspapers and radio stations were more likely to vote for the *Republican* candidate than those who received Democratic exposure. The media seemed to have strongly influenced the voting behavior of both Republican and Democratic respondents. Thus, while voters still might interpret political media fare in light of their biases, there appeared to be more room for media effects than the early researchers had believed.

Another problem surfaced. Lazarsfeld and his colleagues focused only on voting behavior. Had they looked at factors other than voting—for example, discussion, voters' cognitions, or factors operating on the macro level—media effects might have emerged (Chaffee & Hochheimer, 1985). For example, the Republican candidate, Wendell Wilkie, seemed to come from nowhere to become the Republican candidate. Media surely played some part in this. And then there was this—so obvious a problem in the limited effects model that it must have almost embarrassed scholars to mention it: Klapper had based his conclusions on studies that had been conducted before television had become the preeminent medium of political communication. These minimal effect findings could hardly be expected to describe the latter part of the 20th century, an era in which TV had widely diffused throughout society and conveyed so much of the political spectacle.

The limited effects edifice was crumbling, but still standing. In the social sciences, the bottom-line test of a theoretical approach is evidence, and in the early 1970s, the proponents of strong political media effects had yet to amass much evidence. But the facts would not be long in coming.

Influenced by Lippmann's speculations, researchers showed that the media could set the agenda or influence people's perceptions of problems ailing America (McCombs & Shaw, 1972; McLeod, Becker, & Byrnes, 1974). This turned out to be a major revision of the conventional wisdom. Media might not affect what people thought—their basic beliefs—but they powerfully influenced what voters thought about. This turn of a phrase became a mantra in the field. Agenda-setting, as the model became known, offered a different, more optimistic view of media effects, and it became the focal point of the new approach to political communication (see Chapter 6).

Emboldened by this line of research, studies proliferated. Surveys demonstrated that media did not just influence individuals' cognitions, but could affect the dynamics of the larger political system. Thomas E. Patterson (1980), a political scientist who had long argued that media effects in elections were understated, showed that presidential campaigns were organized around the media and seemed to revolve around cultivating reporters. Gladys Lang and Kurt Lang (1983) examined Watergate, the series of events that led to the resignation of President Richard Nixon. They argued that the news media's ubiquitous presence—and the very public impeachment hearings shown on television— encouraged political leaders to hold Nixon accountable for crimes he committed.

Kathleen Hall Jamieson (1984) took readers on a colorful tour of American elections from 1840 to 1980. She showed that candidates had long harnessed communication—primarily speeches and campaign appearances—to mold images. Television advertising followed this rhetorical tradition, emerging as a particularly effective modality by which politicians "package the presidency."

By 1980, when Ronald Reagan, a former Hollywood actor whose communication skills on the small screen became legendary, was elected president, the academic consensus was that media mattered.

In the years that followed, researchers proposed a variety of models of media and public opinion (e.g., agenda-setting, agenda-building, and framing). They explored the content of news, shedding light on the connections among news, journalistic conventions, economics, and political system forces. They examined the impact of news, political advertising, debates, and galloping technological appeals on attitudes and behaviors. Over the past several decades, researchers working in different social science disciplines have coalesced, forging a cross-disciplinary field of political communication. Researchers are united by a fascination with media, an interest in politics, and a conviction that how a society communicates about politics matters. Interest in these issues began with Lippmann, continued through Katz and Lazarsfeld's interpersonal influence research, oscillated in the wake of Klapper's limited effects thesis, rebounded with research on the pervasive impact of news, and continues apace as scholars explore campaign and a host of online communication issues today.

WHAT DO YOU THINK?

Over the course of the 20th century, ideas about media impact on politics have changed. In what ways have scholarly views of media changed over the years?

Pulling It All Together

Let's bring past and present together. What can we conclude from the historical review of political communication research? What do the twists and turns in the intellectual history of American political communication research tell us? What general themes emerge? Threading together Lippmann, Lazarsfeld, Klapper, and rejuvenated scholarly interest in political media effects, we discover several important themes.

First, Lippmann was right: Media shape our images of the world. Lippmann famously suggested that the media form the "pictures in our heads" of the world that lies outside our immediate experiences. His insight was prescient and continues to be true today. We do not experience politics directly. Instead, citizens necessarily rely on the media (and now the Internet) to learn what is happening in Washington, D.C., and in far-off war zones like Kabul, Afghanistan. The media supply us with images that we use to construct beliefs about the political world. This is one reason they are powerful.

Second, social networks matter. Opinion leaders are important. Katz and Lazarsfeld called attention to this in their Decatur study, and it remains true today. In the social media-centric environment, national companies like American Eagle and Hewlett-Packard hire opinion-leading student ambassadors, who promote the brand on Facebook, exploiting their social connections to market the product (Singer, 2011). In electoral contexts, interpersonal influence and discussion can affect political decisions (Huckfeldt & Sprague, 1995). William P. Eveland has shown that how often people talk about politics and who they talk with have intriguing effects on political participation (Eveland & Hively, 2009). In these ways, a concept advanced in 1955—interpersonal influence—plays a vital role in political communication today.

Third, early research was right about some things, wrong about others, but got people thinking. The two-step flow—whereby media influence opinion leaders, who in turn affect others—was a great idea. It still operates today. A study published more than a half-century after Katz and Lazarsfeld found that exposure to a national anti-drug media campaign influenced older siblings, who in turn shaped the beliefs of their younger sisters and brothers (Hornik, 2006).

On the other hand, the two-step flow does not always operate. For some issues, there is a one-step flow: from media to public (Bennett & Manheim, 2006). This was a theme in research on *news diffusion*, the idea that exposure to mass communication spreads new information through society. Where do people learn about important events, like who won a presidential election, a mass shooting, or the targeted killing of Osama bin Laden? Facebook? Twitter? Or through television (e.g., Kaye & Johnson, 2011)? Diffusion is complicated. Increasingly, people are learning about these events through the Internet and social media. Researchers have studied diffusion over the past decades, assembling a variety of conclusions about how people learn about events of national consequence, such as when news diffuses first from media, when it spreads primarily through interpersonal communication channels, and when followers spread information to leaders (Weimann, 1994). These lines of inquiry were generated by the original research on the two-step flow.

Fourth, two different political communication perspectives can be simultaneously true. The media profoundly influence politics. The early work got that right. At the same time, voters harbor strong attitudes. What people bring to media can sometimes trump media content. Klapper got that right. People do filter campaign messages through their attitudes, rejecting communications that conflict with their political attitudes and accepting those that congeal with what they believe. Two different ideas can both be true, with one operating more on certain people or at certain levels of society than the other. Or they can work together.

Thus, Klapper was correct that media work within the context of people's social networks. It is almost literally true in some contexts today. You can be on your Facebook page, reading a news feed or a journalist's blog that a friend posted. Klapper also got it right when he suggested that media effects work in concert with social and interpersonal agents of influence. Media have long been known to supplement, complement, and interact with information that we receive from parents or friends we respect. But where Klapper went astray was in minimizing media effects, suggesting that they were almost trivial. When television advertising strengthens beliefs acquired through interpersonal conversation or from early socialization, this reinforcement matters. Much campaign persuasion focuses on convincing voters to act on their beliefs. If media exposure persuades voters to translate an attitude into action by casting a vote, this can be politically consequential, turning the tide in the advertised candidate's favor in close elections. Political media exert influences on different levels, influencing micro-level voter beliefs about candidates, and macro-level institutions, such as the presidential primaries, which are primarily focused around television and the Internet.

Fifth, concerns about powerful media effects are a pervasive theme in American political communication. There is an interesting continuity in communication research. Early on, observers expressed fear about how the new electronic media, chiefly radio, could exert devastating effects on the public. Then, when comic books came around, fears centered on them. Next concerns focused on television and TV violence, followed by negative political commercials, video game violence, the Internet, and Facebook. As Ellen A. Wartella and her colleagues have perceptively noted, both academics and the public-at-large typically *assume* that the new media will exert powerful effects (Wartella, 1996; Wartella & Reeves, 1985). Over time, as the technology diffuses and becomes part of everyday life, a more modest, complex theory takes hold. Scholars change their tune, recognizing that the medium is not as powerful as they once feared, and they qualify their conjectures (Wartella, 1996).

This has stimulated an interesting "meta-debate" among communication researchers. For many years it was widely assumed that early propaganda researchers believed in a simplistic model of media effects that likened the media to a hypodermic needle that injected a message into audiences. But when scholars tried to find the term in the early research of the 20th century, they could find little evidence that the phrase *hypodermic needle* was invoked to describe mass media effects (Chaffee & Hochheimer, 1985; see also Bineham, 1988). Adding another layer to the discussion, Wartella and Stout (2002) reported that some research conducted during the 1930s adopted a more complex and nuanced view of media effects, hardly what one would expect if all the researchers thought of media in simple terms. Other scholars (Lubken, 2008) have even argued that the hypodermic needle notion served the function of a "straw man" for researchers. It allowed them to pat themselves on the back for coming up with more sophisticated views of media, when in fact no one actually held a simplistic view at the get-go.

Academics aside, there is no question that, across different eras, many members of the general public have *assumed* the media exert powerful effects. In 1922, Lippmann worried that the powers-that-be could instill pictures in our heads and manufacture consent. In 2011, a *New York Times* critic, describing video art, remarked on "the degree to which our world, what we take for reality, is formed by recording and image-making machinery." He noted that "our minds organize incoming information into images and narratives that may or may not be true to the facts," adding "we live in a world of scary, reality-determining technologies" (Johnson, 2011, p. C22).

Amazing! He may be right, but the point is that you could have found a similar paragraph in articles which writers penned in the 1920s, except they would have worried that movies or radio or propaganda controlled us. This represents a common thread in American political history. "The central paradox of America's constitutional tradition," Hogan (2013) observes, "lies in a persistent tension between our commitment to popular sovereignty and fears that 'the people' might be too easily distracted or manipulated to govern themselves" (p. 10). A conundrum of democracy is that democratic government requires organized communication to inform a mass electorate. However, the presence of both institutionalized public relations and mass media industries generate fears of abuse, some based in fantasy, others in fact. When is the public justified in fearing manipulation? When are fears about "brainwashing" and massive media effects out of whack with reality? When should critics worry about White House news management? When do these worries reflect a cynical projection of sinister motives to well-intentioned policies developed by the nation's leaders? These are important questions that thread their way through American political communication.

Sixth, continued debate and dialogue characterize current political communication scholarship. There is not a party line, but continuing questions, the mark of a healthy discipline. Does the Internet facilitate or impede democracy? Do campaigns inform or mislead the electorate? Scholars are not of one mind on these questions. Some scholars are more optimistic about the Internet, arguing that it can strengthen civic engagement (Boulianne, 2009). Others see a more negative picture, arguing that it merely reinforces existing prejudices (Sunstein, 2001). Some researchers point to the deceptive, manip-ulative aspects of campaigns (Le Cheminant & Parrish, 2011). Others argue that campaigns can help voters come up with a more informed choice. Debate among ideas is healthy (see Reflections box). It generates vigorous discussion and helps researchers come up with more sophisticated models of political communication.

All this raises questions. When debates ensue, who is right? Who is wrong? How can we tell? One of the tenets of this book is that we need reliable, valid, and systematically gathered information to answer these questions. This is where social science comes into the picture. It helps us answer questions and assists scholars in reaching more reasoned judgments about normative issues.

REFLECTIONS: PREACHING TO THE CHOIR?

Some years back, several prominent scholars engaged in a dialogue in an academic journal, debating a time-honored question: How powerful are political media? W. Lance Bennett and Shanto Iyengar (2008) argued that the media are *less* likely to exert strong effects today than 20 years ago. When the three broadcast networks dominated the airwaves, viewers of different political stripes all tuned in; they had no choice. And as a result, the networks could shape political beliefs. But today, with Fox News shows on the right, MSNBC's talk shows on the left, along with the politically irreverent *South Park*, conservatives flock to Fox, liberals move to MSNBC, and the irreverent surf to *South Park*. The media don't change these viewers' attitudes so much as act as cheerleaders who strengthen their convictions that they're right and the other side is wrong. As Bennett and Iyengar (2008) noted, "people who feel strongly about the correctness of their cause or policy preferences are more likely to seek out information they believe is consistent with their preferences" (p. 720). Conservative Republicans tune in to Sean Hannity on Fox and liberal Democrats gravitate to Rachel Maddow on MSNBC. Internet-surfing politicos find confirmation of their political worlds from like-minded websites.

Bennett and Iyengar argued that the media do not have sweeping effects. Media reinforce what people already believe, preaching to the choir. In a sense, this thesis harkened back to Klapper's view of limited effects, albeit with new 21st century wrinkles. Bennett and Iyengar also lamented the philosophical shortcomings in the current media scene. In a democratic society, we want citizens to come across views that differ from their own and reflect on alternative perspectives. But if people are tuning in to media that confirm what they already think, and media cultivate an audience of like-minded viewers, no one changes. People just end up feeling all the more strongly about their preexisting beliefs. For example, many of us receive Facebook posts that reaffirm our view of the political world. Rarely do we come across or "like" posts that shake up our preexisting sentiments. Increasingly, people live in customized worlds of political media that allow them to avoid perspectives with which they do not agree (Turow, 1997).

R. Lance Holbert and his colleagues offered an alternative, more optimistic perspective. They argued that media still exert strong influences. Fox News viewers may indeed gravitate to their conservative talk show hosts. However, Holbert, Garrett, and Gleason (2010) noted that a majority of Fox viewers still tune in to one of the big three broadcast news programs, which in turn can shape opinions. What's more, they noted, Bennett and Iyengar neglected the powerful positive role played by social media sites like Facebook, along with Twitter, YouTube, and bipartisan blog posts. These platforms have transformed the political communication landscape both in America and across the globe. Far from exerting a minimal impact, social media technologies can strongly influence political attitudes. The expanded informational environment exposes individuals to a broad array of political information, Holbert and his colleagues argued.

What do you think? Do you believe media mostly reinforce what people already believe? Can you think of instances in which media might have broader effects? How often do you ever hear chin-scratching views that cause you to question what you believe? Thinking more generally about political communication, do you believe that we have entered an era in which people tune in to genres they agree with and come away more convinced that their side is correct? Or, given social media and the seemingly infinite supply of political information on the Internet, perhaps it can be argued that citizens have access to a broader spectrum of views than ever before. What do you think?

SOCIAL SCIENCE AND POLITICAL COMMUNICATION

After tossing different topics over in your mind, you decide that an examination of media bias seems like a pretty good topic for a paper in your political communication class. After all, you think to yourself, "it's a well-known fact the media are biased." It should be an interesting paper, you muse. Almost fun, though that might be stretching it.

Expecting the paper to roll out smoothly, it comes as a surprise when suddenly all these pesky questions grab hold of you and won't let go. Questions like: What do we mean by *bias*? Can the news put a candidate in a negative light without showing bias? How do you measure bias, anyway? How do you figure out if the candidate is described in a way that is favorable, unfavorable, or neutral?

As it turns out, those are good questions, just the kind that social scientists wrestle with when conducting research (see Chapter 9). Research fundamentally focuses on exploring the unknown and uncovering mysteries. It is about finding answers to questions that puzzle us and trying to figure out if a hunch is correct or an observation that is commonly believed to be true actually is. But research is not a walk in the park. **Social science** involves a series of logical and empirical steps (Babbie, 2004). The logic concerns development of theories and hypotheses. The empirical refers to the testing of hypotheses through evidence gathered in actual social settings. Social scientists apply scientific methods to try to uncover regularities or patterns in human behavior. This section describes the social science methods that political communication researchers employ to answer interesting questions about politics and media.

Social science is employed to develop a body of knowledge of the role that political communication plays in society (Holbert & Bucy, 2011). To be sure, the social scientific approach is not the only way to approach the study of politics and media. We can gain insights from investigative articles in the press, film documentaries and even political novels. But social science offers a dispassionate framework in which researchers ideally set aside personal biases and explore issues through the rigorous realm of hypothesis-testing and empirical methodologies.

Social science cannot answer "should" questions. It cannot tell us whether limits should be placed on campaign spending or, alternatively, if a hands-off approach is better for democracy. It cannot say whether presidential debates should be open to third party candidates, if government should devote funds to the ailing newspaper industry, or if WikiLeaks should be shut down. However, it is important to note that, by accumulating research findings, social science *can* provide insights on questions like these. For example, if we find that negative advertising dispirits voters and depresses turnout, this information could be brought to bear on policy decisions. More generally, research can clarify conundrums about the role played by political communication in society, pinpoint falsehoods, and build a body of knowledge of political communication processes and effects. These are worthy pursuits.

Research starts with a theory and hypothesis. To some degree, everyone has theories about politics and media. If you think the media are the primary influence on people's beliefs about politics, you have a theory. If you think the media are irrelevant, and it's our friends who influence us, you have a theory. If you believe that the media bash conservatives, prop up the powers-that-be, or, alternatively, are increasingly irrelevant to how young people experience politics, you have a theory.

At least sort of. These are "lay theories" or intuitions about political communication. Truth be told, they are not formal scientific theories unless they contain a well-developed underlying conceptualization and a series of predictions that describe, explain, and predict events. A **theory** is a large, sweeping conceptualization that offers a wide-ranging explanation of a phenomenon and generates concrete hypotheses about when and why specific events will occur. A **hypothesis** is a specific proposition that can be tested through evidence.

Researchers begin with a theory and hypothesis because they provide a potential roadmap to the territory. Starting a research journey without theory and hypotheses would be like venturing off onto a journey of a foreign land with your eyes closed, or like starting a day's trek through the circuitous pathways of a European city—say, Florence, Italy—with no roadmap, only a desire to see some art. Theories offer a way to interpret the world of human phenomena; hypotheses present a way to empirically determine if these ideas are likely to be true. Together they can help us arrive at a body of factually based knowledge, which in turn can illuminate and help offer insights on normative issues.

Strictly speaking, research tests a hypothesis derived from a theory. When enough hypotheses from different layers of the theory are supported, we no longer call it a theory, but an established body of knowledge. In the biological sciences, evolution fits into this category. We have less certainty in the social sciences, but there are areas where hypotheses have been confirmed with enough regularity and sufficient confirming evidence has been obtained that we can speak with confidence about the validity of the knowledge base.

When you are talking with your friends, you can claim that such-and-such is true and people may politely agree. (Or perhaps not, if you have a particularly contentious group of friends!) When you are working in the domain of social scientific studies of political communication, you cannot say something is true unless there is scientific evidence to substantiate it. And that's the beauty of research. It separates the fanciful wheat from the factual chaff. It tells us what is more likely to be true and what is more likely to be false.

RESEARCH METHODOLOGIES

Methodology is to research as cooking is to the work of a chef. You need ideas to start, but the proof is in the empirical pudding. Methods put hypotheses to the test. There are a number of research methodologies that are harnessed in political communication studies.

Content Analysis

A widely used tool in social science research, **content analysis** is a systematic method to quantitatively examine the characteristics, themes, and symbols of a message. Content analyses can tell us if news covers certain candidates more favorably than others, whether female politicians receive different types of news coverage than male politicians, and how candidates use websites to promote their campaigns. It was an ingenious invention because it gave us a way of saying with certainty just what a message contains. It helped scholars to map the symbolic landscape of a nation's political system.

Content analysis quantifies—or describes with numbers—components of the content of communications. Content analyses usually examine verbal dimensions of media content, such as words and arguments. But they can also quantify audiovisual images, like how frequently candidates display compassion with the kiss of a baby, and similarity through a rolled-up shirt sleeve, as well as how the news media select certain camera shots to emphasize a candidate smiling or frowning (Grabe & Bucy, 2011). Visual images play an important role in political communication, and content analysis offers a way to carefully document these images.

A challenge in content analysis is determining your unit of analysis. Should you search for bias in each paragraph in a news story? Or should you focus instead on the adjectives reporters use to describe a political figure? In addition, you probably will not want to examine each and every news story, political speech, or website. You will need to sample. But what type of sample should you draw, and how? There are criteria researchers employ to help answer these questions.

Finally, you will need to distinguish between *manifest* and *latent* content (Benoit, 2011). Manifest content refers to what is obviously there, right on the surface, like the issues that a politician discusses or sources a reporter quotes. Latent content is the subtle, deeper message that requires more judgment and analysis to ferret out, like the emotion that a candidate expresses, or even the degree to which a news story is biased. A news story can depict a candidate smiling a lot, but this does not mean the story is biased in the candidate's behalf. It may just mean that the candidate smiles a lot or knows how to package herself before the camera. Bias requires an inference that content reflects a reporter's insertion of his or her own attitude into the story. This occurs from time to time, yet can be hard to demonstrate empirically. In addition, a news story that shows a candidate in a favorable light may not cause viewers to develop a positive attitude toward the candidate. This is a question of media effects, the purview of methods that follow.

Experiment

The hallmark of scientific research, an **experiment** is a controlled study that provides evidence of causation through random assignment of individuals to a treatment or control group. A treatment is a stimulus of interest—for example, an experimental drug in a medical study and a news segment in a political communication experiment. A scientific experiment involves at least two conditions: an experimental condition in which the treatment is administered, and a comparison or control group. Random assignment refers to the allocation of individuals to conditions, based on chance factors. Names may be assigned numbers, and numbers are randomly selected from a random numbers table.

Experiments have demonstrated that the news can influence beliefs about national problems; political persuasion shapes attitudes; and political humor can increase cynicism. Although it may seem funny to think about rarefied experiments in the rough-and-tumble world of politics, they are actually extremely useful in helping us to say with certainty whether Factor (or Variable) X causes Outcome Y. Political communication is so complicated that it is good to know for certain if a variable can cause an outcome (Arceneaux, 2010).

The shortcoming of experiments derives from their strength. Precisely because they take place in a controlled setting, they cannot tell us whether the experimental finding actually occurs in the real world. An experiment may tell us that exposure to a negative political advertisement makes people more cynical about politics in the laboratory. But will this hold up in the real world, where people may not even see the commercial in question? Will the effects persist over time? Over the past decades, researchers have perfected a number of strategies to increase the realism of experiments, enhancing confidence that they can apply the results to real-life political contexts (Iyengar, 2011).

Survey

This is a dominant research strategy in political communication (Holbert & Bucy, 2011). A **survey** is a questionnaire or interview-based study that documents a correlation or relationship between two or more variables in a real-world setting, identifying factors that can best predict a particular outcome. A correlation is a measure of the linkage or relationship between two factors. You have taken many surveys yourself, from course evaluations to Facebook polls.

Surveys play a particularly important role in political communication because they are so flexible. Researchers can ask lots of questions about different political variables, and, unlike super-sensitive topics like prejudice, where people don't always tell the truth, people are usually fairly comfortable answering questions about politics on a questionnaire. A survey can tell us many interesting things, like if Internet use leads to more civic participation, whether television news increases knowledge of public affairs, and the degree to which the impact of news on knowledge depends on your educational level.

A key aspect of surveys is *measurement*—measuring your concepts validly in a questionnaire. Let's say you are a journalism major and a news junkie, and believe that news does all sorts of good things, like increasing knowledge of politics and offering voters guidance in making candidate choices. Tired of your friends' cracks that the news is boring and of little value, you decide to conduct a survey to demonstrate that your hypothesis about news effects is supported by evidence. But you need to empirically assess news media use in order to differentiate those who follow the news a lot from those who hardly follow it at all. You ask people how much exposure they have to news.

Alas, exposure to news is a general category. It would be like testing the hypothesis that college increases critical thinking skills by asking students how much exposure they had to college or to college classes. It's not just exposure that could catalyze critical thinking. It is how much attention students pay to the material, how they process the information, how they link up the class to other goals in their life, and so forth. Applying this to news, it would be better to ask respondents how much attention they pay to news, as well as how they reflect on and process what they see (Hoffman & Young, 2011a; Kosicki, McLeod, & McLeod, 2011).

News is also a general category. What type of news? Newspapers? Television? Local, national, political talk, or all of the above? Are they following news online? And if you ask respondents about their online news use, do you mean a newspaper website, a blog, or a news clip viewed on *The Daily Show* which, complicating matters further, could be a combination of actual news with Jon Stewart's fake news? And suppose the news receiver becomes a news sender (Sundar & Bellur, 2011), forwarding the news he or she views to a friend and adding a sarcastic comment? How do you incorporate all this into the measure?

Specificity is a cardinal virtue in research, and you would want to include ever-more specific measures of news use to incorporate these concerns. It is doable, and there is a lot of contemporary research to guide you, as Hoffman and Young (2011a) helpfully note. The payoff is that more fine-tuned measures could help you make a stronger case to your politically apathetic friends that news has positive influences. Recent refinements in political communication survey research have enabled researchers to make more specific and precise statements about media effects (e.g., Eveland & Morey, 2011; Hayes, Preacher, & Myers, 2011; Kenski, Gottfried, & Jamieson, 2011).

Certain problems still bedevil researchers. Respondents may indicate on a survey that they learned a candidate's issue position from a presidential debate, believing this is where they gleaned the information. But they may have acquired the information from news of the debate or a conversation with a friend who attended closely to the debate. The survey information would therefore be wrong. The trick is to tease out the particular factor that caused an effect. There are ways to hone in on this, and there are several additional research strategies that can help pinpoint communication effects (see Box 3.2).

BOX 3.2 METHODS AND MORE METHODS

More than 35 years ago, when the modern field of political communication was launched (Chaffee, 1975), the discipline lacked the methodology and technology to zoom in on a number of important issues. Over the past decades, the intellectual horizons of the field have expanded, and with this have come a proliferation of new and improved methods (Kosicki, McLeod, & McLeod, 2011). These include:

● Secondary analysis, a technique that allows researchers to reanalyze national data sets with a particular focus or innovative twist (Holbert & Hmielowski, 2011);

● Focus groups, a qualitative (or non-numerical) method, in which a trained leader coordinates a group interview that can yield rich insights on a variety of topics, such as how people talk about politics in everyday life, why many young people do not vote, and reactions to political ads (Jarvis, 2011);

● Multiple strategies to explore communication that occurs in deliberative meetings. This includes systematic analysis of discussion at a school board meeting or town hall forum, as well as post-meeting follow-up interviews with participants (Black et al., 2011); and

● Psychophysiological measures of heart rate, facial muscle activation, brain imaging and other bodily arousal that occurs while watching candidate speeches and negative political ads (Bucy & Bradley, 2011).

Complementing these approaches, rhetorical and discourse-focused scholars study political communication with more qualitative methods. Although these lack the precision of scientific techniques, they can illuminate the rich tableau of political communication, as practiced by leaders and ordinary people. Karlyn

Continued

Kohrs Campbell and Kathleen Hall Jamieson (2008) call on elements of classical political rhetoric in delineating characteristics of presidential inaugural addresses, state of the union speeches, war rhetoric, and national eulogies. Other scholars have employed discourse analysis to offer insights into communicative practices and sometimes contradictory political beliefs expressed by ordinary people in community gatherings, such as school board meetings (Tracy, 2010).

The theme underlying this section has been that theories, hypotheses, and research methods are the foundations of political communication research. Armed with these techniques, scholars can make inroads on intriguing questions. The field of political communication takes a cross-disciplinary approach to research. Ideas from communication, political science, psychology, sociology, and marketing are brought to bear in empirical studies. Scholars ask some of the same questions that you do, but couch them in deeper, more conceptually based hypotheses. They try to answer the questions with social science methods. Political communication scholarship cannot answer all the questions about politics and media, but it has provided some helpful answers over the past several decades. It also has helped to raise critical issues about political media that eluded observers. In some cases, researchers' insights have informed policy. Frequently they have helped to clarify and illuminate the "out of reach, out of sight" political world that so profoundly influences everyday life.

WHAT DO YOU THINK?

Think of one political communication issue—involving media content, perceptions, or effects—that interests you. Devise a hypothesis. How would you conduct a study to explore this issue? Which method would you employ?

CONCLUSIONS

If you thought that the history of political communication would be a bland, monotonous story, you may have been surprised by the twists and turns on the historical path. The history of political communication research involves a series of ebbs, flows, conflicts, and continuities. European scholars like Le Bon and Tarde took note of the power of mass psychology and the ability of newspapers to mold public sentiments. In his 1922 book, *Public Opinion*, Lippmann explained that, unlike in past eras, citizens living in the 20th century did not experience the political world first-hand, and therefore had to rely on fallible news media to supply them with information. News was not truth and people frequently received (and believed) inadequate distillations of the world from news media accounts.

In the years to come, social scientists began to study the effects of political media. Lazarsfeld and his colleagues' Erie County, Ohio voting study seemed to indicate that media had only a modest impact. Interpersonal influence and opinion leadership reigned supreme. Based on research of the 1940s and 1950s, researchers concluded that political media had minimal effects.

This perspective was controversial, rankling scholars who believed that media exerted a preeminent role in politics. With the diffusion of television, apparent impact of news, widespread popular belief in media impact, and (most importantly) proliferation of scientific evidence of strong political communication influences, the limited effects model withered away. It gave way to a robust appreciation of the direct, indirect, and subtle ways that media influence politics.

Reviewing the history of political communication scholarship, one glimpses several continuities. The media influence our pictures of the world, molding ideas, helping us construct beliefs about politics, and influencing attitudes. Interpersonal influence, a concept documented in the 1940s and 1950s, remains relevant to today's political communication. In the contemporary view, some of the conclusions of the limited effects model remain valid (Lang, 2011). Media effects do depend on people's attitudes. Social forces interact with media to determine effects. However, the pessimistic conclusion that media have few effects is incorrect and has been revised over the years. Political ads can reinforce attitudes toward candidates, pushing people to turn out to vote on Election Day. In close elections, these messages may make the difference between victory and defeat. Mediated messages also exert an impact on a host of micro-level attitudes, and the media have shaped the development of political institutions and policy. Over the years, researchers have documented many political communication effects, such as agenda-setting, framing, and political persuasion, topics to be discussed in depth in subsequent chapters.

Political communication is a diverse discipline, enriched by different approaches. A social scientific perspective emphasizes that questions are explored systematically through the articulation of theories, posing of hypotheses, and hypothesis-testing.

The cornerstone of hypothesis-testing is research methodology. We test hypotheses through a variety of empirical methods. Content analyses, experiments, and surveys are major strategies scholars use to test predictions and advance knowledge of political communication. Each has strengths and shortcomings.

The three decades since 1980 have witnessed major transformations in political commu-nication research methods. Content analyses, surveys, and experiments are conducted with more precision and real-world flair. A host of other techniques, including focus groups, deliberative discussion analysis, and psychophysiological measures, have been developed and refined, generating new insights on political communication.

Rigorous tests of hypotheses allow us to advance theory and build a body of knowledge of political communication effects. While social scientific studies cannot answer "ought" questions, they can clarify issues, pinpoint falsehoods, and offer insights about the quality of contemporary democracy.

4   Media and Political Knowledge

Several years back, an amusing YouTube video generated a lot of buzz. An Australian reporter interviewed Americans on the street, asking them ridiculously easy questions about politics, and they answered them all incorrectly. I can't show you what the people looked like, but try to visualize Americans of different shapes and sizes, some puzzling over questions, and others spouting confidently whatever popped into their minds. Here is some of the Q&A that is particularly memorable:

Reporter: Name a country that begins with U.
Man 1: Yugoslavia?
Man 2: With U: Utah.
Woman 1: A country that starts with a U? Utopia.
Woman 2: A country? . . .
Reporter: What about this one?
Woman 2: What?
Reporter: United States of America.
Woman 2: (Gasps, recognizing her obvious error.)
Reporter: What is the religion of Israel?
Man 1: Israeli.
Man 2: Muslim.
Man 3: Islamic.
Man 4: Catholic probably.
Reporter: What religion are Buddhist monks?
Man 1: Buddhist monks?
Man 2: Islamic, I don't know.
Reporter: Who won the Vietnam War?
Woman: We did (laughing). Wait, were we even in the Vietnam War?

Reporter: What is the currency used in the United Kingdom?
Man: Possibly American money?
Woman: Queen Elizabeth's money?

Okay: Some of the people may have been pulling the reporter's leg, and the sample is hardly representative of the public. But the example touches on two important issues in democratic theory: What do Americans know about politics? Does it matter?

These two quintessential questions about citizenship in a media age were posed some years back by Michael X. Delli Carpini and Scott Keeter (1996) in a classic book. The answers to both questions are fascinating and may surprise you. Normative democratic theories place a premium on citizen knowledge and competence. You cannot have a functioning democratic society if citizens are ignorant of basic facts of government and cannot grasp the array of problems facing their society. "For democratic decision making to be meaningful and legitimate," political scientists Richard G. Niemi and Jane Junn (1998) note, "citizens must be capable of understanding what is at stake in politics, what their alternatives are, and what their own positions are" (p. 9). Nowadays, the media are the major vehicles that transmit political information to citizens.

This chapter and the one that follows offer an in-depth examination of citizenship in an age of mediated politics. The present chapter focuses on knowledge, and Chapter 5 examines the socialization of political beliefs and attitudes. This chapter is divided into two sections. The first section examines what Americans know about politics, what they don't know, and the reasons why knowledge levels are not as high as they could or should be. The second portion examines the media's impact on knowledge acquisition. Several different approaches to media and political information-holding are introduced, followed by a discussion of political learning in a digital age.

WHAT DO AMERICANS KNOW ABOUT POLITICS?

First, the good news.

In their systematic review of national surveys of political knowledge conducted over the course of a half-century, Delli Carpini and Keeter concluded that Americans are modestly informed about politics and have basic knowledge of a number of aspects of government. In this vast, richly diverse country, marked by striking differences in income and education, there is widespread knowledge of the definition of a presidential veto, the length of a presidential term, and the meaning of *deregulation*. There is also substantial knowledge of key aspects of the U.S. Constitution and civil liberties, such as the fact that the Constitution can be amended, freedom of the press is guaranteed by the First Amendment, and citizens have the right to a trial by jury. Most Americans can name at least one position in the U.S. Cabinet and know the number of senators from their state. Ninety-nine percent of Americans can correctly name the U.S. president, compared to 89 percent of Italians who can name their head of state!

A more recent survey of knowledge of the 2012 presidential campaign, conducted by the Pew Research Center for the People and the Press, reported similar results. There was overwhelming awareness (85 percent) that Joe Biden is vice president of the U.S. More than two-thirds of voters recognized that Obama was the presidential candidate who favored increasing taxes on income higher than $250,000 (Pew Research Center for the People and the Press, 2012a).

But the ignorance and disparities in knowledge, reported by Delli Carpini and Keeter and others, are, well . . . nothing short of breathtaking:

- Less than half the public can accurately define several concepts that are central to democratic politics, such as *liberal* and *conservative*, or know how presidential delegates are selected.
- Just 35 percent could name both senators from their state. Three-quarters of all Americans do not appreciate the difference between a legislator and a judge (Breyer, 2010).
- Just over half believe revolutionary speech is not protected by the U.S. Constitution. A disturbing 45 percent believe that a member of the Communist party *cannot* run for president. Twenty-nine percent think a person can be tried twice for the same crime.
- Only a third of the public can name all three branches of government (executive, legislative, and judicial, in case you forgot). Yet two-thirds could name a TV judge on *American Idol* (Breyer, 2010).
- Only about 25 percent of Americans can identify *more than one* of the five freedoms ensured by the First Amendment (freedom of speech, press, religion, assembly, and petition for redress of grievance). But more than half had no trouble naming two members of *The Simpsons* (Shenkman, 2008).
- Geographical knowledge is staggeringly low. Just over half of the public could locate Central America or France on a map. What's more, only 50 percent of Americans could locate Ohio on a map and 42 percent could accurately locate New Jersey (though with Snooki's fame on MTV's *Jersey Shore*, the percentage may rise)!
- There are widespread inequalities in political knowledge. Educated and wealthier Americans are immensely more knowledgeable than their less-educated and poorer counterparts.

Adlai Stevenson, the Democratic presidential candidate of 1952 and 1956, said it best. A supporter once told him, "Governor Stevenson, all thinking people are for you!" Stevenson replied "That's not enough. I need a majority" (cf. Shenkman, p. 37; see also politics quizzes in the Reflections box and at http://www.pewresearch.org/quiz/the-news-iq-quiz/).

There is a paradox here. We live at a time when we are swamped with information, glutted with facts, and bombarded by political stimuli. Never before has society had so much political information, and never before has it been easier to access information. Yet people are frequently uninformed on political issues and the Internet is awash in falsehoods and misleading statements of political fact. Democracy requires political knowledge, and it is there for the grasping. But citizens' knowledge does not reach the levels deemed appropriate by political philosophers.

REFLECTIONS: WHAT DO YOU KNOW ABOUT POLITICS?

Go ahead. Give it a try. You probably will do better than you think. What follows below is a quiz about politics. There are just 12 questions and the answers appear at the end.

1. The electorate is defined as:

   a. all individuals who are qualified to vote in an election
   b. the entire population of a particular democratic country
   c. individuals who have voted twice in their lives
   d. people who have been elected to political office.

2. How long is a U.S. senator's term?

   a. 2 years
   b. 4 years
   c. 8 years
   d. 6 years.

3. A caucus, a prominent part of the current U.S. presidential nomination process, is defined as a:

   a. state-wide election in which individuals cast their votes for candidates in a secret ballot

   b.   local gathering, where individuals publicly deliberate and decide which of several candidates they support

   c.   local gathering, where individuals decide which candidate to support, casting votes in private

   d.   gathering among top leaders of the party, where leaders decide which candidate should be the party's nominee.

4.   Democratic and Republican political party nominees in the U.S. are formally selected by:

   a.   voters, who cast votes in primary elections in 50 states

   b.   political party leaders, seeking to represent the views of their party

   c.   the news media, primarily Fox and CNN

   d.   delegates.

5.   The controversial Citizens United Supreme Court decision on campaign finance did which of these:

   a.   ruled that it was illegal for political action committees to donate to political campaigns

   b.   prohibited corporations and labor unions from spending money on elections

   c.   ruled that the government may not ban independent political spending by corporations and unions in elections

   d.   barred individuals who made more than a million dollars from donating to any political campaign?

6.   In mid-2012, the Supreme Court ruled on the constitutionality of Obama's health care act, popularly called Obamacare. The Court:

   a.   declared the act unconstitutional

   b.   upheld the act

   c.   deferred a decision until 2014, when it went to effect

   d.   passed it down to a lower court.

Continued

7. Which of these describes its decision?

   a. The Court ruled that the requirement that Americans obtain health insurance or pay a penalty is authorized by Congressional power to levy taxes.
   b. The Court ruled that the requirement that Americans have health insurance can be justified by Congress's power to regulate interstate commerce.
   c. The Court, declaring the entire law unconstitutional, said Americans cannot be forced to buy health insurance.
   d. The Supreme Court deferred action on a technicality.

8. Which of these is true of presidential debates?

   a. The first televised presidential debate occurred between Jimmy Carter and Ronald Reagan in 1980.
   b. Presidential debates have become a ritualized part of the presidential campaign, with questions asked by journalists and citizens.
   c. Congress legally requires that debates occur every four years, with a debate on domestic issues, foreign policy, and social issues.
   d. Debates are judged according to formal political debating rules, with the winner decided by the Senate Majority Leader and Speaker of the House.

9. Who did Mitt Romney choose as his vice presidential candidate in 2012?

   a. Rob Portman
   b. Tim Pawlenty
   c. Newt Gingrich
   d. Paul Ryan.

10. What is this individual's favorite musical group or singer?

   a. Rage Against the Machine
   b. Prince
   c. Beatles
   d. Frank Sinatra.

11. The Occupy Wall Street Movement famously claimed that this is the percentage of Americans whose incomes have stagnated while the very rich have prospered. Those left behind are known as:

    a.   the 5%
    b.   the 60%
    c.   the 99%
    d.   the 17%.

12. An international political controversy occurred in 2013 when Edward Snowden leaked National Security Agency documents. The controversy fundamentally involved:

    a.   whether websites can show how to build a nuclear bomb
    b.   whether government surveillance violates citizens' civil liberties
    c.   whether Americans can get a job with the National Security Agency in Washington, D.C.
    d.   whether advertisers can track consumers' activities on websites through web or browser cookies.

How did you do? Better or worse than expected?

With the quiz in mind, you might consider a few more general issues that researchers ponder. For example: Is a survey like this one a good way to tap into political knowledge, or would broader questions be more appropriate? Do voters really need to know arcane aspects of civics to fulfill their role as citizens? Alternatively, how can citizens competently fulfill their roles if they don't know the most basic of civics facts?

Answers: 1: a; 2: d; 3: b; 4: d; 5: c; 6: b; 7: a; 8: b; 9: d; 10: a; 11: c; 12: b.

WHY DO PEOPLE KNOW SO LITTLE?

Americans' ignorance of basic facts about government is disturbing. Americans know significantly less about political issues, particularly international problems, than citizens from a host of European countries (Aalberg & Curran, 2012). What accounts for the knowledge deficits? Five explanations have been advanced (see Aalberg & Curran, 2012).

One reason is lack of incentive. A key way people make their voices known in democracy is through voting. Yet one person's vote makes virtually no difference in the outcome of an election. From a purely rational perspective, it is not in an individual's self-interest to expend much time soaking up political information when his or her input is of such little consequence.

A second explanation of low knowledge levels emphasizes the way news is presented. Its focus on facts, figures, and jargon can overwhelm people. News about the economic crisis can contain mind-numbing discussion of *mortgage-backed securities*, *over-leveraging*, or *liquidity shortfall*, concepts that most people do not understand and that are explained poorly, if at all, by journalists. In addition, American television networks devote less time to news during peak hours (7 to 10 p.m.) than do European broadcasts (Aalberg, van Aelst, & Curran, 2012). Despite the growth of CNN and Fox, there is actually less news provided during prime time in the U.S. than in six European nations. This helps explain why Americans know less about politics than do their European counterparts.

A third explanation lies in the expansion in media choices. With a multitude of entertaining cable channels, YouTube, and social media sites, news may be swamped by other channels, lost in the mix. "Those who prefer nonpolitical content can more easily escape the news and therefore pick up less political information than they used to," one scholar observes (Prior, 2005, p. 577). Ironically, as the volume of political information has grown exponentially with the Internet, political knowledge may have declined among the less interested members of the public. When television was the dominant medium, even the more apathetic could not avoid the news. When the television set was on, they watched and may have soaked up some facts. Nowadays, politics may be easier to ignore.

Fourth, leaders sometimes deliberately dissemble information, intentionally conveying misleading political facts. Back in the 1990s, some political leaders described Social Security in doomsday terms, talking about the "impending bankruptcy" of the financial program. Policymakers claimed that the program would run out of cash by the 2030s, even though there would actually be enough funds available to pay retirees for another two decades to come. Some leaders may have resorted to hyperbole in an effort to push Congress into acting sooner rather than later. Others may have had more opportunistic motives. Whatever the reason, the political rhetoric did not match the facts. Yet it had demonstrable effects on public knowledge. During the debate about Social Security in 1998 and 1999, about a third of Americans incorrectly believed that Social Security would completely run out of money (Jerit & Barabas, 2006).

The final explanation for low knowledge levels lies in the increasing disconnect between politics and everyday life. To many Americans, politics has become the province of political professionals—consultants-for-hire who manage campaigns that people passively watch, a faraway road show that has little to do with their personal lives.

The Case for a Minimally Informed Citizenry

Maybe it's not so bad. Perhaps the criticism of citizens is misplaced, placing unreasonable expectations on contemporary voters. Perhaps people are doing just fine, when all is said and done.

Although it may surprise you, this is a well-respected philosophical perspective articulated by a number of political scientists. Scholars acknowledge that in an ideal world, people would closely follow politics and formulate thoughtful perspectives on every issue. But this is unrealistic, given the demands on everyone's time and the difficulty of understanding immensely complicated issues. Consequently, people develop shortcuts or **heuristics** to help them make political decisions.

Voters evaluate candidates based on whether short descriptions of candidates' positions are roughly congenial with their own values. They use political party labels as guides, casting a vote for nominees of their preferred party. Voters loosely follow presidential debates, checking to see if their candidate is knowledgeable about the issues and can competently defend positions. They may rely on the views of respected opinion leaders, as expressed in newspaper editorials, on cable TV, or in blogs. People may fall short in their knowledge of basic civics or international issues, but nonetheless remain capable of making reasonable decisions in elections (Sniderman, Brody, & Tetlock, 1991). A majority of voters can accurately identify the Republicans' and Democratic Party's positions on raising taxes on the wealthy, increasing gay rights, restricting abortion, and trimming the size of the federal government (Pew Research Center for the People and the Press, 2012b).

Some researchers also note that tests of political knowledge are flawed, requiring people to supply trivial facts that are peripheral to the actual task of citizenship. Other scholars point out that good citizenship does not require intimate knowledge of every issue covered in the news. Citizens can scan the political environment, looking out for dangers to their personal well-being and the public welfare. They can fulfill their civic duty by simply monitoring the political environment (Schudson, 1998; see also Zaller, 2003).

Some scholars go further, noting that the system can function adequately so long as there is a healthy minority of individuals who closely follow political issues, remain knowledgeable about politics, and partake in activist causes. Everyone does not have to boast top-flight knowledge, so long as some do. According to **elite democratic theory**, politics in industrialized democracies has become so complicated and time-consuming that it requires a class of experts to make high-level political decisions. These experts are elected officials, who are accountable to the people through free and fair elections. The political theorist Joseph Schumpeter (1976) bluntly noted that "democracy means only that the people have the opportunity of accepting or refusing the men who are to rule them . . . Now one aspect of this may be expressed by saying that democracy is the rule of the politician" (pp. 284–285).

As you might expect, this view of elite democracy has generated considerable criticism. Leave democracy to the politicians? That's precisely the problem with modern politics, critics charge. Professional politicians are not responsive to the people, but to lobbyists and moneyed interests who finance their campaigns, skeptics lament. Advocates of deliberative and participatory democracy argue that even in our mediated age, democracy must be based on the active engagement of citizens in decisions that affect their lives. Fair enough. But how much should people know about politics? What does the good citizen to know to fulfill civic duty? What facts can the dutiful voter reasonably ignore? There are not hard-and-fast answers to these questions.

WHAT DO YOU THINK?

Does the public's lack of knowledge of many political issues pose a problem for democracy? Or do citizens manage acceptably, in ways that enhance democratic aims?

MEDIA AND POLITICAL KNOWLEDGE

So, how do people acquire information about government and public affairs? What is the source of their knowledge? The mass media and Internet play an important role, offering the raw materials from which citizens construct beliefs about politics.

We gain insight on the impact media exert on political knowledge by exploring different perspectives on the issue. The approaches emphasize concepts from the fields of mass communication, psychology, and sociology.

Mass Communication Perspective

A mass communication perspective examines the distinctive effects that a particular communication medium exerts on knowledge. Newspapers contain detailed articles with considerable information. Their format allows people to re-read articles, which

Figure 4.1 For many decades, newspaper readership was strongly associated with high knowledge of public affairs. With newspapers on the downswing, will political knowledge dramatically decline? Or will news websites take their place?

iStockphoto

can encourage deeper processing of information. For these and other reasons, newspaper readership has long been associated with high levels of political knowledge (Becker & Whitney, 1980; Robinson & Levy, 1986; see Figure 4.1). Newspapers were supplanted by television in the middle of the 20th century, as TV became the dominant medium for conveying news to the public. There has been much debate over the years about the role television news plays in political learning. Critics charge that frequently simplistic stories do not do justice to complex social problems. Defenders note that television's dramatic format can helpfully communicate symbols and emotionally arousing events, such as national tragedies; TV can also be particularly effective in imparting information to audiences that are deficient in formal education (Graber, 2001; Prior, 2002).

A more specific mass communication approach is **constructionism**, pioneered by W. Russell Neuman, Marion R. Just, and Ann N. Crigler (Armoudian & Crigler, 2010; Neuman, Just, & Crigler, 1992). Constructionism examines how people construct meaning from media messages. It focuses on how individuals form beliefs and political attitudes from exposure to media. Like the limited effects perspective discussed in

Chapter 3, constructionism emphasizes that media rarely have simple, uniform effects on everyone. Unlike the limited effects view, it stipulates that mass media can strongly influence cognitions. Constructionism says that effects depend on the interaction among demographic categories, the psychology of the audience member, and content of a particular medium.

Psychological Approach

A psychological viewpoint focuses more directly on the many cognitive and emotional attributes individuals bring to political media. Like constructionism, the psychological view emphasizes that you cannot appreciate the effects of news media on knowledge without understanding how people process or think about news.

A key psychological factor is a **schema**, defined as "a cognitive structure consisting of organized knowledge about situations and individuals that has been abstracted from prior experiences" (Graber, 1988, p. 28). Political communication scholar Doris A. Graber has extensively studied the types of political schemas citizens employ in processing the news. She shook up the political communication field by showing that viewers do not just soak up whatever happens to be shown on the nightly news. Graber demonstrated that processing the news is active, not passive. People don't start with a blank slate. The act of remembering news involves relating the news to what people already know or believe.

News that resonates with viewers' preexisting beliefs is likely to reinforce and strengthen their attitudes. News stories that shake up or conflict with knowledge structures are apt to be psychologically questioned. This is why many Americans had trouble accepting the fact that Iraq did not possess weapons of mass destruction (WMDs). The White House, thought by many to be a source of factual information, drummed in the linkage between Iraq and WMDs. The linkage had been repeated for many years by both Democrats and Republicans. Thus, even though there was abundant evidence that Iraq did not possess WMDs, it violated long-held beliefs and took a long time to sink in.

Sociological Approach

A sociological view emphasizes the influence of broad demographic and social structural factors. Education is a time-honored predictor of knowledge. With more education comes significantly greater knowledge about politics (Delli Carpini & Keeter, 1996; Fraile, 2011). Social class also exerts a major impact. Wealthier individuals know more about politics than do their less affluent counterparts. This is not to say that those with little education or income lack knowledge about issues that bear directly on their well-being or they have no political opinions. They most assuredly do. However, at least as judged by standard tests of political knowledge, they do not fare as well as those with more money and education.

Social class enhances knowledge for a couple of reasons. First, people with a college degree are better able to understand and process the news. Second, middle- and upper-middle-class individuals are freed from the strains of poverty, which affords them more time to reflect on political issues.

Other research has combined sociological and mass communication perspectives, focusing on intersections between the disciplines. One of the persistent findings in political communication research is that there are **knowledge gaps**, where media exacerbate differences produced by two sociological factors: income and education, called socioeconomic status (see Figure 4.2).

According to the knowledge gap notion, people higher in socioeconomic status are at the outset more knowledgeable about politics than those lower in socioeconomic status.

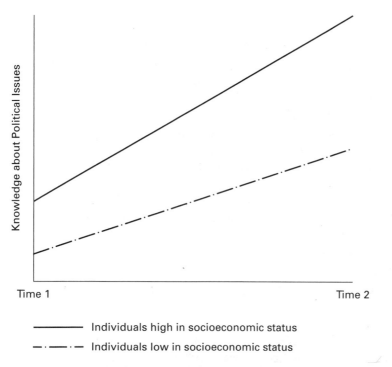

Figure 4.2 Diagram of the knowledge gap in political communication. Knowledge is measured at Time 1, before media publicity of a political issue, and again at Time 2, after the issue has been publicized in the media.

Ideally, publicity, media messages, or an Internet campaign should provide the "have-nots" with more information, leveling the gap. But the knowledge gap hypothesis asserts that the opposite occurs: The high-status, well-informed citizens acquire more information and at a faster clip than their low-status, poorly informed counterparts. The gap widens, rather than closes (Gaziano, 1997; Nadeau et al., 2008; Tichenor, Donohue, & Olien, 1970). The "knowledge-rich get richer," and the less informed fall farther behind (e.g., Brundidge & Rice, 2009). This is unfair and does not comport with the value that democratic theorists—philosophers, scholars, all of us really—place on equality. We want information to level the playing field. When the media accentuate knowledge gaps, the system is not working as it ideally should. This highlights an imperfection in contemporary democracy.

Putting It Together

What do we take from all this? Although mass media are not a panacea, obliterating knowledge deficits and inequities, they have had positive effects. Research offers four general conclusions about media and knowledge levels.

First, the media play an instrumental role in informing Americans. For all their faults, the media provide information that is indispensable to informed citizenship. "Those who follow the news in any medium are more knowledgeable than their peers who do not," observed political communication scholar Steven H. Chaffee (Chaffee & Yang, 1990 p. 138; see also Barabas & Jerit, 2009; Pasek et al., 2006). People who attend to the news know more about politics than those who do not follow the news. Different media have different strengths. Newspapers allow for more complicated discussion of issues. Television can convey vivid, emotional information in compelling ways. The Internet permits cognitively enriching interaction between users and commentators.

Second, we should be suspicious about simple statements about the "powers of media." Media are plural, they have different content, and the particular content can determine what people learn. Effects depend on the particular medium, the content of the depiction, the style the program uses to depict an issue, the age and cognitive skills of the news consumer, and the gratifications he or she derives from political media.

Third, individuals bring a great deal to the media equation. You cannot talk about media effects in the abstract. What people know—or think they know—influences what they learn from media. People who know a lot about politics and possess solid cognitive abilities get more out of the news and process it more thoughtfully than those who know less and have not yet developed strong skills in political thinking. What's more, a voter

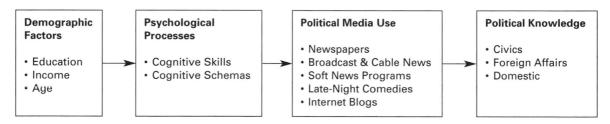

Figure 4.3 Factors that Determine Knowledge of Politics.

does not soak up political information like a sponge. Instead, as constructionist scholars emphasize, "people learn through the development of a composite framework, not by remembering disparate facts. Through the 'barrage' of campaign messages, voters extract and compile information to 'construct' candidates" (Armoudian & Crigler, 2010, p. 310). The news influences what people know, but what people already know affects how they integrate information into their world-views. (See Figure 4.3 for a visual synthesis of the different issues.)

Fourth, the research reminds us of the adage that life ain't fair. The richer and more educated know more about politics, and news can exacerbate these gaps in knowledge.

Political Knowledge in the Age of the Internet

So, you may be thinking, what does all this have to say about the current communication environment, with entertaining news on cable, late-night comedies, blogs, and YouTube political videos posted to a friend's Facebook timeline? To answer this question, it is helpful to know something about trends in young adults' news media habits.

Increasingly, the Internet has supplanted television as the primary news source for young adults under 30 (Pew Research Center for the People and the Press, 2011a). Over the span of just three years—from 2007 to 2010—the number of 18- to 29-year-olds who regard the Internet as their primary news source has almost doubled, growing from 34 percent to 65 percent (see Figure 4.4a). A third of young adults under 30 reported that they saw news on a social networking site the previous day (Pew Research Center for the People and the Press, 2012c).

The Internet is becoming an increasingly important source of news for all Americans, with 41 percent saying they receive most of their national and international news from the Internet. Television remains the main news source for most Americans, but the number citing television as the primary source has dropped over the past several years (see Figure 4.4b).

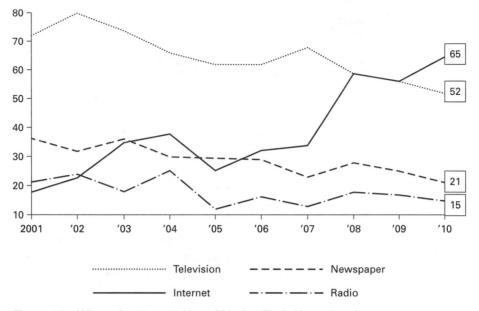

Figure 4.4a Where Do 18- to 29-Year-Olds Get Their News from?

(See Pew Research Center for the People and the Press, 2011a.)

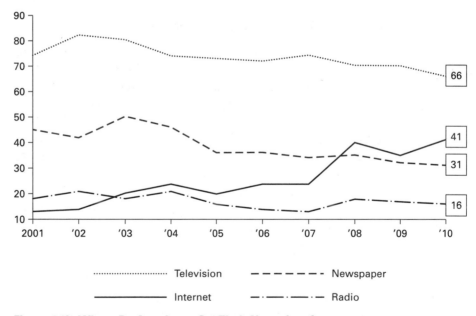

Figure 4.4b Where Do Americans Get Their News from?

(See Pew Research Center for the People and the Press, 2011a.)

Complementing these findings, a more recent survey found that in 1991, approximately 70 percent of Americans reported that they got their news from TV the previous day; by 2012, the proportion had dropped to 55 percent (Pew Research Center for the People and the Press, 2012c). Showcasing the changing landscape of news, nearly 1 in 5 respondents to a 2012 survey said they had been exposed to news or news headlines on a social networking site the previous day, more than twice the number that reported this in 2010. Seventeen percent of Americans reported in 2012 that they got news on a mobile device on the previous day, typically from a cell phone (Pew Research Center for the People and the Press, 2012c).

What does this mean? Remember, the Internet is not a medium per se, but a series of interconnected digital networks that convey information from multiple sources. Many people searching for news on the Internet turn to newspaper and television news sites, as well as news assemblers like Google and Yahoo!, which also get information from conventional sources. Social media can also include news and headlines from conventional news outlets. To be sure, there is wide variation in types of news that young people consume over the Internet, with some viewing newspaper websites, others cable news sites, and still others reading partisan blogs.

When research finds that the Internet is increasingly the transmission channel of choice for young people or that a third of young adults read news on a social networking site, it sounds initially like young people are tuning in to cool genres that are in sync with the contemporary scene. But the content they are using can parallel the content transmitted through more traditional channels. What is different is the manner in which they are receiving it, the interactive capacities the Internet affords news consumers, and the wide diversity in content that was not available in earlier times.

With these facts in mind, we can now return to the question raised earlier: What impact does the new communication environment exert on learning from news? There is currently some debate about this. Skeptics argue that the lure of entertainment, cable television shows to Facebook posts, will pull large numbers of young people from viewing news on TV and on websites (e.g., Prior, 2007). Optimists maintain that newer genres like late-night comedies provide young people with a reservoir of political information. They also note that the advent of newer technologies, such as tablets and smartphones, offers a wealth of opportunities for people to acquire information about politics (see Reflections box).

REFLECTIONS: LEARNING ABOUT POLITICS IN AN INFORMATION AGE

Markus Prior is a skeptic. In an elegant book aptly titled *Post-broadcast democracy*, he argues that:

> Cable television and the Internet clearly do not affect everyone in the same way. Both media offer their audience the opportunity to learn more about politics and find additional motivation to go to the polls, but only people who enjoy the news take advantage of this opportunity. For people who prefer entertainment, the temptations of new media lead elsewhere.
>
> (Prior, 2007, p. 135)

Prior argues that in the old days, when broadcast news dominated the market, television news could make a dent in the knowledge gap. Under some (though not all) conditions, it could reduce the disparity between the well-informed and the less-knowledgeable, and between news junkies and the politically apathetic (Eveland & Scheufele, 2000). With television the only game in town, tens of millions of people were perched before their television sets. But the proliferation of cable channels—as well as all the choices the Internet affords—pulled people away from broadcast television and lured them from the 6:30 news. In particular, individuals who prefer entertainment to news seem less inclined to follow the news today than during the era when network television dominated the media landscape. As a result, political knowledge has decreased for a sizable segment of the electorate: entertainment devotees with access to new media. The lure of entertainment cable shows (and, of course, the Internet) has pulled these viewers away from inadvertent viewing of news (Prior, 2005).

In a similar fashion, one could argue that just because a third of young adults get news from a social networking site does not mean they attended carefully to it or thought much about what they read.

Other scholars take a more optimistic view of young people's exposure to news. They call attention to the virtues of soft news, or stories about public affairs issues that are frequently sensationalized and focus on human-interest topics. These are the focus of attention on late-night talk shows, daytime talk programs, and entertainment TV newsmagazines. There is evidence that these programs can pull the less attentive viewers into the fold, offering up political information they find appealing (Baum, 2002, 2003; Xenos & Becker, 2009). Although many young people tend to shy away from conventional news (Mindich, 2005), close to half of 18- to 24-year-olds surveyed in one study said they watch *The Daily Show with Jon Stewart* at least occasionally (see Baumgartner & Morris, 2006). Viewers of late-night comedies attend more to national network and cable news than do non-viewers (Feldman & Young, 2008; Young & Tisinger, 2006). These fans of political comedy may be the new political junkies.

Others observe that as people get older, get married, and raise children, they become more concerned about the world outside their private lives, paying attention to property tax values, the best schools for their kids, and the state of the world which their children are inheriting. This suggests that the same young people who avoid news today may closely follow it in a decade or more.

It is also possible that the drive to keep informed may drive technology in positive directions. Among the 11 percent of American adults who own a tablet computer, incidental reading of news has become commonplace. Close to 9 in 10 of tablet owners who read long articles over a seven-day period also read news articles they had not sought out initially (Pew Research Center's Project for Excellence in Journalism, 2011). This in turn suggests that, just as inadvertent TV news viewing enhanced knowledge among TV viewers a generation ago, incidental reading of news on the Internet may also increase knowledge in our own era. What's more, entrepreneurs like Kickstarter, a web-based organization that funds creative projects, might find ways of conveying news via the increasing convergence between social media sites and web-enabled mini-technologies, like smart-phones. All of this suggests a more optimistic scenario for political knowledge acquisition in the U.S.

Of course, both sides could be correct, with their theories holding for different population groups. New technologies may enhance political information-holding for the educated, affluent, and the politically involved citizens, who may gravitate to new genres or have the time to attend to political information. Less-educated entertainment devotees may be less motivated to tune in to reading news stories via tablet computer, instead finding themselves lured by cable entertainment fare. Thus, new informational technologies might exacerbate knowledge gaps. Or perhaps something else is going on. Right now, we are at a precipice. With

Continued

older media in flux and newspapers, long the bastion of political information, in free fall, there are legitimate concerns about how media can provide citizens with in-depth knowledge about an ever-more complicated world. Let's hope the optimists are right. (See Figure 4.5.)

Figure 4.5 The majority of young people are getting their news from the Internet and via tablets, smartphones, and other hand-held devices. The verdict is out on whether this will increase or decrease knowledge levels.

iStockphoto

WHAT DO YOU THINK?

With young people getting much of their information from the Internet, mobile devices, and social networking sites, several questions arise. Will the lure of online entertainment distract young adults from attending to news, or will easy access to public information increase news use and knowledge of public affairs? Will instant access to news apps on cell phones and to news on social networking sites enhance information-holding, or will the more typical message-sharing with friends swamp interest in news? Can brief, but constantly updated, snippets of news to which most people are exposed on mobile devices substitute for more extensive print stories?

CONCLUSIONS

"A democracy can't be strong if its citizenship is weak," observed political scientist William A. Galston (2011). A key requirement for effective citizenship is knowledge. Meaningful democratic decision-making requires that citizens understand basic facts of government and the issues that are at stake in elections. National surveys show that most Americans know key aspects of the U.S. Constitution and civil liberties. Happily, they also know the number of senators from their state. But in a testament to widespread ignorance, just 35 percent know the names of both U.S. senators from their state, only a third can name all three branches of government, and 29 percent believe a person can be tried twice for the same crime. This underscores a time-honored paradox of political communication: There is more information available than ever before, yet citizens' knowledge levels do not approach normative ideals (e.g., Neuman, 1986).

There are a number of reasons why Americans lack knowledge of basic facts of government. These include journalists' failure to explain difficult concepts clearly, expansion of media choices, leaders' tendency to deliberately convey misleading information, and cynicism about politics. Do low knowledge levels offer a compelling indictment of the state of political citizenship? There are different views on this issue. Some scholars, with an eye on normative democratic ideals, answer in the affirmative. But a number of theorists make a compelling case that effective citizenship does not require knowledge of arcane government facts. Citizens can fulfill their democratic duties by relying on shortcuts to make political decisions, as well as by scanning the political environment to detect dangers to their personal well-being and the public welfare. Nonetheless, both critics and defenders of the status quo would agree that knowledge levels are not as high as they could or should be, based on normative democratic ideals.

What are the sources of political knowledge? The mass media and Internet impart voluminous amounts of information, providing the raw materials from which people construct political beliefs. There is abundant evidence that individuals who follow the news are more knowledgeable about politics than their counterparts who do not turn to the news media for political information. At the same time, there are striking inequalities in political knowledge, even in a society like the United States, where media are inescapable. Educated and wealthier Americans are significantly more knowledgeable than their less-educated and lower-income peers. Moreover, sociological and communication studies indicate that there are widespread knowledge gaps, where media increase already existing differences in knowledge levels. In these instances, by the end of a media political campaign individuals high in socioeconomic status emerge as even more informed about a political issue than those low in socioeconomic status.

Media do not exert uniform effects on knowledge. What people know influences what they learn from media. The ways that individuals process information and construct events influence the types of effects media exert on audience members. If you want to devise strategies to increase learning from political news, you need to appreciate how people process news. You then devise your strategies so they are in sync with people's information-processing strategies.

Let's end on a philosophical note, harking back to the democracy of knowledge-rich ancient Greece. It is interesting to contrast many Americans' indifference to politics, and lack of knowledge about many issues, with the ethos of the classical democracy of Athens. As the statesman Pericles noted, "We do not say that a man who takes no interest in politics is a man who minds his own business; we say that he has no business here at all" (cf. Held, 2006, p. 14). To the Greeks participation and knowledge were foundations of citizenship, as much a part of the social universe as play, marriage, and child-rearing.

CHAPTER 5

Contemporary Political Socialization

Kate grew up in a liberal Democratic household. Her parents protested the Vietnam War when they were in college, and regaled her with stories of solidarity at anti-war demonstrations, sometimes set off by the firing of tear gas canisters when the protests became violent. (Over the years, Kate began to ritualistically roll her eyes when her parents began nostalgically spinning the tales, retold every Thanksgiving after they listened to the endless Arlo Guthrie ballad, "Alice's Restaurant.") Clearly influenced by her parents' activism, she helped organize an Occupy Wall Street protest near her campus, and she posted blistering blogs berating capitalists, typing furiously on her laptop at the protest site. Pro-union and critical of anything that smacked of Republican politics, she could not believe it when the university dorm lottery system paired her with Olivia.

The first thing Olivia placed in her room, after unpacking her computer, iPod, and favorite novels, was Ayn Rand's conservative classic, *The Fountainhead*. A member of campus Young Republicans and the local Tea Party branch, she is a libertarian who fervently believes that a run-away, out-of-control Big Government is crushing the American spirit. She credits her activism in conservative causes to her parents' encouraging her to explore politics during family discussions at the dinner table.

Jeremy lives down the hall from Olivia and Kate. He is amused by their political passions. Personally, he does not give a hoot about politics. To Jeremy, politicians are cynical and out for themselves. He does not follow politics much at all. Maybe it was because his mother (a single mom, loving, but super-feisty) had such strong views that she would not brook disagreement. She meant well, but you learned it was best not to take the other point of view. Although he steers clear of politics, he is big on volunteering. It's something he picked up in high school, and it has stuck with him.

Talk to Cliff, who lives one floor up from Jeremy, and you enter a different political world. His father grew up in an African American community on Chicago's South Side, gained a graduate degree in theology, and became a well-respected reverend and charismatic preacher in a Black church. Cliff learned some of his politics on his dad's knee, the political lessons fused with a soulful religious spiritualism. He preferred his own generation's music to the traditional hymns favored by his father. Hip-hop music became a source of inspiration and its lyrics an instrument of political education, stimulating him to develop a song describing his own search for political identity.

You may have met young people who fit these descriptions. I have. I combined characteristics of students I know to create these imaginary facsimiles. They were created to highlight a point: People can be very passionate about politics. They also acquire political attitudes as children and adolescents, long before coming to college. How do people develop political attitudes and beliefs? What impact do socialization agents—family, schools, and media—exert on the development of political predispositions? This chapter continues the discussion of the role communication plays in citizenship, focusing on the socialization of political attitudes. The first part of the chapter discusses a prominent theme in political socialization: continuity and change in the development of political attitudes. The second portion describes major approaches to the study of political socialization. The third section looks at key socialization agents—family, schools, and media—and their impact on the development of political attitudes.

THEMES IN POLITICAL SOCIALIZATION

Citizenship is not passed through the genes. It is learned. Indeed, as one scholar observed, "democracy's vitality and continuity greatly depend upon transmitting to each young generation the visions of the democratic life and the commitment to it" (Ichilov, 1990, p. 1). This is the central premise in the study of **political socialization**, more generally defined as "the way in which a society transmits political orientations—knowledge, attitudes or norms, and values—from generation to generation" (Easton & Dennis, 1973, p. 59).

Political socialization performs a valuable function. It helps a society communicate its political heritage to new generations. We want children to understand the storied history of the United States, both its strengths and shortcomings. We want them to appreciate the importance of freedom, tolerance, and duty to country, as well as the importance of civic engagement. Other countries also convey their political lineage to young members of society, emphasizing distinctive national norms and values. Democratic societies in particular seek to nurture four virtues in citizens: *knowledge of the political system*;

loyalty to democratic principles; *adherence to traditions like voting*; and *identification with citizenship* (Dahlgren, 2000).

Two themes weave their way through the socialization of political attitudes: continuity and change.

Continuity refers to the fact that political predispositions that we acquire at a young age tend to persist throughout our lives. Attitudes are formed through macro processes and micro-level experiences.

On the broader, macro level, national events experienced during childhood and adolescence shape political attitudes. Wars, assassinations, political protests, economic catastrophes, and cultural changes that are experienced during the "critical periods" of late childhood, adolescence, and early adulthood can leave a lasting imprint on memories, feelings, and political behavior (Schuman & Corning, 2012). World War II and the Depression were defining political events for "Greatest Generation" Americans born in the 1920s, while Vietnam was important for Baby Boomers. For Americans born over the course of the succeeding decades, the resurgence of conservatism in the Reagan 1980s, culture wars during the Clinton impeachment, 9/11, the 2003 Iraq War, the 2008 financial crisis and recession, and even the diffusion of social media profoundly shaped political attitudes. (For an interesting view of generational effects on politics, see also http://www.economist.com/node/15582279.)

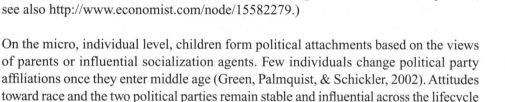

On the micro, individual level, children form political attachments based on the views of parents or influential socialization agents. Few individuals change political party affiliations once they enter middle age (Green, Palmquist, & Schickler, 2002). Attitudes toward race and the two political parties remain stable and influential across the lifecycle (Sears & Funk, 1999).

The continuity perspective emphasizes the powerful impact that early socialization exerts on subsequent attitudes. Growing up in a household that rewards certain viewpoints, or associates political views with strongly held values, can bolster these attitudes and increase the likelihood they are translated into action. "It was once said that the Jesuits could control people's thinking for life if they controlled their education up to the age of five," noted David O. Sears (1990), a proponent of the continuity view.

Social scientific concepts help to explain why political attitudes formed at an early age persist over time. First, individuals (like Kate, the liberal college student) acquire considerable information simply through observation of respected parental, peer, and media role models (Bandura, 1971). Children whose parents display a strong political identification are likely to exhibit the same political identification (Jennings & Niemi,

1968). Second, repetition of political information leads to positive attitudes (Grush, McKeough, & Ahlering, 1978). The more frequently that children listen to adults talking favorably about a candidate, party, or political perspective, the more they come to develop a positive attitude toward this issue. Third, children acquire emotion-packed attitudes via associations. Watching adults solemnly pledge allegiance to the flag, or patriotically sing their country's national anthem in anticipation of a home-town baseball game or soccer match, powerfully links positive feelings with one's country, building national identity.

There is also evidence that some political attitudes may have a genetic basis (Banaji & Heiphetz, 2010). Beliefs about politics can be affected by genes, and ideologically based attitudes may be heritable (Alford, Funk, & Hibbing, 2005; Fowler et al., 2011; Hatemi & McDermott, 2011). However, genes are not the only determinant of political attitudes, and, in any case, nature does not operate in isolation of nurture. Whatever influences genes exert on attitudes interact with the environment, and the intersections are critical. For example, research on twins indicates that heredity affects how strongly individuals feel about partisan politics, but not whether they *choose* to be liberal or conservative (Settle, Dawes, & Fowler, 2009). Your parents and other socialization agents influence your choice of a political party, and partisan attitudes remain relatively stable over the course of the lifecycle.

Yet, complicating matters, some political attitudes do change over time. Americans have dramatically changed their views of race, gender roles, and gay marriage over the past half-century. Media portrayals of prejudice and interpersonal communication have shaken up individuals' assumptions, leading them to reconsider long-held social attitudes. A life-span development view emphasizes that political socialization does not stop in childhood. Instead, it continues over the course of the lifecycle, as people adjust to the procession of new developments on the political stage. In addition, as Zukin and his colleagues note:

> People also change as they grow older because of age-specific experiences. Different stages of the life-cycle bring different politically relevant events, for example, paying income taxes for the first time, choosing a school for a child, or helping an elderly parent deal with Medicare and other health care choices.
>
> (Zukin et al., 2006, p. 11)

STUDYING POLITICAL SOCIALIZATION

In 1965 the Los Angeles Dodgers defeated the Minnesota Twins to win the World Series. If you had been driving to the game, a gallon of gas would have cost 31 cents. You could buy a car for $2,650. Skate boards were big that year. In the same year, a landmark study was published that probed elementary and middle school children's attitudes toward government. The researchers found that children evaluated government very favorably, viewing government as benevolent, protective, and helpful (Easton and Dennis, 1965). Children's positive evaluations of government reflected the insular nature of the times. They showcased a faith in the system to do good things, displaying an admirable, if idealized, view of the country.

You would not find as many children who harbored such uniformly positive attitudes today. On television and the Internet kids are exposed to sordid problems of society, as well as the lascivious acts of politicians and harsh criticisms of the president by the opposition party.

From an academic perspective, the 1965 study of children's attitudes toward government represented a pioneering investigation of political socialization. Scholars began exploring the topic, curious about the political psychology of the 1960s protesters, cultural variations in socialization practices, and the role mass communication played in knowledge generation. Building on this research, this section examines the origins of contemporary political attitudes by describing two scholarly perspectives. The first approach, focusing on media, offers insights into why young people today have a more skeptical attitude toward political authority than their counterparts of several generations ago. The second approach focuses on interpersonal communication dynamics.

Impact of Televised "Backstage" Portrayals

In an intriguing account, Joshua Meyrowitz (1986, 2009) argues that the electronic media, broadly defined, have rearranged our public space, obliterating traditional borderlines between private and public behavior. Years ago, the media covered only the most public of behaviors, avoiding like an electronic plague stories of people engaging in mean-spirited or sexually offensive acts in public. Over the years this has changed, as television exposed—literally it sometimes seems—young viewers to what used to be backstage, backroom behavior, a classic being the widely publicized "wardrobe malfunction" during the televised half-time show at the 2004 Super Bowl, when millions of viewers, young and old, briefly glimpsed Janet Jackson's breast after singer Justin Timberlake accidentally yanked too hard on part of her costume. The episode was termed "Nipplegate."

In the political arena, a news media that for years resisted revealing the "backstage" private behaviors of public officials has changed its tune. Eighteenth century newspaper readers never knew that Thomas Jefferson suffered from rheumatism and migraine headaches. Nineteenth century news aficionados had no idea that Abraham Lincoln may have suffered from depression. Twentieth century radio and TV connoisseurs barely knew that Franklin Delano Roosevelt was paralyzed or had no inkling that John F. Kennedy enjoyed multiple affairs (Meyrowitz, 1986). Over the ensuing decades, the distinction between public and private blurred, as it became increasingly permissible to offer deeper access into the back regions of public officials' lives. Thus, from the 1970s to the present, media consumers learned that President Jimmy Carter had "looked on a lot of women with lust"; Senator Gary Hart departed the presidential race after revelations that he committed adultery; Bill Clinton had sexual relations with Monica Lewinsky; President George W. Bush overcame alcoholism; Democratic presidential candidate John Edwards impregnated a sycophantic videographer, while his cancer-stricken wife enthusiastically campaigned on his behalf; and a capable, promising New York Congressman, Anthony Weiner, sent lewd photos to women he met over the Internet (see Figure 5.1).

You can argue that it is a good (or bad) thing that the news covers every morsel of the private lives of public officials. But most assuredly, according to Meyrowitz's account,

this has left an imprint on children's political attitudes. "By revealing previously backstage areas to audiences," he notes, "television has served as an instrument of demystification. It has led to a decline in the image and prestige of political leaders" (p. 309). This trend has undoubtedly grown, as children have more exposure to political back regions on the Internet and Facebook.

Figure 5.1 The media revealed that Anthony Weiner, a capable, promising New York Congressman, had sent lewd photos to women he met over the Internet. Weiner resigned, raising questions as to whether the media had inappropriately intruded into his private life, or properly revealed information the public had a right to know. Since his resignation, some have argued he should be given a second chance, by hosting a liberal television news show, or otherwise advocating for liberal causes.

WireImage

WHAT DO YOU THINK?

Children today grow up in a no-holds-barred era, in which the media and Internet reveal secrets of public officials. Has this led children to develop a realistic, or overly cynical, view of politics? Do you think the media should ever refrain from showing incidents in which politicians engage in immoral or tacky behaviors?

Interpersonal Communication Dynamics

Other scholars have focused on the role of interpersonal agents in political socialization, adopting a broad, integrative perspective.

University of Colorado researcher Michael McDevitt has articulated a dynamic approach, emphasizing that adolescents can play an active role in family communication about politics. The traditional view is that parents impart their attitudes to children in a top-down manner. McDevitt notes that the direction of influence can go the other way, trickling up from children to parents (McDevitt, 2006; McDevitt & Chaffee, 2002). Teenagers who become animated by politics from exposure to civic programs in schools or via discussions with peers can stimulate parents to rethink their political beliefs. Or adolescents may bring up a perspective gleaned from movies or music that goads parents to defend or forcefully discuss their position on the issue. The result can be a more argumentative, but thought-provoking, series of reciprocal parent–child discussions that transform the family political communication dynamic.

Dhavan V. Shah and his colleagues have examined the ways political socialization plays out in today's era, focusing on the notion of communication competence (McLeod & Shah, 2009; Shah, McLeod, & Lee, 2009; Shah et al., 2005). Communication competence involves an ability to thoughtfully deliberate about political issues, formulate cogent arguments, reflect on information presented in the media, and arrive at a complex understanding of public issues. Children and adolescents ideally develop these deliberative skills through communication with parents and peers, at school, and through exposure to media and the Internet. The skills become the engine that propels participation in civic and political activities.

With these perspectives in mind, let's now review the impact of three major agents of political socialization: families, schools, and media.

FAMILY COMMUNICATION

What was your dinner table conversation like growing up? Was there much conversation about politics? Did your parents trash certain politicians? Did they encourage you to express your beliefs, even if you disagreed with them? Were certain topics—entire categories of politics—off limits? Did you even have conversations with a parent or parents over dinner?

These questions are the centerpiece of a time-honored factor that influences political socialization: **family communication patterns**. There are two core dimensions of parent–child communication: socio-oriented and concept-oriented communication. In socio-oriented families, parents emphasize harmony and deference to adults. These parents may have strong, heart-felt views on social issues that they want to impart to their children. They may believe that the best way to rear competent adults is to teach them to defer to their elders. However, socio-oriented parents tend to be intolerant of dissent. Concept-oriented families, by contrast, encourage open exploration of contemporary issues, facilitating an environment in which there is exposure to diverse perspectives. The child or adolescent is encouraged to challenge others' viewpoints (Chaffee, McLeod, & Wackman, 1973).

Children who grow up in homes where parent–child communication is highly concept-oriented, but low in socio or harmony orientation, are distinctive in a number of ways. They tend to be the most knowledgeable about politics and display the strongest preference for public affairs programs (Chaffee, McLeod, & Wackman, 1973). Children reared in homes that encouraged discussion, but did not place a premium on harmony (like Olivia, the conservative college student mentioned earlier), are especially likely to participate in political discussions (Hively & Eveland, 2009). This has a salutary effect. Children reared in homes with considerable political discussion are more likely to participate in civic or political activities as adults than are kids who grew up in homes with no political talk. More than a third of young adults who were frequently exposed to political discussions while growing up volunteer regularly, compared to 13 percent reared in homes with no political discussion (Zukin et al., 2006; see Figure 5.2).

Presumably, when parents encourage children to openly explore ideas and challenge others' beliefs at home, the kids feel motivated to do the same outside the confines of the family. Turned on to ideas and information, they may explore issues in the media, discuss political topics with others, and become active in civic causes. (Had Jeremy's mother, mentioned earlier in the chapter, discussed political issues more thoughtfully, he might have complemented his social volunteering with more political discussion and participation.)

Figure 5.2 When parents encourage children and adolescents to talk about current political issues, the children are motivated to follow politics in the media. They also are apt to partake in civic and political activities when they become adults.

Shutterstock/ Stephanie Barbary

Research on family communication and politics tends to be conducted in middle-class contexts. There is undoubtedly wide variation in family communication styles as a function of class, race, and the nature of the family (two-parent, single-parent, divorced, and so forth). We do not know whether the findings described above would hold in different sub-cultural contexts. Even so, one can readily agree with Chaffee and Yang (1990) that a child-rearing style that emphasizes concept exploration is conducive to democracy. They lament that "a pluralistic democratic society presumes a citizenry tolerant of divergent viewpoints, but most people are not raised in homes where such tolerance is practiced, so they do not develop mass communication habits that are appropriate to sustaining that pluralistic posture" (p. 145).

SCHOOLS

Political philosophers have long argued that education is of central importance in imparting the values of democratic citizenship. If schools do not provide instruction on civics, such as the right of citizens, nature of political parties, and the structure of government, who will? By the time or slightly before students graduate from high school, they will be able to vote and can be conscripted into military service. Clearly it is important that young people have a functioning knowledge of democratic principles.

Key inputs come from high school civics and history courses. What impact does civics instruction exert on students' political knowledge? Although research results vary, the findings from an extensive national study offer convincing support for the notion that exposure to a high school civics curriculum significantly increases knowledge of American politics and government (Niemi & Junn, 1998). Knowledge is far from perfect, as we have seen, but it is substantially greater than it would be in the absence of civics books and coursework (see Figure 5.3).

Figure 5.3 The books and curriculum to which young people are exposed in high school can increase their appreciation of democratic values. High school civics and history books can help enhance knowledge of democracy, although there has been considerable controversy about different interpretations of historical events. Such controversy is natural and inevitable.

Shutterstock/ maxik

This does not mean that everyone is happy with the content of the curriculum. High school civics and history courses have become a battleground in the cultural wars between liberals and conservatives (see an interesting discussion at http://theweek.com/article/index/207395/-the-great-textbook-wars).

For much of the 20th century, history textbooks offered a puffed-up view of the American past, celebrating conquest of the American West and industrial growth, despite injustices wrought on Native Americans and workers. Textbooks also omitted mention of the scourge of racial and gender prejudice. In order to correct these errors, textbooks written over the past several decades have articulated a different narrative, discussing prejudice and celebrating accomplishments of minorities and women. These books have rankled conservatives, who regard the books as politically correct and an attempt by Baby Boomer historians to rewrite history. Of course, history is always rewritten. There is no objective recitation of past events, for the past is necessarily subject to interpretation, reinterpretation, and revision in light of the present. Still, you do want a pluralistic version of American history, provided that it is based on a consensual view of the facts.

Controversies over the historical content of textbooks are a way that societies come to grips with different interpretations of the past and try to negotiate a common narrative. Indeed, the United States is far from the only country in which controversies over textbooks play out. This issue crosses national boundaries, as can be seen in controversies that have swirled over German, Japanese, Israeli, and Arab textbooks. For many years German history textbooks did not mention the Holocaust and the horrific extermination of Jews that occurred in concentration camps. This has changed, as contemporary German textbooks give extensive coverage to the Holocaust, describing it as one of the darkest periods in human history. In a similar fashion, textbooks used in Japanese high schools had been criticized for distorting and failing to discuss Japan's militant aggression and war crimes. This has changed, as Japan's textbooks now offer a more accurate view of its actions before and during World War II. While Israeli and Palestinian textbooks no longer describe the other side in cruel, dehumanizing terms, they still present the out-group as the enemy and offer glowing descriptions of their own side. Research shows that 87 percent of maps in Israeli texts do not refer to the Palestinian Authority, while 96 percent of maps in Palestinian texts do not mention Israel (Wexler, Adwan, & Bar-Tal, 2013; see IsraeliPalestinianSchoolbooks.blogspot.com). Thus, controversies over the role that American history textbooks play in political socialization should be placed in a larger international context.

If textbooks are a contentious area in which school socialization occurs both in the U.S. and abroad, civic programs sponsored by schools arouse less controversy and can exert positive effects. In recent years, American schools have become increasingly involved in programs designed to encourage civic participation, voting, and deliberative discussion. Some of these programs have exerted positive effects, producing increases in political knowledge, discussion, and even a commitment to activist protest (McDevitt & Ostrowski, 2009).

Unfortunately, many schools, particularly those in lower-income neighborhoods, lack the resources to undertake these activities. Political discussion and deliberative skills are usually more likely to be found in higher-income, better-educated sectors of society, another reflection of life's (or at least this country's) inequality. Political socialization is not absent in lower-class communities, it just takes on a different form. For example, other institutions, like churches, encourage individuals to participate in civic and community activities. This is why it is important to take into account structural factors, such as class and culture, when discussing political socialization.

MEDIA: FROM NEWS TO SATIRE

Unlike parents and schools, mass media and the Internet do not attempt to shape attitudes and beliefs. Yet they most assuredly play a role in political socialization. Think about it: When you were a child, what was your first exposure to the president? Where did you first hear the words "politician," "candidate," "presidential election," and "negative advertising?" From TV, websites, or social media perhaps? What about 9/11 or its tenth anniversary in 2011? Didn't television, websites, or media documentaries shown in school create some of the pictures in your head? And where, if not from satirical media programs or YouTube snippets, did you learn to laugh at politicians' missteps?

Countries have long socialized their citizens, introducing them to social norms and the behaviors that society expects them to perform. Our era is characterized by the overwhelming and (sometimes) overpowering role that media play in political socialization. No one, of course, elected the media to perform this role. You won't find a law prescribing it in the Constitution. Yet, from Cronkite to Colbert (Baym, 2010), the daily newspaper to *The Daily Show with Jon Stewart*, and Mike Wallace (the former CBS reporter) to Michael Moore (who needs no introduction), the media have emerged as important agents of political socialization. What's more, a variety of media genres influence political attitudes. There is news, political advertisements, satirical comedy shows, candidate-mocking YouTube videos, and songs that run the gamut from folk to hip-hop music, the favored genre of the college student, Cliff, mentioned at the outset of the chapter.

In the early 1970s, research began to document that the media—in particular, news—exerted important influences on adolescents' political knowledge (Chaffee, Ward, &

Tipton, 1970). It continues to have this impact today. But news is no longer the only political media game in town. Alternative genres have emerged, exerting important influences on political socialization. Over the past couple of decades, politics has become increasingly inseparable from popular culture, as television dramas, such as *The West Wing* and *24*, became immensely popular; *The Simpsons* cultivated a new generation of viewers; *Saturday Night Live* regained its comedic footing (culminating in Tina Fey's spoofs of Sarah Palin in 2008); late-night comedies continued to attract presidential contenders eager to pitch themselves as showmen and women for a media age; and political satire that dates back to Jonathan Swift's *Gulliver's Travels* found a contemporary home at Jon Stewart' *Daily Show*, *The Colbert Report*, and in the laughter of millions of young viewers turned off by the pretenses of network news. These television programs employ **satire**, a form of humor that employs ridicule to expose people's foibles, and **irony**, a complex comedic device that uses language to suggest an incongruity between the surface and deeper meanings of an event (see also satire in *The Onion* at http://www.theonion.com/).

The popular television show *The Daily Show with Jon Stewart* cleverly blends news and political humor. The program starts with graphics and serious music that suggest an authoritative network news program, but then continues with a quick, entertaining visual display of the studio and an audio soundtrack that pipes in fast-paced rock-and-roll. Building on the format of Letterman's *Late Show* and *Saturday Night Live'*s "Weekend Update," the program cuts seamlessly from host Stewart's sometimes serious, sometimes outraged commentary to edited sound bites and public statements made by actual politicians. The juxtaposition of Stewart's common-sense "can you believe they said this?" statements with in-their-face ludicrous comments from government officials can tickle the funny-bone (Baym, 2005, 2010; see Figure 5.4).

The Daily Show's creators like to call the program fake news to deliberately contrast Stewart's newscast with the supposedly real and factual news programs that appear on national newscasts. The larger point that Stewart hopes to drive home is that the simple distinction between real and false is an illusion; there is much that is false on network news (e.g., misleading statements by politicians that are covered uncritically by journalists). Through satire he seeks to unmask falsehood and encourage viewers to engage in critical thinking about mediated politics (Morreale, 2009).

The Daily Show became famous during the Bush administration, with Stewart using satirical humor to raise serious questions about the Bush administration's credibility and, in Stewart's view, its lack of transparency in perpetrating a preemptive war against Iraq. A particularly memorable newscast occurred after the Abu Ghraib Iraqi prison scandal, when American soldiers tortured and humiliated Iraqi prisoners—for example, forcing a naked detainee to crawl on his stomach while soldiers urinated on him and

Figure 5.4 Jon Stewart's uses dead-pan satire to lampoon public officials and pretense in American politics. The show has attracted a large audience of young adults. Debate has emerged on whether the program increases cynicism or teaches insights about contemporary politics.

Getty Images

later sodomizing him with a police stick as two female officers threw a ball at his genitals. Then-Defense Secretary Donald Rumsfeld was reluctant to call the behavior torture, when it seemed obvious that these, and other even more brutal actions, could only be described this way. The faux newscast went like this, ending with the use of obscene speech:

Rumsfeld: Uh, I think that . . . uh (*scratches his head*). . . . I'm not a lawyer; my impression is that what has been charged thus far is abuse, which I believe, technically, is different from torture (*audience groans*), and therefore I'm not gonna address the torture word.

Stewart: I'm also not a lawyer, so I don't know, technically, if you're *human*, but as a fake news person, I can tell you, what we've been reading about in the newspapers, the pictures we've been seeing . . . it's f......
torture.

(see Baym, 2010, p. 110)

Stewart lampooned Obama too, dogging the president when he appeared on the show in October, 2010. Criticizing Obama for pursuing a more timid legislative approach than was suggested by the "Yes, we can" mantra that accompanied his 2008 campaign, Stewart joked that the new slogan should be called "Yes, we can, given certain conditions, ahem, ahem, ahem." Obama challenged Stewart's description, saying the slogan remained "Yes, we can." But he paused and seemed to hesitate before he declared that his approach was "Yes, we can [pause], but it's not going to happen overnight." His response was met with gales of audience laughter, for it seemed to confirm Stewart's charge to a tee.

Just when you thought that Stewart had taken political humor to a new zenith, along came Stephen Colbert, the paragon of parodying. Colbert had appeared as a comedic character on *The Daily Show* for seven years prior to "spinning off" his personae to his own Comedy Central program. (Colbert, who douses his humor with considerable irony, would appreciate the use of the word "spin" to describe the emergence of his own program. "Spin," after all, is a term used to disparage political marketers, as when one speaks of a consultant putting his own "spin" or interpretation on a candidate's performance.) Colbert savages politicians, pundits, and broadcast journalists who, due to subservience or ambition, slavishly repeat political pronouncements which, he maintains, are frequently false or misleading. Through a combination of parody, irony, and incongruity, Colbert seeks to ridicule the mediated world of politics (Baym, 2009).

During the 2012 campaign, comedy shows had a field day with Romney's flip-flops, Obama's lackluster debate performance, and candidate gaffes. Comedian Jimmy Kimmel satirized presidential debates by asking people on the street about a fictitious political debate between Michelle Obama and Romney's wife, Ann. He professed amazement and got lots of laughs when he showed footage of people who were either sadly gullible or gamely played along with the joke. The respondents unflinchingly claimed that one or the other women won a debate that never occurred.

Saturday Night Live also unleashed a comedy skit during the presidential campaign:

Obama: Our campaign has a secret weapon.

(Camera cuts to Romney, speaking at a rally.) I understand the hardships facing ordinary Americans. One of my horses failed to medal at the Olympics.

Obama (singing): Let's stay together.

Romney: (Frequently satirized as being old-fashioned, sings "Old MacDonald Had a Farm," calling the song "pretty groovy.")

Impact of Media Satire on Youth

Let's turn now from the content of satire to its social effects, as we examine the role satire plays in political socialization. A national survey reported that young adults were more likely to obtain campaign information from late-night comedy shows than were older individuals, and this was back in 2000, when Comedy Central was just finding its stride (see Young & Tisinger, 2006). A 2004 update of the survey, conducted by the Pew Research Center for the People and the Press, found that almost half of 18- to 24-year-olds at least occasionally watched *The Daily Show*, and 54 percent of this group acknowledged that they received at least some news about the presidential campaign from *The Daily Show* and *Saturday Night Live* (Baumgartner & Morris, 2006.). Those numbers are likely to be higher today.

Lots of young adults watch televised political satire. But certain types of individuals are particularly inclined to tune in. Individuals who watch liberal cable television programs like *The Rachel Maddow Show* may be particularly fond of Stewart and Colbert, perhaps because they see similarities in the satirical mocking employed by Maddow, Stewart, and Colbert. Regular viewers of satirical comedy shows say they appreciate political humor because it reveals leaders' weaknesses and helps them to criticize politicians (Hmielowski, Holbert, & Lee, 2011).

But does political satire have any impact? Is it good for democracy? Critics argue that Stewart's and Colbert's programs can increase cynicism. Advocates praise the shows, pointing to evidence that they increase knowledge and offer an antidote to stodgy network news (see Reflections box).

REFLECTIONS: SIZING UP SATIRE

Political satire may amuse the viewers who regularly tune into view Stewart, Colbert, and the host of online purveyors, but it has elicited frowns and raised eyebrows from some communication scholars.

Before a packed audience at a communication convention, communication scholars Roderick P. Hart and E. Johanna Hartelius indicated their displeasure with Stewart's brand of satire. "We accuse Jon Stewart of political heresy," they said, tongue in cheek but with serious rhetorical overtones. "We find his sins against the Church of Democracy to be so heinous that he should be branded an infidel and made to wear sackcloth and ashes for at least two years, during which time he would not be allowed to emcee the Oscars, throw out the first pitch at the Yankees' game, or eat at the Time-Warner commissary. Our specific charge is that Mr. Stewart has engaged in unbridled political cynicism" (Hart & Hartelius, 2007, p. 263).

Drawing on rhetorical principles, they argued that Stewart mocks democratic aims by making cynicism appealing. By skillfully editing public figures' statements, he renders them absurd, debasing the decent intentions that underlie leaders' actions. In addition, by arguing that each individual's vote has no impact on the outcome of an election, as Stewart observed in a book he authored, the critics argued that he diminishes the importance of voting.

Cynicism, Hart and Hartelius suggest, is cool. It allows young people to sound sophisticated, and offers middle-aged adults the opportunity to grasp the heady political elixir of their youth. But in promoting cynicism, Stewart may discourage viewers from doing the hard work of politics, which occurs in neighborhoods, union halls, and legislative sessions, but not perched before a television set.

There is some evidence to support their charges. In a carefully executed laboratory study, Jody Baumgartner and Jonathan S. Morris (2006) showed different experimental materials to three groups of students. One group, a control condition, did not view any television segments. A second group viewed CBS news coverage of the presidential candidates in a recent presidential campaign. Like much network coverage, the portrayals focused on candidate shortcomings, placing candidates in a negative light. The third condition, the experimental group, also watched negative network news portrayals of the candidates' behavior, this time on *The Daily Show*, along with Stewart's mocking, satirical remarks. Experimental group students who viewed *The Daily Show* portrayals gave the most negative evaluations of the candidates. They also displayed the most cynical attitudes toward the electoral system and the news media, exhibiting less faith in the electoral system and the ability of the news media to cover events fairly.

Survey research confirms these findings. Viewing *The Daily Show* and *The Colbert Report* is associated with mistrusting media and believing the political system to be corrupt, regardless of which party is in office (Guggenheim, Kwak, & Campbell, 2011; see also Baumgartner & Morris, 2006). Because the latter studies are surveys, we can't be sure if televised satire causes cynicism, or if individuals who are already cynical gravitate to these shows. Perhaps it is a combination of both.

Harking back to the professors' "charges" against Stewart, the evidence indicates that a hearing is certainly warranted. But an indictment?! What do you think? Stewart's defenders offer three reasons to release him from the servitude advocated by Hart and Hartelius. They believe his satire is good for democracy. What's more, they offer strong evidence in support of this view.

First, there is evidence that *The Daily Show* can enhance political knowledge. More than 1 in 5 young adults reported learning information about a presidential campaign regularly from watching late-night comedy programs like *The Daily Show* (Young & Tisinger, 2006). There is also evidence that viewing *The Daily*

Continued

Show increases young adults' confidence in their ability to understand politics (Baumgartner & Morris, 2006). By piercing the arrogant veneer of television journalists and unmasking politicians' deceptions, Stewart helps young viewers to see through appearances and place greater faith in their own perceptions of political reality.

Second, satire can empower individuals, strengthening their beliefs that they can influence the political system. Researchers Lindsay H. Hoffman and Dannagal G. Young (2011b) found that viewing satirical media fare can enhance political participation by bolstering viewers' perceptions that they can have an impact on contemporary politics. Complementing these findings, a 2009 survey showed that late-night comedy enhances adolescents' political efficacy or belief that they can influence politics; teens' efficacy in turn predicted their civic participation (Hoffman & Thomson, 2009). So, Stewart's fare may not dispirit, so much as activate young people's political impulses.

Third, we need satire. Satirists differentiate right from wrong and are willing to doggedly criticize wrongdoing. They pinpoint absurdities in public life that may go unnoticed and illuminate them so they are visible to the naked political eye. In this way, they can offer citizens a deeper knowledge of politics, while also helping to channel negative emotions into outlets for political change (Gray, Jones, & Thompson, 2009; see Box 5.1).

WHAT DO YOU THINK?

How do you size up satire? Do you agree with critics who charge that Stewart and Colbert's political satire makes young adults more cynical about politics? Do you think that their scathing critiques of contemporary politics discourage viewers from becoming involved in political causes? Or do you believe the programs have more positive effects, perhaps offering insights into politics that conventional news fails to provide?

BOX 5.1 CROSS-NATIONAL APPLICATIONS OF SATIRE

The systemic benefits that satire offers extend well beyond America. Satire appears to exert positive effects in countries with less democratic traditions. In Egypt, Bassem Youssef, a heart surgeon turned comic who modeled his humor after Stewart's, gained popularity by parodying Egypt's ultra-conservative Egyptian sheiks in a popular show called *Al Bernameg* or *The Program*.

Satire also emerged in Russia, where democratic practices co-exist with government authoritarianism. When Russian Prime Minister Vladimir V. Putin likened the white ribbons of Russian protesters to, of all things, condoms, he invited ridicule. Within minutes after his comment, cleverly edited photos of a condom pinned to Putin's label went viral. With many in Russia tired of Putin's rule and his self-aggrandizing style, satire offered a weapon to defuse anger and organize political opposition. After allegations of widespread ballot box stuffing and vote stealing in a December, 2011 Russian parliamentary election spread across the country, a joke gained currency: "The wives of United Russia party members don't fake orgasms. They falsify them" (Yaffa, 2012, p. 4)! The humor galvanized disgruntled members of Russia's urban professional class, enhancing political engagement and producing a vitality that experts believe will continue for some time to come.

China, a country populated by numerous underground whistle blowing bloggers, offers another contemporary example of the positive uses of satire. Journalists have reported that the Chinese government secretly monitors and aggressively censors bloggers who employ humor to expose the coercive structure of the Chinese Communist Party. It devotes more resources to locating subversive content on the web than any government in the world (Larmer, 2011). Yet political humor in China exerts positive effects. As one leading Chinese blogger explained, "jokes that mock the abuse of power do more than let off steam; they mobilize people's emotions. Every time a joke takes off, it chips away at the so-called authority of an authoritarian regime" (Larmer, 2011, p. 37).

Unfortunately, authoritarian regimes use their coercive powers to strike back. They try to silence dissidents who use satire to question authority. Egypt issued an arrest warrant for the Egyptian satirist, Bassem Youssef (Fahim & El Sheikh, 2013). The complaint charged that Youssef's satire disparaged Islam and the Egyptian president.

NEW MEDIA AND POLITICAL ENGAGEMENT

Political socialization is a work in progress, with new media genres that socialize young people emerging in our digital culture. Activists have devised innovative websites in an effort to promote civic engagement and political participation. They have a mixed record of success (Bachen et al., 2008; Bennett, Wells, & Freelon, 2011; Xenos & Foot, 2008). Many sites fail to offer interactive learning opportunities to which young people are accustomed. On the other hand, social media can help stimulate political participation in events like presidential campaigns, protests, such as Occupy Wall Street (which was promoted through an email post), and partisan causes, spanning both sides of the abortion and gun debates. About a third of social media users have re-posted political content previously posted by someone else, employed social media to encourage other people to vote, and used social media to encourage others to take political action on an issue that they viewed as important. Young people are especially likely to use the tools of social media in these ways (Rainie et al., 2012).

As positive as these developments are, it is likely that many of those who use social media for political purposes are already predisposed to get involved in politics. The apolitical social media users probably don't use social media as tools for political engagement. In addition, social media, with its posts from like-minded political friends, is apt to reinforce the views that individuals already hold, rather than exposing them to new points of view.

CONCLUSIONS

Political socialization performs a key function in a democratic society. It provides a way for adults to communicate a culture's political heritage to young people. We want children to understand the storied history of the United States, both its strengths and shortcomings. We want them to appreciate the values of freedom, as well as the virtues of tolerance, duty to country, and civic engagement in causes outside the self.

Examining the ways society communicates politics to children and adolescents, one glimpses continuities and changes. Political predispositions acquired at a young age tend to persist throughout the lifecycle. Attitudes acquired during one's youth can remain influential during the adult years. Just as there is continuity in political socialization, there is also change. As a result of exposure to media and interpersonal communication, Americans have changed their attitudes toward race, gay marriage, and other issues over the past several decades.

Communication scholars emphasize that contemporary socialization to politics is dynamic, characterized by interaction among different socialization agents and growth in communication competence, a generalized ability that ideally should spur civic engagement. Parents are a major influence on children's political views, with family communication patterns exerting a significant influence on children's interest in politics. Schools also socialize children, through textbooks and the increasing number of programs designed to promote voting, deliberative debate, and civic participation.

Contemporary media represent portals that introduce young people to a world of politics that is played and constructed electronically, cinematically, and digitally. News, television dramas, movies, and music—from heavy metal to rap (Jackson, 2002)—introduce young people to the serious and sublime—along with the admirable and absurd—aspects of contemporary politics. Meyrowitz has persuasively argued that electronic media (and the Internet) have profoundly influenced political socialization. By showing the "back regions" of public life and revealing the imperfections, personal shortcomings, and sexual infidelities of political leaders, the media have made it difficult for young people to revere elected officials. News and entertainment media have demystified politics, leading current generations of young people to view political leaders through more jaded, skeptical eyes.

Entertainment genres have come to play a strong role in political socialization. Large numbers of young adults, particularly those between the ages of 18 and 24, report that they receive at least some political information from late-night comedies, such as *The Daily Show with Jon Stewart*. These programs, like other political entertainment genres, blur the boundaries between news and entertainment. Stewart and Colbert use satire and irony to unmask deception and hypocrisy in politics and journalism. There is evidence that satirical comedies can increase cynicism about politics and mistrust of media. The satirical posture of both shows has salutary effects as well, increasing young adults' confidence in their ability to understand politics and providing deep insights into the shortcomings of American politics.

Political socialization continues to be a work in progress. New media genres have emerged that can offer new routes to political socialization and engagement. These developments suggest that dour predictions of the demise of citizenship in a digital era are in need of reexamination. Young people's participation in public life will probably not mirror that of their elders, shaped as they are by different political and technological trends. However, reports of young people's disengagement from civic and political life are greatly exaggerated. We do not know for sure, but it is entirely possible that political engagement will reinvent itself in ever-imaginative ways in the years to come.

PART TWO

Political News

6   Agenda-Setting

The slogan emerged suddenly and mysteriously—seemingly from nowhere. A motley group of protesters, camped near Wall Street in the fall of 2011, chanted and tweeted the phrase until it became a national symbol of inequality and populist outrage at the rich. Seized on by a voracious news media and transplanted onto the ubiquitous Internet, the slogan took on a life all its own. *We are the 99 percent!* The brainchild of the 2011 liberal Occupy Wall Street movement, the slogan was shorthand for an issue that within weeks vaulted onto the national agenda, capturing the attention of citizens, journalists, and policymakers.

The Occupy Wall Street movement began spontaneously in downtown New York City in September, 2011, when hundreds of protesters responded enthusiastically to a series of creative social networking posts. They camped out to demonstrate their anger at a capitalistic system that, in their eyes, had veered off the rails, careening in the wake of the 2008 financial crisis. Using the 99 percent catchphrase, they promoted the idea that the vast majority of Americans had seen their incomes stagnate, while the top 1 percent grew phenomenally richer. The movement spread to a variety of cities, with activists of different ages, ethnic backgrounds, and political banners occupying parks, plazas, and other public sites, protesting corporate greed and gaping economic equality. Supporters applauded the truth of their message. Opponents pointed to its utter simplicity and the movement's inability to translate anger into concrete political action.

Typically, political movements like these are branded by the media as extreme and are ridiculed or ignored by most Americans. But this one caught on, perhaps because the protests spoke to the economic hardship many Americans were experiencing and their perception that government bailouts benefited the rich. In addition, the slogan itself was simple and catchy, daring "listeners to pick a side" (Stelter, 2011, p. A1; see Figure 6.1).

Figure 6.1 The Occupy Wall Street Movement began spontaneously in New York City in September, 2011 as a protest against corporate greed and income inequality. It quickly spread to other cities, capturing the media agenda and offering a frame for economic inequality: "We are the 99 percent."

AFP/Getty Images

The news media picked up on the economic inequality issue, offering a spate of stories devoted to the theme. The 99 percent frame got big play too. There were seven times as many Google searches for the term "99 percent" during September and October, 2011 than prior to this period. The issue seeped into Americans' political perceptions. A national opinion poll conducted in the wake of the protests reported a significant increase in the number of Americans who believed there were substantial conflicts between the rich and poor in the U.S. (Tavernise, 2012).

Democrats invoked the 99 percent phrase to press for Congressional action on President Obama's jobs bill, while Republicans branded the protest as class warfare. The issue surfaced in the 2012 presidential election campaign. It was not long before the catchphrase became the stuff of capitalist merchandising, with stores promoting "gifts for the 99 percent," a folk singer's album calling itself a "soundtrack for the 99 percent," and even humorous Facebook posts inviting friends to attend "one percent parties!"

"The '99 percent,' and the 'one percent,' too, are part of our vocabulary now," declared a New York City university history professor (Stelter, 2011, p. A1).

The political effects of the Occupy Wall Street movement illustrate two central political communication concepts: agenda-setting and framing. Propelled by the activities of protest groups and covered vociferously by the mainstream news media, a problem—income equality—leapt onto the national agenda for a period of months. One among many frameworks for viewing the problem—that the top 1 percent of Americans became richer at the expense of the hapless 99 percent—gained traction. This all raises interesting questions. What is the impact of concentrated media coverage of issues on public opinion and policymaking? What shapes the media agenda, and how does it influence policymakers? What influences do media frames or interpretive slants exert on public opinion and policy? These questions are the focus of the discussion in this chapter and the two chapters that follow. People frequently speculate about the effects that news exerts on society. The discussions in these chapters address just these issues, offering a variety of answers to questions about media impact.

The first section of this chapter defines agenda-setting, and the second portion helps you to appreciate social scientific research that has explored its impact. The third section looks at the consequences of agenda-setting, viewed through the lens of priming, an intriguing political communication concept.

INTRODUCTION TO AGENDA-SETTING

A critical term in the exploration of agenda-setting is agenda. An agenda is defined as an issue or event that is "viewed at a point in time as ranked in a hierarchy of importance" (Rogers & Dearing, 1988, p. 555). Agendas are important. Groups that control a nation's agenda own the keys to the corridors of power. As the political scientist E.E. Schattschneider (1960) famously said, "the definition of the alternatives is the supreme instrument of power" (p. 68).

There are a multitude of problems that afflict individuals and social systems, and governments cannot work on them all at once. Democratic societies must decide which problems to shelve, which ones to tackle, and how to formulate policies to address the problems they have chosen. "Every social system must have an agenda if it is to prioritize the problems facing it, so that it can decide where to start work. Such prioritization is necessary for a community and for a society," explain James W. Dearing and Everett M. Rogers (1996, p. 1) in a thoughtful book on this topic.

This is where the media come into the picture. Do you remember Walter Lippmann, the political writer discussed in Chapter 3? He was the early 20th century journalist who first called attention to the power of the press to create pictures in people's heads. He recognized that the world had changed with the growth of cities, advent of mass media, and exploitation of government propaganda that could shape political sentiments. Observing that "the world we have to deal with politically is out of reach, out of sight, [and] out of mind," Lippmann emphasized that people must deal with a second-hand political reality, one shaped by journalists' perceptions (Lippmann, 1922, p. 29). Lippmann argued that the press serves as our window on the distant political world, shaping our political beliefs.

Some years later, during the television news era, political commentators offered even stronger pronouncements about media effects. Journalist Theodore White observed that "the power of the press in America is a primordial one. It sets the agenda of public discussion . . . It determines what people will talk and think about" (White, 1973, p. 327). Political scientist Bernard Cohen (1963) noted that "the press is significantly more than a purveyor of information and opinion. It may not be successful much of the time in telling *people what to think*, but it is stunningly successful in telling its readers *what to think about*" (p. 13, italics added).

Cohen's pithy statement is the most famous description of agenda-setting in the academic literature. Just about every major article or book on the subject quotes it. His observation highlighted the subtle, but powerful, effects that media could exert on public opinion. It also directed attention away from the popular belief that political communication swayed attitudes and voting behavior. Instead, it emphasized that media influences were felt in another arena—people's perceptions about what constitutes society's most important problems. By simply emphasizing certain problems rather than others, the media can significantly influence opinions and policy.

Agenda-setting is defined as "*a process through which the mass media communicate the relative importance of various issues and events to the public*" (Rogers & Dearing, 1988, p. 555). It is worth reiterating that there are hundreds of issues out there, lots of stories to cover: terrorism, gun violence, unemployment, the budget deficit, climate control, social inequalities. What do you cover? Which ones do you play up?

Journalists employ a host of professional criteria to make these decisions, a complex issue that will be discussed in Chapters 9 and 10. The point right now is this: By allocating space or time to certain issues, the media increase their *salience* or perceived importance. In other words, as David Weaver (1984) notes, "Concentration by the media over time on relatively few issues leads to the public perceiving these issues as more salient or more important than other issues" (p. 682). Historically, by shining the beam of their searchlight on social inequities, the press has done considerable good, exposing political corruption, spotlighting fraudulent business practices, and revealing abuses that caused physical harm (see Box 6.1).

As we will see, agenda-setting sheds light on a host of intriguing and consequential events in the world of politics. It helps explain how a little-known governor from Arkansas named Bill Clinton was elected president in 1992 (see Chapter 15). It explains why, in 1986, the nation "erupted with concern about illegal drugs," although there was no sudden increase in the use of drugs (Kerr, 1986, p. 1). And, turning the concept on its head, it suggests why few Americans thought about or worried about terrorism until 9/11.

But before we can say with certainty that these effects are attributable to agenda-setting, there must be evidence that the media actually set the agenda. You may say that it is obvious that the media set the agenda, based on these examples or your own intuitions. But how do you know that the examples accurately represent the political universe or your intuitions are correct? We turn to social science to determine the truth of hunches and assumptions.

BOX 6.1 MUCKRAKING AS AGENDA-SETTING

The classic image of the investigative journalist was popularized not by a reporter or an editor, but by an American president. It was President Theodore Roosevelt who coined the term, describing investigative writers as men with the "muck-rake." Actually Roosevelt used the term in a pejorative manner, criticizing journalists for focusing on the negative rather than lofty aspects of society. However, reporters came to view the term "muckraker" positively, emphasizing the ways that journalistic investigations could call attention to social problems in need of improvement.

In the early 1900s, investigative journalists or writers were a new and courageous breed, uncovering political corruption and business abuse for the new mass medium of their era, magazines like *McClure's*. Lincoln Steffens exposed urban political corruption in a series called *The shame of the cities*. Ida Tarbell, a crusading female journalist, revealed how Standard Oil bullied rival businesses and railroad companies that threatened their interests. Ida B. Wells, a courageous African American reporter, documented the decades-long horrors of lynchings in the South. These and other exposés called attention to social problems festering under the polite surface of American society. They created an agenda for social reform.

Continued

By the late 20th century, when Bob Woodward and Carl Bernstein broke the Watergate story, investigative reporting had become accepted—indeed revered—in American journalism. But few were prepared for the consequences unleashed in 1972 when these two rookie *Washington Post* reporters painstakingly revealed the break-in at the Democratic National Committee Headquarters at the Watergate Hotel in Washington, D.C.; connected the Watergate burglary to the Nixon White House; showed how Nixon campaign funds had been involved in the break-in; and documented that political sabotage had played a key role in Nixon's reelection campaign. The stories set in motion a series of incredible developments that led to a trial of the Watergate burglars, televised hearings by a Senate Committee, evidence of a White House cover-up, a House impeachment vote, and Nixon's resignation (for website descriptions of the fascinating history, see: http://www.hrc.utexas.edu/exhibitions/web/woodstein/post/, and http://www.fordlibrarymuseum.gov/museum/exhibits/Watergate_files).

Contrary to popular mythology, *The Washington Post* investigations did not cause Nixon to resign. Few other media picked up on the Watergate story in 1972, because it seemed either too unbelievable or too risky to cover. But the drip-drip of *Post* coverage, painstakingly reported by Woodward and Bernstein, helped build the agenda that led inexorably to Nixon's resignation.

Investigative journalists are a rare breed, motivated by a combination of moral zeal (Ettema & Glasser, 1998) and raw ambition. Their articles spotlight social inequities and business abuses, helping to set the agenda, subsequently sparking public discussion and, in some cases, prodding government to correct the problem. The annual Pulitzer Prize in Investigative Journalism recognizes journalistic achievements. For example:

● In 2012, *Seattle Times* reporters Michael J. Berens and Ken Armstrong were awarded a Pulitzer for revealing how an obscure government body in the state of Washington shifted physically vulnerable patients from safer pain-alleviating drugs to methadone, a less expensive but more dangerous medication. The state issued health warnings as a result of the exposé.
● In 2008, *The Chicago Tribune* staff was awarded the prize for exposing inadequate, shoddy government regulation of toys and car seats, leading to a major recall of the products and action by Congress.
● In 2002, Sari Horwitz, Scott Higham, and Sarah Cohen of *The Washington Post* exposed the role played by the District of Columbia in the neglect and subsequent death of 229 children who had been placed in protective care

over a 7-year period. They received a Pulitzer for their article, which led to sweeping reform of the district's welfare system.

- In 1999, *The Miami Herald* staff received a Pulitzer for reporting that revealed systematic voter fraud in a city's mayoral electoral race. The election was later overturned.
- In 1987, John Woestendiek, of *The Philadelphia Inquirer*, received a Pulitzer for prison beat reporting that proved that a man convicted of murder was innocent of the crime.

WHAT DO YOU THINK?

What do scholars mean when they say the media set the agenda? What is a contemporary example of agenda-setting? How have the media set the agenda in ways that curb government power?

DO THE DATA SUPPORT AGENDA-SETTING?

To demonstrate that media set the agenda, researchers need to do three things. First, they must show that there is a relationship between the media agenda—news stories appearing prominently in the media—and the public agenda, the issues people perceive to be the most important in their community or nation. Second, they must show that agenda-setting operates for different issues and in different contexts. Third, researchers need to establish that the media *cause* changes in citizens' ranking of most important problems. To make the case for agenda-setting, researchers conduct content analyses, surveys, and experiments.

The first study—the one that is frequently cited even today, more than 40 years after its publication—was conducted by Maxwell E. McCombs and Donald L. Shaw, then young professors of journalism at the University of North Carolina. McCombs and Shaw explored the perceptions of undecided voters in Chapel Hill, North Carolina during the 1968 election. The researchers asked voters to indicate the issues that most concerned them, the ones that they believed "government *should* concentrate on doing something about." The researchers content-analyzed news stories, editorials, and broadcast segments in the media available to Chapel Hill residents, looking to see which issues the news emphasized. McCombs and Shaw discovered a near-perfect correlation between the ranking of issues on the media agenda, as verified by the content analysis, and citizens' issue rankings on questionnaires. The more the media played up an issue, the more important the issue was to voters.

Talk about a study that set the agenda for the field! Research testing the agenda-setting hypothesis followed, like an avalanche, in the wake of McCombs and Shaw's suggestive evidence of media effects. Empirical research substantiated the researchers' findings.

Numerous studies conducted at a single point in time reported a significant correlation between the media and public agendas. Longitudinal research, conducted over different time points, also revealed a strong relationship between the media agenda and public opinion. For example, Winter and Eyal reported back in 1981 that there was a strong relationship between news coverage of civil rights and the percentage of Americans who named civil rights as the most important problem facing the U.S. over a 23-year period (Winter & Eyal, 1981).

Agenda-setting effects have emerged for numerous issues, including energy, drugs, crime, and foreign affairs. What's more, effects have been obtained across the world, in studies conducted in Argentina, Britain, Germany, and Japan (McCombs, 2004). More than 425 studies of agenda-setting have been conducted. The hypothesis holds up strongly in the bulk of the research, as documented by a statistical analysis of 90 empirical studies (Wanta & Ghanem, 2007).

Evidence for Causation

So far the evidence shows that there is a strong relationship between the media and public agendas. But it does not conclusively demonstrate that the media exert a *causal* impact on the public agenda. As discussed in Chapter 3, one way to establish causation is to conduct experimental research. Shanto Iyengar and Donald R. Kinder (1987, 2010) employed just this strategy, publishing a series of now-classic experiments that demonstrated the impact that television news exerted on perceptions of the most important problems facing the nation.

In one key study, the researchers asked their participants to evaluate the importance of a series of national problems. Over the course of a week individuals viewed television newscasts that had been edited so they focused heavily on one particular problem. One group watched a week's worth of news that emphasized nuclear arms control. Another group viewed news focusing on civil rights, and a third saw news on unemployment. Participants subsequently indicated their beliefs about the importance of national problems.

As agenda-setting predicted, individuals perceived the targeted problem to be more important after viewing the newscasts than prior to viewing the news (see Table 6.1).

Table 6.1 Experimental Evidence for Agenda-Setting.

	Importance Rating of Problem	Pre-experiment	Post-experiment Change
Arms control	76	82	6
Civil rights	64	69	5
Unemployment	75	82	7

(From Iyengar & Kinder, 2010.)

Note: Numbers refer to participants' numerical ratings of the importance of problems, along with pre-post changes.

The results made it abundantly clear that sustained exposure to the news can exert a causal impact on beliefs about the importance of national problems.

Does this mean that the media's choice of top items influences the priorities of each and every newspaper reader, blog scrutinizer, or viewer of television news? No, it does not.

Consider evidence that physical exercise is associated with health and well-being. This indicates that the more you exercise, the better your overall health. However, this does not mean that physical exertion will have an identical effect on the heart rate of each person who exercises frequently each week. Circumstances matter. Amount and type of exercise, time spent exercising, the genetic make-up of the individual, the person's overall health, and the juncture in the individual's life when he or she began exercising influence the strength of the relationship. It is the same with agenda-setting. "Agenda-setting does not operate *everywhere*, on *everyone*, and *always*," Rogers and Dearing explain (1988, p. 569).

You can think of issues the media could cover until the cows come home that would fail to influence the public agenda. Even if the media provided round-the-clock coverage of prejudice against left-handed individuals, it is unlikely this would register as a problem with the public (Iyengar & Kinder, 2010). News coverage during war time that tried to convince the public that the nation faced no threat from abroad would be doomed to failure. When the media direct attention to an "implausible problem," one that flies in the face of common sense, their efforts are not likely to bear fruit (Iyengar & Kinder, 2010; see also Box 6.2).

WHAT DO YOU THINK?

What are different ways that researchers can empirically test the agenda-setting hypothesis? How could you test a hypothesis about media agenda-setting?

BOX 6.2 AGENDA-SETTING WRINKLES: POWER OF CONTEXT

Who is most influenced by the media agenda? When is agenda-setting most likely to operate? Several factors emerge with regularity.

Need for orientation. Agenda-setting is particularly likely to affect individuals who believe politics is personally relevant, but are uncertain who to vote for or what political action to take. The combination of high relevance and uncertainty leads to a need for orientation (McCombs & Reynolds, 2009; see also Matthes, 2006). Engaged by politics but uncertain just which alternative to take, citizens high in need for orientation can turn to the media to help them decide which issues are most important.

News play. Stories that lead off network newscasts have a stronger influence on public perceptions than more ordinary stories (Iyengar & Kinder, 2010). Lead stories are influential partly because viewers assume network news is credible, inducing them to accept journalists' judgments about the important issues. Lead stories also appear early—before people leave the room to get something to eat, text a friend, or fall asleep.

Partisan media. This is a new twist on classical agenda-setting. In the very old days, the mainstream media all focused on many of the same issues. This has changed. Nowadays, in an era of partisan media, Fox News will focus on issues that appeal to conservatives, while MSNBC will tilt toward liberals' concerns. The same dynamic plays out in websites and blogs.

Can partisan media set the agenda? Under some circumstances, they can. Back in 2004, when the Iraq War and terrorism were major issues, partisan cable outlets covered the issues differently. Conservative media outlets—Fox News and like-minded radio shows—emphasized the evils of terrorism, while liberal outlets, like MSNBC, gave more attention to problems in how the Bush administration conducted and administered the Iraq War. Thus, conservative Republicans who relied on conservative media were more likely than others to believe that terrorism was the Number One problem facing the U.S. But individuals who used liberal media were less inclined to view terrorism as the most important problem (Stroud, 2011; see also Johnson & Wanta, 1995). Thus, in an era of fragmented media, news can strengthen beliefs people already hold about which issues are most important. This raises concerns. As Stroud (2013) notes, if "like-minded media use encourages Republicans and Democrats to perceive different issues as important, it may become difficult to bring citizens together to solve the nation's problems" (p. 15).

Political system. Media agenda-setting differs as a function of the political system. In dictatorships, where media are controlled by government, the government controls the agenda, stifling the ability of diverse groups to exert political influence. This illustrates the wisdom of political scientist Schattschneider's comment that "the definition of the alternatives is the supreme instrument of power."

Key characteristics of political systems include the nature of a nation's electoral system, its political culture, and the degree to which the media are autonomous from both government and political parties (Semetko & Mandelli, 1997; see also Peter, 2003). The more freedom media have from government control, the more opportunities there are for journalists, opposition political parties, and dissident activists to challenge the government's political agenda and place other issues on the front burner. These are core aspects of functioning democracies.

Typically, in countries with strict government control over media, the ruling elite sets the public agenda. Yet today, with the penetration of the blogosphere, Facebook, and Twitter, it can be more difficult for even marginally democratic governments to stifle widespread protests. In Russia, where the government typically does not allow television news to criticize its leadership, anger at vote-tampering and corruption in a presidential election some years back diffused throughout society as a result of smartphone-documented films of government authorities bribing subordinates to recruit voters and denunciations of electoral swindling on a popular dissident's blog (Barry, 2011b). This forced even government-controlled television to cover a large demonstration in Moscow protesting the election results, pushing the issue of electoral fraud to the top of the political agenda.

CONSEQUENCES OF AGENDA-SETTING: THE POWER OF PRIMING

What difference does it make if the media set the agenda? True, the effect is interesting because it demonstrates a subtle and pervasive media influence. However, agenda-setting takes on more importance if it can be shown that it affects other aspects of the political system, such as voting behavior and policymaking.

In their theoretical account of news impact, Iyengar and Kinder (2010) articulated an explanation of how agenda-setting can influence voting behavior. It is a five-step process that begins with what people cannot do.

First, individuals can't pay close attention to all or even most of what happens in the political world. "To do so would breed paralysis," the scholars noted (Iyengar & Kinder, p. 64).

Second, rather than carefully analyzing all issues, people rely on the most accessible information, or stuff that comes immediately to mind. Thus, when evaluating the president, Americans do not draw on everything they know about the chief executive's policies, ideological positions, personal traits, achievements, and political mishaps. Instead, people call on a small sample of their knowledge—a snapshot that comes immediately to mind, or is accessible, at the time they must decide how to cast their vote.

Third, the media powerfully determine which issues come to mind. Problems that receive a great deal of news coverage are the ones people invariably mention when asked to name the most important problems facing the country. This, of course, is agenda-setting.

Fourth, once the media set the agenda, they can prime voters. "By calling attention to some matters while ignoring others," Iyengar and Kinder observe, "television news influences the standards by which governments, presidents, policies, and candidates for public office are judged" (p. 63).

Fifth, priming can influence the way people cast their votes.

Priming is a psychological concept that describes the way that a prior stimulus influences reactions to a subsequent message. It stipulates that concepts are connected to related ideas in memory by what are called associative pathways. When one idea is piqued or aroused by a message, it activates related concepts, producing a chain reaction.

Political communication research calls on this concept, suggesting that the media agenda primes other realms of political thought. **Priming** specifically refers to the impact of the media agenda on the criteria voters employ to evaluate candidates for public office.

In theory, it works this way: The issues that the media happen to be covering at a particular time are communicated to voters. Voters—some more than others—then decide these are the most important issues facing the country. With these issues at the top of their political mind-sets, people call on them and decide to evaluate the president based on the chief executive's performance in handling these particular problems. If they approve of the president's performance on the targeted issue, they may cast a vote for the chief executive. If they think the president has done a poor job in that area, they may vote for an opponent or choose not to vote at all. Schematically, in its most basic form, the model looks like this:

Media agenda ——→ Priming ——→ Voters' agenda ——→ Voting

Importantly, there are a variety of factors that determine whether priming leads to voting in a particular election, including the individual's party affiliation. The model offers a pure, simple illustration of the hypothesized pathways.

Researchers have tested priming in a number of studies. Iyengar and Kinder, who conducted early experiments on agenda-setting, were among the first to empirically explore the priming hypothesis. In one representative study, they randomly assigned research participants to one of three experimental treatments. Over a week's time one group of individuals watched newscasts that focused on unemployment. A second group viewed news that emphasized arms control. In a third condition, individuals watched newscasts with a strong focus on civil rights. According to priming, participants who viewed stories on a particular issue should accord more weight to the president's performance on the targeted issue when assessing the chief executive's overall performance. This is indeed what happened. Individuals who viewed unemployment stories gave more weight to the president's performance on unemployment after watching the news than they did before. Similarly, participants who viewed news emphasizing arms control and civil rights placed more weight on these issues when assessing the president's performance.

At the same time, surveys have also uncovered support for priming. Researchers Jon Krosnick and Donald Kinder (1990) seized an opportunity to put priming to a strong real-world test. This was the era of Ronald Reagan's presidency, and during Reagan's second term, in November, 1986, news of a strange series of events leaked out. The United States had secretly sold weapons to Iran in order to facilitate the release of American hostages held by a terrorist group with ties to the Iranian government. The decision violated U.S. policy that banned the sale of weapons to Iran. Even more strangely, the U.S. had funneled a portion of the proceeds from the arms sale to a cadre of rebels thousands of miles away, in Central America, who were fighting what Reagan regarded as "the good fight" against a Communist regime. This also violated U.S. policy. The affair became known as the Iran–Contra scandal (see Figure 6.2).

Krosnick and Kinder reasoned that the news might prime evaluations of Ronald Reagan. The researchers looked at evaluations of Reagan before and after the bombshell announcement of the arms-for-hostages deal, focusing on whether domestic or foreign issues better predicted overall evaluation of Reagan. Prior to the announcement and avalanche of media coverage, Reagan's record on domestic issues better predicted his overall evaluation than did foreign affairs. Afterwards, the tide had turned, and his foreign affairs record, particularly on Central America, forecast overall assessment of Reagan better than did domestic issues. Priming was at work! The media had called attention to the foreign affairs boondoggle, and this now weighed heavily in

Figure 6.2 President Ronald Reagan speaks with the news media during Congressional hearings on the Iran–Contra affair in 1987. The scandal emerged after the press revealed an illegal arms-for-hostages deal involving Iran and a group of Central American rebels. News of the scandal influenced attitudes toward Reagan, and priming helped explain the news media's effects.

Time & Life Pictures/Getty Images

respondents' minds. The avalanche of news coverage had influenced attitudes toward Reagan, and priming helped explain the media's impact.

Of all the issues that could exert a priming effect, perhaps the most explosive—and powerful—is race. Racial attitudes, particularly prejudiced ones, tend to be strong, vitriolic, and connected to other sociopolitical domains. Armed with this insight, Nicholas A. Valentino (1999) embarked on a study of priming, politics, and race. He hypothesized that crime news that centers on racial minorities primes—or accesses—stereotyped racial attitudes. He conducted the study many years ago, when Bill Clinton was president, noting that Clinton was a Democrat and crime is an issue that usually works to the advantage of Republicans. Republicans have historically billed themselves as tough on crime, lambasting Democrats for coddling of criminals. Valentino figured that a news story about gang-related crime that depicted minority suspects would activate racial stereotypes and fears about increasing crime. These negative feelings should spread to, and activate, other attitudes, such as whether Clinton was doing a good job protecting the country from crime. Since Clinton is a Democrat, the concerns accessed by the racially focused news story should adversely affect respondents' evaluations of him.

Valentino assigned research participants in Los Angeles—a city in the throes of gang wars—to one of three experimental conditions. A first group was exposed to a crime story with minority suspects, a second viewed a crime story about non-minority suspects, while a third was not exposed to any crime story at all. He then asked participants to evaluate Clinton and his performance on several issues. Participants who viewed news with minority suspects evaluated Clinton most negatively. These participants were also significantly influenced in another—quite subtle—respect. News of gang crimes with minority suspects primed these individuals' racial attitudes. They then brought this to bear in evaluating Clinton's overall performance to a greater extent than subjects in the other two groups.

A variety of more recent studies have supported priming (Domke, 2001; Kim, 2005; McGraw & Ling, 2003; Moy, Xenos, & Hess, 2005; see also Pan & Kosicki, 1997). Like agenda-setting, media priming has emerged in electoral contexts outside the U.S., for example in Israel, Switzerland, and South Korea (Balmas & Sheafer, 2010, Sheafer, 2007; Kim, Han, & Scheufele, 2010; Kühne et al., 2011). Pointing to findings like these, some scholars argue that the media have a tremendous capacity to influence political thought. Iyengar and Kinder speak of its "insidious" effect.

Priming Revisited

Are citizens hapless victims, manipulated by media marionettes? Do journalists and Internet political communicators implant the criteria people use to select their nation's leaders?

Iyengar and Kinder raised concerns about media power. By covering an issue a great deal, the media make the issue more accessible to voters. Almost without thinking, voters call up issues—and political standards—acquired from casual exposure to political communications.

Other researchers have questioned this notion (Althaus & Kim, 2006; Eveland & Seo, 2007). Scholars argue that the media can temporarily access an issue or place it at the forefront of consciousness. However, this still may not cause voters to alter the criteria they employ to evaluate a political leader.

Thus, accessibility may be a necessary, but not sufficient, condition for priming to operate. Media coverage can influence subsequent evaluations if the news springs to voters' minds, but only if they regard the issue as applicable or relevant to the judgment they have been asked to make (Althaus & Kim, 2006; Roskos-Ewoldsen et al., 2009; see also Price & Tewksbury, 1997). Just because media heavily cover an issue does not mean the issue will exert a priming effect. Voters appear to be less susceptible to media manipulation than critics feared (Miller & Krosnick, 2000; see Reflections box).

Priming is more likely under certain conditions. For example, the more the news suggests that the president is responsible for a particular problem, the stronger effects priming exerts (Iyengar & Kinder, 2010; McGraw & Ling, 2003). If news portrayed a president as responsible for the nation's economic woes, news about the faltering economy would lead viewers to form more negative evaluations of the chief executive than if it suggested that the economy was beyond the control of even the president of the United States. More generally, if the news convincingly suggests that a political leader is responsible for a problem, news coverage is more likely to lead the public to take the issue into account when evaluating the leader's performance in office.

REFLECTIONS: MEDIA POWER AND AGENDA-SETTING

Do the media manipulate voters? Or are voters, and citizens more generally, more stubbornly resistant to media agendas than is commonly believed?

If voters view media stories passively and are relatively uninformed about politics, they may be susceptible to media agendas. If people rely on the most accessible information, they may call to mind articles covered heavily in the media. Political media in turn may prime voters, influencing the way they cast their votes or evaluate leaders. Some theorists worry that this makes people susceptible to influence, in the worst cases, pawns to media gatekeepers who may choose stories to attract big audiences or curry favor with the rich and powerful. Researchers in this tradition worry that these tendencies make it all too easy for the White House to manufacture agendas during war time that can be used to suck in a gullible public.

The other viewpoint is that people are harder to manipulate than is commonly believed. They have their own beliefs and political priorities. Interpersonal opinion leaders, reference group affiliations, and individuals whose political opinions they respect can outweigh media influences. What's more, the media are not a monolith. Individuals may be influenced by particular media genres that resonate with their attitudes, and not by others.

What do you think? Do you think media manipulate citizens or are less influential than is commonly believed? What responsibility do citizens bear for succumbing to political media effects?

CONCLUSIONS

The media set the agenda.

This is the most famous of all political media effects, one that is well known in political and journalistic circles. It is among the most well-documented political communication effects. Agenda-setting is sometimes believed to be synonymous with any and all media influence. It is not. Agenda-setting has a precise meaning. It is the process through which media communicate the importance of specific issues to the public. It occurs when concentrated media coverage of a problem causes the public to believe this is more salient than other problems. By defining a problem as important, media can profoundly influence public opinion and, under some conditions, policymaking. This is the fundamental insight of agenda-setting theory.

There is abundant evidence that the media help set the agenda (McCombs, 2004; Johnson, 2014). Evidence comes from cross-sectional and longitudinal surveys, experiments, and a variety of studies conducted in different countries across the world. It is in some senses a truism that an issue cannot be regarded as important unless stories about it appear in the media and the Internet. But simply because an issue appears in the media does not logically lead to the conclusion that it will increase in perceived importance as a result of media coverage. Yet concentrated media coverage of an issue frequently increases its perceived importance.

Priming, frequently viewed as a consequence of agenda-setting, occurs when the media agenda primes or influences the standards voters use to judge a president or political leader. By calling attention to certain issues and not others, news can affect the criteria voters invoke to judge candidates for office. Priming stipulates that when news concentrates on, for example, health care reform during an election year, voters may accord more weight to the president's performance on health care when judging the chief executive's overall performance. Although media priming effects occur, they are more likely to emerge when voters regard the criteria as applicable or relevant to the decision at hand. Priming and agenda-setting have intriguing implications for the conduct of political campaigns, as we will explore in the third section of the book. They underlie the strategic choices consultants make, and they can play a pivotal role in presidential elections.

CHAPTER

7

Agenda-Building

Painful recollections of the Newtown school shootings persist, even as searing memories of the massacre at the Connecticut elementary school recede into the past. When the nation learned what happened—20 first-graders and six adults killed at point-blank range in a school in a rustic New England town just 10 days before Christmas Eve in 2012—there was shock, anger, and tears. At hastily arranged funeral services, grieving family members reminisced about the young children who loved to sing, learn about whales, gobble down hamburgers with ketchup, and wear shorts in even the coldest weather. Because of the young age and innocence of the victims, the all-too-common school shooting took on different proportions. Large swaths of citizens expressed both sadness and outrage in media forums, from online social media sites to radio talk shows. The media swarmed into the bucolic community, where residents eerily said it was the last place something like this could have happened. President Obama, tearful and visibly moved after meeting with grieving parents, addressed a nationally televised memorial service promising to "use whatever power this office holds to engage my fellow citizens in an effort aimed at preventing more tragedies like this."

There was extensive media coverage of the funerals, capped off by a high-profile CNN news show host's interviews with gun rights and gun control advocates, a spate of news articles probing loopholes in gun restrictions, and reports of new opinion poll findings. Within days of the shootings, pro-gun Democratic senators indicated their willingness to consider new gun restrictions. Less than a week after the massacre, Obama announced that he would submit gun control legislation to Congress no later than January, 2013. The National Rifle Association, for its part, remained steadfastly opposed to assault weapon bans, proposing instead, in an announcement extensively covered in the media, that armed security guards be posted at every school. The media agenda had shifted from near-obsessive focus on Congressional efforts to resolve an economic crisis that put the nation on the brink of a "fiscal cliff" to gun violence. A new agenda had suddenly emerged, with public, media, and policy concerns appearing to converge. A variety of different courses of policy action were suddenly in play on an issue that had lain dormant for years.

As the example illustrates, agenda-setting does not exist in a vacuum. It occurs in the context of society and a myriad of social problems, and intersects with spectacular events, political leaders' priorities, and public opinion. This chapter focuses on the larger macro issues of agenda-setting. Chapter 6 showed that the media can set the agenda and prime voters. This chapter places agenda-setting in a larger context by examining factors that shape the media agenda and the broader policy consequences of agenda-setting. The first portion of the chapter discusses media, policymaking, and agenda-building, using the gun control issue as a case in point. Two boxed sections focus on factors that shaped the media agenda in a classic 1980s case study of drugs (see Box 7.1), and on areas where media failed to set the agenda for pressing national problems (see Reflections box). The second section takes a more contemporary focus by examining broader aspects of agenda-setting in today's digital age.

Several concepts underlie the discussion in this chapter. **Agenda-building** is defined as "a process through which the policy agendas of political elites are influenced by a variety of factors, including media agendas and public agendas" (Rogers & Dearing, 1988, p. 555). The public agenda consists of the issues the general public views as most important at a particular time. The policy agenda refers to the issues that head the priority list of political leaders.

BOX 7.1 AGENDA-BUILDING AND DRUGS

In the colorful history of contemporary news, you can find plenty of examples where the press focused ceaselessly on an issue, helping to transform it into a major agenda item for public and elite leaders. But for scholars and journalists with a long memory, there is one issue that particularly fits the bill. The issue takes us back to a different time: the Reagan 1980s, when a new, disturbing problem seemed to lay siege on the land.

"More than any time in memory," reporter Peter Kerr observed at the end of 1986, "America this year has erupted with concern about illegal drugs." The drug issue

Continued

splashed across the front pages of the nation's newspapers. Weekly magazines plastered it on their covers. Network news broadcast special programs on what was called the *crisis*, *plague*, and *epidemic* in drug use. Suddenly, public concern about drugs skyrocketed. Congress approved more than $1.5 billion in anti-drug legislation.

But there was one small paradox: Quantitatively, the number of Americans using most illegal drugs, such as marijuana, hallucinogens, and stimulants, remained stable from 1982 to 1986. "For many, then, a question about drugs is 'Why now?'," Kerr asked (1986, p. 1). Why did drugs catapult to the top of the media and public agendas? There are a number of reasons, all shedding light on the building of media agendas.

First, journalists, particularly investigative reporters, are motivated by moral values, a desire to ameliorate societal problems. When civil rights leader Jesse Jackson personally appealed to the editors of *The New York Times*, giving a moving speech on the devastation drugs had wrought on minority neighborhoods, he exerted an impact, inducing the *Times* editor to assign a reporter to cover illegal drugs on a full-time basis.

Second, political news frequently involves novel and unusual events. In 1986, crack, a smokable form of cocaine that got its name from the sound emitted when it was smoked, was new and very popular among high-profile segments of urban areas (see Figure 7.1).

Third, the media disproportionately cover celebrities. Celebrities are newsworthy because they attract a fan base that consumes the media. Within an 8-day period in June two celebrity athletes died from ingesting cocaine. The death of Len Bias, the NBA-bound, All-American University of Maryland forward, had an astounding effect "on the nation's capital, where Maryland is virtually a home team" (Kerr, 1986). Days later there was a second casualty: Cleveland Browns defensive back Don Rodgers.

Fourth, as agenda-setting scholars have observed, news is not created out of whole cloth. Events in the real world influence news coverage. By 1985, close to 6 million Americans were smoking, snorting, or otherwise regularly using cocaine, a 38 percent rise from 1982. New York City reported deaths from cocaine jumped from none in 1982 to 137 in 1985 (Kerr, 1986). This increased the newsworthiness of the story.

Figure 7.1 Crack, a new form of cocaine that could be smoked, caught on in certain social groups in the U.S. in the mid-1980s, leading to dangerous addictions and deaths. The media played an important role in building the agenda on the cocaine problem, leading to policy action. Critics charged that policymakers responded more to media-highlighted symptoms than to underlying problems.

NY Daily News via Getty Images

For a variety of reasons—some based on reality, others steeped in journalistic criteria, and still others reflecting cultural forces—the media jumped on the drug issue in the late 1980s. The media agenda exerted powerful effects. In April, 1986, just 3 percent of the American public regarded drugs as the country's most important problem. By August, 1986, after the spike in media coverage, the percentage had jumped to 13 percent. By September, 1989, 54 percent of the American public regarded drugs as the most important problem facing the nation (Dearing & Rogers, 1996; see also Shoemaker, Wanta, & Leggett, 1989).

The issue did not stop with the public. Members of Congress, increasingly concerned by media coverage, decided that legislative action was necessary. Moving

Continued

more quickly than usual, House and Senate leaders developed a sweeping anti-drug bill that increased federal government spending on legal enforcement, treatment, and educational programs. Congress overwhelmingly approved the bill in October, 1986. Critics charged that politicians had been more concerned about doing something quickly to appease public concerns about drugs—which had arisen due to agenda-setting—than with enacting meaningful legislation. "America has gone on another of the goofy benders that so often pass for public policy debate," one magazine editorialized (Kerr, 1986).

THE BIG PICTURE

National leaders face a dizzying array of problems. They cannot focus their resources on all issues simultaneously. They must select among issues, concentrating energies on certain social problems and letting others fall by the wayside. Issues compete for attention, and their proponents—well-heeled lobbyists, activists, and passionate ideologues—must persuade policymakers to devote time and money to their issue rather than someone else's. As David Protess and his colleagues (1991) observed:

> It is no easy matter for social problems to get on policymakers' agendas and produce corrective actions. The number of problems that policymakers might address is virtually infinite . . . Policymakers must decide which problems will receive priority attention.
>
> (pp. 238–239)

Deciding that something is a problem is itself an important—and political—act. If an issue is not defined as a problem by the media or political elites, it cannot move through the series of stages necessary for a problem to be contemplated, considered, discussed, and ameliorated. There are countless national problems, but policymakers' agenda can only accommodate a handful at a given time. There is not a one-to-one relationship between the importance of the issue and its emergence on the policy agenda. What's more, an issue can be important, but never reach media or policymakers' agenda (see Reflections box below).

REFLECTIONS: WHEN MEDIA FAIL TO SET THE AGENDA

Historically, issues that radically challenge a country's power structure or dominant cultural practices have not always been covered in the media. The press should have made these agenda items, but didn't because the events were too unfathomable to believe, contradicted cultural norms, or were not pursued by the powers-that-be.

During World War II, the American media played down news of the Holocaust, frequently placing stories of Nazi extermination of the Jews on inside pages of newspapers and shrouding them in doubt (Leff, 2005). The story was simply too unbelievable to cover seriously (Lipstadt, 1986). Even though President Roosevelt knew of the annihilation of the Jews and could have either acted to prevent it or conveyed the scale of the problem to journalists, the White House refrained from acting, due in part to anti-Semitism. With few official sources in government willing to reveal information about what was going on in the concentration camps, for fear of adversely affecting the war effort, journalists were stymied. But reporters also chose to erect blinders and psychological barriers, allowing them to minimize the horrors of what happened (Lipstadt, 1986). The Nazi atrocities that occurred in the concentration camps were not credibly reported until after the war—when it was too late to rescue anybody (see for e.g.: http://www.hnn.us/articles/10903.html).

In a similar fashion, racism and the plight of African Americans were rarely covered in the media until the civil rights protests of the 1950s and 1960s. Reporters undoubtedly harbored racial prejudices, and the government was loath to tackle institutional racism. When racial prejudice was defined as a *social problem* that required government action, thanks to the many demonstrations during this period, it became a legitimate issue on the public agenda.

During the early period of the AIDS epidemic, the media were also asleep at the wheel. Because the issue did not capture policymakers' attention and focused on groups—gay people and injecting drug users—that were ostracized or viewed by many Americans as deviant, the media refrained from devoting resources to the story (Kinsella, 1988). Although close to 10,000 individuals had contracted AIDS from 1981 to 1985, the issue did not appear on the media agenda. Only after

Continued

celebrities were diagnosed with HIV or died from AIDS, the virus began to insinuate itself into mainstream America, and the Reagan administration made the issue a political priority did the media begin to devote significant attention to AIDS (Dearing & Rogers, 1996). Even then, there undoubtedly was less coverage than there would have been had the story affected primarily mainstream, affluent segments of the American public.

By contrast, on other issues the media present very different portrayals, bringing controversial issues into the open and covering the negative, seamier side of public life. How can we explain this?

According to Daniel C. Hallin (1986), news media coverage can be divided into three distinct ideological spheres: the sphere of legitimate controversy, the sphere of consensus, and the sphere of deviance. Issues that fall into the sphere of legitimate controversy, such as election campaigns, are fair game for press criticism and coverage. In the electoral arena, journalists are afforded enormous freedom to explore candidates' shortcomings. Moral misdeeds, gaffes, mediocre debate performance, and sagging poll numbers are grist for reporters' mill and a constant, legitimate source for news stories.

News in the sphere of consensus—the domain of "motherhood and apple pie"— involves events about which there is cultural consensus. This includes news of Olympic Game victories, soldiers' heroic acts, and military interventions, such as the Persian Gulf War and early coverage of the war in Iraq. When covering these stories, reporters feel less cowed by news media conventions. Putting their identity as Americans before their professional role, they can act as boosters for patriotic causes.

The sphere of deviance is the domain of groups or issues that fall outside the mainstream, raising concerns that are incompatible with cultural norms. When issues are deemed to fall into this sphere, journalists have been reluctant to cover these stories. Sadly, agendas that needed to be built—on the Holocaust, race, and AIDS—never emerged.

This raises questions. Do these spheres still exist today, in our "no-holds-barred" contemporary era? Where do you draw the distinction between the spheres of legitimate controversy and consensus? What constitutes the sphere of deviance? Are revelations more likely today, with blogs and social media?

MEDIA, PUBLIC, AND POLICY AGENDAS

There are complex relationships among the media, public, and policy agendas (Gonzenbach, 1996). Agendas are built in a variety of ways. To shed light on these inter-relationships, scholars develop models. Dearing and Rogers proposed a model, shown below, of the agenda-building process (see Figure 7.2).

Take a look at the model. Whew! Lots of words, boxes, and arrows! It is a complicated model—but an interesting one. It also sheds light on the process of agenda-building. The model emphasizes that the media can affect Washington policymakers' agenda directly or indirectly. It also shows that a variety of forces influence the media agenda.

Sadly, the events that followed the mass shootings in Newtown, Connecticut offer an example of the model in action. An agenda for gun control and ameliorative action was built over a relatively short period of time, beginning with immense media focus on the shootings and a rash of opinion poll results. On the grass roots level, a Newtown gun control advocacy group was formed in the wake of the shootings. Subsequently, families of the victims, banding together to form a group called Sandy Hook Promise, called for a national conversation on mental health and gun responsibility. A bipartisan group of New York City school leaders took out a full-page ad in *The New York Times* to urge

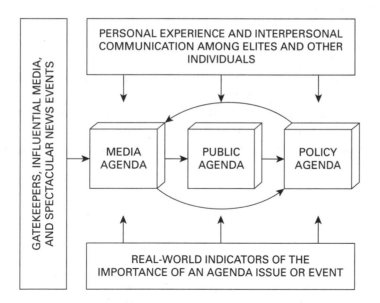

Figure 7.2 Main Components of Agenda-Building.

(From Dearing & Rogers, 1996.)

the president to do everything he could to prevent further gun violence. In the winter of 2013, as bills made their way through Congress and hearings were held, news articles discussed the policy and strategic aspects of gun control. The apparent convergence of media, public and elites' concern with guns helped to push forward an agenda that led to Congressional consideration of policy changes.

What Shaped the Media Agenda?

The news media like to say they hold up a mirror to reality, but this is never true. As was the case with drugs in the 1980s, news about gun control did not reflect all of the facts on the ground. Given the way the media fixated on the gun issue in the wake of Newtown, you might think that violence from firearms was on the rise. Actually, the national rate of gun murders has dropped in recent years, and is at its *lowest* point since 1981 (FactCheck.org, 2012a).

Importantly, media coverage of gun violence did not reflect the areas of the country with a high incidence of crime. In 2012, there were more than 500 murders in the city of Chicago alone, with 87 percent linked to guns. During the 2011–12 school year, 319 Chicago public school students were shot, 24 fatally. Seventy percent of the murder victims were African American, and the homicides took place in lower-income areas of the city (Cole, 2013; Davey, 2013). Yet there was comparatively little national media coverage of these tragedies and no outcry for gun control.

News media focused on Newtown because of the horrific nature of the crime; the number of individuals killed in one shooting; the age of the victims; and the incongruity of the crime with widespread cultural expectations. That a crime of this magnitude occurred in a small New England town defies common expectations, making it news-worthy. None of this is to say that news coverage of Newtown was inappropriate or excessive. The larger point is that news involves series of criteria, judgments, and cultural considerations. It is not a simple mirror of what is happening in public life (see also Chapters 9 and 10).

At the same, the media agenda, once built, came to influence opinions and policy. How did this happen? The model offers insights.

Agenda-Building and Policymaking

Media to Public; Public to Policymakers. As the arrows of the model show, *the media agenda* can directly influence the *public agenda*, or public opinion regarding the most important issues facing the nation. The public agenda can then affect the *policy agenda*, or leaders' priorities.

With legions of journalists encamped in Newtown, non-stop news media coverage in the immediate aftermath of the shootings, and countless Twitter feeds on the topic, the media helped set the agenda. The heart-felt stories of young children gunned down, told by grieving parents as they spoke lovingly of their kids, moved Americans. In early 2013, news stories profiled reactions of victims of other gun violence, with CNN's Piers Morgan aggressively challenging gun rights supporters on his widely watched program. (Fox News steered clear of the issue, illustrating the partisan nature of the agenda-setting process, as noted in Chapter 6.)

Saddened and shocked by the massacre, millions of Americans alternately displayed anger and despondency, suggesting their dissatisfaction with a situation in which 26 innocent people could be gunned down in a small town elementary school (Steinhauer & Savage, 2012; see Figure 7.2). The school massacre influenced the public in a manner that other public shootings did not. A *USA Today*/Gallup poll taken shortly after the shootings revealed that 58 percent of the public favored tighter gun laws, marking a 15 percent increase from October, 2011 (Madhani, 2012). A *New York Times*/CBS News poll found that 53 percent of the public favored a nationwide ban on semiautomatic weapons, 63 percent supported a ban on the sale of high-capacity magazine ammunition, and 92 percent endorsed background checks on all potential gun buyers. Support for stricter gun control cut across social and partisan lines. Republicans, respondents who indicated a member of their household owned a gun, and those whose households included members of the National Rifle Association, all supported requiring background checks on all gun buyers. "I see no reason for high-capacity magazines if you want to go hunting," said Sally Brady, a retired teacher from Virginia who owns a rifle. "You don't need a whole big bunch of bullets to shoot a deer or a squirrel. If you're that poor of a shot, stay out of the woods," she said (Cooper & Sussman, 2013, p. A14; Steinhauer, 2013a).

Obama and Biden, recognizing they had a once-in-a-generation moment to curb gun violence, sought to "seize on public outrage" to launch a multifaceted initiative to push for sweeping gun control legislation (Baker & Shear, 2013, p. A1). In late January, 2013, California Senator Dianne Feinstein introduced legislation that would ban the sale and manufacture of major semiautomatic firearms.

The agenda-setting media coverage seemed to have left an imprint on the policy agenda. In February, 2013, members of Colorado's House of Representatives, still recalling the Aurora, Colorado movie theater shootings of July, 2012, approved a bill that limits high-capacity magazine ammunition to 15 rounds. The governor later signed the bill, making it one of the toughest anti-gun laws in the country. On the other end of the political spectrum, in March, 2013, South Dakota became the first state in the U.S. to enact legislation that permitted school employees to carry guns in a school setting (Eligon, 2013).

Gun-related bills were introduced in a variety of state legislatures in the wake of the Newtown shootings.

Media to Policymakers. The model also depicts a direct path from the media agenda to the policy agenda. This indicates that media coverage can influence policymakers directly, without the mediating role of public opinion. Elites read the newspapers, follow the news on television, and keep up with trends on social media. The horrific school shootings immediately captured the attention of leaders. Liberals, like New York City Mayor Michael R. Bloomberg, demanded that the president take a leadership role and spearhead an assault weapon ban. A day after *The New York Times* revealed that a private equity company had major ownership of a gun company that manufactured the semi-automatic rifle used in the Newtown shootings, the private equity firm announced it would sell its controlling stake in the gun company. Thus, media coverage seems to have directly influenced policymakers in a number of cases, without the mediating influence of public opinion.

Policymakers to Media. The model depicts an arrow from the policy agenda to the media agenda. Policymakers' priorities can be communicated to media, which lavish coverage on their announcements. With leading Democratic senators indicating a willingness to consider gun control legislation, reporters rushed to cover the stories. Indexing coverage to reflect elites' sudden interest in gun restrictions, journalists devoted considerable coverage of Congressional willingness to reopen the gun control debate. West Virginia Senator Joe Manchin III, a National Rifle Association member who two years earlier had run an ad in which he fired a gun at pro-environmental legislation that served as a target, said that "everything should be on the table" in the gun control debate.

Policymakers' plans and legislative packages became the fodder for media attention. Early in 2013, when New York State approved sweeping changes in gun laws, including stiff restrictions on assault weapons and measures intended to keep firearms away from the mentally ill, the media picked up on the story, giving it big play. When Obama unveiled a broad campaign to curb gun violence, including universal background checks for all gun purchases, eliminating loopholes for gun shows, and an assault weapon ban, the news media dutifully covered the story, sparking analysis, pro and con commentaries, and a national dialogue on the issue.

External Factors. Arrows at the left, top, and bottom of the diagram identify other factors that build agendas. Clearly, the actual tragedy, horrific and spectacular as it was, captured media coverage. Personal experiences of family members of victims of gun violence were shared on national television (see Figure 7.3). Interpersonal communication among national leaders also increased the salience of the story. With the influential, elite national media covering the story, state and local media followed suit,

Figure 7.3 The Newtown, Connecticut shootings saddened and outraged many Americans. Media coverage helped build the agenda, with images like these propelling the issue upward on the public and policy agendas.

Getty Images

an example of **intermedia agenda-setting** (see, e.g., Reese & Danielian, 1989). However, real-world indicators—the actual amount of gun violence in the U.S.— did not shape coverage. With gun murders at their lowest point since 1981, the spectacular nature of the massacre, coming as it did on the heels of other shootings, stoked coverage.

Policy Impact

When media, public opinion, and a bipartisan collection of elite leaders converge in one direction, a new agenda can be built. But the media agenda does not necessarily lead to policy change.

Gun control is a case in point. Agenda-building propelled elected officials to consider policy solutions. In some cases, action was taken. New York State implemented an assault weapons ban. But on the national level, despite the flurry of media attention and building of an agenda around gun control, Congress did not enact any of the sweeping recommendations put forth by the Obama administration. In April, 2013, the Senate defeated a ban on assault weapons, limits on the size of high-capacity gun ammunition magazines, and even expanded background checks, which had significant public support.

There are many reasons why Congress refused to take stringent action on guns. First, some legislators strongly believe that the Second Amendment guarantees Americans an absolute right to bear arms. Second, policymakers gleaned from media coverage that the public was not of one mind on gun control. Trying to be balanced, journalists covered concerns voiced by gun owners. Scores of stories described gun rights activists' concern that the Obama administration was trampling on their Second Amendment rights, the National Rifle Association's opposition to any gun control, and the surge in gun sales in the wake of possible restrictions on firearms. One gun rights activist wrote that the Second Amendment "protects the right to shoot tyrants, and it protects the right to shoot at them effectively, with the same instruments they would use upon us" (Blow, 2013, p. A17). And while some polls showed considerable support for gun restrictions, others did not. A *USA Today* poll showed that 51 percent of the public opposed an assault weapons ban (Madhani, 2012). These stories offered up a complex view of public opinion, conveying to policymakers that a ban on assault weapons would face opposition from many Americans and would especially incense gun rights lobbyists.

Lawmakers, whose voting decisions are shaped by the political predispositions of their constituents, were sensitive to pro-gun rights views of voters in their districts or states. Gun lobbies like the National Rifle Association also wielded enormous power, for they have bankrolled advertising campaigns against legislators who favor gun control. As a *New York Times* editorial noted, "the gun lobby has exerted so much pressure on Republicans and red-state Democrats that the Democrats have dropped an assault weapons ban" (Keep guns out of criminal hands, 2013, p. A18). In order to counter these pressures, the Obama administration needed to use its influence to push key senators to vote for a ban on assault weapons. In the old days, a president like Lyndon B. Johnson would have pulled out all stops, using hard-nosed persuasion strategies to change the minds of members of Congress (Caro, 2012). But these are different times, and legislators are less deferential to the president. Obama, for his part, is an eloquent speaker, but less skilled in the art of bare-knuckles political logrolling.

This case study leaves us with several conclusions. The media are not all-powerful. They cannot force the hands of policymakers. Political factors also intervene. This is sobering to those who believe social change simply requires media attention. The news operates within a highly politicized policy nexus, and a host of high-profile political factors shape policy agendas. Some of these involve power politics: the influence of powerful lobbies like the National Rifle Association, whose political muscle intimidates lawmakers.

Others factors are rooted in an uneasy combination of hard-core electoral politics and raw ambition: Republican senators sought to reflect the strong gun rights positions of their vocal constituents, while a handful of Democrats from conservative-leaning states feared they would lose the election if they backed gun control measures. What's more, pro-gun control senators needed to surmount a high bar. According to complex Senate procedures, 60 votes were required to pass this major piece of legislation, and gun control advocates fell shy of this hurdle.

To be sure, the media exerted influence, helping push the gun issue to the forefront of the public and policy agendas. Congress considered serious legislation on guns for the first time in two decades, and several states—Colorado, Connecticut, and New York—approved sweeping gun legislation. To gun rights supporters, Congress's refusal to approve gun control legislation reflected a common-sense appreciation of the Second Amendment. But to the Newtown parents who tearfully pushed for strengthened gun control laws and the bulk of the public that backed tougher background checks, Washington's refusal to approve gun control laws represented a failure of Congressional will. It also showed that, for all its visibility and apparent power, the media are only one force in the political calculus, not the mighty behemoth they are often assumed to be.

WHAT DO YOU THINK?

How did the media build an agenda on gun control after the Newtown massacre? How did media work in concert with other forces, such as public opinion and elite policymakers, to influence the agenda? Does gun control illustrate how media can influence policy, or the inability of the media to make a difference on issues where powerful interests are at stake?

WHAT'S NEXT? AGENDA-BUILDING IN THE DIGITAL AGE

Let's switch gears to examine the ways agenda-setting and agenda-building are changing in the contemporary digital environment. McCombs and Shaw developed the agenda-setting model during a time when mass media had enormous impact. Journalists were the primary gatekeepers; they decided, based on journalistic conventions, whether and what information would reach the public. The media could present a fairly consistent and uniform agenda at any particular time (Metzger, 2009). But these assumptions are no longer tenable. People no longer rely exclusively on the conventional media for information. They can also turn to online information that reflects tastes and political priorities. The media's ability to convey a singular agenda to hundreds of millions of

Americans has slipped. During the 20th century, mainstream journalists exclusively decided which issues would dominate the media agenda. Nowadays, blogs and other online genres can influence media, public, and policy agendas.

Old media first felt the shockwaves back in January, 1998, when an ambitious Internet gossip columnist broke a story that took the political world by storm. Matt Drudge, who publishes an online newsletter consisting primarily of hyperlinks to other news sites, revealed that *Newsweek* magazine had killed a story detailing a sexual relationship between a White House intern and President Bill Clinton. *Newsweek* subsequently published the story, but *The Drudge Report* was the spark that lit the journalistic fire, propelling the world's media to focus on what became known as the Lewinsky affair.

The next celebrated case of the Internet setting the media agenda occurred during the presidential election campaign of 2004. CBS revealed a journalistic bombshell, announcing that it had proof that President George W. Bush had pulled strings to enlist in the Texas Air National Guard rather than face possible deployment to Vietnam. However, the story did not pass the smell test, in the view of conservative activist Harry MacDougald. He questioned the authenticity of the documents on a right-wing forum, Freerepublic.com, and other conservative bloggers, presumably outraged by "Liberal Media's assault" on a Republican president, directed their attention to the issue as well. *The Drudge Report* picked up the story, and within several days the counterclaim that CBS had failed to authenticate the documents was a big national story in the American media. Ten days later CBS backed down, saying that it could not prove the memoranda were authentic.

This is not to say that blogs regularly determine the media agenda. They don't. In some cases, the media determine the agenda of blogs. The point is that Internet blogs—sometimes written by citizens, not professional journalists—can enter the public fray, influencing the media agenda.

The lynchpin of agenda-setting is media power to decide what to cover and how to cover it. Increasingly, this power is becoming diluted, as Internet outlets give users more control over news content. Some years back, Internet techies created social news sites like Reddit and Digg, their names capitalizing on word games (read it and dig, if you want to find the information). These sites allow users to post content, links, and pictures. Users collectively decide which content they like best, and a computer formula or algorithm uses the popularity data to determine the order in which stories will appear on the site's front page. In other words, people set the agenda. (The content includes stories about politics, technology, and gross, weird-but-true stories like "Man robbed while peeing in North Beach alley." This story included the uncomfortable pun that if you are a robber searching for an easy mark in San Francisco, "urine luck!")

But here is the news for us: People, sitting before computers, are voting with their thumbs, determining the hierarchy of items in online news agendas. Individuals, rather than journalists, are exerting an ever-increasing influence on the news agenda. As writer Eli Pariser (2011) notes:

> Now the *Huffington Post* can put an article on its front page and know within minutes whether it's trending viral; if it is, the editors can kick it by promoting it more heavily . . . At Yahoo's popular *Upshot* news blog, a team of editors mine the data produced by streams of search queries to see what terms people are interested in, in real time. Then they produce articles responsive to these queries. . . .
>
> (pp. 70–71)

Reddit goes further. Articles that do not receive consistent voices of approval drop off its pages. A particular individual's page consists of stories favored by the group of registered users, and those which the person likes. The agenda is set by the group and is exquisitely tailored to fit users' preferences. The old model in which media gatekeepers determine the agenda is passé on these websites, replaced by one which awards power to the audience, with special consideration to each person's idiosyncratic tastes.

This raises policy questions. On the one hand, blogs and social media give grass roots groups, previously relegated to the margins, increased ability to influence the public agenda. Isn't that good for democracy? Or is it better if journalists, whose judgments are based in breadth and expertise, decide which stories should get the most play? What's more, if personalized news ever becomes the norm, how will citizens ever be exposed to agendas that differ from their own?

Conventional Media Still Matter

As you ponder these questions, you should also recognize that political communication has not yet reached this juncture. Sites like Reddit and Digg cater more to entertainment than to political information preferences. Even the increasing numbers of citizens who get their news from the Internet click onto websites from conventional media outlets (Takeshita, 2006).

News aggregators like Google News rely on automatic computer algorithms, rather than human decision-making, to select news items for display. But Google scans thousands of major news sites to determine which items to display online. These are typically conventional news outlets, like *The New York Times*, *The Washington Post*, Reuters, BBC, and Voice of America. Thus, choices made by gatekeepers at established media outlets continue to influence the agenda of Google and other online aggregators.

In sum, mass media agenda-setting still matters. But the political communication world is changing, and new media are changing the relationships among the media, public, and policy agendas. Current scholarship indicates that:

1. Conventional journalists no longer solely determine the media agenda. In some cases—the specific conditions have not been yet specified—blogs and online news sites can influence the news agenda that diffuses across the political world.
2. Social media can strengthen the role that established political forces play in the policymaking process. Well-heeled lobbyists have the resources to connect instantly with legislators via social networking sites, and they can harness social media to increase access to policymakers.
3. By the same token, the Internet offers citizens and social protest groups more opportunities to influence the public and policy agendas. Social media posts helped to launch and forge the Occupy Wall Street protests. They also may have helped to spread the message of dissidents who helped topple the Egyptian government in 2011, although we need to be careful about making simple statements about social media effects (Wolfsfeld, Segev, & Sheafer, 2013). In early 2012, social media flexed its viral muscle again, as people deluged Twitter, Tumblr, and Facebook to protest a decision by America's leading breast cancer advocacy group to end most of its financing of Planned Parenthood. A day after the protest was widely reported, the organization reversed itself and restored its partnership with Planned Parenthood.
4. Conventional media are still very much alive and important. Occupy Wall Street, the Tea Party, the Arab Spring of 2011 and other social movements egged on by social media penetrated the mass public and influenced policy elites because the traditional media spread their message and carried their stories. The messages may have diffused to the public through new online gatekeepers, but media coverage helped set the agenda and influenced policymaking elites. Researchers Shehata and Strömbäck (2013) concluded, after conducting systematic research, that "despite major transformations in media environments, the media are still surprisingly successful in influencing what issues the public perceives to be important" (p. 252).

WHAT DO YOU THINK?

In a digital age of blogs and social media, do mainstream media still set the agenda? Or are they largely irrelevant, taking their cues from social media? What does the research suggest? If social media and blogs become key forces in agenda-setting, what are some of the benefits and drawbacks?

CONCLUSIONS

The media do not exist in a vacuum. Media agenda-setting operates in the context of a larger culture, society, and political environment. Deciding that something is a problem is itself an important—and political—activity. If an issue is not identified as a problem by the media or political elites, it cannot move through the series of stages necessary for the problem to be contemplated, considered, discussed, and hopefully solved. These broader questions are the purview of agenda-building, which examines the intersection among media agendas, public agendas, and policymaking. Agenda-building is the process by which media and public opinion influence the policymaking agenda of political elites. There are complex relationships among the media, public, and policy agendas, with media influencing policymakers' agendas directly, and indirectly via public opinion.

Just because a problem exists does not mean it will gain substantial media attention. A variety of journalistic, political, and sociocultural factors shape the media agenda.

Media agenda-setting is a part—a substantial one, to be sure, but not the only component—of the larger policymaking process. It is never a sufficient condition for the implementation of a change in policy; media can cover an issue until the cows come home, but unless there is a ripe climate, receptive policymakers, and feasible proposals, no action will be taken. Agenda-building is, at its core, a political process.

It is important to emphasize that an issue does not remain on the agenda forever. It stays on the shelf for only so long. The Occupy Wall Street issue, which garnered so much attention in the fall of 2011, dropped off the radar screen by March, 2012, recruiting virtually no coverage (Schmidt, 2012). With substantially fewer people participating in the protest and the story bereft of novel, newsworthy aspects, journalists lost interest.

This is typical. After a story dominates the national agenda for a time, it inevitably slips out of view. Other problems come up. The media loses interest. The public becomes enamored by the issue *du jour*. Policymakers respond to lobbyists peddling other policy proposals. The president focuses attention on matters that can pay political dividends, and grass roots groups emerge to direct attention to new problems. The shelf life for a problem that is in need of improvement is short, and if action is not taken when the time is ripe, change may not occur for years, if at all (Downs, 1972). This was one reason why Obama sought to move quickly after the Newtown shootings.

There is debate among scholars as to how democratically the system operates. Some argue that the system is exploited by wealthy individuals and corporations, who can hire lobbyists to persuade policymakers to place their issue at the forefront of their agendas. Others point to the ability of grass roots groups like Mothers Against Drunk Driving to commandeer media attention, solicit public support, and propel policymakers to take political action.

In a digital age, the role of the news media in agenda-building has been supplemented by blogs and social media. Bloggers and social media now can influence the media, public, and policy agendas. But we should be realistic about their agenda-setting impact. As Shehata and Strömbäck (2013) concluded, based on their research, "The traditional news media agenda still matters for public opinion dynamics at the aggregate and individual levels . . . At the same time, the results also support the idea that the growing availability and use of alternative online news sources reduce the agenda-setting impact of traditional news media" (p. 251).

The struggle in agenda-building is to control the direction the country takes and to shape a policy agenda. It is a high-stakes battle. While many lament that "political games" must be played, the fact is that these are endemic to democracy. Democratic societies must determine which problems to prioritize, which to put on the back burner, and how to reach consensus on public policy questions. The media play an important role in agenda-building. The development of blogs and social media offers hope that citizens unconnected with powerful lobbies, but concerned about social and economic issues, can exert a greater impact on the process.

CHAPTER

8   **Framing**

The conflict caught everyone off guard.

A group of American Muslims announced plans to construct an Islamic community center about two blocks from Ground Zero in lower Manhattan. A day after a New York City community board unanimously approved the $100 million project in May, 2010, a take-no-prisoners blogger, Pamela Geller, issued a vitriolic denunciation of the project. "What could be more insulting and *humiliating* than a monster mosque in the shadow of the World Trade Center buildings brought down by Islamic attack?" she asked (Geller, 2010). A week later, an influential New York City newspaper columnist picked up the banner, using Geller's terminology to call the project fundamentally wrong, titling the column "Mosque Madness at Ground Zero." Some of the relatives of 9/11 victims followed suit, calling it a "gross insult to the memory of those who were killed on that terrible day" (Jacoby, 2010).

The "insensitivity to 9/11 victims" frame began to diffuse, and it sent shockwaves through the conservative media. Conservative Fox News host Sean Hannity invited Geller on his program and a right-leaning Washington, D.C. newspaper expressed outrage about the mosque. Former New York City Mayor Rudy Giuliani, who had done so much to unify New Yorkers on September 11, 2001, spoke out, calling the mosque a "desecration." With Republican leaders like Sarah Palin and Newt Gingrich issuing condemnations and tempers flaring, there was suddenly a major conflagration to cover.

Criticisms mounted during the spring and summer of 2010. Then came August, and a counter-frame entered the national conversation. Two luminary political leaders—New York City Mayor Michael Bloomberg and President Obama—offered stirring defenses of the mosque project. Bloomberg and Obama viewed the issue differently than had conservatives, emphasizing religious freedom. Bloomberg, in particular, was especially passionate, exhorting that on September 11:

> 3,000 people were killed because some murderous fanatics didn't want us to enjoy the freedoms to profess our own faiths, to speak our own minds, to follow our own dreams, and to live our own lives. Of all our precious freedoms, the most important may be the freedom to worship as we wish . . . Whatever you may think of the proposed mosque and community center, lost in the heat of the debate has been a basic question: Should government attempt to deny private citizens the right to build a house of worship on private property based on their particular religion? That may happen in other countries, but we should never allow it to happen here.
>
> (Elliott, 2010b)

Two strikingly different perspectives on the issue resounded across the land. And the different viewpoints—or frames, as scholars call them—led to very different interpretations and outlooks toward the mosque controversy.

Supporters, emboldened by the freedom to worship argument, emphasized that the Islamic cultural center was part of a world-class community center that would welcome all comers, regardless of their religious faith. They pointed out that two other mosques not far from Ground Zero had operated for years. Opponents countered that the proposed cultural center would nonetheless include a mosque, a place for Muslims to pray. "Ground zero shouldn't be about promoting Islam," an American Islamic physician observed (Jacoby, 2010; see Figure 8.1).

The proposed center is still a work in progress. Developers opened the space with a photo exhibit in September, 2011 and hope to finish the larger project in the next several years. But the tangible emergence of the center is less interesting than the controversy it stimulated and the different frameworks that emerged through the combative process of political communication.

The controversy over the mosque speaks to the power of what is known as *the frame*. The battle for public opinion and policy change can be seen as a jousting among different political frameworks, a struggle to see which will command the most popular and elite support. Framing has generated considerable research over the past decades (D'Angelo & Kuypers, 2010), and for good reason. It cuts to the core of the meanings people attach to political communication, pinpoints the roles symbols play in the process, and sheds light on political campaign strategies. This chapter will introduce key aspects and effects of framing, beginning with an introduction to the concept and several examples. The second section, emphasizing social scientific issues, compares

Figure 8.1 The proposed construction of an Islamic community center about two blocks from Ground Zero in Manhattan elicited controversy, generating two very different interpretive frameworks. The conflict speaks to the power that frames exert in spearheading public debates.

Getty Images

framing with other terms and helps you to appreciate the evidence for framing effects. The third portion takes a broader look at framing, exploring how it works in the policy sphere, where frames can have real consequences. The focus is on the way frames operated during the post-9/11 war on terrorism, providing a window on the interactions between frames and power politics as they unfolded on the international stage.

WHAT FRAMING MEANS

Let's start with the English language.

Frame is a noun. A picture frame encloses the picture. The frame of a house is the foundation that provides essential support.

Frame is a verb. You can frame a response, frame a policy, or frame an innocent man.

Framing is a present participle. A trendy California store promotes its business by noting that it does needlework framing, antique photo framing, and even sports jersey framing.

What all these different grammatical forms have in common is they denote the ways that an entity defines and structures subordinate physical or verbal objects. In the social sciences, where framing has been invoked to explain a variety of phenomena, a frame is defined as "a central organizing idea or story line that provides meaning to an unfolding strip of events, weaving a connection among them" (Gamson & Modiglini, 1987; see also Kuypers, 2006; Nisbet, 2010; Reese, 2007; Schaffner & Sellers, 2010). Political communication scholars have a more precise definition. They define **framing** as:

> selecting and highlighting some facets of events or issues, and making connections among them so as to promote a particular interpretation, evaluation, and/or solution.
> (Entman, 2004, p. 5)

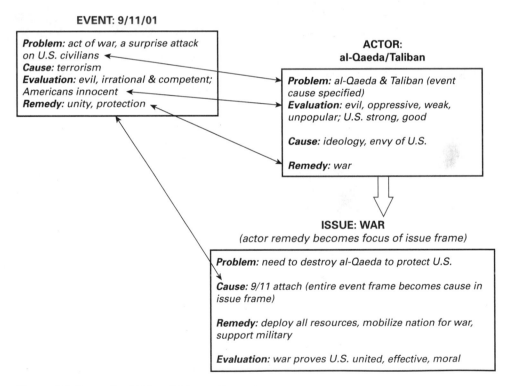

Figure 8.2 Frame for 9/11 and War on Terrorism.

(Adapted from Entman, 2004.)

Frames, like social beliefs, contain different attributes. According to Entman, fully developed frames are composed of different elements, with four core characteristics: (1) problem definition; (2) hypothesized cause; (3) moral evaluation; and (4) proposed remedy. All this is abstract, but, as we will see, frames call on a host of colorful, strongly held beliefs. You can appreciate this by reviewing a frame for 9/11 and the war on terrorism (see Figure 8.2).

The figure shows that a frame can have different components: an event, actor, and issue. Each contains sub-components: a perceived problem, cause, evaluation, and remedy. While this diagram offers only broad contours, it suggests the different dimensions that frames contain.

Framing operates at different levels. Political elites harness frames in an effort to advance a particular definition of a problem, hoping this will propel a bill into law or appeal to voters during an election campaign. Journalists use frames when they employ broad themes to structure factual details. Citizens interpret political issues in terms of broad principles that help them structure and organize the political world. The relationships among elite, media, and citizens' frames are complex, just as the relationships among these actors' different agendas are complicated.

Framing is at the heart of political discourse. As Donald R. Kinder (2007) notes:

> The issues taken up by government and the events that animate political life are always subject to alternative interpretation; they can always be read in more than one way . . . Frames (or something very much like frames) should be ubiquitous in political communication. Frames suggest how politics should be thought about, thereby encouraging citizens to understand events and issues in particular ways. By defining what the essential issue is and suggesting how to think about it, frames imply what, if anything, should be done.
>
> (p. 158)

And that is the essence of politics.

If you are looking for a simple, contemporary term to describe "frames," think of "spin." If you want a broader synonym, think "perspective."

Offering a more scholarly approach, communication researchers David Tewksbury and Dietram A. Scheufele (2009) point out that frames are the rhetorical devices that make linkages among concepts. Information provides the starting point, but frames connect the dots and build critical associations, inviting citizens to view the issue in particular ways. "Frames link issues to particular beliefs that carry with them concepts for interpreting the origins, implications, and treatment of the issue," they thoughtfully observe (p. 20).

If you think about some of the most important—and contentious—issues on the political horizon, you readily see frames in action. For example:

Affirmative action has been the subject of considerable debate, with framing a centerpiece. Supporters passionately frame affirmative action around the responsibility to once and for all remove the stain that racism has left on the nation's heritage. They note that, given the sins of the past, the egalitarian American ethos requires that the United States render justice to today's minorities. Opponents frame the issue around fairness, noting that it is not fair to offer benefits to minority citizens that are not available to equally qualified individuals who happen not to be minorities. Opponents also note that it is un-American to treat an individual differently on account of race or ethnicity and wrong to discriminate against one person in order to help another.

Birth control has been the site of some of the most contentious framing wars. In 2012, the Obama administration touched off a firestorm when it announced new regulations that required employers to provide coverage for contraception in health care plans they offer to their employees. Framing the issue around women's access to health care and the medical benefits that contraceptives offer women, the administration believed it had a strong philosophical case. Not so, said many Catholic bishops. Adopting a freedom-of-religion frame, they argued that the rules violated women's First Amendment rights, requiring them to pay for birth control, a practice they strenuously oppose on religious grounds. In response, the Obama administration modified its proposal, stating that religious institutions would not have to provide the coverage. Instead, free contraceptives would be offered directly to women through their insurance carriers. This plan, which also earned the ire of Catholic bishops, ultimately became official policy, though not before comedian Stephen Colbert joked that "a woman's health decisions are a private matter between her priest and her husband!"

Gun control is a time-honored touchstone of controversy. In the wake of the mass murder of 20 young children and six adults at an elementary school in Newtown, Connecticut in December, 2012, as discussed in chapter 7, frames sharply diverged. Liberals blamed the prevalence and easy accessibility of high-powered firearms; they called for bans on semiautomatic weapons and stricter background checks. Conservatives, concerned with restrictions on gun owners' freedom and arguing that gun control laws have not reduced crime, pointed to the need to allow people licensed to have concealed weapons to carry them in schools and college campuses. Others argued that the problem was deeper, rooted in a culture that romanticized violence in media and video games. Still other critics framed the tragedy in terms of a crisis of the spirit, lamenting that the nation was unmoored and lacking in the moral values that kept violent inhibitions in check.

As these examples suggest, frames are wellsprings of controversy, with divergent frames tapping into different problem definitions. In elections, frames are the focus of debate. Elections can be won or lost, based on the cogency and resonance of the frames candidates select. This is exciting and important stuff, but is worthy of a separate discussion. It will be discussed in Chapter 15, which examines political advertising.

SOCIAL SCIENTIFIC UNDERPINNINGS

To appreciate framing, it is helpful to differentiate it from two related concepts previously discussed: agenda-setting and priming. All three concepts explain how political media can influence citizens in subtle ways. All three also highlight cognitive effects, pointing to how media exert an impact on how individuals think about politics. But there are differences that might elude us if we lump them together.

Agenda-setting examines the salience of issues—their brute importance in voters' minds. Agenda-setting extended previous research by illuminating how political media could exert significant effects without necessarily changing voters' attitudes. But it neglected the rich ways that people construct the political world, as well as the many ways that leaders and media harness communications to define a problem in a particular fashion (Kosicki, 1993; Takeshita, 2006).

When it comes to policy debates that dominate mainstream media or whip across the web, there is not much question that the agenda is important. What makes for a colorful and consequential political debate is how different political actors describe the debate, the metaphors they use, and the spin they put on the issues at stake. Agenda-setting examines "*whether* we think about an issue." Framing explores "*how* we think about it" (Scheufele & Tewskbury, 2007, p. 14).

On the macro level, agenda-setting and priming examine *the particular story* the media select, stipulating that more coverage of the story bolsters perceptions of issue importance and priming of political standards. Agenda-setting frequently operates by pushing particular stories to the top of voters' minds, *accessing* them.

Framing is less concerned with the particular issues the media decide to cover than with "the particular ways those issues are presented" (Price & Tewskbury, 1997, p. 184). Framing suggests the *applicability* of certain ways of thinking about the problem, calling attention to certain values and not others (Hertog & McLeod, 2001; Price & Tewksbury, 1997; Scheufele & Tewksbury, 2007). This can be powerful stuff.

Poverty did not catch anyone's attention when it was framed as part of the natural order of things, an unfortunate byproduct of survival of the fittest. This is the way the issue was implicitly framed in the first decades of the 20th century. When activists framed poverty as a social problem with human consequences, one that merited government action, the media, the public, and policymakers took notice.

While most scholars view framing as distinct from agenda-setting, some prefer to think of framing, agenda-setting, and priming as spokes within a common conceptual umbrella, viewing framing as a type of agenda-setting effect. However, this approach is unwieldy and cumbersome, obscuring differences among the concepts (Scheufele, 2000; Scheufele & Iyengar, in press; Takeshita, 2006).

WHAT DO YOU THINK?

Think of issues currently in the news or the focus of social media conversations. How do different individuals or political groups frame these issues differently? What impact might these frames exert on public opinion?

Theory and Research

Psychological research offers a theoretical basis for political framing effects. The psychologists Amos Tversky and Daniel Kahneman theorized that frames guide processing of different choices, and direct individuals to define problems in subtly different ways (see Kahneman, 2011).

Scholars argue that the social world contains a rich array of different perspectives and viewpoints. Any of these can be evoked by framing a message in a particular fashion. Applied to politics, framing suggests that the way a political issue is framed can influence how people think about an issue, as well as the connections they make.

Some scholars worry that framing gives political leaders and journalists immense power to mold public opinion. By simply choosing one slant rather than another, and adroitly spinning the issue with focus group-tested words, elites can manipulate political opinions (Brewer, 2001). Critics lament that in the real world of political marketing, consultants play word games, trying to figure out if voters will respond more favorably to reductions in taxes when they are described not as *tax cuts*, but as *tax relief* (Lakoff, 2004). Republicans derisively framed Obama's health reform legislation *Obamacare*, hoping that the creation of a two-word neologism would invoke the specter of government health care run amuck, where patients are mere puppets in a health care system steered by the president. Democrats, for their part, like to frame educational programs designed to help underrepresented groups disadvantaged by society as *affirmative action*. Opponents prefer the term, *reverse discrimination*.

It is not just a frame game—it's a name game as well. One political writer emphasized the role that language plays in framing:

> Call it what you will—enhanced interrogation or torture, collateral damage or civilian deaths, pro-life or anti-reproductive rights, global warming or climate change, homosexual marriage or marriage equality, assault rifles or "semi-automatic small-calibre sporting rifles with plastic accessories"—it's all the same . . .
>
> (Hertzberg, 2013, p. 23)

Do frames influence beliefs? We cannot know for sure until research examines framing effects. A number of experiments have varied the frame, holding information about the issue constant. These studies have found that beliefs can be altered merely by varying the frame, or the way the story is told. For example:

- Research participants were informed that the Ku Klux Klan had asked for a permit to hold a rally on campus. For one group, the request was framed in terms of the right of a racist group to exercise its right to free speech. For another group, the emphasis was on the public safety and violence that might result. Individuals who read a *New York Times* article emphasizing free speech expressed more tolerance toward the rally than those who read a public safety article (Druckman, 2001).
- A mock newspaper story offered two frames of a land development controversy in south Florida. The information was the same, but the slants differed dramatically. An economically framed article claimed that the project would create thousands of construction jobs, noting that creating jobs "is more important than protecting frogs and snakes." The environmentally framed article stressed how regional wetlands would be harmed by the development, arguing that "we shouldn't sacrifice planet Earth's diversity for the sake of yet another hotel." Participants who read the economic frame held a more positive opinion toward the development than those in the environmental framing condition. Individuals who read the environmental frame were less likely to believe that the project would exert a positive environmental impact (Nelson & Oxley, 1999).
- A series of field experiments framed poverty in terms of either anecdotes or thematic explanations. In the anecdotal or episodic frame that focused on a single poignant episode, individuals viewed a news report describing two homeless Black adolescents living on New York City streets or a homeless White couple forced to live in their car in San Diego. The focus was on the personal plights of these

individuals. A thematically framed story juxtaposed a description of national increases in poverty with discussion of reductions in federal social programs. Participants who viewed the episodic story attributed poverty to individualistic factors, blaming poverty on character and education. Those who watched the thematically framed story attributed poverty to societal conditions (Iyengar, 1991). (These findings take on political importance. Noting that much news is episodic, focusing on a personal anecdote, liberal critics argue that the news does society a disservice. It shifts responsibility for poverty from social conditions to poor individuals. Conservatives counter that to a large degree individuals, not society, are responsible for poverty. Thus, they would not be troubled by Iyengar's findings.)

When Do Frames Work?

The studies above suggest that frames conveyed by the media will sway the public. Intriguing as these studies are, they are experiments and tell us only that frames exert these impacts in theory, everything being equal. Everything is never equal, especially in politics. Constructionist research reviewed in Chapter 4 reminds us that citizens are not a blank slate when it comes to framing. Instead, they have a rich repertoire of ideas about issues, some of them highly developed, others more carelessly put together. Media frames should exert the greatest influence on individuals when they are consistent with—or resonate with—individuals' preexisting beliefs.

Research conducted by Edy and Meirick (2007) offered support for this notion, with the study focusing on two different ways of framing the events of September 11. A war frame stipulated that September 11 was an act of war. According to this view, the Americans killed on that tragic day were casualties, and the aggressors should be killed on a battlefield of war. A crime frame emphasized that the dead should be viewed as murder victims and the perpetrators held accountable in a court of law. Contending that frames should be more influential when they resonated with individuals' preexisting viewpoints, the researchers predicted that support for the Afghanistan War in the fall of 2001 would be stronger among those who employed a war frame than among those employing a crime frame for punishing the perpetrators of 9/11. Edy and Meirick found strong support for this hypothesis.

They also found that people did not slavishly accept frames emphasized by the media. Although broadcast television networks framed the events of September 11 primarily in terms of war, respondents were most likely to frame the issue as a crime, treating it as a heinous crime indeed. Some individuals adopted a mixed frame, for example viewing the dead as war casualties, but preferring to see the perpetrators tried in a court of law.

Just as media cannot create agendas out of whole cloth, so too they cannot implant frames in audience members' minds. Research has found that media framing effects intersect with the values individuals bring to the media. Framing effects are more likely when frames are consistent with individuals' core values and beliefs about the political world (Boyle et al., 2006; Brewer, 2001; Keum et al., 2005; Shen & Edwards, 2005).

Reviewing these and other studies, one can reach several conclusions about the impact political frames exert on individuals:

1. Media frames probably have a greater impact when the issue is new or novel. On many issues, people bring their own framework to the media and do not necessarily accept media or elite frames lock, stock, and barrel.
2. Frames do not usually change the attitudes of strong partisans (Shah, McLeod, Gotlieb, et al., 2009).
3. Framing has a stronger effect when the frame is consistent with the audience members' political values. Thus, communicators frequently attempt to convince audience members that an ambiguous frame is congenial with what they already believe.
4. A frame does not operate in a vacuum. Frames operate in a political arena characterized by multiple voices. When there is competition among frames, the effect of a particular frame may be reduced (Chong & Druckman, 2007a).

MACRO ASPECTS OF FRAMING

Framing is a multi-layered concept. It can operate individually, on the micro level, in terms of how citizens frame political issues. This has been the focus of the discussion up to this point. Framing can also operate on a macro level. Political frames selected by journalists can influence citizens and policymakers. Political elites strategically choose frames, harnessing them to gain power, push issues, and control the policymaking process.

Just as we examined agenda-setting and agenda-building, we can examine frame-setting and frame-building (Baumgartner, Linn, & Boydstun, 2010; Scheufele, 1999; Scheufele & Scheufele, 2010). Just as many issue agendas compete for U.S. policymakers' attention, so too do multiple frames compete on the national stage. Power involves persuading political elites, media gatekeepers, and citizens to adopt one frame rather than another. Certain frames never make it to the national stage, precluding the possibility that a problem can even be defined in a particular fashion. Thus, power is not simply the ability to define the alternative, as Schattschneider said. It also involves the ability to frame and spin the alternative in a particular way.

But who exerts the power? Does the government call the shots, with White House frames influencing the way the media frame issues? Do media buy into government's frames, thus failing to offer up the kind of skepticism upon which democracy depends? Or do the media frame issues in alternative, oppositional ways?

Three theoretical perspectives shed light on these questions. They are:

1. **Hegemony**, the notion that political leaders can enforce their will on the mass public by manufacturing consent, harnessing mass communications in the service of their political objectives (see Chapter 10).
2. **Indexing**, the idea that political media index news so that it closely matches the range of voices expressed by political elites (Bennett, 1994; Bennett, Lawrence, & Livingston, 2006). According to this view, the news media calibrate coverage so that it reflects the assertions of key elite policymakers.
3. **Cascading activation**, a model stipulating that frames flow downward from the White House, through other key elites, the media, and to the public, with each actor in the process affecting political communication, as well as being influenced by it (Entman, 2004). According to a cascading activation model, influence moves from the White House to other major elite groups, like Congressional leaders and via news media frames, to the public, as measured by opinion polls. Interestingly, influence can flow upward, from the public to the White House (see Figure 8.3).

Of the three approaches, hegemony assumes that government has the most control over mass communications and can manipulate public opinion through a variety of techniques, including coercive political influence. Hegemony commonly operates in non-democratic societies, where government can engineer popular consent through deception and force. However, hegemony can also occur in democratic societies, like the U.S. You can argue that lack of press coverage of the Holocaust, of racism until the mid-20th century, and AIDS in the early 1980s followed a hegemonic pattern. As will be discussed in Chapter 10, there is rarely a simple hegemony, in which government uses coercive and persuasive strategies to influence the media. In democratic societies like the U.S., news rarely follows government dictates lock, stock, and barrel; instead, journalists exercise considerable autonomy by relying on news judgments and media routines.

Indexing grants media more autonomy, but says the media essentially reflect or parrot back what elites discuss. If government officials are in general agreement on an issue, the media present the dominant government frame, shelving alternative viewpoints. When government is divided and different elites frame the issue in different ways, the media will offer critical viewpoints, reflecting the diversity of elite debate.

The cascading model is more fluid. Likening political communication to a cascading waterfall, it emphasizes that influence frequently flows downward: from the White

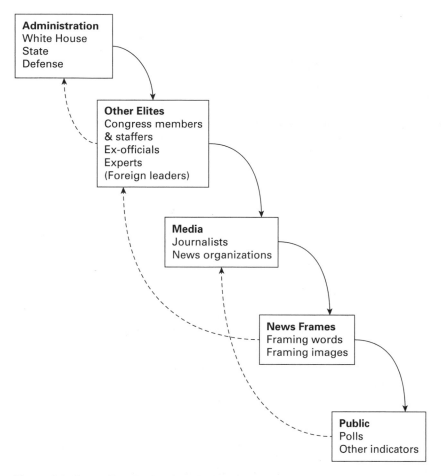

Figure 8.3 Cascading Activation Model of Framing

(From Entman, 2004.)

House through elites and media to the public. However, influence can also flow upward, with media or public opinion influencing policymakers' frames (as we saw with agenda-setting). Of the three models, the cascading view gives media the most autonomy, arguing that, under some circumstances, journalists are motivated professionally to present dissenting frames on foreign policy issues.

In order to grapple with these issues and help you appreciate the interplay of frames on the national stage, I focus on how frames operated in a particularly contentious issue.

FRAMING WARS: THE WAR ON TERROR

Initial Horror and Response

Immediately after the terrible attacks on September 11, America was in a state of shock and stunned disbelief. Innocent people—thousands, perhaps more—were dead. People wanted to know what happened, how to explain it, who to blame, what to do next. As Jim Kuypers (2006) observed:

> Graphic images were repeatedly seen on television and in print, searing them into the collective consciousness of Americans who were hour by hour increasingly wondering about their safety: were more attacks lurking around the corner?
>
> (p. 18)

The government had to quickly determine cause and consequence, and communicate these to its citizens. If ever there was a situation that needed framing, it was this one.

As President George W. Bush and his aides deliberated and reached consensus on how to respond, the president articulated his views in an address to the nation. The Bush administration determined that the nation must embark on a war on terrorism, one framed in terms of good versus evil. The press followed suit, lending support for the "symbolic significance" of an American president addressing his citizens on the night of September 11 (Kuypers, 2006). The public backed the president wholeheartedly. Bush received high marks for his strong, resolute response to the attacks.

Did the government enforce consent through coercive social influence, as hegemonic critics might suggest? No. But it did not need to. The Bush administration relied on adroit political persuasion and showed sensitivity to public sentiments. Public support for Bush also followed the time-honored tendency of the public to rally, at least for a time, around the president. As a result, the White House could wield control of how events were defined, framed, and interpreted (Reese, 2010).

Indexing and News Media Subservience during the Military Build-Up

During the months that followed 9/11, the Bush administration resolved to proceed with a war on terrorism by sending troops to Afghanistan and making a case to attack Iraq. Recognizing that it needed Congressional approval to attack Iraq, and knowing that members of Congress would be reluctant to support military action if their constituents opposed it, the Bush administration embarked on a full-court press, devising a campaign to promote the Iraqi military action. Supporters praised the administration for making a forceful case to the public. They argued that the U.S. needed to respond aggressively to the 9/11 attacks, and Bush had formulated a coherent plan. Critics charged that the Bush administration deceptively marketed a "sales pitch, which was delivered loud and clear throughout the news media" (Bennett, Lawrence, & Livingston, 2007, p. 19). The journalist Frank Rich (2006) called it "the greatest story ever sold."

The administration dispatched key leaders to make the case that there were plausible connections between Iraq and the 9/11 hijackers. Vice President Cheney and other Bush Cabinet officials charged that Iraq had weapons of mass destruction (WMDs) that could cause the deaths of tens of thousands in a mushroom cloud. Clandestine intelligence

Figure 8.4 President George W. Bush addressed the United Nations General Assembly, stating the U.S. planned to attack Saddam Hussein's Iraqi regime, unless he eliminated his weapons of mass destruction. It turned out Iraq did not have WMDs, unleashing a series of framing conflicts and controversies.

NY Daily News via Getty Images

reports obtained years before Bush became president had suggested as much, and the Bush administration argued that it had drawn on information gathered when his predecessor, Bill Clinton, had been president. The Bush administration argued that war was necessary in order to force regime change in Iraq, which would offer a democratic framework that could serve as a model for other states in the Middle East (see Figure 8.4).

As it turned out, much of the classified information about Iraqi WMDs turned out to be suspect. The news dutifully reported that Iraq possessed WMDs, but it turned out there were no WMDs. During the run-up to the war, the news offered a narrative consistent with the Bush administration's pro-war frame (see http://www.pbs.org/wgbh/pages/frontline/newswar/part1/wmd.html).

The indexing hypothesis helps to explain the news media's reluctance to criticize the war. Indexing emphasizes that the media index news coverage so that it closely reflects the range of frames articulated by leading policymakers. Few members of Congress, including leading Democrats, had strongly challenged the war. With an abundance of legislators and officials rallying behind the president, journalists could locate only a handful of government sources who publicly questioned the administration's master-frame. It pointed up what the scholar Leon Sigal (1986) famously observed: "News is not what happens, but what someone says has happened or will happen."

As a consequence, the American public was heavily exposed to pro-war views. (This could be good or bad, depending on your position on the issue.) In their extensive study of CBS, NBC, and ABC network news coverage of the march to the Iraq War, Danny Hayes and Matt Guardino (2010) found that Bush administration officials were quoted twice as many times as competing sources. Opposing Democratic legislators "were barely audible, and the overall thrust of coverage favored a pro-war perspective" (p. 59). However, contrary to indexing, there was ample coverage of dissenting frames. Officials from foreign governments who advocated a diplomatic settlement were frequently quoted on network news reports.

News, Indexing, and the Horrors at Abu Ghraib

During the war in Iraq, a handful of U.S. soldiers humiliated and abused Iraqi prisoners. They dumped phosphoric liquid on prisoners and beat them with a chair and broom handle. In one instance soldiers left a prisoner naked in his jail cell and forced him to crawl on his stomach and bark like a dog as soldiers urinated on him. Later he was sodomized by a police stick, while two female police officers hurled a ball at his genitals (see Figure 8.5, and also http://www.newyorker.com/archive/2004/05/10/040510fa_fact).

Figure 8.5 Iraqis walk past a mural showing humiliation of Iraqi prisoners by U.S. soldiers at the Abu Ghraib prison in 2004. News framed the incidents as abuse, but shied away from applying the torture label. Critics charged that by choosing to frame the events in this way, the news media reflected the prevailing, dominant U.S. government view of the incidents.

AFP/Getty Images

As photographs of the events at the Abu Ghraib prison were made public, the Bush administration launched a framing offensive. The president said he was sorry for the humiliation experienced by Iraqi prisoners, but emphasized these were isolated examples of "mistreatment and abuse" on the part of low-level American soldiers. Human rights experts and independent journalists expressed outrage, describing the events as torture, even part of a more sustained U.S. policy of coercive interrogation against prisoners in the war on terrorism. Yet members of Congress, including leading Democrats, shied away from strong condemnations of U.S. interrogation policy, refraining from labeling the events as torture (Bennett, Lawrence, & Livingston, 2007). Either because they did not want to seem unpatriotic or because they feared the consequences of a political firestorm, legislators followed the president's lead, shying away from challenging his overall frame.

Journalists rely on sources to reveal information. With few high-level sources willing to invoke the *torture* label, the news media could not frame the Abu Ghraib events in

Table 8.1 Primary Story Labels Used to Describe Abu Ghraib, by Type, *Washington Post*, April 1–August 31, 2004.

	Abuse	*Torture*	*Mistreatment*	*Scandal*
News (N = 242)	81% (188)	3% (9)	3% (7)	12% (29)
Editorials (N = 52)	61% (32)	17% (9)	3% (2)	13% (7)

* These data area based on the *first* label used in each article. Numbers in parentheses are the counts for each cell; percentages are not rounded and may not add up to exactly 100 percent in all cases.

(From Bennett et al., 2007.)

this manner. The indexing hypothesis suggests that the press will index its coverage so that it reflects prevailing elite sentiments on the topic, and this is exactly what happened.

In a content analysis of news stories in a leading national newspaper, *The Washington Post*, Bennett et al. (2006) found that just 3 percent of the stories labeled the events as torture. Yet the events included gruesome images, such as a picture of a hooded man standing on a box that was hooked up to electrical wires. Notably, 81 percent of the stories described the events with a less pejorative label, calling them *abuse*. About 3 percent labeled the incidents *mistreatment,* and some 12 percent described them as a *scandal* (see Table 8.1). Editorials in *The Washington Post* and news in other outlets displayed a similar tendency (Bennett, Lawrence, & Livingston, 2007). Reflecting the dominant voices in the political establishment, the press chose a frame that downplayed the severity of the abuses.

Cascading Frames: News Media Challenge the Status Quo

Media frames changed after 2004, becoming increasingly critical of the Bush administration's prosecution of the war in Iraq (Kuypers, 2006). Indexing explains some of this. An influential Republican senator, John McCain, himself a victim of torture during the Vietnam War, led a serious Congressional debate on terrorism and torture in 2005. This provided journalists with an opening, allowing them to formally report a hearing that featured criticism of Bush's policies. With leading members of Congress challenging the president, there was debate among elite leaders. When the government is divided and leaders disagree among themselves, the disputes offer legitimate fodder for media coverage. There is a legitimate public controversy to cover, and policymakers on both sides are publicly saying different things. As a result, the media, indexing coverage to divided government, present critical coverage of the issue. But more than indexing was involved.

Throughout the Abu Ghraib controversy, the press offered vivid, visual frames of the incidents, trumpeting the photographs across newspaper pages and the nightly news. The appalling, despicable treatment of detainees spoke volumes, conveying a more visceral and brutal message than any words could, even if they emphasized *abuse* more often than *torture*. Over the period of the next year, investigative journalism kicked into high gear, propelled by: (a) the moral outrage that drives crusading journalists; (b) professional press norms that emphasize exposing the negative underside of government policy; (c) media routines that favor stories showcasing drama and conflict; and (d) professional rewards that are bestowed on journalists who expose White House wrongdoing.

Following the revelations of Abu Ghraib, several national publications published extensive stories that explored the use of torture in the War on Terror, vividly describing violent mistreatment of Iraqi prisoners. Other critical coverage soon followed. *The New York Times* received a Pulitzer Prize for revealing that the Bush administration had secretly authorized the National Security Agency to eavesdrop on Americans to search for possible terrorist activity without acquiring the court-ordered warrants usually required for domestic spying.

The press began to reframe the issue, no longer emphasizing the freedom versus tyranny frame that characterized early post 9/11 coverage, or the contention that the Iraq War was a necessary battle in the long war on terrorism. Instead, the new frame seemed to suggest that the peril to America lay not only in violence threatened by terrorists, but also in the civil liberties-endangering activities of the United States government.

The diffusion of alternative counter-frames by the news media is consistent with the cascading activation model. The journalists' frames cascaded upward, raising questions that policymakers were forced to consider. At the same time, with Iraq casualties rising, Americans' support of the war dropped precipitously from more than 75 percent in 2003 to under 50 percent in 2006 (Bennett, Lawrence, & Livingston, 2007). Public dissatisfaction with the war contributed to the Democratic sweep of the 2006 Congressional elections. Public opinion likely exerted a cascading effect upward, causing both media and elected officials to take note of public disapproval of the war effort. However, as is typical in contemporary media democracy, the public was primarily reactive, responding to frames wielded by policymakers and press.

Summary and Evaluation

The discussion shows the complex, dynamic interplay among frames harnessed by the president, Washington, D.C. elites, the media, and the public. Frames shift and slide, with different parties exerting a different controlling influence on framing. This leads to several conclusions:

1. In the wake of a national crisis and perceived threat to security, the president can exert control over the dominant frame used to define events.

2. The news media index coverage to reflect the range of elite debate, reinforcing the dominant White House frame when there is consensus among national leaders and offering more critical coverage when debates break out among policymakers. In this sense, the media mirror the views held by key policymakers.

3. Once debate reaches a certain level, the news media become active players in the framing process, challenging elite frames and offering critical perspectives on policy (e.g., Lawrence, 2010).

4. The public can also influence the framing process, through elections and opinion polls. However, the public is ordinarily reactive, taking a back seat to frames wielded by policymakers and the press.

What is the verdict? Did framing serve democracy during the foreign policy crisis that followed 9/11? Did the media enhance democratic functioning? Much depends on the criteria used to evaluate political communication. You can argue that everything worked just fine, with some coverage overly critical of the war (Kuypers, 2006), other coverage too positive, but the bulk of the stories just right, offering skepticism and criticism. Indeed, the media broke the story of Abu Ghraib, displaying the grisly photos for the world to see, and continued to investigate abuses long after public interest in the story waned. However, it is the job of academic critics to hold the media's feet to the fire, and there is little question that the media could have performed better.

Rather than simply mirroring official debate, critics argue, the media should have moved more quickly to present alternative frames to the dominant version. "When an administration is working hard to sell its policies to the public—even in the name of national security—" Bennett et al. (2007) note, "the press can and should provide the public with coherent counterperspectives" (p. 194).

WHAT DO YOU THINK?

Who do you think controlled the frame during the early war on terrorism, marked by the Iraq War and Abu Ghraib scandal? How did frames change over the course of the Iraq War? Did the media effectively counter government frames? Finally, the big, underlying question: Did framing advance or hinder democratic ideals during the war-time period?

CONCLUSIONS

Framing helps explain how power is wielded. Unlike agenda-setting and priming, which focus on the perceived importance and accessibility of issues, framing takes a different tack. It looks at how issues are presented and the organizing principles that are employed to structure the political world. Agenda-setting and priming explain how particular issues become centerpieces of national deliberation. Framing takes it one step further by exploring what happens as issues start to reach the vortex of national debate. It explores how the frameworks employed by different political actors influence public opinion and policy.

A frame is the central organizing theme that is employed to lend meaning to political events. Framing involves selecting certain facets of issues and weaving connections so that particular interpretations and remedies are promoted.

Frames work on multiple levels. They are spun by elites, promulgated by the news media, harnessed by activists, and harbored by citizens, who use them to make sense of the political world. The frames invoked by these diverse groups can clash and collide. Politics is a battle for the frame, with different actors attempting to influence the way issues are presented and highlighted.

Frames are not magic bullets. They are more likely to influence citizens when they are consistent with their preexisting political orientations.

Frame-building occurs in the macro arena, where citizens, policy elites, activist groups, and media jockey for influence and power. Three models—hegemony, indexing, and cascading activation—have been proposed. Hegemony may explain, to a limited extent, the tendency of White House frames to exert influence early in a foreign policy crisis, but its heavy, ham-handed terminology minimizes the wide degree of latitude and autonomy that media and other actors have in a media democracy.

Indexing argues that the news media play a predominately passive role in frame-building, taking cues from the level of conflict expressed in elite circles and calibrating coverage to fit the dominant public voices in the debate. There is some support for this view. Cascading activation maintains that frames frequently flow downward from the White House, but can also flow upward. This model assigns media a more active role in frame-building. It offers a more dynamic view of the frame-building process.

The White House typically has an easier job controlling the frame when the issue is a foreign policy crisis that threatens national interests. Yet the president can potently influence framing of domestic issues as well. The overwhelming majority of television news stories on the Bush tax cuts of 2001 and 2003 quoted Bush administration officials and Republican legislators. The coverage emphasized tax cuts' potential to stimulate economic growth more than the possibility that they would increase economic inequality (Bell & Entman, 2011). (Of course, policy analysts differ on the long-term benefits of tax cuts, with some arguing that they increase inequality between the rich and poor, and others maintaining that they grow the economy, providing across-the-board economic benefits.)

Scholars differ in their views about how well frame-building serves democracy. Conservative scholars frequently criticize the media for undercutting the president in cases when a country faces a foreign enemy. By contrast, liberal critics point to instances where the media shied away from promoting frames that challenged government authorities. Normative theories suggest that a democratic society needs a wealth of frames that offer a diverse reading of a contemporary policy. As discussed throughout the chapter, there are legitimate questions about the degree to which the media helped to circulate frames that challenged the government's definition of the problems facing the U.S. after 9/11. To be sure, news stories broke new ground in questioning excesses of U.S. government anti-terrorism policies. Journalistic investigations definitely uncovered government abuses. Hindsight being 20–20, there also were areas in which the media could have acted more quickly to challenge the dominant version of events. In this way, they could have placed other viewpoints on the national tableau (see also Reflections box).

In any case, power is unquestionably wielded in democratic societies, occasionally in heavy-handed ways, but usually more dynamically and reciprocally. How much influence the public exerts and to what degree key elites manipulate public opinion are matters for debate. The news is a key factor, a catalyst of influence, setting the agenda, building the agenda, framing issues in disparate ways for the public and elite leaders. Thus, it behooves us to understand what makes news tick. This question forms the focus of the next two chapters. Get ready: When you talk about news, you introduce a cacophony of views, lots of chatter. The discussion will be noisy, filled with clamorous, sometimes clashing, perspectives on what shapes news in a contemporary media democracy.

REFLECTIONS: WHAT'S A SCANDAL? IT'S ALL IN THE FRAME

This is a story of two Republican presidents who engaged in two ethically problematic actions that led to two national outpourings of anger and dismay. But there was only one scandal. Why? This Reflections box explores the issue and invites you to ponder the broader questions involving the role framing plays in political scandals.

First, the tale of two Republican presidents. The first president in our story is Ronald Reagan. During his second term, Reagan presided over a strange, controversial deal. The United States secretly sold weapons to Iran in order to facilitate the release of American hostages held by a terrorist group that had ties to the Iranian government. The decision violated U.S. policy that forbade selling weapons to Iran. Even more strangely, the Reagan administration funneled a portion of the money from the arms sale to a cadre of rebels thousands of miles away in Central America, who were fighting what Reagan regarded as "the good fight" against a Communist regime. This too violated U.S. policy, as well as a Congressional amendment—and was conducted so secretively that few in the Washington, D.C. power elite knew what was going on. The revelations rocked the nation's capital, ricocheted across the country, and led to Congressional and public outcry, along with the formation of a presidential commission to uncover the truth. A national scandal ensued.

The second Republican president is George W. Bush. In 2002 and early 2003, in the tragic wake of 9/11, the Bush administration embarked on a full-throated national campaign to make the case that Iraq had weapons of mass destruction that could launch a second, even more serious, attack on the U.S. It turned out that Iraq did not possess WMDs. What's more, the Bush administration may have known this from the get-go, but opted to use WMDs as a galvanizing argument to propel forward the case for war. The American public bought the argument, and Congress authorized the use of military force against Iraq in 2002, to some degree based on a false set of facts. The Iraq War had devastating human consequences: More than 4,000 Americans and well over 100,000 Iraqis lost their lives. Critics argue that the Bush administration's deliberate distortion of facts about WMDs, its authorization of torture in Iraq in violation of the Geneva Convention, and ineffectual U.S. responses to ethnic civil war in Iraq were scandalous (Entman, 2012). But no scandal developed. Why?

Continued

Political communication scholar Robert M. Entman, in a book aptly titled *Scandal and silence*, proposes a framework to help answer this question. Entman argues that scandals are not objective events calibrated to the actual existence of moral wrongdoing. Instead, they are socially constructed by journalists and other participants in the political communication process. A critical factor is how reporters frame the events. An avalanche of media coverage that frames public officials' misdeeds as scandalous can create the political momentum necessary to hold elected officials accountable for their actions. But—and this is the important point—journalists cannot do this on their own. News is not created out of whole cloth, but emerges from a web of relationships between journalists and public officials, formal events, and legitimizing public activities. To build and frame an agenda, reporters require cooperation from government institutions that hold hearings, form commissions, and otherwise begin a formal process of remedial action. This legitimates news stories and allows journalists to frame misdeeds as scandals.

Government took official actions in the wake of Iran–Contra. A presidential commission was appointed, members of Congress actively spoke out, and leaders of the opposition party publicly denounced Reagan's actions. This allowed journalists to frame Iran–Contra as a scandal. None of this happened in the case of the WMDs and Iraq. Initially, there was much less finger-pointing and there were no formal investigations that journalists could cover and harness to frame a series of stories. Leaders from both parties had long believed Iraq had WMDs, so it was dissonant for them to change their minds on a dime. Democrats were sensitive to being seen as "soft" or "weak" on defense. Consequently, Congress did not demand that a presidential commission be formed to examine the Bush administration's conduct. Thus, there was little elite disagreement to which stories could be indexed. In addition, the public, still reeling from the tragic aftershocks of 9/11, was inclined to accept the White House's version of the facts. This impeded any activation of cascades moving from the public to policy elites to the White House.

Frames help us to understand why there was a scandal in the case of Iran–Contra, but not for WMDs and the Iraq War. (Conservatives would take issue with this analysis, arguing that the scandal metaphor is inappropriate. Given the president's sovereign duty to protect the citizens of the U.S., he had reason to fear another attack on U.S. soil in view of the accumulation of considerable evidence, mistaken as it turned out, that Iraq had WMDs. Furthermore, conservatives would contend that the Iraq War achieved important benefits, such as neutralizing a U.S. enemy and producing a more democratic Iraqi government. To conservative activists, what was scandalous perhaps was Bill Clinton's refusal to aggressively pursue al-Qaeda during his term. But this too illustrates that scandals are socially defined, with frames playing an important role.)

What do you think? Can you think of other misconduct that did not become a scandal, but should have? What about the 2008 financial crisis, which had grave implications for the U.S. economy, global repercussions, and was abetted by government decisions and Wall Street greed? Yet although Treasury, the Federal Reserve, and Wall Street bore responsibility, no one was held accountable, and no scandal developed. Entman provides an explanation that is consistent with the models discussed earlier in the chapter. "The more powerful the individuals and interests implicated by the allegations, then—all else being equal—the less, not more, likely they are to spark a major scandal," he writes (2012, p. 8). Thus, Anthony Weiner's titillating tweets, which did not violate the law or cause any physical harm, generated more media interest than a number of other, more substantive public misdeeds.

Can you think of other examples? What about on the local level? Have local media been reluctant to frame officials' behavior as scandalous, for fear it would alienate powerful institutions? Do you think that blogs, investigative journalism websites, and social media can frame events as scandalous, and therefore deserving of remedial action? Or, even today, do conventional media still play a critical role in promoting a scandal frame? With some old media, like daily newspapers in various cities, dying out, who will pick up the slack if the mainstream media no longer have the muscle to frame political transgressions as scandalous?

9

Behind Political News: Myths and Realities

Admit it. You can come clean. You're among friends.

If someone asked you to describe news, you would say it's biased, wouldn't you? You like to think of yourself as objective, but on this one, it's pretty clear, right? Wouldn't you say that bias is a part of today's news? If you said this, you would have lots of compatriots. When pollsters ask Americans what they think of news, they are of one mind: It's biased! Two-thirds of the public believe that news stories are frequently inaccurate. More than three-fourths of Americans perceive that news media tend to favor one side, and 8 of 10 Americans believe the press is often influenced by powerful interests (Pew Research Center for the People and the Press, 2011b; see also Ladd, 2012). What exactly does it mean to perceive news as biased? Does it signify a belief that news is inaccurate, negative, or tilts toward a particular political position? Or does bias mean something entirely different?

These questions raise broader issues, such as: What makes news tick? What shapes political news? Does news certify the status quo or does it challenge authorities? These questions cut to the heart of contemporary news. They help us understand whether and how news is biased. They help us unpack political news.

Now that you appreciate the effects of news—how it sets agendas and frames events— it is fitting to turn to the content of the frequently consequential news. This chapter unpacks myths of political news, explaining why common conceptions of news over-simplify the notion of bias. With the mist of popular conceptions of news cleared, Chapter 10 explores the broad factors that underlie contemporary news.

To help grapple with these issues, I turn to theory. Pamela J. Shoemaker, Stephen D. Reese and their colleagues developed a comprehensive perspective on news (Shoemaker,

1991; Shoemaker & Cohen, 2006; Shoemaker & Reese, 1991, 1996; Shoemaker & Vos, 2009). Shoemaker and Reese began by asking if the news media "hold a mirror up to society and try to report it as faithfully as possible," as a CBS network executive famously stated (Epstein, 1973, pp. 13–14). If the news holds up a mirror to reality, then questions about bias and macro determinants of political journalism become moot. News simply tells us the way things are. Bias is an illusion because news is essentially equivalent to truth.

Beginning with the mirror notion, this chapter and the one that follows examine the multiple forces that impinge on news. Forces work in different ways, lying on different levels of the social structural continuum and moving from micro, individual-level factors to broader, macro determinants. As Figure 9.1 shows, the first level is the individual: the social, psychologically oriented, and demographic factors that influence how reporters construct news. In some ways, this is the liveliest and most controversial arena; it demands that we confront the question of liberal and gender bias in the news. The second level focuses on the routines, or the professional practices journalists employ

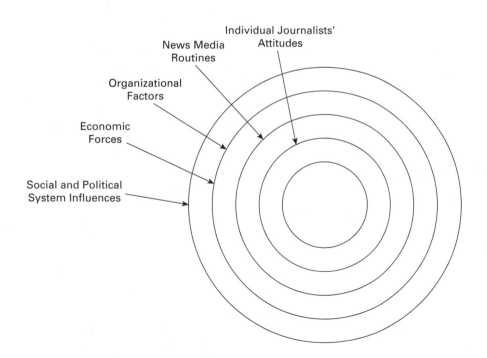

Figure 9.1 Determinants of Political News.

(Based on Shoemaker & Reese, 1996.)

to do their job. Moving up the sociological hierarchy to more macro forces, we then explore the influences of organizational, economic, and social system factors on news. This chapter focuses on individual-level determinants of news and controversial issues of news bias. Chapter 10 looks at broader forces that influence news.

The first portion of this chapter begins with a case study of an unusual news story, designed to question the idea that news closely reflects reality. I then explain why news does not, and should not, offer a simple reflection of events in the world. The second section focuses on the meaning of the controversial term, news bias. In the third portion of the chapter, I discuss the case for and against liberal bias. The fourth section explores gender bias in presidential election news.

DOES NEWS REFLECT REALITY? WELL, NOT EXACTLY

The story blanketed the news. The local media couldn't get enough of it. All the Cleveland TV stations covered it big time. So did Cleveland's daily newspaper, *The Plain Dealer*. It seems what happened on September 18, 2012 is that 25-year-old Shidea Lane and a bus driver, Artis Hughes, who was more than twice her age, got into a screaming match, and things got out of hand. Lane apparently boarded the bus, saying she had forgotten her backpack and couldn't pay the fare. She paid the bus fare but called Hughes a name. An argument ensued, with Lane apparently cursing Hughes and allegedly grabbing his throat. That was the last straw. "She want to be a man, I'm gonna treat you like a man," Hughes told the passengers on the bus. Which he proceeded to do, swinging his arm ferociously at the woman, delivering an uppercut to the young woman's chin, and then hurling her onto the street. A passenger's cell phone apparently caught the melée, the video was posted on YouTube sometime later, and went viral on October 11, capturing national attention. It became a major item in the local news, with the local broadcast stations lavishing coverage on the story.

No one denies the incident occurred. But let's appreciate that people board Cleveland buses at all hours of the day, drivers take their money, and then steer the bus through countless streets across the city. They have been doing this for years. The reality of bus travel is deemed too boring and mundane for the evening news. Suddenly, a bizarre, deviant incident is given big play on local news and becomes a front-page story in the next morning's *Plain Dealer*. It obviously is not the only event that happened in Cleveland, nor is it even the most consequential, when compared to the host of other problems that afflict residents of Cleveland and Northeast Ohio, such as educational inadequacies in Cleveland schools, housing foreclosures that are destroying the fabric of urban neighborhoods, or even the hapless record of Cleveland professional sports teams, especially the Cleveland Cavaliers after LeBron James took his talents to the

Miami Heat. Nor does it measure up in social significance to positive regional developments, such as the ways the auto bailout reduced unemployment in Northeast Ohio, and concurrent political events, like the ripple effects of the vice presidential debate that coincidentally occurred the night before the story went viral.

These issues, as well as more ordinary events, are also part of everyday reality, but they did not get a whiff of the local coverage the bus driver incident received. To be sure, a male bus driver punching a young female passenger is bizarrely out-of-the-ordinary and deserving of attention. But the lead item discussed endlessly on the news and in national media no less? If news accurately and closely depicted the reality of life in Cleveland, Ohio, one would have to assert that this incident was the central, most significant event, with the broadest implications for Clevelanders, on this particular day. But, of course, it was not. The news media covered it because it was novel, dramatic, and a YouTube sensation, the latter signifying another way mediated genres influence news judgments.

On a broader level, there is considerable evidence that news does not reflect reality. More than 70 percent of news stories focus only on the handful of people who are known or already prominent, rather than on the entire population (Gans, 1979). Television network news focuses more on the East and West coasts than other regions of the country, because these regions are where the financial and cultural elites conduct their business (Shoemaker & Reese, 1991). The problem of gun violence in America blanketed the airwaves after the 2012 Newtown massacre, but household gun ownership has actually dropped over the past four decades (Tavernise & Gebeloff, 2013).

In the political realm, news does not mirror reality. There are dozens of third and fourth party candidates who run for the presidency—many kooky, a few intellectually provocative—yet they do not get a nod or whisper from the nation's journalists. News devotes enormous resources to covering the Iowa caucus and New Hampshire primary, but the demography of these states does not reflect the diversity of the U.S., and they account for a small proportion of the delegates needed to gain the major party nominations (see Chapter 13). Every year across the U.S., there are thousands of city, county, and state-wide election campaigns that produce outcomes—such as property tax increases and changes in school funding—with more tangible effects on people's lives than the presidential race. But it is the presidential election that gets nearly all the attention.

News is not stenography. It is not equivalent to courtroom transcriptions, dutifully transcribed by a court stenographer. News involves a series of judgments about the important events of the day and issues to which citizens in a democracy should attend. Every event that transpires in real life cannot possibly be covered. For example, as interesting as people's everyday activities are, the public would not be well served if news devoted more time to, for example, the pursuits of soccer moms and dads, cheering on their kids' sports teams, than to income inequalities or to family instability in the working class that threatens the fabric of the culture (Murray, 2012). In 2012, the electorate would have been poorly served if journalists decided their coverage should precisely mirror the entire reality of American political campaigns, leading them to lavish as much attention on Jerry White, the goateed Socialist Equality Party candidate for president, who pledged to emphasize the resistance of the working class to capitalism, and to Jack Fellure, the candidate of the Prohibition Party, which aggressively opposes the sale of alcoholic beverages, as on the campaigns waged by Barack Obama and Mitt Romney.

News inevitably involves a process of excluding certain stories, selecting others, deciding how much time or space each selected story should be allocated, and shaping the message according to certain criteria. Scholars call this **gatekeeping**, noting that a mass communication system is the keeper of society's informational gates, determining in the aggregate which information will be passed along to its citizens. "Simply put," Shoemaker (1991) notes, "gatekeeping is the process by which the billions of messages that are available in the world get cut down and transformed into the hundreds of messages that reach a given person on a given day" (p. 1).

In a study conducted more than 60 years ago, David Manning White (1950) chronicled the behavior of a specific keeper of the gates. He focused on a wire editor at a morning city newspaper, who culled through the national and international stories from the Associated Press, United Press International, and International News Service teletype wires, as they were called, selecting stories to appear in the next day's newspaper. Of the approximately 12,400 inches of national and international news that came across the wire, the editor earmarked just 1,297 inches—a tenth—for inclusion in seven issues of the newspaper. His choices were based on a host of criteria, some professional (he deemed a particular story to be insufficiently national in scope) and others more aesthetic (he deemed the writing in a story to be dull). Some 40 years later, a researcher replicated White's major findings, this time with a female wire editor (Bleske, 1991).

There is nothing wrong with media gatekeepers making choices. Citizens and leaders depend on the media to sift through billions of messages and transform them into meaningful synopses of the world-at-large. Analytical stories can enlighten, and investigative reports can shed light on political malfeasance.

Some readers, particularly those who obtain their news from Yahoo! or partisan blogs, may say that gatekeepers are old-hat. Nowadays, you may note, people decide which stories to read and links to click. We are our own gatekeepers. But this ignores the fact that much of the political information you read online comes from news organizations, such as newspapers, magazines, and network news, that have filtered and selected the news that streams across your computer. News aggregators like Google use computer algorithms to decide which news to display. But the population of news stories that the algorithms examine includes many stories transmitted by the traditional news media.

How does it all work? If news does not offer a literal reflection of reality, what determines its content? Which factors influence the decisions media gatekeepers make each day, as they reject some stories and carefully edit others that are slated to be published, broadcast, or transmitted over the Internet? The discussions that follow examine these issues. The next section explicates the concept of news bias.

A DEFINITION OF NEWS MEDIA BIAS

Do journalists project their own attitudes into the news? Is there bias in the news? To many people, the answers are obvious. Just read Paul Krugman's columns in *The New York Times*. His comments are thoughtful, but his liberal opinions are transparent. He once told an ABC News interviewer that all the 2012 Republican candidates, except Mitt Romney, "are fools and clowns!" On the other side of the political ledger, conservative columnist George Will is equally thoughtful, but every bit as opinionated. Comments by cable talk show hosts go straight for the jugular. Conservative Glenn Beck compared Obama's economic program to Nazi Germany (Leibovich, 2010). Not to be outdone, in 2010, Keith Olbermann, the liberal ex-MSNBC host, called Scott Brown, a Republican candidate for a U.S. Senate seat from Massachusetts, an "irresponsible, homophobic, racist, reactionary, ex-nude-model, tea-bagging supporter of violence against women and against politicians with whom he disagrees." Oh, and let's not forget radio, where Rush Limbaugh famously called a Georgetown University law student, who defended an insurance mandate for contraception coverage in 2012, a "slut" and "prostitute." These are nothing if not intensely partisan, biased comments that continue the proud—or vitriolic, depending on your viewpoint—tradition of partisanship that dates back to the Revolutionary War (see Box 9.1).

BOX 9.1 ROWDY AND IRREVERENT: THE JOURNALISM OF EARLY AMERICA

There was no such thing as objectivity in the colonial press. Some newspapers remained loyal to the British Crown, appealing to the minority of Americans who sincerely believed in the British cause (Emery & Emery, 1992). On the other extreme were the radical newspapers devoted to fomenting revolution. Journalists like Sam Adams of the *Boston Gazette* and Isaiah Thomas, proprietor of the aptly titled *The Massachusetts Spy*, saw their roles as propagandists or mass persuaders. They were ideologues whose hearts burned with the zeal of moral righteousness. Neutral, fact-bound, dispassionate observers they were not.

To promote rebellion, Thomas used as the newspaper masthead a famous picture depicting a divided snake that represented the disunited colonies; above the snake was the slogan "Unite or Die." So, right there on the front page, for everyone to see, was a persuasive message advocating rebellion (see Figure 9.2). Sam Adams went further, inventing facts that advanced the colonists' cause and planning media events, as a member of the partisan Sons of Liberty revolutionary movement. In the autumn of 1773 he planned the Boston Tea Party. As Eric Burns writes in a book colorfully titled *Infamous Scribblers*, Adams and his fellow patriots sat in the newspaper's backroom, hatching plans for the Tea Party.

> On the night in question, in the same back room, they darkened their faces, disguised themselves as Mohawk Indians, and set out for the harbor. After the raid, it is possible that some of them returned to the *Gazette*'s backroom for a cheerful postmortem. The Boston Tea Party was at least as much the newspaper's as it was the town's.
> (p. 159; see also this description of early American newspapers at http://www.historypublishingco.com/articles/articles_188.php)

To be sure, not all journalism crossed an ethical line. Some prose, such as Tom Paine's *Common Sense*, was eloquent and inspirational. Beginning with the justifiably famous line "these are the times that try men's souls," Paine offered forceful, breathtaking arguments in favor of American independence. His words impressed General George Washington and profoundly moved public opinion. His pen was truly mightier than the sword (Streitmatter, 2008).

When revolution came, the press was there to offer its own impassioned perspective. Before presenting an excerpt of how *The Massachusetts Spy* covered

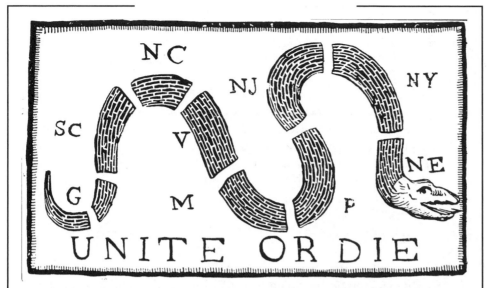

Figure 9.2 The earliest American newspapers were full of bias, in some cases advocating rebellion. The slogan "Unite or Die" became a rallying cry for revolution and was prominently featured in pre-revolutionary political communications. Compared to the colonial press, the contemporary news media are relatively tame.

Getty Images

the Battle of Lexington, it is worth noting that if the battle occurred today, the media would be there in force, covering it as breaking news, but careful to convey an imperious, above-the-battle neutrality. Claims would be qualified, opinionated statements would be strictly attributed to confidential sources, and reporters would steadfastly avoid any appearance of bias. A newspaper story appearing on the paper's 21st century website might begin by stating that:

> Gunfire erupted in the streets of Lexington, Massachusetts earlier today as British soldiers and colonial insurgents clashed in what some observers viewed as the first battle of a protracted struggle. Colonists claimed that British militia—derisively termed "redcoats"—burned down homes. However, the British commanding officer called this another sorry example of "American propaganda."

Continued

Alas, *The Massachusetts Spy* account that appeared two weeks after the battle occurred took a different approach, one in keeping with the values of the era. Here is how Isaiah Thomas described the event on May 3, 1775:

AMERICANS! Forever bear in mind, the BATTLE OF LEXINGTON!—where British Troops, unmolested and unprovoked, wantonly and in a most cruel manner fired upon and killed a number of our countrymen, then robbed them of their provisions, ransacked, plundered and burnt their houses! Nor could the tears of defenceless women, some of whom were in the pains of childbirth, the cries of helpless babes, nor the prayers of old age, confined to beds of sickness, appease their thirst for blood!—or divert them from their DESIGN of MURDER and ROBBERY!

(Burns, 2006, p. 189)

The press played an important part in the American Revolution. Colonists probably placed more trust in press reports than do the media-savvy citizens of today (Sloan & Williams, 1994). Pro-revolutionary colonial newspapers, abetted by Paine's literary prose, stirred public opinion, inspired soldiers, and united the colonies around a common cause (Burns, 2006; Stephens, 2007). But there was moral nuance in the behavior of colonial journalists. Some scribes, motivated by ideology or zeal, were willing to compromise the truth—lie—in the service of what they viewed as noble ends. They grossly exaggerated events, claiming, for example, that British soldiers physically attacked merchants, possibly with bayonets, and sexually assaulted women. Sometimes their claims were true; in other instances they were demonstrably false. The ends did turn out to be noble; but did that justify the means they used to achieve them?

The apparent upsurge (or greater accessibility) of media-transmitted opinionated comments in recent years is probably a reason why the public perceives more media bias today than 25 years ago (Pew Research Center for People and the Press, 2011b). But does this actually mean that the public affairs information that news organizations deliver to Americans is politically biased? Does it indicate that journalists' partisan views shape the news they report? Many critics assume it does, but the answers are more interesting and complicated than is frequently assumed.

For one thing, the individuals mentioned above—Krugman, Will, Beck, Olbermann, and Limbaugh—are not news-gathering reporters, but commentators paid to offer opinions, and sometimes the more incendiary the opinions, the more the people who tune into their programs. Do journalists, the reporters and editors who gather and interpret the facts, slant the news? This is a different question, and there is not a simple one-to-one correspondence between journalists' political attitudes and news. As for bias, it too is a complex, and frequently elusive, term. Is favorable coverage of an upswing of the national economy that occurs on a president's watch biased because it offers an abundance of positive press? Or is it simply fair and appropriate, in light of journalists' obligation to report the facts in a given situation? Is news coverage of a political scandal biased because the stories are salacious and negative? Or is it precisely the kind of coverage that the situation requires?

At the most basic philosophical level, there is bias in all news. No one is objective. There is bias when a reporter picks one adjective rather than another to describe a candidate's performance in a political debate. Bias occurs when a photographer selects a camera angle that depicts a candidate in a more, rather than less, flattering pose. Bias emerges when news covers negative rather than positive aspects of public life. Everybody agrees that there are biases in the news. But these are not the types of biases that animate critics. They are referring to politically motivated or ideological biases that emphasize one view of politics rather than another. And this is where it gets messy.

Bias is complicated because it involves more than simply counting whether a news organization presents more stories on one side of the issue than another. A stringent case for bias requires two daunting elements, as researcher C. Richard Hofstetter (1976) notes: (1) "there must be a source of knowledge about reported matters that is independent of the reporter under scrutiny and is regarded as authoritative; and (2) there must be evidence that the reporter (or someone who participated in the news story's production) was aware of a difference between the authoritative version and the account under scrutiny" (p. 4).

Based on this and other scholarship (e.g., Entman, 2010) a definition of news bias is offered that helps sort out fact from fiction in this controversial area. **News bias** occurs when there is a consistent media pattern in the presentation of an issue, in a way that reliably favors one side, or minimizes the opposing side, in a context where it can reasonably be argued that there are other perspectives on the issue that are also deserving of coverage. There are several things to keep in mind.

First, there must be a consistent pattern in the nature of the coverage. One story that favors Democrats over Republicans does not necessarily reflect bias. Second, there are many ways that bias can materialize. It can occur through systematic exclusion of material, disproportionately more coverage of one side than the other, tone of coverage, word choice, and even the ways that a news organization chooses to set the agenda or frame the issues. Third, the pattern in coverage must be subject to reliable verification through empirical methods. The biases should be subject to scientific investigation, employing the systematic methodologies of content analysis. Observers from different vantage points should detect the same pattern in news coverage. Fourth, there must be other reasonable perspectives on the issue, which are minimized or excluded due to an apparent political disposition on the part of the individual journalist or media organization. Fifth, and in a related vein, the other perspectives *should* be deserving of coverage. We would not claim that news coverage of the grisly murder of an innocent person was biased because it was infused with sympathy for the victim. It would not make sense to charge that the story harbored bias because it failed to offer a sympathetic version of the man who had admitted stabbing the victim 50 times. The perspectives deserving of coverage must be ones that mesh with cultural values and common sense.

With a definition of bias in mind, let's move to consideration of the question of whether journalists' attitudes shape news, as well as the role of partisan bias. The first part of the next section puts forth the argument that news contains a liberal bias, while the second portion critically reviews and examines these claims.

WHAT DO YOU THINK?

How is media bias defined? Can bias be in the eye of the beholder? Are there ever times when media bias can be a positive force? In what ways is news bias a problem in today's no-holds-barred, 24/7 cable and digital media era?

THE CASE FOR LIBERAL MEDIA BIAS

The media are so partisan that many people are under the impression that they must take their marching orders directly from the Democratic National Committee.

(Coulter, 2008, p. 19)

The problem comes in the big social and cultural issues, where we (television journalists) often sound more like flacks for liberal causes than objective journalists. Why were we doing the work of the homeless lobby by exaggerating the number of homeless people on the streets of America? . . . Why did we give so much time on the evening news to liberal feminist organizations, like NOW, and almost no time to conservative women who oppose abortion?

(Goldberg, 2002, p. 22)

Annoy the Media—Reelect Bush.

Republican bumper sticker

If you watch Fox News, you have heard the charges. If you read *The Wall Street Journal*, you are familiar with the allegations. Critics frequently charge that the news media display a liberal, left-of-center bias (see Figure 9.3). As students of political communication, we need to see if these charges hold up when the claims are examined systematically and carefully.

The liberal bias thesis consists of two parts. First, reporters and editors are believed to hold liberal, left-of-center attitudes. Second, journalists are said to project their attitudes into news stories, causing news to contain a liberal bias. As a result, the news is said to project a distinctively liberal slant on everyday events.

There *is* evidence that elite journalists—the national press corps that resides in Washington, D.C.—harbor liberal political attitudes. Some of this may be a result of reporters' natural identification with the underdog, embodied in the journalistic credo that news should afflict the comfortable and comfort the afflicted. Another factor could be that reporters are more critical of authority and identify to a greater degree with society's victims than do other professionals. Third, reporters may simply be more liberal

Figure 9.3 Critics frequently charge that the news media display a liberal, left-of-center bias. Do they? The truth is more complicated and, in the main, casts doubt on this thesis.

CBS via Getty Images

politically. And in fact the top tier of national reporters do hold liberal political attitudes, with large majorities reporting that they vote for Democratic rather than Republican presidential candidates (Lichter, Rothman, & Lichter, 1986; Rivers, 1962). Journalists who gave money to presidential campaigns in 2008 were significantly more likely to donate to Obama than to Republican candidate John McCain (Groseclose, 2011).

In a systematic study some years back, Robert Lichter and his colleagues (1986) found that the majority of elite journalists from major print and broadcast media held left-leaning views on political issues, such as nuclear power and the oil industry. Interestingly, the researchers also discovered what looked to be a parallel between reporters' political attitudes and the way that news organizations covered these issues. News stories offered a consistently negative portrayal of nuclear power, raising questions about nuclear reactor safety, in contrast to scientific experts, who viewed nuclear plants as very safe.

So, here was evidence that seemed to palpably link reporters' left-leaning attitudes to news coverage on a host of domestic issues. The findings were bolstered by quantitative and qualitative research (Groseclose, 2011; Kuypers, 2002). Even widely respected liberal commentators, such as Eric Alterman (2003), have acknowledged that there are "undeniable" instances where "a fair-minded observer might point to a pervasive liberal bias" (pp. 108–109). For example:

> The Associated Press, *Washington Post*, *Boston Globe*, and *Time* Magazine, among others, have referred to those who oppose abortion "even in cases of rape and incest" (circumstances under which most people approve of abortion). But the media almost never refer to those who favor abortion rights "even in the final weeks of pregnancy" (circumstances under which most people oppose abortion).
>
> (Alterman, 2003, p. 108)

Another liberal commentator, Michael Massing, provided similar testimony:

> National news organizations have produced a flood of stories questioning how the death penalty is administered in this country. These accounts have documented the poor legal representation available to death-row inmates, the extra-harsh treatment minorities generally receive, and, most dramatically, the growing number of innocent people who have been condemned to death. As an opponent of capital punishment, I applaud such stories. Yet I also believe that they lean toward one side of the issue, and that the coverage would be enhanced if more attention were paid to, say, the families of murder victims and the ordeal they must endure.
>
> (Alterman, 2003, p. 109)

Scholars also have acknowledged that news coverage of a host of social issues, for example, homelessness, gay rights, religion, and gun control, may tilt to the liberal side of the political spectrum (Entman, 2010).

Truth, alas, is complex, and as engaging as the liberal bias thesis is, it contains short-comings that call into question the sweeping allegations propounded by its proponents.

POSING CRITICAL QUESTIONS ABOUT LIBERAL BIAS

Remember that there are two components to the liberal bias thesis: (1) journalists are liberal; and (2) they project their liberal attitudes into their work, such that news contains a left-of-center bias. Let's now review each contention carefully and critically.

A systematic research review upholds the view that the elite Washington journalists do hold liberal attitudes toward a host of social issues. But what about reporters and editors from across the country? Are they also liberal? A series of answers emerges from the research David H. Weaver and his colleagues (2007) have conducted over the past three decades on the characteristics of U.S. journalists. Their results suggest that jour-nalists from across the country are more conservative than Washington, D.C. reporters. While 36 percent of journalists they queried in 2002 were Democrats, 18 percent were Republican and approximately 32.5 percent regarded themselves as Independents. With more than 50 percent of respondents regarding themselves as Republican or Independent, you can hardly describe journalists as radical liberals! What's more, reporters' bosses—media executives and owners—are business people who hold more conservative attitudes and are concerned with the economic bottom-line. Their directives can push liberal reporters to emphasize more conventional positions in their stories. But there is a more important factor at work. Journalists are professionals, or they try to be. They recognize that interjecting their own biases into a news story is unprofes-sional and flies in the face of journalistic canons. It also will turn off conservative consumers, and can get them fired.

Let's look at the second contention: news stories advance a liberal agenda. A problem is that much of the evidence advanced in its defense is anecdotal. Although interesting and suggestive, it does not provide compelling scientific support for the hypothesis. Ann Coulter and Bernard Goldberg, quoted at the beginning of this section, offer a litany of examples in their books, but these appear to be cherry-picked to support their argument, or could be outweighed by a flurry of counterexamples. For example, in the second extract listed at the beginning of this section, Goldberg asserted that the media lavish attention on feminists but neglect conservative opponents of abortion. How do we know he is correct? He might be, but he also could have conveniently neglected all the instances in which television favorably portrayed pro-life opponents of partial-abortion. Or his thesis might have been true at one time point, but could be swamped by more recent coverage that favored a pro-life viewpoint.

The only way to convincingly document that the volume or tone of coverage favors one political position over another is to conduct content analyses in the scientific fashion discussed in Chapter 3. You would not want to depend on one person to code content, as that individual might see reality in a particularly skewed fashion. Instead, one would ideally employ a variety of different individuals, and they would be instructed to follow a rigorous code guide that used objective procedures to measure favorability of coverage. When researchers have followed this strategy, they have obtained considerably different findings from those suggested by conservative critics.

Two researchers conducted a penetrating study of how a broadcast network, CBS News, and news service, United Press International, covered the key 1980 campaign between Democratic President Jimmy Carter and Republican challenger, Ronald Reagan. Reagan won the election and he actually received slightly more positive press coverage than Carter. The researchers concluded that "the majority of stories were neutral or in balance. Both CBS and UPI were fairly fair in their treatment of the individual candidates, and of the field" (Robinson & Sheehan, 1983, p. 138).

Stronger evidence against liberal bias came from a thorough investigation, conducted by Dave D'Alessio and Mike Allen (2000). The authors conducted a meta-analysis, a study of studies, in which social scientists look at a large number of empirical research investigations and use statistical techniques to figure out whether the findings across studies are solid or weak. D'Alessio and Allen's meta-analytic study found that the evidence for bias was weak. After analyzing many quantitative studies of media presidential campaign news from 1948 through 1996, D'Alessio and Allen found no newspaper biases that favored Democrats or Republicans. Biases for newsmagazines were negligible, although there was a slight pro-Republican bias in coverage. Television news contained a modest, though not entirely consistent, trend that favored Democratic candidates.

Even if the media portray a particular individual or group in a negative light, it does not mean the coverage is *biased*. Bias involves a conscious (or unconscious) intention on the part of a communicator to slant the news in a particular way. For example, Lichter and his colleagues assumed there was bias in news stories that raised critical questions of nuclear power plant safety. But this need not have telegraphed an intention to discredit the nuclear issue in order to push through a liberal anti-nuclear agenda, so much as an attempt to raise awareness of a social issue, a role that journalists perform for society. Articles raising concerns about radiation effects, environmental hazards, and catastrophic accidents could have been motivated by a desire to inform the public about an issue that journalists believed had been swept under the rug by authorities, especially in the wake of a 1979 accident at the Three Mile Island nuclear power plant in Pennsylvania that led to a leak of radioactive gases into the environment.

In other instances, events create their own narrative. In 2008, outgoing President George W. Bush and Republican presidential nominee John McCain faced tough questions in the wake of the 2008 financial crisis, which occurred on Bush's watch. Democrat Bill Clinton was subjected to a torrent of negative coverage after his sexual affair with Monica Lewinsky and failure to own up to his activities. But these did not constitute biases so much as journalistic impulses to hold officials accountable for consequential outcomes: the financial melt-down and a president's lies told under oath.

Finally, the liberal bias thesis is overstated. Conservatives are well-represented in the American media. For every liberal opinion piece in *The New York Times* by Paul Krugman one can read a matching column by conservative David Brooks. Sean Hannity and Bill O'Reilly offer conservative perspectives on Fox. Traditionally liberal newspapers like *The New York Times* and *The Washington Post* command considerable credibility among liberal progressives, but Fox is credible among conservatives. What's more, it has garnered higher audience ratings than the other popular 24-hour news networks—CNN and MSNBC. On the web, the blog DailyKos commands a considerable following on the Left, but take a look at RedStateDiaries on the Right, and you will find plenty of persuasive liberal-bashing.

During the spring primary season of the 2012 campaign, Mitt Romney trotted out the usual charge that the media doled out negative coverage to Republicans, complaining that he was the victim of a "vast left-wing conspiracy." In fact, a content analysis conducted by the Pew Center's Project for Excellence in Journalism revealed that in the first week of April, 2012 Romney garnered substantially more positive press than his Republican opponents, and all of them received more favorable news coverage than Obama (Project for Excellence in Journalism, 2012a). During the 2012 general election campaign, Obama received lots of bad press for his stewardship of a sagging economy.

In sum, the ever-popular liberal media bias thesis has many shortcomings. There is scant evidence to support it. Political news in the American media does not so much reflect a liberal viewpoint as a variety of conflicting perspectives. On the other hand, conservatives are correct that journalists hold more liberal political attitudes than the bulk of the public (Weaver et al., 2007). They have also provided instructive anecdotal examples of cases where reporters have taken a liberal slant on social issues. And, truth be told, by relentlessly holding reporters' (sometimes liberal) feet to the fire, media critics have forced journalists to view their work from a different perspective than they might ordinarily, in many instances producing more thoughtful analyses of contemporary politics.

STEREOTYPES AND GENDER BIAS

Critics have pointed to other journalistic biases besides political ideology. Racial prejudice has influenced reporters over the years. In the 19th and early 20th centuries, when waves of lynching swept across America, the press celebrated the barbaric practice, sensationalizing coverage and refraining from condemnation (Perloff, 2000). Years later, in 1984 and 1988, when African American civil rights leader Jesse Jackson ran for president, the news media shied away from taking his candidacy seriously. The press framed him as a performer and gifted orator, treating him as "an almost ornamental presence" (Achter, 2009, p. 119) Although some defended the coverage, noting that Jackson was never a viable contender for the Democratic nomination, other scholars suggested that subtle racial biases may have been at work. Twenty years later, during the 2008 campaign, the Internet was abuzz with racist drivel about Obama, along with false claims that he was a Muslim.

The mainstream press offered a very different, much more balanced, and even favorable, portrayal of Obama's 2008 candidacy (Lawrence & Rose, 2010; Wolfsfeld, 2011). Race rarely entered the fray in 2012, although it entered the picture in a different way, in the context of coverage of how Obama complexly balanced the presidency and policies directed at addressing the needs of African Americans (Kantor, 2012; see Chapter 14).

Now comes the issue of gender. Critics, scholars, and feminists have argued that the news media are full of stereotyped coverage of female candidates, offer patronizing assessments, and couch stories in sexist language. Other scholars, however, contest this view, contending that biases against contemporary female candidates have largely disappeared; they maintain that differences in how male and female candidates are covered are attributable to news values and standard journalistic practices. The discussions of gender roles and presidential politics draw on a wealth of scholarship: books by Erika Falk (2010) and Regina G. Lawrence and Melody Rose (2010), as well as an array of empirical studies (Braden, 1996; Bystrom et al., 2004; Bystrom & Brown, 2011; Jamieson, 1995; Kahn, 1996; Norris, 1997). The researchers' conclusions should help us sort through the thicket of these controversial issues and emerge with some answers.

Historical Background

This is the way it used to be.

In 1972 the Women's Movement began to gather steam, and egalitarian supporters of women's rights wanted more women to run for political office. Some spoke of the day a woman could be elected president. But this was the 1970s, and sex-role prejudice was pervasive. Typifying the view held by many Americans, one man noted that:

> Women are not qualified for this high office. If one is ever elected President, she would have to depend 100% on the advice of the men she appointed to high executive positions. Heaven help us in the event of a war. She couldn't handle the awesome responsibilities.

(Falk, 2010, pp. 37–38)

Journalism contained many of the same biases. In 1984, when Democratic vice presidential candidate Geraldine Ferraro triumphantly stood before the delegates to the 1984 Democratic National Convention, NBC anchor Tom Brokaw announced: "Geraldine Ferraro . . . The first woman to be nominated for Vice President . . . Size six" (Braden, 1996, p. 15). News also gave less coverage to female than male candidates running for the Senate between 1982 and 1986 (Kahn, 1994). Women candidates running for Senate stressed their masculine traits, such as strength, over 90 percent of the time in ads, but news stories described these characteristics only about 40 percent of time (Beail & Longworth, 2013; Kahn, 1996).

Female presidential candidates garnered less coverage than their male counterparts in 1972, 1988, 2000, and 2004. News portrayed female presidential candidates' campaigns as less likely to succeed than the campaigns of comparable male candidates (Falk, 2010). News offered up stereotyped descriptions of female presidential and vice presidential candidates, describing women candidates in more emotional terms and taking note of their clothing and gender, while focusing more on men's age and appearance.

This brings us to 2008. Was this stereotyped coverage still present when Hillary Clinton ran for president and Sarah Palin ran for vice president? Or had it disappeared, a relic of an earlier age? Two approaches shed light on these questions. The first emphasizes journalistic norms and practices. The second stresses the impact that gender-role stereotypes and prejudices exert on news-gathering.

CLINTON AND THE PRESS

"I'm in. And I'm in to win."

With those words, announced on her website on January 20, 2007, two years before the day that a new president would take the oath of office in 2009, Senator Hillary Clinton electrified millions of supporters, particularly women, who had long awaited the moment when a woman could capture the reins of the American presidency. Her candidacy also presented the news media with a series of challenges. Clinton was smart and experienced; few doubted that. A Yale-trained lawyer and former First Lady who had shepherded her husband's health reform legislation in the heady days of 1993, she had been twice elected senator from New York. Clinton possessed the intellectual acumen and political moxie to become the Democratic nominee. But she was also an intensely polarizing figure, who had annoyed many voters holding traditional sex-role attitudes when she told an interviewer at the outset of her husband's 1992 presidential campaign that she would not sit passively "like some little woman standing by my man like [country singer] Tammy Wynette." Yet, over the course of the ensuing years, Clinton seemed to have mollified many of these voters, earning kudos from Senate colleagues. As the 2008 campaign neared, she was regarded as the clear front-runner for the Democratic presidential nomination (see Figure 9.4).

Figure 9.4 As the front-runner for the 2008 Democratic nomination and the first female presidential candidate to have a real shot at winning the nomination, Hillary Clinton received intense press scrutiny. Did the news media cover her fairly or did the old sex-role biases surface in subtle ways?

Getty Images

A Journalistic Perspective

So, how did the press cover Clinton? The journalistic view emphasizes that journalists had come a long way from sexist biases of the 1970s and 1980s. It emphasizes that news values and professional journalistic conventions ultimately determine the news, and these steered journalists to focus on factors other than gender.

There is evidence that supports this view. In the main, Clinton received significantly better coverage than her female predecessors. What's more, the quantity of her coverage scarcely differed from that of Obama, her chief competitor. She received approximately the same amount of TV news coverage as did Obama, her positions on the issues were discussed as often as his, and there was no overall difference in the number of physical descriptions that she and Obama received in the print media (Falk, 2010).

But quantity was only part of the story, and this is where the more gnawing, controversial questions come that require a careful, multifaceted look at news.

During the period before the 2008 primaries and throughout the primary season, Clinton's press was significantly more negative than that of Obama and John McCain, the eventual Republican nominee. During the period between October, 2007 and June, 2008, 23 percent of the stories contained at least one negative comment (e.g., a quote from a party official or voter) about Clinton, in comparison to 16 percent for Obama and 13 percent for McCain. Significantly more paragraphs in a news story included a negative remark about Clinton than about Obama and McCain (Lawrence & Rose, 2010). The tone of Clinton's stories was more unfavorable than the tone of news for Obama and McCain.

According to a more sociological view emphasizing journalistic conventions, Clinton's more negative coverage did not reflect sexist bias. There are several reasons other than gender bias that explain the nature of her press.

First, she was the Democratic front-runner. This meant that she had a very good shot at becoming the party's nominee. Reporters believe it is their duty to subject front-runners to tough questions, noting that voters have a right to know the fallibilities of their party's potential nominee so that they can weigh these factors when they vote. This is one reason why news stories focused more on Clinton's missteps or political short-comings than they might have had she been viewed as an underdog.

Second, her campaign committed strategic errors that were deemed newsworthy. Clinton let her husband, ordinarily the consummate political strategist, meddle in her campaign, overshadowing her candidacy. He offended African Americans by ridiculing Obama's long-held opposition to the Iraq War and then dismissing the significance of his huge victory in the South Carolina primary, which had been bolstered by his ability to capture three-quarters of the Black vote. An Obama aide, delighted by the turn of events, called this "divine intervention" (Calmes, 2012)! Clinton's campaign also began to unravel as a result of highly publicized interpersonal conflicts and destructive in-fighting among staffers (Balz & Johnson, 2009).

Third, as the Obama campaign gained momentum after a series of stunning victories in Democratic caucuses and the endorsement of the party's royalty—Caroline Kennedy, daughter of President Kennedy, and her uncle, the late Edward Kennedy, former senator from Massachusetts who carried titanic weight among rank-and-file Democrats—Clinton lost her footing. As momentum began shifting in Obama's favor, Clinton began losing ground, her status as front-runner suddenly evaporating as Obama began to gain gravitas in the view of party leaders.

Obama's relatively positive coverage stands as a counterpoint to the more negative press Clinton received. Some of the reasons for the differential *were* steeped in professional journalistic norms. Obama was a fresh face, a charismatic candidate with a compelling narrative, and reporters gravitate to the new and novel. "He was simply a great news story," political communication researcher Gadi Wolfsfeld observed (2011, p. 69).

A Gender Role Perspective

There is another interpretation. A contrasting view of Clinton's 2008 press emphasizes that the same old sex-role biases were there, sometimes displayed subtly, other times quite blatantly. The gendered interpretation draws on theory and research showing that language influences behavior. The labels that journalists use to categorize politicians can influence how voters evaluate candidacies. If reporters differentiate candidates on the basis of gender, and conjure up stereotyped attributes when discussing male and female candidates, their descriptions can leave residual effects. Moreover, if the news media refrain from covering a candidate because she is female or dismiss a politician's chances of winning election because they perceive that voters will never choose a woman, their accounts may cause voters to treat female candidates less seriously than their male counterparts. At the same time, the gendered viewpoint stipulates, female candidates face a psychological double-bind that arises from the sexist notion that women cannot be both professionally competent and feminine (Edwards, 2009; Jamieson, 1995). Voters expect candidates to display stereotypically masculine traits, like strength, power, and decisiveness. If society deems it inappropriate for women to display these characteristics, preferring instead that they behave in stereotypically feminine ways, then women face a daunting obstacle at the get-go. If the press conveys and cultivates this double-bind, it adds to the difficulty that female candidates face in gaining election to public office.

How did the news media cover Clinton? An in-depth look at 2008 press coverage shows that news contained some of the same sex-role stereotypes that appeared in elections past.

Although print articles offered about the same number of physical descriptions of her as of Obama, Clinton was described early on in more physical terms than the average for previous male presidential contenders (Falk, 2010). Some of those physical descriptions raised eyebrows. A frequently discussed *Washington Post* article remarked that "the neckline [of a black top] sat low on her chest and had a subtle V-shape. The cleavage registered after only a quick glance" (Falk, 2010, p. 158). Articles were also more likely to refer to Clinton by her first name than they were to call Obama "Barack" or her other major competitor, John Edwards, "John."

Radio and cable television commentaries took off the gloves. They unleashed the b-word with impunity. Conservative radio host Glenn Beck called Clinton a "stereotypical bitch." The late liberal columnist Christopher Hitchens said she was "bitchy" on an MSNBC program. When a McCain supporter openly asked, "How do we beat the bitch?" and McCain affirmed it by responding, "That's an excellent question," the news clip was shown repeatedly, perhaps legitimizing the use of an offensive term to describe a presidential candidate. Tellingly, the use of a dehumanizing animal metaphor would seem to suggest that female leadership is unnatural, accessing the double-bind that sees femininity as precluding competence (Falk, 2010).

Castration images also were invoked. Clinton was the recipient of many gender-based insulting messages. For example, Tucker Carlson, a former host of the CNN program *Crossfire*, remarked that "There's just something about her that feels castrating, overbearing, and scary," and on another show noted that "I have often said, when she comes on television, I involuntarily cross my legs" (Douglas, 2010; Falk, 2010, p. 165). When you look at the multitude of opinionated commentaries on radio, television, and particularly the Internet, you find evidence that vicious, virulent sex-role biases still exist. Social media sites offered a slew of degrading portrayals. A Facebook group called "Hillary Clinton: Stop Running for President and Make Me a Sandwich" recruited more than 41,000 members in March, 2008. Another, saying that "Clinton Shouldn't Run for President, She Should Just Run the Dishes," had more than 3,000 members (e.g., Anderson, 2011; Jamieson & Dunn, 2008).

Now, let's be clear: Blogs, YouTube, and Facebook sites are not the conventional media. They can represent fringe groups, the Wild Wild West of contemporary communications that do not reflect mainstream media. Reporters did not cover Clinton this way. Indeed, some journalists were quick to criticize those who used the b-word to describe Clinton. The journalistic perspective discussed earlier makes a cogent case that Clinton received approximately the same volume of coverage as did her main competitor, and that differences in quality of coverage can be explained on the basis of the conventions of political journalism. But the gendered perspective calls attention to the operation of subtle biases, particularly in certain more opinionated regions of the political media. Reflecting on Obama's and Clinton's 2008 candidacies, Lawrence and Rose concluded that:

> The painful and public collective memory of struggles over race trumped the nation's more clouded memory of (often private) gender inequalities . . . We must consider whether Obama embodied and symbolized racial progress for many people in the United States (or at least many pundits and commentators) in a way that Clinton did not symbolize progress on sexual equality.
>
> (2010, pp. 217–218, 216)

PALIN AND THE PRESS

How did the press cover Sarah Palin? More colorfully and vibrantly, that's for sure. Palin played a central role in the presidential campaign, as the first chapter discussed. She captivated the media, energized conservative Republicans, including women who could identify with her life story, and served as a touchstone for criticism among liberals, as well as conservative media commentators, who believed she was unprepared for the vice presidency (see Figure 9.5). There has been less scholarly work on Palin's candidacy than on Clinton's. But the research sheds light on how Palin was covered and framed in 2008. We can view Palin's press coverage through two perspectives: journalistic and gender roles.

A Journalistic Perspective

Was Palin's press biased? The journalistic viewpoint says it was not. Unlike female candidates of previous eras, who could be marginalized by the media, she received more than twice the amount of coverage on Internet blogs than her Democratic opponent, Joe Biden. So, why was the commentary about her so negative? For one thing, as researchers Amy M. Bradley and Robert H. Wicks (2011) noted, "because Palin was new to the political sphere, journalists may have attempted to 'dig up the dirt' on her life and career" (p. 816). And there was plenty of "dirt" to unearth, juicy tidbits that are the fodder of political news, like her teenage daughter's pregnancy and the embarrassing revelation that the Republican National Committee had paid for Palin's expensive campaign wardrobe. But they didn't dig it up because she was a woman, but because news is primarily negative and focuses on unexpected, novel issues.

Figure 9.5 Sarah Palin was the first woman to be nominated as the Republican Party vice presidential candidate. She generated considerable press coverage, an outgrowth of journalistic criteria and gender roles. A variety of frames described her multifaceted candidacy.

MCT via Getty Images

A Gender Role Perspective

Palin's gender played a central role in some of the news coverage. But the depictions were more complicated than Clinton's, because Palin combined muscular issue positions with a feminine style. She took traditionally masculine issue positions, while displaying the "trappings of femininity—stiletto heels, silk shirts, and pearls", and, of course, lipstick (Lawrence & Rose, 2010, p. 221). She endorsed stridently Republican values while embracing the conventional feminine virtue: motherhood. Some working-class women identified with this self-proclaimed "hockey mom," who seemed to epitomize their struggles and values. Some men unabashedly carried signs proclaiming "Palin Is a Fox."

A gender approach adopts a nuanced view of Palin's coverage, emphasizing the diversity of media frames. Sarah Palin was many things to many people, framed by the media in strikingly diverse ways, as Linda Beail and Rhonda Kinney Longworth (2013) note. The news framed her as *a rugged frontier woman*, *a political outsider*, and *a former beauty queen* comfortable in her own skin as well as in chic wardrobes. News stories also described her as *a hockey mom.* As one media commentator put it, "Senator Clinton is a politician who also happens to be a wife and mother; Ms. Pain is a wife and mother who also happens to be a politician" (cf. Lawrence & Rose, 2010, p. 222). Palin exuded a down-home, one-of-us, hearth-and-home appeal, a frame that resonated with many working-class mothers who felt marginalized by elites. Yet to others, she remained a freighted, controversial image, one who evoked conflicting media frames: a contemporary achievement-oriented woman, competing in a masculine political world, but not afraid to display the conventional trappings of femininity, yet also a throwback to another era, when women cared only about conforming to male images of beauty.

It is difficult to disentangle the frames that Republicans highlighted, Palin cultivated, and the news distinctively emphasized. Conservative critics argued that the news media marginalized Palin, snobbishly putting down her gaffes, conveniently ignoring her down-home religious appeal, and playing up her physical features. While some media commentators displayed these traits (and Internet posts could be viciously sexist), there is little evidence that mainstream news reflected this caricature. At the same time, the media presented Palin in a variety of lights, some generated by her own self-presentation, others emerging through journalistic conventions, and still others from the intersection of her gender role and political perspectives (Kahl & Edwards, 2009).

WHAT DO YOU THINK?

Do media provide primarily fair coverage of female political candidates? Or does the news reflect a subtle sexist bias? Thinking about media coverage in 2008 and recent elections, do you see any examples of journalistic gender prejudices? And how can media do a better job of covering female and male political candidates?

CONCLUSIONS

This chapter unpacked the concept of bias, viewing it from different vantage points. Most Americans say that the news is biased, but it is not clear exactly what they mean. They probably have different things in mind. Some may believe that news is biased because it so frequently presents the seamy, unpleasant sides of life. This is not really a bias, for it is journalists' job to expose portions of the world that people do not often see or would rather shut their eyes to. Others may call to mind outspoken anchors, shouting matches on cable TV, or partisan bloggers. They may understandably call this biased, which it is, and generalize this perception to the rest of the news, which is frequently more even-handed, or at least more blasé. For others, bias is in the eye of the beholder. Some news consumers harbor strong political views and display the all-too-human tendency to project bias onto content with which they disagree (Feldman, 2011; Perloff, 2009). In still other cases, people are right: News does display a bias toward a powerful interest group. And in other instances, people may claim the news media are biased because this is what they have heard spouted out so many times. Media bias has become an urban—and rural—legend, and when you have heard people claim that the news is biased, you may repeat this statement yourself when an interviewer asks you to give your opinion on the topic (see Reflections box below).

A social scientific approach clarifies matters by articulating a specific definition of news media bias. News media bias occurs when there is a consistent media pattern in presentation of an issue, in a way that reliably favors one side, or minimizes the opposing side, in a context where it can reasonably be argued that there are other perspectives on the issue that are also deserving of coverage. A story that portrays a political figure in a positive or negative manner is not necessarily biased. Bias requires the deliberate and consistent intrusion of gatekeepers' opinions into the news story.

REFLECTIONS: EXPLORING MEDIA BIAS

Bias is a hot topic. It probably is the issue most frequently mentioned when political media are discussed. Now that you have read some different perspectives on the concept, what do you think? Here are some questions you might mull over:

1. What kinds of biases do *you* see in the media?
2. Do you believe news reflects a liberal or conservative bias?
3. Do you think that female candidates are still treated differently than male candidates, and in ways that suggest subtle stereotypes?
4. Taking into account social scientific definitions offered in the chapter, how would you define and measure bias?

You might put your hunches to empirical test. Decide what would constitute a liberal or conservative news bias. Or compare the ways male and female politicians are covered, deciding what would count as favorable or unfavorable (or sexist) coverage. Read a week's worth of national newspapers, watch seven nightly newscasts of a broadcast or cable network, or code an online news site, for example, Politico or RealClearPolitics. See what you find.

One view is that journalists' personal political attitudes determine the news that is displayed in print, broadcasting, and online. A corollary of this notion is the popular view that news reflects a left-liberal bias. In fact, journalists, particularly Washington, D.C. reporters, are more liberal than the rest of the populace. It is also true that media outlets have framed some social issue stories with a left-liberal focus, emphasizing a definition of the problem more congenial to a liberal than conservative viewpoint. But the liberal bias thesis oversimplifies and distorts. Proponents of the liberal bias thesis tend to cherry-pick examples that support their case, citing evidence gathered by partisan organizations rather than social science studies. When you look at the media as a whole, rather than particular media outlets, you are hard pressed to find that the news offers a systematic bias in favor of liberal causes. By the same token, the popular— if flawed—argument that news contains a liberal bias has had the salutary effect of helping journalists consider alternative perspectives in their stories, encouraging the inclusion of multiple points of view.

Critics have also argued that news presented other biases, such as race and gender-based. In the past, news presented a series of offensive stereotypes of African American and female candidates. The picture has clearly improved, but there remains debate, particularly on the question of gender bias. A journalistic perspective emphasizes the role played by journalistic conventions; a gender-bias approach contends that the legacy of sex-role prejudice remains, leading to subtle and striking biases on female candidates. The journalistic approach calls attention to the quantity and favorable quality of coverage that both Clinton and Palin received, indicating the progress that has been made in recent years. The gender-bias perspective highlights the ways that journalists viewed Clinton and Palin in gendered terms and calls attention to the virulent sexist language on websites and in social media. With more women likely to run for president and a record 20 female senators now serving constituents, it will be interesting to see how media portrayals change in the years to come.

Unpacking Political News

The political reporters knew the drill. Heck, they had heard the speech dozens of times before. They knew the key words, intonations, and moments when the candidates—Obama and Romney—would cut to the chase and utter a phrase that would evoke cheers and applause. They also knew how to write the story when they returned to their laptops. There would not be much time and they would need to write quickly.

They would briefly note the location where the speech had been delivered, size of the crowd, and any crowd reactions. They would be certain to quote a red-meat line of the speech. If something unusual happened, like a heckler shouting out a hostile question, they would be sure to describe the incident. Any conflicts that occurred—say, between the heckler and the candidate or maybe between two members of the candidate's staff, arguing about whether the optics would play well on television—would make it into the story for sure. This being Ohio, the swing state of swing states (that phrase might even find a place in the piece), the reporters would note how important it was for a candidate to capture Ohio's 18 electoral votes.

These are my reflections, penned after listening to three Ohio journalists describe their experiences covering the 2012 presidential campaign. They offer a rough portrait of the ritualistic, routine journalistic conventions that the reporters implicitly called on as they recollected their coverage of the presidential race in Ohio.

Routines are among the key factors that influence political gatekeeping. Extending the discussion of Chapter 9, this chapter takes a broader sweep, examining the ways that media routines, organizational forces, economics, and social systemic variables influence political news. The discussion may surprise you, as it examines issues that people do not ordinarily consider when thinking about news. Yet these factors—news values, economics, and aspects of the political system—exert important influences on contemporary political journalism.

The first portion of the chapter reviews the impact of journalistic routines on political news-gathering. The second part looks at the role played by organizational forces, a topic that brings us eyeball to eyeball with controversies involving Fox News. The third section explores the ways that an array of economic factors shape news, and the final portion describes the complex ways that the larger political system influences news, particularly coverage of recent wars. Critical issues are discussed at the end of each section. The different journalistic processes, derived from Shoemaker and Reese's work, help illuminate why news takes the color and hue it does.

MEDIA ROUTINES

Routines probably call to mind a host of mundane images: the ordinary and predictable errands of everyday life; employees performing the work-a-day activities of a 9 to 5 job, shuffling papers, checking email, sending attachments, and engaging in the necessary, but monotonous, tasks that a job requires. Well, journalists are no different from other professional workers in this respect. Their job entails a host of prosaic rituals that scholars frequently place under the umbrella category of "news work." But make no mistake: These activities are important. Research indicates that the day-to-day routines that media gatekeepers perform predict newspaper coverage of political issues better than do reporters' individual-level characteristics (Shoemaker et al., 2001). This is a critical finding, for it empirically demonstrates that job-related demands exert a stronger impact on the construction of political news stories than do reporters' (supposedly biased) attitudes.

What are **media routines**? They are defined as "those patterned, routinized, repeated practices and forms that media workers use to do their jobs" (Shoemaker & Reese, 1996, p. 105). From a professional perspective, routines enable reporters to gain information efficiently, providing tried-and-true methods to determine which information should pass through the informational gates and which should be discarded. There are three key routines: (1) ethically based and journalistic news values; (2) reliance on sources; and (3) dependence on informational channels.

News Values

News values draw on ethical precepts. The ethics code of the Society of Professional Journalists emphasizes that reporters should:

- seek truth and report it, in ways that are honest, fair and courageous;
- act independently, by remaining "free of obligation to any interest other than the public's right to know"; and
- minimize harm, showing respect to sources and compassion to those who might be adversely affected by news stories.

(Society for Professional Journalists, 1996)

News values are also influenced by journalistic norms and conventions. Journalistic news values are criteria that govern reporters' selection of information and crafting of news stories (Galtung and Ruge, 1965; Shoemaker and Cohen, 2006). Major values include:

1. *Social significance.* News covers events that are deemed to be high in social significance, with significance referring to issues bearing on the political system, the economy, and the health and well-being of citizens. In addition, the media devoted considerable coverage to the 2012 Supreme Court decision on the Obama health care plan, given its sweeping implications for the delivery of critical health services, insurance, and doctor–patient relations.

2. *Deadlines.* A newspaper must come out the next day, a television network's web or Facebook pages need to be regularly updated to reflect changing events, and journalists continually update blogs (Pavlik, 2000; see Figure 10.1). In the age of Twitter, where reporters tweet updates constantly, deadlines come every hour, not several times a day (Enda, 2011). Events that mesh with the deadline structure of the media are more likely to be covered. Faced with deadline pressure, journalists can make mistakes. This happened in June, 2012, when Fox and CNN, trying to be the first to break the story of the Supreme Court's decision on the constitutionality of Obama's health care law, jumped the gun and reported that the Court had overturned the health care law when it actually declared that it was constitutional.

3. *Novelty.* This emerges from the old saw that if a dog bites a man (or woman), this is not news because it happens—not every day, but enough such that its occurrence would not cause surprise. But if a man or woman bites a dog, this is a story because it is unexpected, deviating from the norm. (Men have actually bitten dogs! Some years back, a man in southern India wrestled down a rabid dog and bit the dog in the throat.) Information is newsworthy when it emerges from new, novel, and unusual developments. This is one reason why the story of the Cleveland bus driver punching out a passenger got such big play.

4. *Conflict.* News thrives on conflict. Conflicts between groups—such as Republican and Democratic Congressional leaders, labor and management, and Occupy Wall Street activists and authorities—are the stuff of news. Conflict suggests that something important is going on, signifies that there is a problem worthy of attention, and offers an entertaining, dramatic framework for covering issues. News weaves

a coherent narrative around conflicts (Wolfsfeld, 2011), sometimes reducing conflicts to just two sides when there are multiple views of an issue.

5. *Pack journalism and feeding frenzies.* When reporters smell a scandal or controversy involving a public official, they can move voraciously, collectively pursuing new leads, and covering the story non-stop, until the official replies or resigns, or there is no longer news to report. The story is presumed to be more newsworthy because a host of journalists judge it to be worthy of their pursuit. Scholars call this a "feeding frenzy" (Sabato, 1991).

6. *Negative information.* Events are deemed newsworthy when they deviate from the norm. Because people expect or hope that life will turn out nicely in the end, favorable outcomes are not newsworthy. Positive events are the norm; bad news is unexpected and, consequently, it receives more coverage. Thus, candidate pratfalls, missteps, and crass behavior are emphasized. Economic downturns can receive more press attention than increases in domestic productivity.

Figure 10.1 Journalists' daily job-related routines influence the content of news. Deadlines are particularly important. In today's 24/7 online journalism era, reporters constantly update news stories to keep up with current developments. Deadline pressure also can lead journalists to commit factual errors.

AFP/Getty Images

Reporters' ethical precepts and news values shape newsgathering. These can be power-fully influenced by other factors, such as the profit motive. Economic pressures on news media have caused many news organizations to cut staff and resources allocated to travel, sometimes making these organizations more dependent on wire services or elite media outlets that have a larger financial base.

Who Says It: Sources and Channels

"News is not what happens, but what someone says has happened or will happen," Leon Sigal (1986) famously observed (p. 15). Reporters rarely are able to witness events first-hand, but instead must rely on the observations of others. The others on whom they depend are called sources, and these sources are invariably highly placed government officials. In a classic study, Sigal found that close to three-fourths of all news sources quoted in *New York Times* and *Washington Post* stories were domestic and foreign government officials, key members of the political elite. As Bennett (1996) observed, "By any accounting, the conclusion is inescapable: Even the best journalism in the land is extremely dependent on the political messages of a small spectrum of official news sources" (p. 108).

In a related fashion, journalists frequently turn to formal or routine channels to obtain political information. There are three informational channels: formal, informal, and enterprise.

Formal channels include official proceedings, like Congressional hearings, government press releases, White House press conferences, and pre-scheduled events, like speeches and ceremonies.

Informal channels consist frequently of background briefings. A government press officer releases information "on background," allowing it to be described, but not attributed to a particular source. Informal channels also include reports from other news organizations and leaks—information that a government official deliberately reveals to a reporter for a variety of reasons, ranging from blowing the whistle on corruption to embarrassing a political enemy.

The third information channel is the one we associate with a feisty press: enterprise reporting. Enterprise channels include investigative reports, such as in-depth exposés of corruption, as well as long interviews with an elected official, initiated by the reporter, and spontaneous events witnessed first-hand.

In a study of front-page stories in *The New York Times* and *The Washington Post*, Sigal found that formal channels accounted for 58 percent of the stories, enterprise reporting

Figure 10.2 Reporters rely on official sources, who deliver information through formal channels, like a press conference. Robert Gibbs (shown here), who served as press secretary during Obama's first term, relays information to reporters at a White House news conference. Formal channels provide an efficient, routinized way for reporters to get information. However, they also allow the White House to dominate the news cycle.

AFP/Getty Images

explained 26 percent, and informal channels about 16 percent of stories. When he looked at stories that came exclusively from Washington, D.C., he discovered that 72 percent of the channels were formal, 20 percent informal, and just 8 percent enterprise. Later research has substantiated these findings (Perloff, 1998; see Figure 10.2).

Critical Questions: Media Routines Pros and Cons

Routines are functional. They help journalists do their jobs. "News organizations and news workers are faced with an overwhelming stream of events and information that must be culled and crafted into news. Routines economize effort," Shoemaker and Vos (2009) observe (p. 60; see also Berkowitz, 1997). News values simplify journalists' daily activities, helping them decide what is newsworthy, what is not, which stories should be played prominently, and which should never see the light of day. On the other hand, they have drawbacks. As will be discussed in Chapter 13, the press's incessant focus on strategic conflicts between political candidates can push out news of more enduring significance, such as the merits of candidates' stands on the issues. Pack journalism allows the press to descend en masse on a political figure enmeshed in controversy, helping to ferret out dirt and corruption. On the other hand, by focusing the spotlight on a candidate's private foibles, it can focus attention on unseemly issues not worthy of public scrutiny.

In a similar fashion, new technologies give reporters instant access to information, helping keep the public in the loop and in touch with new developments. But they also can lead to inaccurate reporting. Some years back, a false report from an obscure blog stated that South Carolina Governor Nikki R. Haley faced indictment on charges of tax fraud. Within a couple of minutes after a blog published the report, it went viral, traveling via Twitter to mainstream journalists. The governor had to defend herself in response to a rumor that should never have seen the light of day.

Adding another layer to the role technology plays in routine political journalism is *the increasingly porous boundaries between journalists and citizens.* When big events or crises happen, it's not just professional reporters who write stories, based on journalistic routines and news values such as deadlines. Online users post, tweet, retweet others' posts, and transmit pictures. These messages then ripple across the Internet, influencing other citizens and professional journalists. News is thus created and spread by ordinary people sitting before a PC or a cell phone. Sometimes, this can have positive consequences. Shortly after the July, 2012 shooting massacre in Aurora, Colorado, popular social news website speedily transmitted accurate information about the names of victims and the number of individuals admitted to nearby hospitals. Once again, there have been other cases where serious errors have occurred. Three days after the Boston Marathon bombings, a Reddit user posted pictures that suggested that one of the perpetrators was a 22-year-old university student who seemed to resemble one of the actual bombers. Egged on by the post and other online activities, a reporter and hundreds of Twitter users including Perez Hilton, who has millions of followers, sent out the student's name, leading to a veritable and virtual explosion of tweets and comments (Kang, 2013). But the student had nothing to do with the bombings and the revelations exerted a variety of untoward—and devastating—effects.

WHAT DO YOU THINK?

What are the major media routines? How do routines help media to critically inform the public, and how can they be co-opted by government authorities? How have routines adapted to the digital age?

ORGANIZATIONAL FORCES

Organizational factors complement routines. They refer to the many ways that a media organization can influence the direction reporters take on stories and the particular theme that a series emphasizes. If you have ever worked for a big company or a large downtown firm, you can appreciate that organizations have their own rules, rituals, prescribed practices, sometimes called norms, and power dynamics (Bantz, McCorkle, & Baade, 1981). It is the same with news media.

There can be an organizational chain of command, a division of labor where reporters may be assigned to certain specialized areas, called beats, and role differentiation between reporters, who may be unionized, and editors, who may be classified as management (e.g., Fishman, 1997). Large news organizations are bureaucracies, with an administrative structure and different departments, each with distinct social rules and even a turf that needs to be respected. A growing number of news organizations have blurred role distinctions by forming news-gathering teams that develop a series on a particular topic, with staffers contributing expertise in different areas, such as in-depth reporting, research, visual design, and website editing.

Socialization

When journalists begin working at a news organization, they quickly learn what is expected of them, internalizing the explicit and implicit rules of the organizational culture. More than half a century ago, sociologist Warren Breed conducted a landmark study of "social control in the newsroom," exploring the processes by which a news organization socializes its reporters, communicates social roles, and conveys rules for advancement. Breed concluded that "when the new reporter starts work he is not told what policy is. Nor is he ever told." Instead, he learns policy "by osmosis," Breed (1955/1997) famously concluded, noting that reporters come to appreciate roles and rules through observation and subtle directives from management (p. 109).

Reporters develop an identity as a journalist at a particular news outlet, feeling a kinship with journalistic colleagues, while gradually learning the preferred modes to gather and stylistically convey news. Reporters, like members of other organizations, are exquisitely aware of organizational policies and practices that can hinder chances for career advancement. For example, a political reporter at a suburban newspaper may shy away from critically covering a sacred-cow, high-profile local business for fear of alienating the highly connected upwardly mobile publisher.

An Application at Fox News

You can appreciate how organizational processes operate by exploring the inner workings of Fox News, the popular news network. Fox's *raison d'être* was to cultivate "an audience of news consumers being underserved in the marketplace—people who lived between New York and Los Angeles, who waved their flags with pride" and saw the world differently than Washington elites (Brock, Rabin-Havt, & Media Matters for America, 2011, p. 56). Fox achieved this goal through a combination of strategies: symbolic (linking the American flag to the network news logo shortly after the September 11 attacks); personnel-based (promoting a number of articulate, opinionated, unrepentantly conservative broadcasters, like Bill O'Reilly, Sean Hannity, and Glenn Beck); and, in some cases, tilting news coverage of the Iraq and Afghanistan Wars to the right (Aday, 2010).

During the national debate over Obama's health care plan in 2009, Fox's managing editor, Bill Sammon, who had achieved prominence at conservative news outlets, sent reporters a memo that included this directive:

> Please use the term "government-run health insurance" or, when brevity is a concern, "government option," whenever possible.

> Here's another way to phrase it: "The public option, which is the government-run plan."
>
> (Brock et al., 2011, p. 86–87)

Many health economists would have been hard pressed to describe Obama's health care plan—with its preservation of private sector insurance companies and emphasis on competition among different insurance plans—as government-run health care. To be sure, the Obama plan, which took effect in 2010, did enact new federal rules governing health insurance, such as prohibiting insurance companies from dropping people with pre-existing medical conditions. But journalists traditionally are not expected to take sides in these debates. By encouraging reporters to refer to the Obama heath care plan as "government-run health insurance," Fox proclaimed its sympathy with conservatives, implicitly associating the plan with Big Government, a boogeyman in the minds of conservatives and many Americans. From an organizational perspective, the Fox News directive likely had the effect of communicating to reporters that they were expected to describe Obama's health care plan in this, somewhat politicized, manner.

Critical Questions

There is evidence that Fox gave a negative slant to some of its coverage of the Obama health care plan, while also giving Republican candidates somewhat better press than other outlets (Brock et al., 2011; see also Iyengar & Hahn, 2009). The organizational bias continued throughout the 2012 election, and it cut both ways. A Pew Research Center study reported that from the end of August through the end of October of 2012, just 6 percent of Fox News's stories about Obama were positive, compared to 46 percent that trended negative. On the other side of the political ledger, the Pew study found that during the fall election, only 3 percent of MSNBC stories about Romney were positive, while 71 percent were negative (Peters, 2012d). Both Fox and MSNBC seemed to apply an organizational bias to some of their reporting. There has been a blurring of fact and opinion in cable news coverage of politics (see Figure 10.3).

It is important to differentiate a news organization's tilting of news in a particular direction with bias displayed by individual journalists. In the main, reporters work hard to keep their private opinions out of stories. However, news media organizations, led by editors, sometimes have pushed for particular positions, implicitly or explicitly suggesting that reporters frame stories in ways that further these perspectives. This practice has a time-honored history in American journalism. It encompasses *Time* magazine, whose editor Henry Luce pushed a pro-U.S., anti-Soviet Communist line in foreign news reporting; *The New York Times*, which, adopting a liberal perspective, may focus more on the inequities of capital punishment than on victims' plight; and even bloggers, who may direct their assistants to rely too much on partisan sources (Alterman, 2003; Baughman, 1987; Shoemaker & Vos, 2009).

Figure 10.3 Fox anchor Bill O'Reilly and MSNBC anchor Rachel Maddow put their spin on the news. The values and political orientation of news organizations can influence the content of political news.

Getty Images and NBC via Getty Images

Different organizational factors operate in different media outlets. The type of medium, size of the newsroom, leadership style of the news media executive, and organizational culture shape news. We do not often think of something as abstract as "the organization" influencing news. But it most assuredly does. As any employee who has found herself donning an appropriate wardrobe, consulting colleagues on how to deal with an impolite client, and going out of her way to compliment a supervisor in an email can attest, the place we work can sometimes influence the attitudes we adopt and behaviors we perform. It happens in factories, banks, high-tech computer firms, and storied newsrooms.

ECONOMIC INFLUENCES

In a free enterprise capitalist system, economic factors shape the news in a host of ways. At a basic level, as two scholars note:

> Markets are the mechanism whereby supply and demand are brought into balance. The marketplace rewards news media which produce a product that meets market demand . . . If the market demands sensationalism, then that's what it gets. If the market demands a particular political interpretation of events, that's what it gets . . . This is simple media economics.
>
> (Shoemaker & Vos, p. 76)

Three market factors influence news content: audiences, economic development interests, and macro financial markets.

Audience Factors

In stark economic terms, audience exposure to media programs is sold to advertisers. Generally speaking, the larger the audience, and the greater their buying power in the marketplace, the more money media outlets can charge advertisers. Thus, local news is filled with fires, drive-by murders, along with updates on how to protect your kids from predators and how to increase longevity, because this what the bulk of the audience likes to watch. Or, given the limited news menu of local news, these are the stories that grab the greatest attention from television viewers.

What about the political marketplace? Because audiences seem to enjoy the salacious and the titillating, the media—cable television in particular—revel in scandals. They blanketed the airwaves with coverage of the Clinton–Lewinsky affair in the late 1990s, and more recently extensively covered the "sexting scandal" in 2011, in which a member of Congress sent a slew of sexually suggestive photos to women via social media.

During the 2012 French election, French gossip magazines could not get enough of Carla Bruni, the wife of ex-French president Nicolas Sarkozy, herself a former super-model who dated rockers Mick Jagger and Eric Clapton. When Sarkozy was defeated in May, 2012, the magazines asked, "Will she stay with Sarko?" Prior to this, the French press, like the media world-wide, had devoted considerable coverage to the fall from grace of French politician Dominique Strauss-Kahn, who had been accused by a New York hotel maid of sexual assault in May, 2011. The British newspapers were consumed by the continuing saga of the phone hacking scandal that developed when executives at newspapers owned by media magnate Rupert Murdoch were widely accused of monitoring the voice mail of a teenage murder victim and relatives of deceased British soldiers in Iraq, as well as hacking into the phones of politicians and celebrities, all to pursue stories that they suspected would play well with the British public.

Critics note that we have a chicken-and-egg question here: Do the media cover scandals because people follow them, or do people follow scandals because they are the most captivating stories covered in the media? If the media played up more news items in appealing ways, would viewers attend to these stories?

Economic Development Interests in Local Communities

When most of us think about political media, we think about the Big Media—Fox, CNN, ABC, *The New York Times*, and TV news websites. We do not think about local news, covered in community newspapers, broadcast stations, and on websites. We should. Local media can exert an outsized impact on politicians and public opinion. And economics plays an important part in the ways they cover political issues.

News media play important functions in local communities (Tichenor, Donohue, & Olien, 1980). Far from serving as crusading muckrakers or bastions of investigative journalism, news media are frequently metropolitan boosters, serving up positive press on new civic projects. News executives are acutely aware of the ways that civic develop-ments, like convention centers, sports stadiums, and museum complexes, can help the metropolitan region. They also recognize that these developments can benefit the newspaper or local TV station. In a 1991 book on this topic that remains relevant today, Phyllis Kaniss notes that:

> Since the news firm's profits are dependent on audience size and advertising revenues, the greater the total population of the locality and the healthier the econ-omy, the more potential readers or viewers and advertisers the news firm can hope to attract . . . As a result of this interest in growth, it is argued, the local news media often take on the role of a booster, much like an arm of the local chamber of commerce, actively promoting the kinds of policies and projects that would generate

economic growth of the area. According to this theory, publishers or media owners at times muzzle their reporters' critical coverage of certain sacred cow public development projects that may promote growth at the expense of environmental quality or the sacrifice of other socially valuable uses of public funds.

(p. 52)

Examples are plentiful. Several decades back, in the late 1960s, *The San Jose Mercury* actively backed airport expansion, even though it would have adverse consequences for the environment. The editors seemed to have reasoned that the airport would enhance air travel, which would bolster the region and increase airline advertising for the newspaper (Kaniss, 1991; Rubin & Sachs, 1973). In 1975, *The Los Angeles Times* supported redevelopment of LA's downtown, despite criticism that it was a "tax rip off" that would offer substantial assistance to downtown economic interests, while harming

Figure 10.4 Cleveland's Rock and Roll Hall of Fame was a big deal for the city of Cleveland. It offered an opportunity for Cleveland to rebuild its sagging downtown and attract tourists' dollars to its anemic economy. When the Rock Hall opened in the mid-1990s, the city's news media gave it good press, emphasizing its positive features. Metropolitan news media frequently act as boosters for civic developments, focusing more on their social and economic benefits than environmental or human costs.

Getty Images/ Barry Winiker

the region as a whole (Gottlieb & Wolt, 1977). Some years later the newspaper went further, sharing profits of a special Sunday magazine spread about the Staples Center, an LA sports arena, with the facility's owners (Schudson & Tifft, 2005). In Cleveland, the local media, including the city's daily newspaper, *The Plain Dealer*, lavished enthusiastic coverage on projects that promised to bolster the sagging downtown, like the Rock and Roll Hall of Fame and a gambling casino (see Figure 10.4). Although both do offer benefits to downtown business, critics question whether the projects meet the claims promised by developers and whether, in the case of the casino, social costs outweigh material benefits.

You may ask: What is wrong with the news media doing its utmost to bolster the interests of the city? Isn't it good if they help the downtown grow and invigorate the spirit of the metropolis? Well, this raises a question of just what we mean by "good." Certainly, new civic projects can have positive economic and social consequences. But this must be balanced against costs to the environment and neighborhoods. One may argue that these projects produce more overall good than harm, and, in many cases, proponents may well be correct. However, this elides other questions: Is it the news media's job to bolster the status quo? If the news does not raise questions about the viability and social costs of projects, who will? If local news functions more as a lapdog than a watchdog looking for problems on the horizon, who will ensure that worst case scenarios do not crash through the city's gates?

Macro Economic Forces

News media are big corporations that make profits not just from advertising, but also from stock dividends and the financial markets. The media are conglomerates that reap benefits when their stock increases value on Wall Street and when they buy out other companies. This can translate into handsome bonuses for owners and top media executives (Bagdikian, 2004).

Over the past decades, newspaper concentration has increased as big newspaper chains, like the Gannett Company, have gobbled up more daily newspapers. The 21 major group owners control nearly 70 percent of daily newspaper circulation in the U.S., and seven chains own most U.S. newspapers (Dominick, 2009). Ninety-nine percent of chain-controlled newspapers are monopolies in the cities where they circulate. Increasingly, big media conglomerates have merged: Capital Cities Communications acquired ABC and then merged with Disney. General Electric bought RCA and, as a result, NBC. Westinghouse acquired CBS, selling the storied network four years later to Viacom. Five global companies, notably the Walt Disney Company and Time Warner, own the majority of newspapers, magazines, broadcast stations, and film studios in the U.S. (Bagdikian, 2004).

Firms like Tribune, McClatchy, and Avista Capital Partners, which own many U.S. newspapers, frequently function more like Wall Street companies consumed by the bottom line than groups committed to the values of a free press. For these publicly-owned newspaper companies, which control more than 40 percent of daily newspaper circulation, "the business of news is business, not news. Their papers are managed and controlled for financial performance, not news quality" (Cranberg, Bezanson, & Soloski, 2001, p. 9). Increased profitability, strong stock performance, maintaining a solid credit rating, and conformity to market demands have become the *raison d'être* of many media companies, causing them to steer clear of controversy, to avoid risky journalistic exposés, and to rely instead on safe, status quo-enhancing stories (An & Jin, 2004; Cranberg et al., 2001; Napoli, 2003).

Critical Questions

Have current economic trends led to more homogenized news? Has political news become increasingly risk averse, shying away from investigative reports that would jeopardize the corporate bottom line? Has preoccupation with financial markets led to a reduction in alternative voices?

Strong advocates of economic determinism (e.g., Bagdikian, 2004) would have you answer these questions in the affirmative. There is no doubt that news is powerfully influenced by economic and corporate forces. There also is a numbing similarity in American political news. With local television stations in some markets sharing videos and scripts to cut costs, you may actually see identical segments on fires, high-speed chases, and candidate sound bites on different stations (Stelter, 2012).

It is true that the media are allergic to investigative reports and probably are less capable of mounting journalistic exposés today than a couple decades back, thanks to the reduction in resources that has resulted from declining advertising revenues. Indeed, a systematic study of televised investigative reporting found that journalistic exposés are all but absent in TV news (McChesney, 2004). This is a serious problem. But it is a mistake to conclude that, in the face of economic pressures, *all* of the media outlets are asleep at the investigative wheel, afraid to annoy powerful business interests.

In the span of less than six months, *The New York Times* published a couple of rocketing exposés. A first story vividly documented how Apple, one of the richest corporations in the world, had displayed callous indifference to safety problems at Chinese manufacturing plants, where workers assembled iPhones and iPads. Apple turned a blind eye to hazardous working conditions that led to the injury of more than 200 workers and the deaths of four people. Another article revealed how Wal-Mart had systematically used bribery to gain dominance of the Mexican market. *Time* magazine published a

36-page cover story that revealed the outrageously high prices hospitals charge for ordinary medical procedures. New non-profit groups like ProPublica also have written hard-hitting investigative reports of business abuses. Revelations by news outlets like these have forced corporations to implement remedial actions. The Chinese manufacturing plant that was exposed in the *Times* article subsequently cleaned up its act, pledging to improve working conditions and substantially increase wages. Acknowledging the effects of the newspaper exposé, the director of corporate social responsibility at Intel, which makes semiconductors in China, said that no one at Intel "wants to end up in a factory that treats people badly, that ends up on the front page" (Bradsher & Duhigg, 2012, p. A10). Articles such as these speak to the abiding ability of the media to expose corporate wrongdoing and ameliorate social wrongs.

POLITICAL AND SOCIAL SYSTEM INFLUENCES

Communication scholars remind us that "the press always takes on the form and coloration of the social and political structures within which it operates (Siebert, Peterson, & Schramm, 1973, p. 1). Political news is profoundly shaped by the nature of a nation's economy, its political system, relations among economic and political institutions, and an ideological world-view (Hallin & Mancini, 2004).

In a country with a capitalist economic system, like the U.S., audience demand will exert a major impact on news, and this in turn will cause news organizations to steer clear of stories that they fear will turn off audiences, such as complex interpretive pieces on a nation's financial crisis. In Mediterranean countries, like Italy, where political parties exert a strong influence on electoral politics, election news will tend to revolve more around parties than in the U.S., in which a candidate-centered entrepreneurial model dominates. In countries like Greece, where newspapers are ideologically driven and linked to parties, news is apt to be more opinionated and overtly partisan. And in countries like China, where government stifles a free press, you will find far less news that criticizes the nation's leaders, let alone government decisions.

Proponents of a social system view of news take this argument further. They argue that, even in so-called free societies like the U.S., the media are not entirely free. They must bend to the whims of the marketplace if they are to survive. They must respect the political power structure if they are to continue obtaining stories from powerful sources (as the source routine emphasizes), and they can't go out on a political limb if they want to maintain credibility with their more politically moderate audience members. The umbrella concept that is invoked to describe the tendency of a nation's news media to follow and transmit the perspectives of the power structure is hegemony, described in Chapter 8. In a complementary fashion, Edward S. Herman and Noam

Chomsky (2002) have argued that the American media "serve to mobilize support for the special interests that dominate the state and private activity" (p. lix). Do the media prop up the powers-that-be, as these approaches argue? Or do they speak truth to power?

One way to examine the questions is to focus on news coverage of issues that pose a threat to the nation's dominant interests, in particular foreign policy crises and wars. If hegemony is correct, media should hunker down and present a one-sided view of war that favors the nation's leaders. Three wars provide vantage points from which to examine this thesis.

Vietnam

Vietnam was a paralyzing, tragic war that devastated the small Southeast Asian country and killed hundreds of thousands of civilians and more than 58,000 Americans from the early 1960s until the South Vietnamese city of Saigon fell in 1975. Concerned about the threat posed by Soviet and Chinese communism, a succession of U.S. presidents committed resources and troops to Vietnam. Proponents of hegemony, and others who maintain that the media prop up the powers-that-be in military conflicts, argued that, given the massive infusion of U.S. troops into Vietnam in the mid-1960s, the media would serve up a positive portrait of the war. And for a long time, this is exactly what happened. Reporters described the American soldiers as "brave men" and "the greatest soldiers in the world." The U.S. and its South Vietnamese allies were the good guys, the North Vietnamese the bad guys (Hallin, 1986, pp. 138, 140).

Then, in 1968, things changed when the North Vietnamese launched a massive offensive in a series of battles known as the Tet Offensive. Although the U.S. eventually defeated the North Vietnamese on the battlefield, the heavy casualties, grisly battle-scene footage viewed by millions on television, and official estimates (exaggerated as it turned out) of North Vietnamese military strength led a number of journalists to view the battles in decidedly negative terms. The leading television broadcast anchor, Walter Cronkite, broke out of the objective journalism bubble, making the extraordinarily pessimistic pronouncement that, based on his observations from South Vietnam, the U.S. was "mired in stalemate." Egged on by Cronkite and other leading journalists, as well as by the grisly battlefield reports, reporters moved from an optimistic rendering of battles to more skeptical coverage of the war. It was no longer our "national endeavor," one steeped in the tradition of World War II, but instead a conflict enshrouded in controversy and palpable costs to America (Hallin, 1986). With sources releasing negative information about the war and new technological routines allowing television to offer more immediate coverage of battles, news presented critical portraits of military activity.

The drumbeat of negative news—including vivid footage of daily carnage—makes it difficult to argue that America's ruling elite controlled the media or the media followed the party line, lock, stock, and barrel. Three presidents expressed frustration and anger about press coverage of Vietnam. The negative news underscores the fact that, after a long honeymoon of pro-war coverage, the press split with the nation's leaders in its portrayals of the conflict, offering a more complicated picture of media portrayals than that suggested by hegemonic proponents.

Persian Gulf War

The next major war after Vietnam was very different in that it was short and filled with old-fashioned feelings of community, patriotism, and American valor. The 1990–91 Persian Gulf War was launched with the stated aim of liberating Kuwait from Iraq after Iraqi President Saddam Hussein invaded the country in 1990. The war was delightfully short. It took only seven months for the U.S. to free Kuwait from Iraqi clutches. The news was a weapon in the battle. In their conversations with journalists, White House emissaries sought to frame the war in ways that they hoped would serve U.S. interests. In many ways the news promoted the White House's definition of the war, although there were twists and turns in the ways the story was covered.

President George H.W. Bush compared Iraqi President Hussein to Hitler, noting that Hussein had brutally oppressed his people and during previous wars unleashed poison gas attacks against his enemies in a manner that called up memories of Nazi experiments in World War II. The press, invoking the news value that what the president says is news, played up the Hitler analogy (e.g., Dorman & Livingston, 1994).

With the stage set for the likely deployment of U.S. troops to liberate Kuwait, Americans everywhere flew the flag, wore yellow ribbons, and gave blood. The news, taking up the banner of popular culture, rallied behind the troops, as the cascading model described in Chapter 8 suggests. In Buffalo, TV anchors wore yellow ribbons (Hallin & Gitlin, 1994). When the war began, the incredible U.S. military technologies—Patriot missiles in particular—became technological heroes of the war, their awe-inspiring success showcased in live media reports by wide-eyed television reporters (Hallin & Gitlin, 1994). The news had rallied around the war, cultivated patriotic themes, and helped to promote what many—though not all—Americans viewed as a justified military undertaking.

The White House had not coerced news organizations to go along. Rather, the administration had waged an impressive battle for symbols that took into account news values and journalists' understandable desire to be in sync with the bulk of public sentiments. The news media did not stifle voices of dissent. It publicized the views of Congressional

Figure 10.5 President George H.W. Bush warmly greets the military servicemen and women who fought on behalf of the country during the 1990–91 Persian Gulf War. The news media put a positive spin on the war, celebrating the endeavor and U.S. victories. The role that the press should play in war time is complex and contentious. Critics lament that the news typically focuses more on a war's positive aims and benefits than on dissenting perspectives.

Gamma-Rapho via Getty Images

representatives who urged a more cautious policy toward Iraq. There was no hegemonic media, marching in unison behind the president (Entman & Page, 1994). Nonetheless the media gave more press to information that supported, rather than opposed, the White House version of the facts. Throughout the seven-month war, the news media celebrated U.S. victories and military prowess (see Figure 10.5).

The War in Iraq

A dozen years later, in 2003, the United States was fighting Iraq again, with the war ironically spearheaded by a second President Bush—George W., the son of President George H.W. Bush, who had led the successful effort to liberate Kuwait in 1991. This time, the circumstances were different. Arguing that Iraqi President Saddam Hussein—dislodged from Kuwait but still firmly in power—had stockpiled weapons of mass destruction that posed a threat to the United States, the Bush administration waged a strategic political information campaign to persuade the public and key elites to support an invasion of Iraq. Once again, gaining supportive press coverage played a pivotal role in the administration's effort.

Strategically leaking information to *The New York Times*, whose reporters were more than happy to be the first to break the story, Bush administration officials claimed that Iraq would soon obtain nuclear weapons, which could have catastrophic implications for the Middle East and the United States (Boehlert, 2006). With information about nuclear weapons development coming from high-level White House sources through informal channels, the information was deemed credible and highly newsworthy. The news helped make a strong case for the necessity of war. But, as noted in Chapter 8, there was a problem, one that strikes to the heart of the fallibility of journalists' reliance on the sources routine. The facts about Iraqi acquisition of nuclear weapons turned out to be wrong, dead wrong. Iraq had not acquired weapons of mass destruction. The news media had accepted the White House line, reflecting a pro-war bias that was consistent with hegemony.

But the hegemony model was half-correct at best. During the run-up to war, the television networks did cover Bush administration sources much more than opponents (Hayes & Guardino, 2010). When war came, the news provided graphic images that showcased the stunning successes of U.S. troops in pushing back the Iraqi Army. For a time, the press cultivated time-honored myths of U.S. military prowess. In 2003, the media duly transmitted the dramatic story of Private Jessica Lynch, who, reporters were told, had fought off Iraqi attackers, sustained serious wounds, and then had been rescued from an Iraqi hospital by a special army unit. It turned out that the story was not entirely true. Lynch did not have bullet injuries and knife stab wounds. The special unit had stormed into the hospital where she was recuperating, but also to locate other U.S. troops. While the factual errors were corrected, the war effort had received a media-assisted boost.

Yet, as the battles wore on, opposition political leaders and citizens grew restive. Criticism of Bush administration strategic efforts mounted. Anger about the loss of American and Iraqi civilian lives intensified. Responding to elites' criticism and the visible carnage of war, the news presented substantial critical coverage of the war in Iraq (Hayes & Guardino, 2010; Kuypers, 2006). Television networks vividly displayed photographs of American soldiers' torture of Iraqi prisoners at Abu Ghraib, although the media shied away from applying a torture frame. As noted in Chapter 8, newspapers published exposés of arguably illegal acts that the Bush administration performed to stem the tide of terrorism.

Critical Questions

Political system forces do influence media coverage. Even in a country as fiercely democratic as the U.S., news media can take on the trappings of government ideology. During times of war, the press can serve up news that favors the White House's version of events. This can be troubling if the news neglects to present alternative views of a policy issue. Presentation of a diversity of viewpoints is important in a democracy because it illuminates complex policy issues and can enhance the quality of deliberative debates. But the governing metaphor here is persuasion, not coercion: News media are not forced to cover events in ways that favor the American government. Instead news outlets choose to do so, influenced, as they are, by information cultivated by elites and their harnessing of routine channels.

Although hegemony offers an explanation of egregious media coverage in the past, such as the Holocaust and race, it is a less reliable model of contemporary news. The problem with the hegemony model is that it simplifies a rather complicated process (Benson & Neveu, 2005a and b; Bourdieu, 2005). Moreover, it is notoriously difficult to prove false (Shoemaker & Vos, 2009). In social science research, where hypotheses must be capable of being tested with empirical evidence and proven false based on statistical tests, hegemony has emerged as a nettlesome concept. It can be stated so vaguely that you can interpret the evidence as either offering support or disconfirmation. Proponents of hegemony sometimes refuse to be open to data that show hegemony is wrong. In many cases, media stories do contradict official positions and undermine government initiatives.

The indexing and cascading models, described in Chapter 8, offer more plausible views of news coverage of foreign wars. Indexing coverage to reflect the range of voices expressed by political elites, the press will offer dissenting views when national leaders break from the White House mold, as occurred in the case of all three wars discussed above. When public opinion begins to turn against a war effort, the news offers ample coverage of these developments. What's more, an increasingly feisty press has provided critical exposés of government activities during war time. The 24/7, global media, abetted by social media, also provide the public with pictures and behind-the-scenes information that was not available to citizens of earlier generations. WikiLeaks is a case in point.

In 2010, *The New York Times* and leading newspapers in European countries published a series of investigative reports, obtained from WikiLeaks, a non-profit organization, dedicated to revealing classified documents. Convinced that the stories offered citizens valuable information on the inner workings of the foreign policies of democratic governments, the editors published the articles. The articles disclosed untold civilian casualties during the war in Afghanistan and revealed information about secret government activities. The information offered up a different picture of U.S. foreign policy than the government wished to present, once again poking holes in approaches that claim the press always props up the powers-that-be (see Reflections).

REFLECTIONS: WIKILEAKS AND PRESS FREEDOM: YOU DECIDE

WikiLeaks aroused considerable controversy in 2010 when it released a cache of classified documents on sensitive issues. These included revelations of civilian casualties during the war in Afghanistan, delivery of armaments to militant groups, secretive U.S. efforts to remove uranium from a reactor in Pakistan, a systematic sabotage campaign directed by the Chinese government to hack into Google's computer system, intriguing alliances among foreign leaders, and backroom diplomatic discussions of critical foreign policy problems (see the WikiLeaks website, http://wikiLeaks.org). Several leading newspapers, including *The New York Times*, decided to publish stories based on the secret files, arguing that they offered a treasure trove of information on classified, secretive government dealings.

Suppose you were editor of *The Times* and it was your call. What would you do? Here are two positions to consider:

On the one hand, diplomats and observers of foreign policy were outraged by the decision. They argued that some information should be kept secret because, if it were made public, it could undermine sensitive negotiations between diplomatic representatives, negotiations that are intended to break logjams and produce long-term benefits for the nations themselves. Critics questioned whether it is the media's role to intrude in sensitive international issues. Even in a democracy, they argued, government has a right to classify sensitive information. Some worried that release of the information could endanger Afghan aides who helped the U.S., while at the same time discouraging diplomats from conducting sensitive negotiations, out of fear that someone with a misguided missionary zeal would release the information to the press.

WikiLeaks supporters vehemently disagreed. They cited Jefferson's dictum that "information is the currency of democracy." A free flow of information inevitably advances democratic aims, they argued, noting that citizens have a right to understand the bases on which their governments make decisions. WikiLeaks advocates emphasized that secrecy undermines the flow of information that is endemic to democracy. Besides, they argued, that much of the time, governments classify information that has no business being kept secret. Information is frequently classified not because it bears on national security, but because it serves bureaucratic needs, thus denying people access to controversial decisions. *The Times* noted that it was careful not to publish information that could jeopardize the lives of foreign diplomats.

What do you think? If it was your call to make, would you recommend publication? And, if so, why?

What role should the news media play during war time? Radical critics seem to suggest that a nation's news media should generally oppose a government when it wages war, focusing instead on revealing the facts that the government would rather not acknowledge. Others, particularly conservative critics, would take a more patriotic stance, noting that the duty of a nation's media to is to back leaders and the troops in war time. Surely, there are times when war represents the only way that a nation can settle problems that are central to its national interest or can protect its citizenry. In these cases, revelations by media can imperil the military effort. On the other hand, when leaders fabricate facts or launch ventures that serve their interests, rather than those of citizens, the media are virtually the only available check on power. There are no simple, glib answers to questions about the proper role media should play during war time. These issues point up the complex, multifaceted roles the news plays in a democratic society.

WHAT DO YOU THINK?

Are the news media primarily watchdogs or lapdogs? Do they serve as a powerful check on government power? Does local media coverage of civic developments and national media coverage of war merely uphold the status quo? Thinking of major national events, are there examples of when political media curbed government power and when they were too subservient to government?

CONCLUSIONS

This chapter continued the exploration of political news determinants by focusing on several broad, macro-level factors.

Media routines exert a strong influence on news content. News values, reliance on sources, and informational channels shape the quantity and quality of political news. As employees working in a bureaucracy, journalists are also influenced by organizational forces, their news stories shaped by the nature of the workplace, and, in some cases, the political priorities of news executives. It is frequently assumed that reporters' day-to-day activities reflect their own personal biases, but this understates the ways that contextual and organizational forces shape news.

Economic factors influence news in several ways. In a capitalist society, the local news media cater to audience interests and tend to support civic projects that promote the larger metropolitan region. Macro-economic forces, such as the corporate goal to increase profitability for stockholders, can influence news. Conformity to these demands can propel news organizations to steer clear of controversy and transmit safe, homogenized coverage of a political issue. Powerful as these forces are, there are news outlets that defy conformity and publish hard-hitting exposés. There is a tension in the press between catering to system-maintaining economic forces and cultivating the time-honored ethos of speaking truth to power.

The news does reflect the political structure and ideology of the social system. This too is complex. News can prop up established interests, offering a wealth of positive coverage when the country is at war. However, news does not march uniformly to the drumbeat of the White House, and in recent wars it has offered substantial criticism of the military ventures, albeit after a flurry of positive coverage helped to seal the case for war.

Thus, the question of news bias is considerably more complicated (and interesting) than is commonly assumed. In one sense, you could say there are a number of biases, set in motion by reporters' attitudes, routines, organizational factors, economics, and the social system. While journalists do decide what is newsworthy and how to frame stories, they are not isolated from these larger social forces.

Next time someone asks you what makes news tick, you can bring a wealth of factors to the discussion. And perhaps also you can appreciate that, for all their faults, the news media frequently shed light on flaws in official policies, bringing dissident and alternative views to the surface. Journalism, as an institution, seeks to attain laudatory goals. Bill Kovach and Tom Rosenstiel (2007) note that "journalism's first obligation is to the truth, [and] it must serve as an independent monitor of power" (pp. 5–6). As media critic David Carr (2012) points out, "the constancy of a daily paper"—and consistent presence of other media in living rooms and streamed across a computer screen—offers salient reminders "that someone is out there watching" (p. B2).

PART THREE

Communication and the Election Campaign

11 Political Campaigns Past and Present

In Hollywood's latest stab at politics, a movie called (what else?) *The Campaign*, Will Ferrell played a slick politician, Cam Brady, who admired his hair locks early in the film and boasted that "my hair could lift a car off a baby if it had to." Brady looks like he is a shoo-in for a fifth term until he is caught making an obscene phone call, raising questions among the fat cats who support him. Not long after, a pot-bellied, ungainly challenger named Marty Huggins, played by Zach Galifianakis, announces his intention to challenge Cam Brady. As the campaign unfolds, the initially earnest Huggins become a typical pol, willing to use dirty tricks to embarrass Brady, who retaliates by seducing Huggins's wife (which seems to increase Brady's poll numbers). In the end, Huggins takes office, determined to serve the people. As the film closes, Huggins announces his commitment to work on an issue that he believes is critical to the community. But in doing so, he reveals that he is still clueless about just how he will serve his constituents. "Let's get rid of daylight savings time because I hate when it gets darker earlier," he tells an enthusiastic crowd of supporters.

The film is funny, and garnered positive reviews. Like all good satire, it captures some truths: Consultants play to win, some politicians will say anything to get elected, media feed on political scandals, and voters can be bamboozled. But Hollywood celluloid is not Washington, D.C. reality and the movie simplified politics, preferring a clichéd version to the more granular, complicated reality. It picked on easy marks: politicians' sexual temptations, suggesting they are the major cause of political scandals, and big money's contaminating influence on politics. But scandals have a host of causes, of which sex is just one, and the relationship between money and politics is more complex than fat cats calling the shots from atop Money Mountain. The film misses the ebb and flow of presidential politics: the dynamic relationships between candidates and news media; dedication shown by political party activists; the role ideas play in campaigns;

candidates' efforts to devise mediated appeals that voters find compelling; bitter partisan disputes showcasing ideological differences; and the wrenching domestic and foreign policy problems that are at the center of campaigns.

The chapters in this part of the book delve into the core issues in campaigns, focusing on the fusion of politics and communication in America's four-year election extravaganza. The next two chapters offer an introductory sweep. This chapter presents a breezy review of the historical forerunners to the present campaign and describes the key features of today's mediated campaign. Chapter 12 extends this discussion, describing in more detail the campaign's main components, such as polling, political parties, and campaign finance.

This chapter begins by introducing the historical forerunners to the present campaign. After describing continuities and contrasts between past and present, the chapter describes seven features of contemporary campaigns, with special focus on online campaigning.

PRESIDENTIAL CAMPAIGNS PRIOR TO THE AGE OF TELEVISION

Today we have come to expect that our presidential candidates will announce with much fanfare more than a year before the election that they want to be president of the United States. It was not always this way. As historian Gil Troy (1996) notes:

> Originally, presidential candidates were supposed to "stand" for election, not "run." They did not make speeches. They did not shake hands. They did nothing to betray the slightest ambition for office. Candidates were supposed to stay on their farms in dignified silence, awaiting the people's call, as George Washington had done.
>
> (p. 7)

The Founding Fathers looked down their noses on campaigning for public office. Openly soliciting votes? Aggressively seeking political office? These smacked of an obnoxious ambition that the idealistic early Americans felt was unbecoming of citizens of the new nation. What's more, they feared that a handful of unscrupulous, ambitious campaigners would manipulate the masses. "Popular campaigning was not only dangerous, it was improper, illegitimate, and unnecessary," the early leaders maintained (Troy, 1996, p. 8).

This did not last long. Political acrimony, fierce attacks between contenders for office, and unabashed, slug-it-out presidential campaigns soon became the order of the day. A courtly, aristocratic model of presidential politics was gradually replaced by a persuasion model, in which candidates publicly campaigned for election. Three eras preceded today's media-centered campaign: (1) elite party and press politics; (2) popular, prejudiced politics; and (3) party-managed whistle-stop campaigns.

Elite Party and Press Politics

During the late 18th and early 19th centuries, presidential candidates symbolically jousted through the medium of the newspaper. Politics was a rich man's game, waged with a courtly veneer that hid the fierce underbelly of presidential politics. During the 1800 election, the candidates, President John Adams and challenger Thomas Jefferson, never left their farms. But their supporters were not so passive. The two new political parties of the era—Alexander Hamilton's Federalists and Thomas Jefferson's Republicans (no relation to the current Republican Party)—operated newspapers that brandished their ideology.

Pro-Jefferson newspaper editors smeared President John Adams, a Federalist, alleging that he plotted to create a "dynastic succession with his sons" (Troy, 1996, p. 13). Federalists called Jefferson an atheist and a traitor. "The engine is the press," Jefferson acknowledged. "Every man must lay his purse and his pen under contribution," he added, suggesting that if they wished to reach elite newspaper readers, candidates had to avail themselves of the power of the pen. And so, candidates penned harsh words lambasting their opponents, as the two political factions—the more pro-government Federalists and libertarian Republicans—diverged sharply on the issues. Yet there remained a silver lining. Despite the partisan conflicts, developments of considerable importance were occurring (Fischer, 1965). Political parties were beginning to form and leaders were using established organs to express their ideas. Unlike in the French Revolution, opponents were not beheaded by guillotine. The opposition party did not mount a coup. Power passed from one party to the other, peaceably, amid fervent, colorful political disputes.

But we would be remiss if we did not point out that there lurked a fundamental inequity just beneath the surface. Only property owners could vote. Blacks and women could not cast ballots. By the definition of democracy advanced in Chapter 1, the U.S. was not a fully democratic country.

Popular, Prejudiced Politics

In 1828 another negative campaign ensued. Andrew Jackson, nationally known for his military prowess in the War of 1812, faced an aristocratic candidate, John Quincy Adams, the son of the second president. Jackson's newspaper-editor friends concocted lies about Adams, charging that he had referred to the Dutch as "the stupid Dutch."

Pro-Adams editors counter-attacked, charging that "General Jackson's mother was a common prostitute." But politics was becoming more personal, as Jackson's macho military persona thrilled masses of people, who invented a nickname ("Old Hickory") they never would have dared to affix to a Southern gentleman like Jefferson or James Madison. Jackson's supporters devoted themselves to gaining backing from the political power-brokers of the era: newspaper editors. More than half of the 600 American newspapers supported Jackson, offering him a forum to attack his opponent.

Jacksonian democracy, as it became known, expanded the parameters of politics, stimulating scores of citizens to follow politics more actively than they had in the past. The number of eligible voters rose dramatically as many states removed the rules restricting voting to property owners. The French writer Alexis de Tocqueville, touring America in the early 1830s, was impressed by the tumult and the obvious pleasure Americans took in forming social groups to discuss political issues. Politics was no longer the exclusive province of super-rich and educated elites; ordinary people were becoming involved. The organizing mechanism was the political party. Parties began connecting with and organizing the mass public, mobilizing citizens around party nominees (Pessen, 1985).

It came together in 1840. "Popular politics became the new American religion, as two and a half million men streamed to the polls—ten times the number enrolled in churches," Troy notes (1996, p. 20). Any strategy, no matter how goofy, that engaged the electorate was deemed acceptable. The beneficiary was William Henry Harrison, in truth a mediocre candidate, but the first to deliver a stump campaign speech on the campaign trail. Branding himself as a man of the people, Harrison positioned himself against the incumbent, President Martin Van Buren. He brandished himself "as the log cabin-hard-cider candidate who, unlike the high-falutin' Martin Van Buren, was plain, simple, down-to-earth, and very much of, by, and for the people" (Boller, 2004, p. 66) (see Figure 11.1). The campaign was quite a spectacle, with thousands descending on Whig Party rallies, gabbing at parades that went on for miles, and brandishing campaign paraphernalia, like coonskin caps, Tippecanoe badges, and Tippecanoe shaving cream named after Harrison's now-controversial battle against Shawnee Indians in a place called Tippecanoe, Indiana.

Had this occurred today, it would all have been mocked as image-based campaigning or laughable political branding by a cynical political press (Jamieson, 1984). But in 1840 the press was not cynical and was funded by political parties; many party newspapers supported Harrison.

Harrison died in office, but he left an imprint on the political campaign process. His campaign stimulated interest in politics, bringing more people into electoral politics

Figure 11.1 Let the branding begin! In the first image-based, political brand-focused campaign, party professionals promoted presidential candidate William Henry Harrison as a log cabin, hard cider-drinking candidate in 1840. In this depiction, Harrison, left, is shown as he might have been during the campaign, standing outside his cabin, a man of the people, greeting a wounded war veteran.

Getty Images

than had participated before. It also signaled that popular, slogan-filled campaigns geared to the populace were here to stay. But there were serious downsides. As in the vast majority of 19th century campaigns that would follow, the candidates failed miserably to place important issues on the political agenda. There was no mention of inequality, urban squalor, or the scourge of slavery.

Increasingly, political parties became the mechanism that connected the public and its elected leaders. Parties developed structures—professional organizations, ideological platforms, conventions, and exuberant campaigns—that connected people to political leaders. During presidential campaigns, they helped to organize spectacular rallies and enthusiastic marches through the streets, called torchlight parades. Coordinated by political clubs composed of immigrants toiling in blue collar jobs, the parades featured barbecues, and thousands of men marching, military-style, through the streets, kerosene torches lit, a brass band leading the way. As many as 25 percent of voters participated actively in campaigns during the last half of the 19th century, and 77 percent of the electorate—primarily White men, to be sure—voted in presidential elections (Dinkin, 1989; McGerr, 1986). Issues were debated passionately, yet frequently with prejudice, as discussions focused on immigrants' rights and petty resentments, such as hostility toward Germans because they drank beer on Sundays (Perloff, 1999). Throughout the many parades and interpersonal discussion of the era, talk about horrific rules that disenfranchised African Americans voters, such as poll taxes and literacy tests, was probably off the table, deemed inappropriate for public conversation.

Party-Managed, Whistle-Stop Campaigns

As the 20th century approached, change in style, if not substance, became the political order of the day. The 1896 campaign served as an early model for the national, party-organized campaigns that would follow. By 1896, loud, rambunctious, military-style street rallies were out-of-fashion. The spectacle of men marching through the streets seemed out of sync as the country approached a new century (Dinkin, 1989). The Civil War-era armies of the night had given way to a business model of campaigning, and political parties' national committees played a more centralized role in campaign planning. During the 1896 campaign, Republican Party Chairman Mark Hanna employed modern bookkeeping practices, kept track of campaign developments by telephone, and raised corporate funds for the campaign. Although the campaign raised important monetary issues—the gold standard versus free silver, the latter symbolizing justice to Democrats and fiscal disaster to Republicans—Hanna ran a tightly organized campaign that reduced complex issues to clever phrases, advertising candidate William McKinley "as if he were a patent medicine," in the words of Theodore Roosevelt (Perloff, 1999).

While McKinley pursued a quiet, but effective, campaign strategy, delivering carefully scripted speeches to audiences gathered at the front porch of his Canton home, his opponent, William Jennings Bryan, embarked on a national speech-making tour, traveling more than 18,000 miles and giving 600 speeches, nearly falling victim to exhaustion at campaign's end. Although Bryan lost, his strategy became the model for 20th century campaigns. No longer adhering to antiquated notions that candidates should stand for election, not run, candidates crisscrossed the country. Theodore Roosevelt traveled to more than 550 towns in 24 states. Franklin Delano Roosevelt and Harry Truman whistle-stopped the country by train. National campaigns were de rigueur, and party managers developed strategies to promote candidates, distribute information, organize field operations, and raise money from wealthy individuals. As radio and television grew, campaigns were set to move to the next stage. Television news and increasingly negative TV ads came to occupy a preeminent role in contemporary political campaigns.

Summary

By reviewing key features of past campaigns, we see continuities and contrasts with today. There are four similarities. First, campaigns then and now provide an institutionalized mechanism by which candidates for public office can communicate with citizens, and by which citizens can evaluate candidates. Second, media—newspapers in the 18th and 19th centuries, print and broadcast media in the 20th, and the variety of media technologies today—are a time-honored feature of the American presidential campaign. Third, negative campaigning is not new, but dates back to the earliest campaigns. Fourth, campaigns always have been short on substance, prone to skirt key national issues.

Campaigns are vastly different in form and content from their 19th and 20th century predecessors. Today's campaigns are more democratic, no longer shutting out minorities and women. Party bosses no longer choose party nominees; instead, nominees are selected democratically, through primary elections. Media have replaced political parties as the tissue linking candidates and the electorate. Communication among candidates, media, and citizens is incredibly quicker, with messages to and fro landing instantly on technological devices that would have been unimaginable two centuries ago.

THE CONTEMPORARY MEDIA CAMPAIGN

The media are the centerpiece of today's campaign. As Stephen J. Wayne (2008) observes, "The road to the White House is long, circuitous, and bumpy. It contains numerous hazards and potential dead ends" (p. 2). It also wends its way through the media, via the news and across the pathways of advertising, debates, and blogs.

"The mass media are the main channels through which politics is communicated," and the ways media convey electoral reality substantially influence how voters perceive politics, political communication researchers Jesper Strömbäck and Lynda L. Kaid observed (2008, p. 2). Scholar Thomas E. Patterson (1980) recognized this more than three decades ago, titling his book *The mass media election*. An academic journal on political communication underscores the point, calling itself the *International Journal of Press/Politics*. And you know this too, because your knowledge of presidential campaigns is probably based almost exclusively on what you glean from the media, regardless of whether you read about it in ink-stained newspapers, watch advertisements on television, or peruse the Internet, clicking on websites and watching candidates' images flicker across your computer screen. There are seven core characteristics of today's media and technology-centered presidential campaigns.

First, campaigns focus on the cultivation of images. During the 2012 campaign, Mitt Romney's strategists recognized that their candidate had an image problem: He was seen as uncaring and unsympathetic with the problems of middle-class Americans. Consequently, Romney went to great lengths to soften his image in the presidential debates, moderating some of his more conservative positions, and congratulating Obama on his wedding anniversary. He even joked that spending an anniversary on a debate stage with his opponent was not the most romantic way to celebrate the occasion. Obama, for his part, sought to reinforce perceptions that, despite his stewardship of a sagging economy, he was a likable, "in-touch" president. During the height of the fall campaign, he appeared on *The Tonight Show* and *The View*, as well as on MTV.

When you watch a presidential candidate on television or watch a candidate in a YouTube video, you are not seeing the true essence of his or her personality. What you have viewed is a snapshot, a stylized presentation, a picture that has been crafted by the candidate and consultants in an effort to influence the impression of the candidate that you carry in your mind. Politics is about creating and molding those impressions. It is concerned with convincing voters to accept the positive impressions, integrate them with their own perceptions, and remix them mentally so they form a favorable attitude. Image-construction and image-management play a central role in contemporary political communication.

Scholars have offered a precise definition of the term, image. A candidate's image is defined as the constellation of perceptions "based upon both the subjective appraisals made by the voters and the messages . . . transmitted by the candidate" (Nimmo, 1975, p. 771). In some sense, concern about images—and politicians' beguiling of citizens with appearances rather than realities—dates back to fears articulated by the Greek philosopher, Plato. Many years later, historian Daniel J. Boorstin (1961), in a book simply titled *The Image*, warned of the ability of politicians to contrive artificial activities, called pseudo-events, that are pre-planned for media coverage. His book gained traction because it challenged the widespread belief—which seems incredibly naïve to contemporary observers—that political content contained in the media was, in some sense, "real."

In the 1960s and early 1970s, politicians and journalists commonly differentiated between a "real" campaign event, like a Labor Day speech, and media coverage. This distinction began to break down during the 1970s and 1980s, as candidates became more adept at manufacturing appearances for television. Soon it became clear that the "real" campaign occurred on the media and involved a battle to craft political images. In 1988, journalists "often portrayed the candidates as rival image makers, competing to control the picture of the campaign that would play on the evening news" (Adatto, 2008, p. 73). The image became the story, and journalists became part of the story. With politicians manipulating pictures to gain the best possible pose and television journalists editing political images, sometimes to recruit viewers, voters seemed to lose respect for the process, viewing it all as a matter of artifice and packaging.

WHAT DO YOU THINK?

Do political campaigns revolve too much around image-making? Should viewers distrust any candidate speech, recognizing that it is an attempt to manufacture image? Is it all artifice, manufactured for the camera? If so, what are some ways to inject more authenticity into political campaigns?

Second, campaigns are focused more around candidates than parties, elevating the role of media. Party identification has declined over the past decades, with the growth of ticket-splitting, advent of Independent voters, and increased education, which encouraged people to move away from reflexive support of a political party (Dinkin, 1989).

Television helped to precipitate some of the weakening in partisan ties, replacing parties as the primary communicative link between candidates and voters. Candidates—beginning, to some degree, with Jimmy Carter in 1976—have become independent entrepreneurs, who hire their own staffs, raise political money independently of the parties, employ pollsters, devise strategies, and attempt to wage a campaign that communicates their ideas and ambitions. Parties are still important: They structure campaigns and influence voter attachments. But they are nowhere near the kingmakers they once were. During the first half of the 20th century, candidates had to break bread with the big city mayors—for example, Richard Daley of Chicago and David Lawrence of Philadelphia—hoping the mayors would lend their support and deliver delegates at the nominating convention. Nowadays, candidates must win primaries and caucuses to secure the nomination, and news media coverage exerts an outsized impact on the nomination process, as candidates must depend on the news to secure publicity for their campaigns.

Third, media-age presidential politics is increasingly personalized. Television is an intimate medium that people watch in their living rooms and bedrooms. It takes shattering events in faraway places—wars, assassinations, and famines—and personalizes them, showing the human sides of tragedy. The electronic media reveal the back regions of political lives, revealing personal details of candidates' sex lives, infidelities, and psychological foibles. As noted in Chapter 5, earlier media maintained a traditional boundary between the private and public, showing only the most socially acceptable public behaviors of political officials. This boundary dissipated with the development of technology (faster film, videotape, online media) that allowed journalists easier and less obtrusive access to politicians' activities.

Cultural changes also eviscerated the boundary between private and public. With the growing public appetite for political gossip, and journalists' acknowledgment that they had covered up presidents' private misdeeds (like JFK's affairs), there was virtually no private behavior a politician could perform that did not seem suitable for mass media coverage (Meyrowitz, 1986). Political candidates, for their part, adjusted to the new era, recognizing that there could be political mileage and rhetorical benefits in revealing aspects of their personal lives.

In a book aptly titled *Seducing America: How television charms the modern voter*, Roderick P. Hart (1994) offers telling examples of how candidates try to personalize themselves in media appearances. The 1984 Democratic convention keynote speaker Mario Cuomo spoke emotionally about his father, "a small man with thick calluses on both hands [who worked] 15 and 16 hours a day." Democratic presidential candidate Jesse Jackson revealed that "at 3 o'clock on Thanksgiving Day we couldn't eat turkey because Mama was preparing someone else's turkey at 3 o'clock . . . then around 6 o'clock she would get off the Alta Vista bus; then we would bring up the leftovers and eat our turkey" (Hart, 1994, pp. 29–31). These personalized examples would have been unusual in the pre-television campaign. Personalization of politics has yielded benefits, but also raised critical questions (see Reflections box).

REFLECTIONS: THE PERSONALIZATION OF POLITICS

Candidates like to appear folksy on television. They strive to convince voters that they are decent, ordinary guys and gals who can appreciate your problems and feel your pain. While candidates have always sought to appear likable, the attempt to appear "warm and fuzzy" has everything to do with the television age. Does this have merit? Is it nothing more than inauthentic sham?

Case in point: Al Gore, who served as vice president from 1992 to 2000 and has become widely known for his concern with global warming. Gore, who could appear stiff before the cameras, went to extremes to humanize himself when he was Bill Clinton's running mate in 1992. During his acceptance speech at the Democratic nominating convention, he shamelessly discussed his son's brush with death in a car accident, while the cameras panned to his son, who appeared visibly embarrassed and uncomfortable. Four years later, Gore was back again, this time poignantly relating his 46-year-old sister's death from lung cancer, right up to her last dying breath. As he spoke at the Democratic national convention, the camera showed women wiping away tears. And when he ran for president in 2000, he planted a kiss on his wife's lips before accepting the Democratic nomination, a passionate smooch that lasted so long it left even television aficionados feeling uncomfortable.

In 2012, Ann Romney—seeking to humanize her husband, Mitt, described as "a perfectly lubricated weather vane" (cf. Cassidy, 2012)—lovingly narrated a biographical video on the campaign website. With the gushing sounds of airplanes in the background, she took us back to right before Christmas, 1968, when she and her husband-to-be landed at the Detroit airport. He said "oh gosh, why don't we just get married right away." She thought that was a great idea, and they decided to tell everybody, she recalled, as the camera panned the verdant Michigan countryside. Later, as adorable pictures of Romney's young sons appear on the screen, we watch as Romney kisses his wife affectionately, while she holds one of their babies. Later viewers are shown a family video, in which Romney plays patty-cake with the kids.

There is certainly merit in offering voters personal information about the men or women who would be president. It can help voters make a more informed choice. The electronic media are at their best when they bring "persons of great magnitude into our own modest living rooms [and] they share themselves with us, persons whom they have never met, persons whom they will never meet" (Hart, 1994, pp. 29–30; see Figure 11.2). But should a candidate break ethical norms of decorum by revealing a child's brush with death or share the story of the last breath of a dying sister? Of what value is it to voters to learn that a presidential candidate played patty-cake with his children? Alternatively, does it matter if Mitt Romney is not a "warm and fuzzy" candidate? Should voters downgrade him for this reason? Or, in a media era, is it reasonable to evaluate candidates based on their television skills? Does contemporary leadership involve the ability to project empathy and convey likability to voters via technological platforms? What do you think?

Continued

Figure 11.2 Politics is increasingly personalized, as candidates, their spouses, and children share personal, loosey-goosey reflections on television and on websites. Ann Romney, shown above, sought to humanize her competent, but frequently standoffish, husband, Mitt, during his 2012 presidential campaign, relating personal tidbits of their courtship and children in a web video. Do personalized appeals offer voters useful information or are they inauthentic ploys designed to tug at the heartstrings?

AFP/Getty Images

A fourth characteristic of today's politics is campaigns' near-obsessive focus on obtaining favorable coverage in the media. Staffers scope out the auditorium where a candidate is scheduled to speak, to make sure that the size of the venue matches the number of people expected to be in attendance. On the eve of the critical Michigan primary in 2012, Mitt Romney found himself speaking to 1,200 supporters in a football stadium that seated 80,000. Much to his chagrin, news stories emphasized that his message was dwarfed by the size of the arena. Later in the campaign, he improved his optics, as his strategists planned campaign appearances days in advance, searching for the most visually appealing location for Romney to speak and working hard to build crowds so photographers could click pictures of throngs of enthusiastic supporters as the candidate spoke in a picturesque locale. They hoped to time a rally in an Ohio town so precisely that Romney would speak at "the exact moment when the event's backdrop, the municipal building, would be bathed in an alabaster glow from the setting sun" (Parker, 2012, p. A14).

Fifth, in a related fashion, campaigns are orchestrated to comport with the media's logic for covering events. Candidates must adapt to television's time compression, its focus on speed and a clip-clip packaging of information to maintain viewers and tell a story. The average sound bite or length of time devoted to a candidate's speech on the news shrunk from more than 40 seconds in the late 1960s to less than 10 seconds in the 1980s and 1990s to about 7.5 seconds in 2004 (Baum, 2012; Bucy & Grabe, 2007; Hallin, 1992; Lowry & Shidler, 1998). Television forces candidates to speak glibly and swiftly, compressing their thoughts, and reducing the complexity of issues to . . . well a simplistic sound bite. Voters frequently blame candidates for glib, artificial speech, but the fault also lies with TV news.

Strategists recognize that people form impressions of candidates from media. In close elections, these impressions can be critical. Candidates are exquisitely sensitive to negative portrayals on the news. The one thing they want to avoid is a gaffe or obvious pratfall, blunder, or misstatement.

As Roger Ailes, the director of George H.W. Bush's 1988 media campaign and current president of Fox News, famously explained:

> Let's face it, there are three things that the media are interested in: pictures, mistakes, and attacks. That's the one sure way of getting coverage. You try to avoid as many mistakes as you can . . . It's my orchestra pit theory of politics. If you have two guys on stage and one says, "I have a solution to the Middle East problem," and the other guy falls in the orchestra pit, who do you think is going to be on the evening news?
> (quoted in Runkel, 1989, p. 136)

A sixth characteristic of media politics is its pictorial focus: Visual images are critical. Television is a visual medium that prizes pictures and pleasant images. Candidates are necessarily concerned with how they look, because voters form impressions of political figures from appearances in the media. Didn't impressions always matter? Weren't voters concerned with how candidates looked when they gave stump speeches on the campaign trail or in candidate debates? Yes. In an 1858 debate with Stephen Douglas, Abraham Lincoln replied to Douglas's charge that he was two-faced by quipping, "I leave it to my audience. If I had another face, do you think I'd wear this one?" (Jamieson, 1986, p. 10). However, a smaller proportion of voters saw candidates on the stump than see them on TV today. Evaluations of whether a candidate "seemed presidential" were probably less salient when there were no visual media.

Ronald Reagan elevated visual image-making to an art. As an actor, Reagan appreciated the power of artifice, and his aides understood the need to orchestrate images so they appealed to a mass audience. New terms came into the lexicon during the 1980s: staging the news, presidential image-making, and photo-op (for photo opportunity). For example, the public relations pros in the Reagan White House arranged to have Reagan "hoisting a few beers . . . in an Irish pub at two o'clock in the afternoon . . . with a bunch of blue collar workers and an Irish priest." They recognized that the picture instantly communicated that Reagan "was just a regular guy," perhaps also prompting them to conclude that his controversial economic policies would benefit the working class (Hertsgaard, 1988, p. 26; see also http://archive.pressthink.org/2004/06/09/reagan_ words.html for a discussion of the Reagan administration's preoccupation with visual images).

Finally, campaigns are organized around contemporary online technologies. There was a time not so long ago that political consultants focused endlessly on how their campaigns played on television. No longer. To be sure, TV is still a player; it is the primary source of political information for older Americans, and campaign managers pay close attention to how network news covers their candidates. But today, as political management expert Dennis W. Johnson (2011) observes, campaign consultants are likely to be equally if not more consumed with questions like these:

> What are yesterday's poll numbers posted on Polling.com showing? Did you see that Twitter posting from our opponent? Are we following that potentially damaging rant on RedState.com blog site? Did you see how much traffic that YouTube posting is getting? Are we getting any traction from our pop-up ads on Google? What are they doing on our opponent's Facebook page?
>
> (p. 22)

As exciting as it looks from the outside, the Internet- and social media-based campaign is not a perfect fit for candidates. "The whole idea of a campaign is a centralized message, vetted for potential backlash and communicated to the right people, in the right way," observes Stephen F. Frantzich (2009, p. 146). "Campaign managers are control freaks," he points out. But the interactive genie is out of the bottle, and campaign consultants recognize that they must harness online media to reach voters and influence opinion leaders. Online campaigning is a central part of a candidate's strategic plan, with extensive use of websites, social media, and YouTube.

Background: 1996–2008

These developments did not happen overnight (see timeline in Figure 11.3). Back in 1996, presidential candidates created websites, and by 2000 candidate websites, with informational and biographical features, were relatively commonplace (see Davis et al.,

1996	2000	2004	2006	2008	2012
• Presidential candidates create websites.	• Campaign websites become commonplace.	• Democratic candidate Howard Dean becomes first presidential candidate to develop blog. • Dean changes the nature of fundraising, raising money online from many small contributors.	• YouTube videos become more powerful as a video sinks Virginia Senate candidacy of George Allen.	• Obama brings campaigns into the digital age, raising record amounts of small online donations; creating a campaign social network; posting numerous YouTube videos; and harnessing social media to link campaigns to volunteers.	• Social media use grows, becoming a regular part of campaigns. • Twitter becomes a major force in campaigns. • Microtargeting matures and expands.

Figure 11.3 Timeline of Campaign Changes in the Digital Age

2009). Candidate websites focused heavily on informing users of candidates' issue positions, offering biographical background and trying to forge a connection between the campaign and the site visitor (Schneider & Foot, 2006). But the sites were primitive by today's standards.

In 2004, online communications received a seismic boost when Democratic presidential candidate Howard Dean became the first presidential contender to develop a blog. He innovatively brought campaign volunteers and supporters together via the Internet. Dean also changed the nature of campaign donations, raising more than $40 million online, primarily from small gifts donated by many online contributors. In this way, he consummated a shot-gun marriage between new technologies and the time-honored constant of politics, money (see Stromer-Galley & Baker, 2006).

In 2004, video files entered the political world in a big way when a JibJab video depicting John Kerry and George W. Bush in cartoon-like form singing a political variant of "This Land is Your Land" garnered 65 million hits. (The video was hilarious, with the animated Bush singing, "This land is your land, this land is my land. I'm a Texas tiger, you're a liberal wiener," and Kerry reprising, "This land is your land, this land is my land. I'm an intellectual, you're a stupid dumb ass!"; see the video at http://www.youtube.com/watch?v=z8Q-sRdV7SY). More generally, online political videos took on more importance in the 2004 election.

In 2006 political cyberspace erupted when the front-runner for the Virginia Senate race, incumbent George Allen, insulted an American student of Indian ancestry, a staff member of an opponent's campaign, who had been following Allen around the state. Frustrated by the repeated sighting of an opponent's staffer, holding a digital recorder, Allen used a little-known racial slur, calling the young man a "macaca," an arcane word defined as a female monkey. The comment, uploaded to YouTube and widely covered in conventional media, sank Allen's reelection bid (Johnson, 2011). The lesson: Micro-media could diffuse messages across cyberspace, initially circumventing the mainstream media and ultimately propelling conventional journalists to cover the story big-time.

Two years later, during the 2008 presidential election, technology exerted a transformative effect on campaigns. The 2008 Obama campaign harnessed online media in many ways. The campaign transformed the methods that presidential candidates use to mobilize supporters, raise money, and influence voters. Making big financial and staff investments in digital communications, the campaign surpassed Dean's 2004 effort, raising record amounts of small online donations and even creating its own social network, MyBarackObama.com, a virtual hub that allowed the campaign to request money, enlist volunteers, and encourage people to participate in the campaign in numerous ways, from registering to vote to adding an Obama "Yes We Can" ring tone to their cell phones (Jones, 2011). The tech-savvy staff innovatively exploited YouTube, as Obama posted more than 1,800 videos, including a music video by hip-hop singer Will.i.am that set Obama's "Yes We Can" campaign words to music, recruiting more than 10 million hits. Online political messages also helped Obama to reach young people, who use Internet political messages in political decision-making; research also suggests that Obama's sophisticated digital barrage mobilized young supporters, strengthening their beliefs that they could influence politics (Owen, 2006; Tedesco, 2011; Towner & Dulio, 2011).

YouTube essentially provided the campaign with free advertising and delivered a double bang for the buck when ads were covered by the mainstream media, no doubt causing some staffers to conclude, "Yes We Did!" By campaign's end, Obama boasted more than 2 million supporters on different Obama Facebook sites and an email list of 13 million adherents (Johnson, 2011). In addition to forging connections between supporters and the campaign, the use of interactive technology offered the Obama campaign a tangible benefit: It provided an inventory of grass roots supporters who could be contacted and mobilized throughout the campaign and for future Democratic Party efforts.

The Obama campaign had successfully mobilized young people, who were accustomed to social networking and pleasantly surprised that the technology had been harnessed by an established political candidate. Looking back at three important candidates in the 2008 campaign—Obama, Clinton, and Republican nominee John McCain—we might say, in the lingua franca of computer-savvy youth, that "Obama was the Mac, of course: youthful, creative, nimble, forward-looking, and sleekly stylish; Clinton was the PC— massive, corporate, sitting atop a huge pile of capital . . . and market share that favored a conventional, risk-averse strategy. . . . John McCain, though . . . who had never sent an email . . . was an IBM Selectric" (Friedman, 2009; cf. McKinney & Banwart, 2011, p. 3).

Online Environment

The 2008 election was distinctive and historic. By 2012, Obama's techniques were no longer novel. If in 2008 he was a Mac, by 2012, he and Romney were well-known iPads, cool, handy, but not particularly distinctive.

Online campaigning is now a centerpiece of presidential elections, with each election becoming ever-more interactive than the one that preceded it. In many instances, conventional media follow online buzz rather than vice versa. This makes sense when you look at the stats. Eighty-seven percent of Americans have a cell phone, 81 percent of 18- to 29-year-olds are wireless Internet users, and 72 percent of the online 18- to 29-year-old group use social networking sites (Brenner, 2013; Lenhart et al., 2010). Much of the younger voting population lives online. Campaigns cannot reach these individuals through newspaper, radio, or TV. To reach and influence them, they must communicate via websites and social media.

There are five characteristics of the contemporary online campaign.

First, candidate websites are sleek and interactive, bearing no resemblance to the dull, clunky, linear websites of elections gone by. Obama and Romney's websites included the standard biographical and issue information, but were supplemented by videos and blogs; contests; invitations to demographic and occupational groups to join the campaign (e.g., Rural Americans for Obama; Educators for Obama); apparel to purchase (a Romney "Believe in America" water bottle); stories to share; and multiple, easy opportunities to contribute money.

Second, social networking plays a key role in the online campaign. In 2011, former Minnesota governor Tim Pawlenty announced he was forming an exploratory committee for the Republican nomination via Facebook. During the 2012 Republican nomination process, Romney claimed close to 1.5 million fans, far more than his competitors. However, he trailed libertarian Republican Ron Paul in the number of "likes" and comments (West, 2014).By forging connections with supporters via social networking sites, candidates can gain large amounts of personal data on users. Consulting firms like Aristotle, Inc. (that's actually its name!) can also put some of this information to use in sophisticated online persuasion campaigns, directed at voters under 30, two-thirds of whom have an online social networking profile (Frantzich, 2009; Pilkington & Michel, 2012).

Twitter plays an outsized role in the electoral campaign. The social networking service has diffused rapidly since 2008, allowing campaigns to instantly send messages to supporters, update information quickly, and even sell political messages to candidates. Called promoted tweets, these pop up on the user's screen when particular search terms are punched in.

Campaign consultants habitually use Twitter, allowing them to communicate with supporters, the press, and other political strategists. In 2012, both Romney and Obama managers tweeted regularly. Obama senior campaign adviser David Axelrod posted numerous tweets about Romney during the primary campaign. For example, when Romney seemed to have difficulty answering questions about when he would release his tax returns, Axelrod punned, "Why is this question so taxing?" (Shear, 2012)! During the Republican and Democratic Party conventions, about 16.5 million tweets flitted through cyberspace (West, 2014).

Twitter has changed the nature of campaign reporting. Rather than spending time schmoozing with candidates on the chartered bus or shooting the breeze on the long, red-eye flight from the West Coast, reporters may be furiously searching social media sites for the latest information or tweeting away on their BlackBerries to beat the opposition (Enda, 2011). What they gain in speed and access may be offset by what is lost: press-the-flesh stories that give readers a feeling for the personality of the candidate and texture of the campaign.

Third, contemporary campaigns regularly place videos and political ads on YouTube, guaranteeing publicity in the online world and avoiding the costs of television ads. Celebrity appeals that might have appeared on TV now come online. In 2012 Obama invited supporters to enter a $3 online lottery to dine with actress Sarah Jessica Parker of *Sex and the City* fame; Romney invited his backers to enter a similar $3 lottery to have dinner with Mr. Celebrity Apprentice, Donald Trump.

Fourth, the speed and pulse of campaigning have quickened, producing a fast-paced environment characterized by instantaneous messaging. Candidates answer opponents' charges in video attack spots conveyed soon after a charge has been leveled. Political email, social networking sites, and the 24/7 news cycle are "informational amphetamines, a cocktail of pills" that consultants pop and promote at warp speeds (Partnoy, 2012, p. 5). This offers flexibility, but can also increase the probability that mistakes will be made.

Fifth, contemporary political campaigns are increasingly characterized by ever-more specialized uses of political persuasion techniques. The 2012 Obama campaign spent $100 million on technology, measuring voters' political preferences, and tailoring messages to fit different voter profiles (Tufekci, 2012). The new buzz word is **micro-targeting**, in which candidates target niche audiences, tailoring the appeal to match a targeted group's characteristics and online preferences (see http://www.nytimes.com/2012/02/21/us/politics/campaigns-use-microtargeting-to-attract-supporters.html).

During the 2012 general election campaign, campaigns relentlessly mined voters' personal information, hoping to tailor persuasive messages that fit them like a political glove. With the aid of demographic data that consultants had purchased, they had access to swing voters' age, race, party affiliation, and even shopping preferences. By planting cookies on targeted voters' computers, strategists could discover if voters frequented religious or partisan websites. They could then use this information to tailor appeals to fit a particular voter's characteristics, perhaps by emphasizing that the candidate shared

Figure 11.4 Presidential candidates now use a variety of high-tech, microtargeted, online appeals to reach voters. The 2012 Obama campaign harnessed interactive technologies, sending messages promoting its "Four More Years" appeal to the cell phones of targeted voters.

AFP/Getty Images

the voter's concern with religious issues. Campaign workers also asked supporters to grant them access to their Facebook profiles to offer a glimpse of their interpersonal networks. Armed with this information, a union supporter in Ohio who visited a Big Labor website was asked to contact a colleague from work who might be susceptible to a pro-Obama appeal from a trustworthy, politically similar source (Duhigg, 2012). In this way, campaigns combined online microtargeting techniques with good old-fashioned persuasion to try to influence undecided voters' presidential choices (see Figure 11.4).

During the 2012 primaries, Mitt Romney directed a family appeal at voters who had not yet made up their minds, and a very different "red-meat" message emphasizing that this election was an attempt "to save the soul of America" to partisan Republican activists (Vega, 2012). Obama campaign aides spent considerable time adapting technology so that the campaign website fit seamlessly into the screen of an iPhone, Android, or BlackBerry. With immediate access to tens of millions of individuals via email, Twitter, and Facebook, campaign specialists hoped to tailor messages to recruit an army of active volunteers (Rutenberg & Zeleny, 2012a).

Yet, as pivotal a role as online media play in contemporary campaigns, conventional media still matter. It is widely believed that Obama won the 2008 election as a result of his political mastery of interactive technologies. Online communications undoubtedly helped him net the Democratic nomination by mobilizing a wide swath of campaign volunteers. However, online messages played a less critical role in the general election campaign, in which candidates had to reach a heterogeneous mass of voters through conventional media: news, debates, and TV ads.

Summary and Evaluation

Today's campaign is a hybrid: old and new media, print and social networking, with sophisticated data-gathering and online microtargeting techniques leading the way. Clearly, online strategies are changing the nature and focus of contemporary campaigns. But are they good for democracy?

Online practices offer several benefits. First, enhanced interactivity has enabled voters to communicate more directly and personally with candidates and campaign staffers. Second, online political activity can promote participation in traditional offline political arenas (Edgerly et al., 2013). Third, political participation via social media can invigorate political participation and reduce cynicism.

There are also drawbacks, primarily on the macro level. First, digital campaigning can facilitate knowledge gaps, as many, presumably less affluent, voters lack high-speed access to the Internet (Edgerly et al., 2013). Second, online practices promote instant communication, prioritizing instantaneous candidate responses at the expense of vision. Political columnist David Brooks (2012) observed that:

> Technology is making campaigns dumber. BlackBerrys and iPhones mean that campaigns can respond to their opponents minute by minute and hour by hour. The campaigns get lost in tit-for-tat minutiae that nobody outside the bubble cares about. Meanwhile, use of the Internet means that Web videos overshadow candidate speeches and appearances. Video replaces verbal. Tactics eclipse vision.
>
> (p. A19; see also Hart, 2013)

WHAT DO YOU THINK?

How have the Internet and social media changed political campaigns? In what ways have they improved campaigns? In what ways have they made campaigns worse?

CONCLUSIONS

Presidential campaigns have changed dramatically over the years. In the 18th century, presidential candidates did not campaign for office. Fearful and distrustful of partisanship, leaders stood in the shadows, while their followers unleashed scathing attacks in newspapers. Something good emerged from all the hue and cry: Political parties evolved, offering civilized mechanisms to express political disagreements.

This elite phase of presidential elections gave way to popular politics, with campaigns waged on behalf of colorful contenders, in particular Andrew "Old Hickory" Jackson. With voting no longer restricted to property owners, masses of voters streamed into political campaigns, organized by the newly established parties. With the 1840 presidential campaign, presidential politics took off as rallies sparked interest and candidates promoted themselves with simple and, by today's standards, goofy nicknames and populist strategies. A national presidential campaign marked an American innovation. Parties connected people to leaders, and party newspapers provided a mechanism by which parties could influence voters. But dark clouds circled above as parties nominated mediocre candidates, and neither parties nor candidates nor the bulk of newspapers did much to discuss the scourge of problems facing America, from urban squalor to slavery.

Popular, prejudiced politics gave way to party-managed, national whistle-stop campaigns. Party leaders orchestrated campaigns and made backroom deals that secretly advanced the prospects of candidates they favored. With the growth of candidate-centered politics and television, presidential campaigns became inextricably linked with media.

Media campaigns are about the construction of images, with candidates using persuasion and technology to cultivate favorable impressions. This has raised knotty questions about the degree to which artifice and packaging have replaced authenticity in politics.

Today's presidential campaigns have seven core characteristics. First, campaigns try to cultivate images. Second, they are candidate-centered, with image-oriented messages revolving more on candidates than parties. Third, they are highly personalized, as candidates share aspects of their personal lives, a development with drawbacks as well as benefits for the electorate. Fourth, campaigns strive to obtain favorable stories in the news media, and, fifth, they necessarily revolve around the media's logic for covering campaign events. Sixth, candidates focus heavily on cultivating favorable visual images, and finally, campaigns are organized around online technologies: websites, YouTube, and social media.

Campaigns conducted over the past two centuries reveal continuities, as well as contrasts. From the late 1800s to the present day, campaigns have been negative, misleading, frequently deceptive, and sometimes dirty. They also have ceaselessly sought to sell candidates, using popular motifs of the era (Tippecanoe shaving cream in 1840, campaign buttons in the 1960s, an Obama ring tone in 2008). For all its shortcomings, the American presidential campaign represents a political innovation: a national spectacle designed to activate voters, renew national hopes, and give candidates with different visions an opportunity to make their persuasive case to a mass electorate. The campaign is loud, raucous, and sometimes elides important issues. As we will see throughout this section, there is a yin and yang in contemporary campaigns: Campaigns flow from the yin of aggressively and sometimes deceptively marketing candidates to the yang of providing an opportunity for candidates, voters, and media to collectively discuss national issues.

12 The Main Players in Political Campaigns

Election campaigns play a critical role in contemporary democracy. "Elections are arguably the single most important event in American democratic life," observed political scientist James A. Thurber. Elections, he explained, provide "an opportunity for Americans to both give their consent to be governed and to hold their representatives accountable for past performance" (Thurber, 2000, p. 1). In a similar fashion, Paolo Mancini and David Swanson (1996) noted that election campaigns "select decision makers, shape policy, distribute power, and provide venues for debate and socially approved expressions of conflict . . . Symbolically, campaigns legitimate democratic government and political leaders, uniting voters and candidates in displays of civic piety and rituals of national renewal" (p. 1).

In short, elections fulfill democracy's purpose, giving citizens the opportunity to select their leaders (Trent, Friedenberg, & Denton, 2011). Campaigns are the key. They provide the vehicle by which candidate information is conveyed to voters. They symbolically bring citizens and leaders together in rituals of debate, discussion, and dialogue.

This chapter introduces the main players in the election campaign and describes their role with concepts, data, and occasional anecdotal examples, the latter in an effort to help readers appreciate the human aspects of campaigns. The first section introduces media, candidates, and political consultants. The next portions describe the roles played by opinion polls and political parties. The final section examines the role money and campaign finance plays in presidential campaign politics. While the focus is on the presidential election, the players described in this chapter are mainstays on the stage of other campaigns.

MEDIA

A theme of this book is that the media and politics are, for all practical purposes, inseparable. Media are the road by which presidential campaigns travel every four years.

The last chapter described the ways that media and interactive technologies have influenced the trajectory of contemporary campaigns. Television has personalized politics. Candidates tailor coverage to fit the logic of mass media and online social networking sites. Campaigns are a battle to control the image, with candidates attempting to convey visually compelling images, journalists offering their own frame on candidate constructions, and voters sorting through candidate presentations, news coverage, and their own biases to settle on an image they carry with them into the voting booth.

Let's remember then that media serve dual functions. They are channels of communication between political candidates and citizens, conveying images that candidates present. But they also interpret, bolster, and challenge these images, with journalists, commentators, and bloggers introducing a multitude of messages and frames through news stories, talk shows, commentaries, blogs, and Twitter feeds (Jakubowicz, 1996). Not only do media intercede between political leaders and citizens, they are also the playing field on which campaign politics occurs, "our primary points of access to politics" (Jones, 2010, p. 23). Media are the place where political encounters take place, and are constructed, reconstructed, and deconstructed.

The paid media play an important role in presidential elections. However, in lower-level electoral contests—local races, state contests, and some Congressional races—candidates do not always have the budget to afford TV ads. They therefore push to get favorable news stories in media outlets, promote candidates on the web and in social media, and rely on an army of volunteers to get out the vote. Old-fashioned retail campaigning, amplified by the buzz of digital media, can play an important role in lower-level elections.

CANDIDATES

What it takes: The way to the White House.

These are the words that greet a reader of Richard Ben Cramer's voluminous book on presidential politics. They are the title of his more than 1,000-page book, and they aptly illustrate his theme: It requires a lot to run for president, takes a great deal for someone to say "not only should I be president . . . *I am going to be President*." Candidates must "see in themselves a figure of size to bestride a chunk of history" (Cramer, 1992,

p. viii). Presidential candidates need an outsized ego, and immense ambition. "Wanting to be president," John F. Kennedy reportedly remarked, "is not a normal ambition" (Strother, 2003, p. 2). Candidates also need tremendous confidence, political vision, love of country, and passion for the political process. Like activists who partake in political causes, candidates probably gain considerable psychological rewards from the grander social purposes of politics: making a difference in issues that help others and transcend the self (Stone, 2010). In voters' view, the ideal candidates are those who display these traits with integrity, displaying honesty, compassion, and a determination to talk about core issues (Trent et al., 2010).

In his journalistic account, Cramer profiled candidates running for president in 1988. One of the candidates Cramer profiled was Dick Gephardt, the long-time Congressman from Missouri, who made a valiant, but unsuccessful, run for the Democratic presidential nomination (see Figure 12.1). Cramer traced Gephardt's rise in politics, and by reviewing an episode from his first run for Congress, we appreciate the burning political desire and immense commitment to political action that propels candidates to run for political office, whether it is an election for state representative, U.S. Congress (as it was in Gephardt's case), or the presidency. In the passage below, Cramer describes Gephardt's determination and grit.

> [Gephardt] He was out the next day, and the day after that, and after that . . . door to door: "Hi, I'm Dick Gephardt, and I'm running for Congress. Everything okay in the neighborhood?"
>
> He'd do it all day . . . he'd spend two minutes at a door, or an hour, depending on what they wanted to say. . . . Gephardt nodded, listened. He never argued, never fogged over. His blue eyes were clear, locked on their faces. . . .
>
> "How many doors did we hit today?"
>
> That's all Dick wanted to know.
>
> There wasn't a day off. There wasn't an hour off. If he had thirty minutes between appointments—well, he might get one side of a block. They had the blocks numbered, and they'd hit them one by one . . . every house . . . hundreds every day . . .
>
> Gephardt tried to make it look like he was everywhere at once—out on the fringe of the countryside, Tuesday; Wednesday, up the tight streets of South St. Louis . . . [His opponent] mailed into all of those houses. But Dick showed up on their porches . . .
>
> (Cramer, 1992, p. 783)

Figure 12.1 Politicians like Dick Gephardt, who served for more than 25 years as a member of Congress from Missouri, call on zeal, passion, and ambition in their efforts to gain election to public office.

Getty Images

Gephardt's gritty work paid off. He defeated his opponent by 18 percentage points and was on his way to Congress.

The same dedication was on display nearly 20 years later, in the fall of 2006. Barack Obama was contemplating a run for the White House—mulling over the pros and cons—when political aide David Plouffe explained the choice to his boss:

You have two choices, he told Obama. You can stay in the Senate, enjoy your weekends at home, take regular vacations, and have a lovely time with your family. Or you can run for president, have your whole life poked at and pried into, almost never see your family, travel incessantly, bang your tin cup for donations like some street-corner beggar, lead a lonely, miserable life. That's your choice, Plouffe explained. There's no middle ground, no short cuts . . .

(Heilemann & Halperin, 2010, p. 63)

Presidential candidates endure more than emotional tribulations. The road to the White House is a test of physical endurance: greeting automobile workers when the plant opens at 7 a.m.; attending rallies and meetings with apathetic, even hostile voters; spending grueling afternoons working a crowd; chomping fatty hot dogs and pirogues with the locals; crafting a speech at midnight; and punching out a tweet at 2 a.m. when you can't see straight. Bob Dole, the former senator from Kansas and 1996 Republican presidential candidate, put up each day with gripping pain he still felt from a battle injury sustained during World War II, pain that caused his arm to ache for hours, even an entire day, but he never let anyone see what he felt, barreling ahead, pressing forward with a grin and a snarl. Dole never got to be president. Clinton trounced him in 1996, but, as Cramer notes, he showed through his grit "what it takes" to run for the White House.

To be sure, candidates are imperfect, their libidos causing them to break marital vows (Bill Clinton) and their ambition leading them to violate moral and legal pacts with the American public (Richard Nixon). But each candidate has personal strengths that distinguish him or her from equally, if not more intelligent, colleagues who choose not to pursue the presidency. Through it all, they try to concentrate on the big picture—the "vision thing," as George H.W. Bush inimitably put it: governing, policy analysis, and pulling together diverse constituencies to get a Congressional bill passed into law. The everyday tasks of practical persuasion are left to consultants, pollsters, and campaign strategists—the all-important "symbolic handlers who routinely organize, plan, and manage the communications of political actors" (Rose, 2010, p. 257).

POLITICAL CONSULTANTS

The Seattle interior designer, who had recently announced her candidacy for the U.S. House of Representatives, freely acknowledged she was clueless.

Heidi Behrens-Benedict had penned a newspaper commentary in response to a school shooting, expressing outrage at the political influence wielded by the National Rifle Association. Less than a week later, impelled by her newly discovered political outrage, she decided to run for Congress. She set out to challenge long-time Republican Congresswoman Jennifer Dunn for a seat in the U.S. House of Representatives. Behrens-Benedict hoped to run as the Democratic nominee and then defeat Dunn in the general election.

One day after meeting with a group of gun control advocates, whose cause sparked her decision to run for Congress, she called it a night and prepared to leave, knowing that a series of campaign tasks awaited her. That's when the thought careened across her mind. "I'm getting ready to drive home, and I realize I have no idea how to run for Congress," she recalled (Dulio, 2004, p. 2).

Enter political consultants, stage left.

Behrens-Benedict, the new candidate on the block, contacted political consultants, who helped her wage the Congressional campaign. This is no Cinderella success story. Behrens-Benedict lost to veteran Congresswoman Dunn. But she garnered the Democratic nomination for the House seat and obtained more than 40 percent of the vote in her first run for Congress. She also called attention to the incumbent's voting record on issues that mattered to voters and pushed the incumbent to attend more closely to issues that were important to constituents. And none of this would have happened if she had not hired consultants.

Political consultants—frequently criticized for exploiting television attack ads and emphasizing style over substance—are a mainstay of contemporary campaigns. As political parties declined and party leaders assumed a smaller role in campaign management, consultants filled the void. No longer able to solely depend on parties to organize volunteers and wage campaigns, candidates turned to consultants. And consultants, consumed by the adrenalin rush of media campaigns, a desire to advance a political cause, and (yes) the handsome profits they earn for their services, were more than happy to enter the fray (Dulio, 2004).

When people think of consultants, they may call to mind the big-ticket, internationally famous ones, like Democrat James Carville and Republican Ed Rollins (see Figure 12.2). A 1993 New Jersey gubernatorial race was called a contest between "two campaign titans," and the titans in question were not the competing candidates, but Carville and Rollins. Or one may think of the legendary Karl Rove, George W. Bush's political "architect," or Dick Morris, the one-time pollster for Bill Clinton who became an ardent Republican consultant and a frequent guest on Sean Hannity's Fox News talk show—perceptive, but capable of hurling brutal invective at candidates from the other camp.

Figure 12.2 James Carville (left) and Ed Rollins (right) are two of the most well-known political consultants in the U.S. Over the past decades, political consultants have played an increasing role in presidential elections, plying their communication skills to devise strategies that have helped candidates win elections but raising questions about whether gimmickry plays too much of a role in contemporary politics.

Getty Images and Time & Life Pictures/Getty Images

Consultants are a diverse lot, and few are as famous as the consultants mentioned above. There are hundreds of political consulting firms, specializing in different areas of political campaigns. As a field, political consulting has grown over the past 50 years. During the mid-20th century, consultants were primarily generalists. But today the profession has become more specialized, with growing numbers of experts in tele-marketing, fundraising, data analysis, and global political marketing (Johnson, 2012; see the American Association of Political Consultants website at http://www.theaapc. org/).

One survey reported that about 49 percent of consultants described themselves as Democrats, 37 percent indicated they were Republicans, and the remainder could be roughly categorized as Independents (Dulio, 2004). Consultants typically work for candidates from their preferred political party. Pro-Republican consultants are guns for hire in Republican races, and pro-Democrat consultants work for Democratic candidates.

What do political consultants do? They develop campaign strategies, conduct polls, craft messages, coordinate media-focused, technology-driven efforts, as well as interpersonal get-out-the-vote drives, and oversee online responses to an opponent's advertisements. Consultants typically specialize on one or several of these tasks. Their work can be artistic, or scientific and highly statistical (Johnson, 2000).

Consultants are primarily driven by one goal: victory. Political consultant Raymond D. Strother (2003) bluntly observed:

> In political consulting winning is everything. There is no good second place. No runner-up award. As a result, no cost is too great. Survival depends on it. A win, even a fluke victory over a scandal-ridden opponent, throws the spotlight on the consultant and allows him to prosper. A noble and principled campaign that did not use negative ads and talked about issues of substance turns into ashes if it loses by even one vote.
>
> (p. 1)

A controversial key to victory is opposition research. Opposition research—uncovering the opponent's record (strengths and shortcomings), personality quirks, and even skeletons in the political closet—troubles critics and newcomers to the political campaign. However, as Johnson (2007) observes, it is important—particularly for challengers who want to explain to voters why the incumbent should be booted out of office. "Thousands of hours can be spent on candidate and opposition research in any major campaign," Johnson notes (p. 75). It can, he observes, provide embarrassing, politically consequential items, such as "a member of Congress who portrays herself as being tough on drugs, but has a string of citations for driving while under the influence of alcohol" (p. 73).

Discovering personal skeletons in a candidate's closet is unusual, and consultants must be sure their information is accurate, of reasonably recent vintage, and won't come back to bite the candidate or consultant later on. More typical is opposition research that locates inconsistencies in a candidate's record or positions taken that, when made public, could alienate key constituencies. For example, in 2012 seasoned pro-Obama consultants labored over Republican nominee Mitt Romney's record as the leader of a private-equity investment firm, Bain Capital, making a case that the firm bought companies that later went bankrupt, laying off workers, while Bain cashed in, earning hundreds of millions of dollars (Draper, 2012; Koff, 2012). The consultants tracked down several people who had been laid off by Bain Capital, convinced them to relate their stories, and used these as the grist for negative ads that would try to raise doubts about Romney in the minds of middle-class voters. Some of these ads were accurate; others made claims that turned out to be highly suspect (see Chapter 15). The deceptions point to a broader problem with contemporary consulting: the tendency for consultants to work as hired guns for unscrupulous, deep-pocketed political action committees.

Defenders of opposition research point out that it can provide compelling information to challengers hoping to unseat a popular incumbent who has not kept his word or who has said things in private that belie her public statements. Consultants also are paid to devise strategies that will get their candidate elected, and, so long as their tactics are not illegal, they are professionally obligated to run an aggressive campaign. However, when consultants lie, mislead, or choose to reveal sleazy tidbits about the opposition candidate's background, they have crossed an ethical line. Thomas A. Hollihan, a political adviser and communication professor, argues that consultants should fulfill the ethical canons of their profession. "Consultants who fail to live up to these expectations, as well as the candidates who retain their services, should be punished when voters go to the polls on Election Day," he states (2009, p. 50).

While there are dishonest consultants, the overwhelming majority adhere to professional canons. Many work for local, state, and Congressional candidates with limited budgets, and they offer a strategic perspective on contemporary politics that policy-focused candidates lack. The broader, more enduring question is whether the institution of political consulting advances or belittles democratic aims. Political scientist Larry Sabato, a long-time critic of the consulting industry, notes that "consultants have emphasized personality and gimmickry over issues, often exploiting emotional and negative themes rather than encouraging rational discussion" (Sabato, 1981, p. 7). Defenders of consulting argue that providing negative information about a candidate's record is fair game in an election, especially if it contradicts the candidate's previous claims. Once again, there is no simple answer to this question, and different normative philosophies offer different perspectives. Libertarian philosophers, who emphasize the rights of the individual, affirm the role of consultants, arguing that they help candidates make a strong case for election. Deliberative democrats are more critical, emphasizing that consultants have cultivated a corrosive, crash-and-burn style of campaigning that hardly promotes a thoughtful dialogue on issues.

POLLING

Can you imagine an election without a poll? Can one even conceive of a presidential campaign story that did not mention the latest tracking, trial heat, or CBS/*New York Times* poll? "Politics without polling has become as unthinkable as aviation without radar," a political writer observed (cf. Johnson, 2007, p. 87). Polls have proliferated, with a 900-fold increase in trial heat polls from 1984 to 2000 alone (Traugott, 2005).

Polling is an important aspect of political consulting, but is a highly specialized, scientific arena. Presidential campaigns hire private pollsters or keep them on retainer. Candidates poll and incessantly follow polls conducted by professional polling organizations (e.g., Gallup, Pew, and Rasmussen) in the months before presidential primaries and during the primary season. Polls play a pivotal role in news media coverage and decisions by wealthy donors to finance a candidate's campaign (see Chapter 13).

Why do candidates conduct polls during the primaries and general election phases? They want to know where they stand with voters so they can adjust campaign strategies to fit the attitudes of key constituent groups. They may be especially interested in test-marketing campaign messages so they can see if certain words grab voters or particular frames resonate with key voting blocs. They also want to appreciate how voters evaluate the opponent; this can help them to select among various counterattacks before it is too late and advertising-produced perceptions harden into convictions in voters' minds.

Presidents also poll, typically judiciously, to appreciate how the public views a presidential policy initiative, a controversial program, or the president's overall priorities (Hillygus, 2011). But presidents also conduct polls on topics that bear on their political futures. As president, Bill Clinton asked consultant Dick Morris to poll public attitudes toward his impeachment in the wake of his affair with Monica Lewinsky. Morris reported back that the public could tolerate adultery, but not perjury. Clinton ignored his pollster, lying to a grand jury. (He should have listened. The House impeached Clinton on the grounds of committing perjury to a grand jury and obstruction of justice.)

So . . . what exactly is a poll? A poll, note two experts, is "literally, a counting of heads." And just what is a pollster? "A person who conducts polls" (Traugott & Lavrakas, 2008, p. 191)!

Just what you thought, right? Why can't we keep it simple!

In a basic sense, a poll and a pollster can be defined just as Michael W. Traugott and Paul J. Lavrakas defined them. But, as they point out in a thoughtful book on election polls, there is more to scientific polling than this. A **poll** is "any political sample survey of the electorate conducted by the media, politicians, or political interest groups that aims for a relatively quick and somewhat cursory tally of the public's political opinions and preferences" (Traugott & Lavrakas, 2008, p. 191). The key word here is *sample*. A sample is a scientifically selected subset of a larger population.

You might wonder why researchers sample. Why not just bite the bullet and talk to everyone? This is a virtual impossibility. Interviewing everyone in the population, what is known as a census, is expensive, time-consuming, and fraught with problems. It can be nigh impossible to locate certain individuals, such as those who are homeless or extremely mobile. As a result, pollsters sample. And sampling is remarkably accurate, as Traugott and Lavrakas (2008) note:

> A well-drawn, scientific sample allows a pollster to conduct interviews with only a very small fraction of a population but to draw inferences with confidence from the sample's responses back to the attitudes or behavior of the entire population of interest (such as the voting eligible population). But this can be done reliably and with confidence only if the sample is drawn according to certain laws of probability. When these procedures are followed, pollsters can accurately estimate the opinions of the more than 200 million American adults who are citizens or the candidate preferences of the more than 120 million Americans who are expected to vote . . . with a sample of only a few thousand respondents.
>
> (p. 59; see also Box 12.1)

Four major polls are used to study voters' attitudes. They are:

1. benchmark surveys that offer general baseline information about level of candidate name recognition and perceived public image;
2. trial heat surveys, pitting candidates against one another by asking "If the election were held today, would you vote for Mitt Romney or Barack Obama?";
3. tracking polls, conducted on a daily basis toward the end of a campaign to determine changes in public sentiments; and
4. exit polls, based on face-to-face interviews with voters as they exit voting booths.

Polling has become increasingly scientific over the past decades, offering more sophisticated and fine-tuned ways of tapping the pulse of the electorate. In 2012, reputable election polls offered stunningly accurate predictions of the outcome of the presidential race. *The New York Times*'s Nate Silver, who writes a polling blog for the newspaper, accurately predicted the results in all 50 states based on statistical analysis of poll results, even putting himself out on a limb by boasting about his predictions long in advance.

Still, other—non-scientific—problems surround contemporary polling. Unscrupulous consultants have abused polls, constructing "push polls" that are designed to mislead, not inform, respondents (see Box 12.2). Critics argue that polls have come to exert a disproportionately large effect on elections, causing candidates to become unduly concerned with pleasing the public and journalists to incessantly cover every numerical wrinkle in new poll results. But this is not a problem with polling per se, but with how polls are exploited by participants in the contemporary campaign. Like all methods of gathering information, polls can be harnessed for both positive and pernicious purposes. Used wisely and thoughtfully, polls offer useful insights into public perceptions of candidates and can advance democratic aims.

BOX 12.1 PITFALLS AND CHALLENGES IN POLITICAL POLLING

Scientifically conducted election polls are remarkably accurate. But they are not without shortcomings. By reviewing several contemporary challenges that polls face, we gain insight into the modern science of political polling. Listed below are several problems that political pollsters face.

First, respondents, consumed with other tasks when the pollster calls, sometimes hang up before the interview has been completed. This creates methodological problems. Researchers must make certain that they replace respondents who decline to be interviewed with demographically equivalent individuals. Usually, this can be done, but occasionally problems creep in. A now-famous example occurred in 2008, when polls taken before the New Hampshire primary gave Obama a double-digit lead over Hillary Clinton. Yet Clinton won by about two percentage points, raising questions about the accuracy of pre-election polls. One reason the polls failed is that some of Clinton's stalwart supporters, union members and those low in education, were not adequately represented in earlier interviews, partly because they were hard to reach. Rather than continuing to call these individuals, and catching them at a later point in time, some pollsters gave up, replacing them with new randomly selected respondents, individuals who were easier to reach, and who likely supported Obama (AAPOR, 2008).

Continued

A second problem involves likely voters. Polls frequently focus on *likely voters*, those who are predisposed to go to the polls on Election Day. It is they—not all registered voters—who can be expected to take the trouble to vote. On some occasions, though, it can be difficult to estimate just who is likely to vote, either because turnout is much higher or lower than expected.

Third, although individuals rarely lie outright to pollsters, they may prevaricate when the questions concern socially sensitive subjects, like voting for a white-supremacist candidate or voting against an African American contender (Johnson, 2007). A survey taken shortly before the 1990 Louisiana Senate primary suggested that between 22 and 28 percent of Bayou state voters favored the racist David Duke. He actually received 44 per cent of the vote. Conversely, tracking polls taken late in a 1989 Virginia gubernatorial campaign indicated that African American candidate Douglas Wilder led his opponent by about 10 points. It turned out that Wilder won in a squeaker (Asher, 2007). These difficulties are likely to dissipate as prejudice continues to decline in America. However, given that some voters will always harbor prejudices of one sort or another, the tendency to distort answers in a socially desirable direction will continue to present problems in elections featuring minority candidates.

Fourth, the way questions are worded can influence responses to polls. Striking changes in the way pollsters ask questions, such as the use of double negatives, inflammatory phrases and semantically charged words, can alter opinion poll responses. For example, a 2006 CBS/*New York Times* poll on presidential use of wiretaps in the war on terrorism obtained different results, depending on how the question was asked.

> Version 1: After 9/11, President Bush authorized government wiretaps on some phone calls in the U.S. without getting court warrants, saying this was necessary in order to reduce the threat of terrorism. Do you approve or disapprove of the president doing this?

> Version 2: After 9/11, President Bush authorized government wiretaps on some phone calls in the U.S. without getting court warrants. Do you approve or disapprove of George W. Bush doing this?

> (Asher, 2007, p. 65)

Which version do you think elicited more favorable answers? If you said, Version 1, you were correct. In the first case, 53 percent of the public approved and 46 percent disapproved. In the second case, 46 percent approved, while 50 percent disapproved of government wiretaps. As you may have noticed, the first version offers a justification, arguing "this was necessary in order to reduce the threat of terrorism." It also referred to the president rather than George W. Bush. In general, experts argue that pollsters should use simple language, steer clear of ambiguous questions, and appreciate how subtle wording changes can influence survey responses.

A final and nagging contemporary dilemma involves cell phones. In the past, pollsters relied exclusively on a random digit dialing procedure to scientifically sample residential, landline telephone numbers. This provided a reliable way to accurately sample voters. Then came cell phones. More than a fourth of U.S. households have only a wireless or cell phone and can't be reached by pollsters calling on a conventional landline phone. With so many people relying exclusively on cell phones, a residential landline phone sample runs the risk of excluding these respondents. What's more, cell phone only users differ in several ways from landline users. Cell-only users are younger and more likely to be men than their landline counterparts (Jackson, 2008).

In addition, compared to young adults with landline phones, cell phone or wireless-only young adults are more likely to be lower in income (Blumberg & Luke, 2007). From a political point of view, polls that rely only on landline samples produce somewhat more support for Republican than Democratic candidates, perhaps because some landline users may be a little wealthier and more supportive of traditional Republican issues than cell phone only voters (Pew Research Center for the People and the Press, 2010).

Here's the rub: Scientific polling requires that the sample reflects the population. Landline-only samples clearly don't, and this can yield skewed and distorted results. So, what to do? Researchers have dialed up a new strategy, devising methodologically intricate ways of combining landline and cell phone only samples. Pollsters also have developed reliable random digit dialing procedures to sample cell phone users (AAPOR Cell Phone Task Force, 2010). Pollsters are working hard on the problem, devising new methodologies to scientifically sample cell phone only users and developing ever-more contemporary ways to accurately tap the electorate's political attitudes. In any event, their techniques seemed to work. Major, scientific polls accurately predicted the outcome of the 2012 presidential election.

Continued

On a normative level, we want election polls to be transparent, with clear information about how pollsters selected their sample and conducted the survey. Citizens, who have a clear stake in political polling, should seek out a variety of different polls that are taken at different points in time and word questions in different ways.

BOX 12.2 PUSH POLLS

Did you ever pick up the phone and agree to answer one of those political surveys, only to hear the voice on the other end of the line quietly trashing a candidate and following up by asking you how you evaluate the candidate's fitness for office? Well, if you were living in Maryland in 2006, you might have received an automated call from a conservative organization that asked you which candidate you supported in a U.S. Senate race, and then whether you thought medical research should be performed on unborn babies. Wow, you might think, reacting in part to the semantics of the question, "Research on unborn babies? No way!" When you said out loud that you did not believe that such research should be performed on babies still in the womb, you would hear the voice tell you: "Fact. Ben Cardin voted to allow stem cell research to be done on unborn babies. Fact: Michael Steele opposes any research that destroys human life" (Asher, 2007, p. 157). This was a deceptive persuasion ploy. By using loaded language—terms like "unborn babies" and "destroys human life"—supporters of Michael Steele sought to rile the emotions and deliberately paint the opposition candidate, Ben Cardin, with the brush of negative association.

This is a **push poll**, a highly unethical pseudo-poll, defined by the American Association of Public Opinion Research as

> a telemarketing technique in which telephone calls are used to canvass potential voters, feeding them false or misleading "information" about a candidate under the pretense of taking a poll to see how this "information" affects voter preferences.
>
> (Asher, 2007, p. 156)

Unlike legitimate polls, which are designed to obtain knowledge, push polls offer up propagandistic information. They attempt to trick voters, goading them into believing that the pollster is interested in their views when the actual purpose is to feed them biased information that can influence their voting behavior.

Push polls are not the norm. Reputable pollsters would not think of using them. However, there are many instances of unscrupulous consultants putting them to use in elections. Unfortunately, they work, probably exerting a greater impact on late-deciding, low-involved voters. For example, some years back, an unmarried Congressman from Ohio received reports about push polls that would ask his supporters, "Would you still vote for him if you knew he was gay?" The candidate said he was not gay, but acknowledged the technique placed him an untenable position. "What do you do?" he asked. "Do you hold a press conference and say, 'I'm not gay!'?" (Sabato & Simpson, 1996, p. 265). The candidate did not hold a press conference. He also did not get reelected to another term in Congress.

Push polls are also used in presidential campaigns. The most famous and dirtiest was harnessed by supporters of George W. Bush during the 2000 South Carolina Republican primary. Hoping to soil the reputation of their main challenger, Senator John McCain, backers of Bush circulated a push poll that asked: "Would you be more likely or less likely to vote for John McCain for president if you knew he had fathered an illegitimate Black child?" Besides its racist content, the poll was particularly unseemly because it obliquely referred to McCain's adopted Bangladeshi daughter. During the 2008 presidential election, a push pollster asked Jewish voters in Florida if they would be more or less inclined to vote for Obama if they knew he had given money to the Palestine Liberation Organization and met with leaders of the anti-Israel terrorist group, Hamas (Asher, 2012). (He hadn't.) Apparently, the push poll had virtually no effect, as most Florida Jews voted for Obama in 2008.

Concerned about the ethics of push polling and the damage it could do to the consulting profession, the American Association of Political Consultants has condemned the practice. This is a positive step that may deter its use. But, given the nature of campaigns, condemnation of push polls will not stop unscrupulous purveyors from putting the technique to use.

WHAT DO YOU THINK?

What are the main scientific features of opinion polls? How can polls serve democracy, and how can they be abused?

POLITICAL PARTIES

They're not dead.

Political parties do not exert the outsized effect on the electoral process that they did a half-century ago, but they still play an important role in presidential politics. The U.S. has had a vibrant two-party system throughout its more than 200-year history. While the parties have changed over the years—the underlying ideological visions and political coalitions of today are much different than they were 50 years ago—the Republican and Democratic Parties continue to be the mainstays of contemporary American party politics. For the last 150 years, American politics has been a two-player competition (Brewer, 2010).

Over the years, the two-party play has been amplified by bit players and supportive actors from alternative political factions. In 2000 liberal activist Ralph Nader ran for president as the candidate of the Green Party, capturing enough votes in Florida to contribute to George W. Bush's pivotal victory in the state. In 2009, frustrated by Obama's federal government initiatives, large numbers of committed conservative activists formed the Tea Party, named after the iconic pre-revolutionary tea-dumping in Boston Harbor (Zernike, 2010). Less a bona fide political party than a movement with loose (and sometimes antagonistic) relations with the Republican Party, the Tea Party helped Republicans achieve Congressional and statehouse victories in 2010 (Busch, 2012).

The two major parties have different positions on many issues. Viewed through the lens of its platform, the Republican Party emphasizes reining in federal government spending and repealing the health care law, popularly known as Obamacare. The Republican Party, commonly known as the GOP (for Grand Old Party), supports lower taxes, vows to reform Medicare by giving a fixed dollar amount to future beneficiaries of the program, staunchly supports Americans' right to own guns, and supports a strong pro-life position on abortion that makes no exceptions for rape or incest. The Democratic Party platform sees virtues in government spending, argues that the federal government should continue the federal Medicare program, and has strongly supported higher taxes on wealthier Americans to reduce the budget deficit. There are stark differences on social issues, with Democrats supporting same-sex marriage and reaffirming support for abortion rights.

The parties also share certain similarities, such as taking strong positions against terrorism, preventing Iran from gaining a nuclear weapon, and backing Israel in the Middle East. In addition, as radical critics are at pains to emphasize, both parties vigorously support the American capitalist system, with each happy to embrace multi-million dollar political action committees (PACs) that bankroll their candidates' advertisements.

Parties play a critical role in presidential nominations. A candidate runs as a Democrat or a Republican and must capture his or her party's nomination. Parties run the nominating conventions that certify the nominee (see Chapter 13). Even in a candidate-centered era, parties recruit viable candidates, furnish candidates with staff assistants, provide resources to mobilize voters, and help solicit campaign dollars for the presidential campaign. Even in a media-focused election, retail door-to-door campaigning still occurs, with assistance provided by national party staff.

In sum, although parties do not control campaigns like they did more than 50 years ago, they are still important politically. On the individual level, parties are brands that guide voting decisions. If I am a Republican, I feel loyalty to my brand and want to see my candidate emerge victorious. If I'm a Democrat, I view a candidate through the lens of my brand, deciding to vote for him or her because s/he displays the Democratic label. Parties can serve as repositories of thought and feeling; and strongly held party attachments, formed through socialization, influence political behavior (Hetherington, 2012). At the macro level, parties help to structure the long presidential campaign, offering different visions of contemporary issues. When parties convey misleading messages or avoid taking stands on issues, they do not advance democratic aims. When the two parties offer contrasting viewpoints on campaign issues, they can advance democratic goals. But when they are unable to reach agreement on issues dividing the nation, they produce deadlock rather than the compromises that are necessary to govern.

CAMPAIGN FINANCE

Sheldon Adelson, a billionaire casino mogul, shelled out more than $16 million to a PAC that supported Newt Gingrich's 2012 candidacy for the Republican presidential nomination (Confessore, 2012a). Adelson appreciated Gingrich's disdain for labor unions and liked his strong pro-Israeli position. The Koch brothers, Charles and David, both billionaire conservative businessmen, raised an estimated $200 million for independent political groups opposing Barack Obama's reelection. Over on the Democratic side, well-heeled liberal donors, like billionaire financier George Soros, pumped some $100 million into independent liberal organizations that supported Democratic candidates in the 2012 election (Confessore, 2012b). Unions and other Democratic groups were on board, presumably spending hundreds of millions of dollars on national, state, and municipal elections. And on both sides of the political aisle, huge donations given to independent liberal and conservative groups now can be kept secret, passed through organizations that hide the names of the donors who write the checks.

All this is legal—a result of a controversial 2010 Supreme Court Citizens United decision that stipulated the government could not ban independent political spending by corporations and unions in elections.

To be sure, campaigns need money. They use it to pay for political ads, but also to send out old-fashioned political mailings. They need bucks to hire consultants and pollsters, but also to field grass roots campaign offices across the country, where staff members must be hired to solicit volunteers, train them, make telephone pitches to undecided voters, and register sympathetic voters in critical, swing states. Campaigns are expensive, and during each electoral cycle costs seem to rise to a new, unprecedented level. Recognizing this fact, in 2008, Obama became the first major presidential candidate to reject public campaign funding. By doing this, he could avoid federal spending restrictions and spend unlimited amounts of money on his campaign. His decision represented an abrupt—some would say hypocritical—departure from his criticism of politics-as-usual and earlier suggestion that he would opt for public campaign funding.

What role should money play in politics? Should government restrict the ability of rich donors—aka fat cats (or big dogs, if you prefer a canine metaphor)—to make lavish donations to political campaigns? It is a time-honored question, one that goes back to previous eras, where bagmen laundered money to candidates they favored. One thing is clear: You cannot understand contemporary presidential politics without appreciating the role that money and campaign finance play in the process.

The battle lines have been sharply drawn. Conservatives argue that government does not have the right to bar corporations from trying to influence electoral outcomes, emphasizing that corporations have legal rights, like people. Liberals respond that corporate money corrupts the political marketplace, exerting an undue impact on elections and elected officials' decisions while in office. To understand the current era, a brief historical review is helpful.

Watergate

Jaw-dropping ethical abuses occurred in the wake of the Watergate scandal, which unfolded after a team of burglars, their actions sanctioned by President Nixon's attorney general, broke into the Democratic National Committee headquarters at the Watergate Hotel in Washington, D.C. in June, 1972. Incredibly, Nixon's presidential reelection campaign earmarked money to pay the burglars and paid them hush money to keep quiet. Thus, secret campaign funds helped finance the Watergate burglary and cover-up. During this period, in the early 1970s, other abuses occurred. The dairy industry donated $2 million to Nixon's campaign and was awarded with an increase in price supports for milk, allowing it to make more money off dairy products. The telephone conglomerate, known then as International Telephone and Telegraph, promised $400,000 to fund the 1972 Republican convention in San Francisco. In exchange, the Justice Department settled an antitrust case in a manner favoring ITT; Nixon personally went to bat for ITT (Wertheimer, 2012).

Post-Watergate Reforms

It takes a lot for the two houses of Congress to pull together and pass sweeping campaign reform. Watergate served as a massive impetus. In 1974, Congress implemented major changes to campaign finance laws in an effort to curtail the parties' dependence on wealthy donors, discourage secret campaign contributions, and reduce the high cost of presidential campaigns. The new legislation stipulated that in any election contributions from an individual donor could not exceed $1,000 to a candidate and $20,000 to a political party committee; contributions of $200 or more must be publicly identified. It established an independent government agency, the Federal Election Commission, to enforce election law, created an optional mechanism for public financing of presidential campaigns through federal and matching funds, and required substantial disclosure of campaign spending.

Over the next decades, campaign finance ricocheted back and forth from court action favoring liberals, who wanted government to set strict limits on campaign expenditures, to decisions congenial with the values of conservatives, who argued that campaign reforms threatened free speech. However, court-ordered reforms failed to stop the diffusion of big money into political campaigns. Moneyed interests found ways of circumventing the post-Watergate reforms, propelling Congress to pass major legislation, known as the Bipartisan Campaign Reform Act of 2002, or McCain–Feingold Act, after its two champions in the Senate, John McCain and Russ Feingold.

The Supreme Court Expands Free Speech and Opens the Floodgates

Conservatives were furious. Believing that the First Amendment was sacrosanct and brooked no exceptions, they could not, for the life of them, see why there should be any limits on advertising whatsoever. This was America, after all. Liberals responded that yes, this is America, and the "m" in America stands for money. Big money talks, drowning out smaller voices, giving powerful interests easy access to the corridors of power. But money has a right to talk, conservatives said, and it would violate the constitution to restrict campaign expenditures. "Money is speech," they declared, and candidates "can spend as much as they want of their own money on their campaigns; it would be unconstitutional to limit their expenditures" (cf. Toobin, 2012, pp. 43–44). An earlier Supreme Court decision agreed (at least in the realm of campaign expenditures). Liberals responded that the decision was unwise. So the argument went.

On the lookout for an opportunity to challenge the McCain–Feingold law that placed limits on campaign contributions, conservatives found one, and an odd case it was. In the run-up to the 2008 election, a conservative non-profit corporation called Citizens

United produced a documentary, *Hillary: The Movie*, that used news, interviews, and creepy music to undermine the candidacy of Hillary Clinton. The McCain–Feingold Act stated that any communication which mentioned a candidate and ran it a month before a primary was "electioneering" and illegal. The Federal Election Commission said this was true of *Hillary: The Movie*. Thus, it could not be broadcast. Arguing that this was unconstitutional, conservatives took the case to the Supreme Court.

This time conservatives won. In a 5–4 decision in the **Citizens United** case, the Court ruled that that *the government could not prohibit spending by corporations and unions in elections.* Corporations, unions, and rich individuals—the Court said there was no difference among these three entities—could give as much money as they wanted to develop an ad that mentions a candidate and could run the ad up to Election Day. They could sponsor the ad themselves or funnel the money to an independent political group, a PAC, which could develop the advertisement. "Speech is an essential mechanism of democracy," Supreme Court Justice Anthony Kennedy wrote in defense of the decision, adding that "the First Amendment protects speech and speaker" (Toobin, 2012, pp. 45–46). "Speech is . . . constitutionally protected," noted conservative law professor Michael W. McConnell—"not because we doubt the speech inflicts harm, but because we fear the censorship more" (2012, p. 14). The ban on corporate and union contributions to parties and candidates remained. But the Citizens United decision shattered post-Watergate era restraints on campaign spending and key aspects of the 2002 McCain–Feingold law. It was a victory for unrestrained free speech.

Liberals thundered back, arguing that the Supreme Court decision "unleashed a torrent of money from businesses and the multimillionaires who run them, and as a result we are now seeing the corporate takeover of American politics" (Bai, 2012, p. 14; see Figure 12.3). Critics pointed to five unintended consequences of the Supreme Court's Citizens United decision:

1. Spending by outside groups has increased astronomically since the Supreme Court's decision. Independent non-political party spending on campaigns has risen in recent years, with the growth of super-PACs. Importantly, the amount spent by independent groups in the first election since Citizens United, the 2010 mid-term elections, approached the $240 million expended in the 2008 presidential race. In 2012, independent groups, like super-PACs, spent a record $600 million (see Figure 12.4).
2. Certain individuals with immense fortunes can exert an outsized effect on the process. Some 26 billionaires have given over $61 million to super-PACs (Blow, 2012). Public officials will feel naturally beholden to these donors, feeling an obligation to return the favor by supporting policies their financial benefactors favor. (Why else would billionaires donate if not to gain influence?) This increases the

possibility of unseemly favor-trading. It also diminishes the impact that ordinary citizens can exert on the electoral process.

3. Many donations given to super-PACs are kept secret. A $250,000 contribution to a super-PAC supporting Romney in 2012 came from a group that had a post office box for a headquarters, but no apparent employees (Confessore & Luo, 2012). Donations are frequently passed through tax-exempt advocacy organizations that can legally hide the names of the donors who write the checks. Because they are technically not political groups, they are not required to reveal the names of their donors to the Federal Election Commission (McIntire & Confessore, 2012). This runs counter to the ethos of transparency that guided post-Watergate campaign finance reforms. The upshot is that the identity of big donors to campaigns can be hidden from the citizens of the country.

4. Candidates can outsource controversial, marginally ethical ads to independent groups. These PACs can shroud themselves in patriotic-sounding names like Working for Working Americans, Priorities USA Action, American Crossroads,

Figure 12.3 Conservatives hailed the Supreme Court's Citizens United decision, which prohibited government limits on corporate and union spending in elections, calling it a victory for free speech. Liberal and other groups, such as those shown here, opposed the decision, arguing that it gave billionaire businesses too much influence in politics.

Roll Call/Getty Images

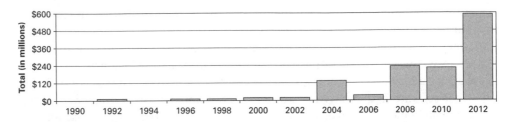

Figure 12.4 Increases in Independent Political Spending from 1990 to 2012. Notice that independent political spending increased in 2004 and 2008, rose to a high off-year presidential level in 2010 with the growth of super-PACs, and increased dramatically in 2012, the first presidential election since the Supreme Court's Citizens United decision. A number of PACs act secretly, and some get money from billionaire donors, raising serious questions for a democratic society. (Adapted from chart developed by Center for Responsive Politics, 2012.)

and Restore Our Future. Attack ads can be paid for and developed by PACs, such as these, which operate independently of campaigns, but with campaigns' tacit acceptance. This allows candidates to benefit from effective, sometimes deceptive, advertisements without having to take responsibility. While this is not new, it may have been exacerbated by the Supreme Court decision (e.g., Confessore & Rutenberg, 2011).

5. Presidential campaigns are crossing ethical lines. Federal law bans super-PACs from working directly with candidates. This is to help prevent the possibility that big donors can gain inappropriate influence over elected officials. But candidates' campaign staffs and PACs share a number of ties and overlapping professional roles. For example, back in 2012, a consulting firm, Black Rock Group, was located in the same Alexandra, Virginia office suite as the Romney campaign; its co-founder was a top Romney aide in 2008 who helped to direct a PAC that supported Romney in 2012. A super-PAC that supported Obama was created by two ex-White House staffers, and Obama officials helped to raise funds for the group. These overlapping roles may maintain the letter of the law, but they violate its spirit (McIntire & Luo, 2012; see also Reflections box).

INCREASES IN POLITICAL ACTION COMMITTEE SPENDING SINCE CITIZENS UNITED

What to Do?

These problems may raise red flags in your mind, causing you to wonder about the state of American democracy. Or you may retort that these are hypothetical problems: We do not know for sure that big donors always influence elected officials' policy decisions; if the overlapping roles between super-PACs and candidates have caused actual conflicts of interest; or whether the hundreds of millions of dollars spent on political ads converted any voters. You may approve of Citizens United because it enshrines free speech. That's a legitimate argument, and the majority of the Supreme Court agrees (see also a conservative essay at http://www.nationalreview.com/bench-memos/49332/citizens-united-decision-means-more-free-speech/paul-sherman).

However, critics are troubled by the ways that Citizens United reduces transparency and encourages secretive political activities (see Bai, 2012; Lessig, 2011a,b). Appreciating these problems, reformists have suggested some intriguing ideas (Ackerman & Ayres, 2002; Lessig, 2011b).

Among the most interesting ideas was one proposed by Lessig. He emphasizes public funding of Congressional elections. Lessig suggests that the first $50 of the tax revenue each American pays the U.S. Treasury each year be converted into a "democracy voucher." Each voter could decide to allocate the voucher in whatever way he or she wanted, giving the entire $50 to a particular candidate, or dividing it among different candidates. Candidates could take the money, provided they agreed the only money they would use to finance their campaigns would be democracy vouchers or small citizen contributions. They could not accept money from PACs. Lessig calculates that if every registered voter participated in the system, it would yield millions of dollars in campaign funds for each electoral cycle. This could remove the taint of corporate contributions and ensure that campaigns are funded by all citizens, not just the richest 1 percent, helping to restore trust to the political process.

Conservatives would cry foul as the plan seems to implicitly bar corporations and unions from spending unlimited funds on campaigns. This could be construed as a violation of the First Amendment. Similarly, libertarian scholars would object to the notion that voters could be coerced into giving "their tax revenues" to any political candidate. At the very least, the plan offers a constructive way to launch a new conversation on this topic.

WHAT DO YOU THINK?

Defend and criticize the Supreme Court's Citizens United decision on campaign finance. After thinking it through, what is your opinion on the case? Do you think the case advanced or hindered democratic aims?

REFLECTIONS: MONEY AND POLITICAL ACCESS

What do you make of the role money plays in politics? Figure 12.4 shows that spending by outside groups not connected with candidates or political parties has grown exponentially since the Supreme Court decision. What's more, there is great inequality associated with campaign donations. During campaigns and in the years between elections, people with deep financial pockets give more to public officials than those with less money, raising questions of equality. Well-heeled political lobbies can vastly outspend their less financially well-endowed counterparts. Since 2011, the National Rifle Association has spent not twice, not five, but 10 times more money on lobbying than all of the gun control groups combined. As political scientists Kay Lehman Schlozman, Sidney Verba, and Henry E. Brady point out:

> Policy makers hear from a limited, and unrepresentative, set of people who are, on average, better educated and more affluent. Campaign contributors are much more affluent . . . Political activity by organized interests, which spend huge sums outside campaigns on policy influence, reinforces unequal voice. Organizations representing those with deep pockets vastly outnumber advocates for the middle class and the poor. And of the billions of dollars spent annually on lobbying in Washington, 72 percent comes from organizations representing business interests, and no more than 2 percent from organizations representing the vast majority below the very top.
>
> (2012, p. 2)

We want individuals and groups to have equal access to their elected representatives. This is an ideal canon of democracy. If certain people and organizations give more money, they are likely to have more access and influence. On the other hand: You can argue that the fact that groups are willing to spend money to support their cause is an example of free speech in action. Giving does not guarantee influence. Shouldn't people have the right to use resources to try to persuade public officials of the wisdom of their point of view? As the conservative law professor Michael W. McConnell noted earlier, speech is protected by the Constitution, not because we doubt that speech can cause harm, but because we fear the costs of censorship more.

What do you think? How do you balance the different values?

INTERSECTIONS AMONG PLAYERS

As actors on the volatile stage of political theater, the players described in this chapter crisscross each other's paths and intersect in a number of ways. Candidates try mightily to influence media agendas and frames, but they must adapt to the routines of the press. Some turn to partisan bloggers, and many candidates reach out to social media to cultivate voting blocs. Media reflect and refract candidate themes, offering publicity to consultants, but sometimes framing their strategies with disdain. Polls play an indispensable role in campaigns, offering candidates feedback on whether they are reaching voters and helping them to modulate their message so that it is in sync with broader themes. Polls are a ubiquitous presence in the media, sometimes pushing out more substantive stories. Special interest groups poll, and hire consultants to push their agendas, with PACs increasingly bankrolled by million-dollar donations that may be shrouded in secrecy.

Candidates spend immense amounts of time raising money, cultivating well-heeled donors and sympathetic partisan organizations. Parties depend heavily on media to communicate their political message, recognizing that they function as brands in an era of digitally based political marketing. It's all politics: combative, partisan, and a high-stakes attempt to leverage influence in order to assume the reins of power. In the best cases, it results in elected officials calling on a mandate to implement policies that improve people's health and standard of living. In the worst instances, the process advantages the rich and powerful, ensuring that moneyed interests maintain their lock on the status quo.

CONCLUSIONS

There are six main forces that impinge on the political communication process: media, candidates, political consultants, opinion polling, political parties, and campaign finance. The media—conventional channels and social media—play a key role in conveying and interpreting statements transmitted by candidates. Candidates, for their part, are motivated by a combination of brute ambition, ideological vision, and a desire to work for the public good.

Political consultants—often criticized for emphasizing superficial style over substance—are major players in contemporary campaigns. Campaigns have become so complex—so focused on communications, centered on polling, and necessarily revolving around attracting diverse constituent groups—that political consultants have become an indispensable part of presidential politics. Consultant-coordinated opposition research has generated considerable controversy. Proponents argue that, if ethically based, it is legitimate campaign persuasion. Opponents lament that it is frequently dishonest and corrodes the political process.

Polling plays a critical role in campaigns. Polls are sample surveys of the electorate that include benchmark, trial heat, and tracking surveys. Polls help candidates to understand voter perceptions and to adapt strategies to fit voter needs. Polls too have been a source of controversy, but, used prudently, they can offer useful insights into voter attitudes, serving democratic ends.

Political parties continue to play an important role in presidential politics, even if they are no longer the arteries through which campaigns pass. Parties recruit viable candidates and certify them through nominating conventions. Parties also exert effects on voters, serving as brands to help guide voting decisions.

Finally, you cannot run campaigns without money, and lots of it. The 2010 Supreme Court decision loosened campaign finance restrictions, ruling that the federal government cannot ban independent spending by corporations and unions in candidate elections. This has opened the floodgates to unprecedented corporate spending, pleasing First Amendment advocates but distressing critics who worry about the possibility that corporate groups can control the direction of presidential politics.

Yet the electoral impact of Citizens United remains in doubt. Anti-Obama PACs poured hundreds of millions of dollars into the 2012 campaign, outspending Democratic PACs. However, Obama won reelection by a broad margin and the Democrats retained control of the Senate. Pro-Democratic PACs spent bundles to oust Republicans, but Republicans kept control of the House. Unrestricted political spending does not buy elections outright. Voters remain stubbornly resistant to blatant attempts to exploit advertising to win elections.

But more subtle problems in campaign finance remain. Donations to political action groups can be kept secret, violating democratic principles of transparency. Inequality in political influence continues, as organizations with deep pockets have greater access to public officials than advocates for the middle class and the financially downtrodden.

13 Nominations and the News

"Whatever happened to President Rudy Giuliani? And what about President Hillary Clinton?"

Political scientist Samuel L. Popkin (2012) posed these questions, noting that a year before the 2008 election Giuliani was the odds-on favorite to win the Republican nomination, his poll numbers more than doubling those of his competitors and his fundraising dollars shattering previous records for Republican candidates. Giuliani was mayor of New York City during the 9/11 attacks and earned plaudits for his courageous leadership on September 11 and during the weeks that followed the terrible tragedy. With an impressive record as New York City mayor and a reputation for no-nonsense toughness that called on Republican values and seemed likely to inspire voters, he appeared destined to win the nomination.

But Giuliani fizzled. He failed to win a primary in 2008 and withdrew from the race in late January, months before the Republican convention (see Figure 13.1).

Why no President Hillary Clinton? A virtual juggernaut, a member, by dint of marriage and her own political accomplishments, of Democratic Party royalty, a political leader who inspired reverence among legions of her compatriots, and a twice-elected senator from New York, Clinton was favored by many to capture the Democratic nomination. She led the polls, boasted a huge campaign war chest, and commanded a campaign team that glittered with political panache. By contrast, Obama launched his campaign with virtually nothing. When he filed papers to explore presidential candidacy in January, 2007, only four staffers coordinated a meager Washington, D.C. office. On the day before the announcement, they rushed out to buy a wireless router so everyone could have access to the Internet. Obama had a strange name and a thin record, having

Figure 13.1 Rudy Giuliani, the celebrated former mayor of New York City, was a front-runner for the 2008 Republican nomination. But his campaign fizzled amid strategic errors and critical media coverage, illustrating the perilous path to the nominations in a media age.

AFP/Getty Images

served less than two years in the Senate (Balz & Johnson, 2009).

Yet, in what was a crushing personal disappointment, Hillary Clinton failed to gain the 2008 Democratic presidential nomination. Few would have predicted this outcome during the cold winter months of 2007, when Clinton, polished and precise, seemed poised to capture the nomination, while Obama, sluggish and overwhelmed, struggled to stay on message.

And why didn't Rick Perry become the 2012 GOP nominee? The three-term Texas governor was popular, gamely, handsome, and an adept campaigner. Popular in Texas, he had an uplifting narrative that could inspire voters, and what's more, took reliably conservative positions on issues such as abortion and gay marriage. Polls taken in 2011 gave him a double-digit lead over Mitt Romney, suggesting he could build a coalition that could defeat President Obama in 2012. Yet he too failed to gain his party's nomination, the victim of self-inflicted verbal wounds few could have anticipated.

Campaigns involve a series of strategic choices, nettlesome decisions, and the complex challenges involved in leading a campaign organization. Some candidates rise to the occasion and some fail. At the outset it seems obvious who will capture the party's nomination, until reality sets in, and then it becomes equally obvious when the candidate withdraws that he or she did not really have a lick of a chance at the get-go. Communication plays an important role in the nomination process. News media coverage influences voters' beliefs about who is a serious candidate, while also shaping fundraisers' perceptions of candidate viability. Opinion polls and primary debates can alter the trajectory of a campaign in ways that would have been unheard of in the political party-dominated nomination process of yore. The distinctive process by which America selects its nominees for president has shortcomings, but also strengths, and has unquestionably evolved into something far different than the country's founders would have anticipated.

This chapter describes the role political communication plays in the presidential nomination process. The first section introduces the rules of the game, with an explanation of the formal procedures that govern presidential nominations and the logic that underlies the all-important news coverage. The next sections explore the different phases of the campaign: pre-primaries, the first critical caucus and primary, and the subsequent state primaries. An evaluation of the nomination process and news media coverage follows. The final portion describes conventions, which have evolved from pivotal events to week-long advertisements for the parties.

I am sure you have followed presidential nominations in the media—a lot or a little, depending on your interest. Perhaps you have been curious or even puzzled about the legion of primaries that candidates contest, the ways they trudge through small states in quest of votes, and the seemingly endless poll-based, strategy-infused media coverage. This chapter will help you to make sense of it all, develop a more critical understanding, and appreciate the methods behind the madness.

FORMAL RULES AND PROCEDURES

The primaries are a fixture in presidential politics. Candidates must win primaries—and caucuses—if they want to gain the nomination of the Republican and Democratic Parties. Needless to say, it was not always like this. In the 19th century, party bosses selected the nominees, bartering and making deals among themselves in smoke-filled backrooms. In the early 20th century, frustrated by boss control over parties, a group of political reformers, the Progressives, helped to initiate primaries in order to give voters an opportunity to select presidential nominees. Primaries took off slowly. About 12 states held primaries in 1912. The number of state primaries fluctuated over the next five decades; on the average, 15 states held presidential primaries, and no more 40 percent of the convention delegates at the nominating conventions came from primary states (Wayne, 2008). Party leaders still wielded considerable influence over the nomination process. John F. Kennedy entered primaries in 1960 to demonstrate to party leaders that voters would accept his presidential candidacy, even though they knew he was a Roman Catholic. He did not contest primaries to amass delegates based on the number of primary victories. Instead, he entered to impress the party honchos.

By 1972, the Democratic Party was forced to democratize its procedures, after it became clear the nomination process was controlled by party leaders, who could strong-arm dissenters. A blue-ribbon commission called for a fairer, more open process of choosing delegates, one that was less beholden to the dictates of party elites. The commission recommended that popular elections—primaries, held during the year of the general presidential election—should serve as the major mechanism by which convention delegates would be selected. The Democratic Party adopted the report, and state legislatures subsequently passed laws that made the changes binding for both Democrats and Republicans. As a result, the overwhelming majority of delegates to the nominating conventions are essentially selected by voters in primary elections and caucuses. Before going further, let's define three key terms.

A **presidential primary** is a state-wide election that gives voters the opportunity to select the party's presidential nominee. Voters cast votes in a secret ballot, just as they do in a general election.

Caucuses are different. As the name suggests, a caucus involves talking, discussing, and caucusing together about issues. A **caucus** is a local, public gathering where party members publicly deliberate about candidates, decide which presidential candidate they will support, and choose delegates to the nominating convention. A caucus is a public event, where party members try to persuade one another to support one or another candidate. In the end, caucuses vote, selecting a preferred candidate and a slate of delegates to represent their views at a nominating convention.

A **delegate** is a member of a political party, an individual who attends the convention and formally casts a vote for a candidate. Delegates tend to be political activists and hold more extreme political views than both rank-and-file-party members and typical voters (Polsby et al., 2012). (This may not be bad: Strong positions on issues propel people to become involved in presidential elections, and that's a good thing.)

In practice, delegate voting is a formality. The winner of a primary or caucus typically secures all (or a large proportion) of the convention delegates, who are honor-bound to support the candidates that voters selected in primaries and caucuses. (Increasingly, primaries have adopted proportional representation procedures, so delegates are allocated in proportion to the number of votes received.) There is also a special, smaller category of delegates: superdelegates. Superdelegates are national committee members of the party and (in the case of the Democrats) elected officials (governors and members of Congress).

You might wonder why we still have delegates at all. The practice seems arcane and old-fashioned. The tradition harks back to the 19th century, when party leaders dominated nominating conventions and delegated certain individuals to perform the nitty-gritty tasks of running the convention and selecting nominees (Wayne, 2008). In the 19th century, party leaders selected delegates; today, they are chosen via the results of primaries and caucuses. But the tradition remains. Some experts ardently defend the concept of a convention delegate, noting that it gives rank-and-file party members an opportunity to participate in the convention, rewarding their hard work and helping to cement party loyalty. There is a complex formula for translating primary and caucus votes into delegates. It fundamentally ensures that delegates will support the choices voters made at the polls.

THE NEWS MEDIA IN THE PRIMARIES

Horse Race and Strategy-Based News

> The national press is entirely concerned with "horse race" and popularity . . . If thermonuclear war broke out today, the lead paragraph in tomorrow's *Washington Post* would be, "In a major defeat for (the president) . . ."
>
> (Robinson & Sheehan, 1983, p. 140)

The news media cover presidential politics as if it were a game, a sporting event, a horse race. Journalists focus incessantly on the candidates' strategies to vanquish their opponents, electoral battle plans, poll ratings, and come-from-behind tactics to over-power political rivals. Political communication scholar Thomas E. Patterson was among the first to explain and document this tendency. Indefatigable in his criticism of media for reducing the campaign to a horse race, Patterson has argued that the media trivialize the serious business of presidential elections. He and colleague Robert D. McClure observed that:

> Network reporting treats a presidential election exactly like a horse race. The camera follows the entries around the country trying to capture the drama, excitement, and adventure of a grueling run for the November finish line. The opinion polls are cited frequently, indicating the candidates' positions on the track. The strengths and weaknesses of all the participants are constantly probed, providing an explanation for their position and creating drama about how the race might change as they head down the homestretch.
>
> (Patterson & McClure, 1976, pp. 41–42)

The horse race metaphor dates back years, reflecting an era in which horse races were popular spectator sports. You find horse racing out of date? Fine. Replace it with the baseball pennant race, pro football playoffs, or March Madness. Whatever sport you choose, the import is the same: The news media treat electoral politics as a competitive game, characterized by a battle over tactics for the prize of victory, rather than a more serious endeavor that involves a debate among different policy ideas, a contest among leaders who have articulated different visions for their country, or a critical exercise in the deliberation of ideas among citizens and leaders.

Every four years you will come across headlines like these in major news media: Polls show late surge by Kerry and Edwards; Dean now third (as in *USA Today*, January 18, 2004); Clinton and Obama locked in tight race in Indiana (*U.S. News & World Report*, May 2, 2008); and Shifting tactics, Romney attacks surging Gingrich (*The New York Times*, December 15, 2011). That's just during the nomination phase.

During the general election campaign, the build-up of **horse race news** is inescapable: nearly every day a national poll, a new prognostication, and, when the election is projected to be close, as was 2012, the tightness of the race is the main story (the only story, it seems), as network anchors breathlessly count down the days until the race begins. Horse race news is a key part of the nominations, arguably more important during this phase because projections of who is ahead exert a more critical impact on fundraising and a stronger influence on voters, who are less engaged in the nominations than they are in the fall campaign.

Thus, before the onset of a debate among candidates for a presidential party nomination, you will hear an adrenalin-filled, chest-stomping description of an upcoming face-off. If you were not listening closely to the names, you might be forgiven for mistaking CNN's preview of a 2012 Republican presidential primary debate, held in the fall of 2011, for one of those dramatic, storybook segments that accompanies the football playoffs, where the announcer dramatizes and romanticizes the teams and their players. The CNN montage began with scenes of cowboys, cattle, luscious streams, and mountains, befitting the western debate locale, as woodwind musical instruments chirped a musical melody. Here is what a deep-throated CNN anchor intoned before a Republican debate in Las Vegas, showcasing all the trappings of horse race, competitive drama-infused political journalism:

> From the mountain majesty of the Rockies to the deserts sands of the Mojave, the American frontier is a historic land of opportunity for Republicans. Tonight the fight for the GOP presidential nomination comes here: to a region where Barack Obama made inroads four years ago [cut to picture of Barack Obama]; to a state that could be decisive in the primary season and the general election [camera pans to casinos and Las Vegas traffic]; for a Las Vegas event for Republican presidential contenders, on stage and in depth after a dramatic reshuffling of the pack [picture of playing cards]: Herman Cain, now among the leaders surging in recent weeks; Rick Perry, trying to get back on track after a meteoric rise; and Mitt Romney, steady holding his place at the top of the tier. Now with nothing less than America's future [cut to Statue of Liberty], the presidential campaign goes west. [Dramatic music played, followed by cheers, and the voice of CNN's Anderson Cooper.] Welcome to our viewers from the U.S. and around the world. Let's meet the 2012 Republican presidential contenders. Joining us on stage: Minnesota

Congresswoman Michele Bachman [she walks out like a star athlete decked out in a white dress, to much applause]; the former Speaker of the House Newt Gingrich [he strolls out like a titan and waves to the crowd]; Texas Governor Rick Perry [spoken like he was the power forward of an NBA team amid lots of cheers] . . . former Pennsylvania senator Rick Santorum; former Massachusetts Governor Mitt Romney; former President and CEO of Godfather's Pizza Herman Cain [he pounds his chest]; and Texas Congressman Ron Paul [the candidates announced like a celebrity-studded starting basketball team in the NBA playoffs].

Corroborating these examples, there is abundant empirical evidence that the news media focus on the game aspect of politics, particularly in the nomination stretch of a campaign (e.g., Lavrakas & Bauman, 1995; Miller & Denham, 1994; Patterson, 1993; Sigelman & Bullock, 1991). Findings emerge from careful content analyses of election coverage, where researchers code stories to compare the proportion that focus on the horse race with those that examine policy issues, such as where candidates stand on the economy.

From 1988 through 2012, an average of 64 percent of news stories centered on the horse race, compared to 28.1 percent that delved into policy issues. For example, in 2000, a whopping 78 percent concerned the horse race, compared to 22 percent that examined policy issues (Farnsworth & Lichter, 2012; Project for Excellence in Journalism, 2012b; see Table 13.1).

Just months after the 2012 election had been certified, press speculation turned to 2016. Journalists discussed which Republican hopefuls had the edge: New Jersey's Chris Christie? Florida's Marco Rubio? Or 2012 vice presidential candidate Paul Ryan from Wisconsin? Speculation about Hillary Clinton become so intense in media circles six months after the election that columnist Maureen Dowd (2013) declared bluntly, "Please don't ask me this anymore. It's such a silly question. Of course Hillary is running" (p. 1).

Why do horse race stories dominate news coverage, notably during the nomination period? There are four reasons: (1) the proliferation of opinion polls; (2) the fact that polls offer an easy, routinized way to present news, one filled with statistics, which offer an imprimatur of scientific respectability; (3) increased journalistic skepticism about politics, which encourages reporters to view politics as nothing more than a strategic power game; and (4) the fact that the election *is* a horse race, with candidates strategizing, focusing on early primary victories, and incessantly following polls.

Critics have lamented the media's obsession with the horse race, arguing that there are more instructive ways to view the campaign. Their criticisms, along with alternative ways to frame the campaign, are discussed toward the end of the chapter.

Table 13.1 Horse Race Coverage in Primary Election News: 1988–2012

Focus of coverage (percent of stories)*	1988	1992	1996	2000	2004	2008	2012
Horse race	49	55	56	78	77	71	64
Policy issues	16	72	44	22	18	14	10

*Stories coded could include horse race and a policy focus, or neither; thus the numbers do not add up to 100%. (1992 was an anomaly, with news media offering more policy coverage in response to candidate discussion of economic policy, and perhaps also to atone for criticism of press shortcomings in coverage of the 1988 campaign.)

(1988–2008 analyses based on ABC, CBS, and NBC News, with some other news supplemented, e.g., Fox News in 2004 and 2008 and the PBS NewsHour in 2000. 2012 analyses based on analyses of print, network TV, cable, online media, and radio news.

1988–2008 data and chart from Farnsworth & Lichter (2011). 2012 data from Project for Excellence in Journalism, 2012b.)

Favorite Media Storylines

The press is not a conveyor belt that simply relays electoral information to the public. It does not hold up a mirror to politics, but presents particular slices and perspectives of presidential campaigns. As discussed in Chapter 9, the news is not filled with partisan biases, but is instead shaped by professional routines. One routine is the tendency to spin campaign narratives. Like all communicators, journalists tell stories—not lies or fictions, but narratives that frame politics around particular themes. Naturally, the themes differ in different election years, but it is remarkable how similar the storylines are over the course of a variety of elections. The intent is *not* to push particular presidential contenders, although it can sometimes seem this way to thin-skinned campaign aides. Instead, the purpose is to select out a theme, among the dozens that could be chosen in an effort to shed light on the dynamics of particular nomination races.

In his work over the years, Patterson has identified major journalistic storylines that dominate in presidential nomination news (e.g., Patterson, 1993). They include:

The front-runner scenario: News favors the candidate who, according to polls, expert opinions, and influential endorsements, leads the pack. Front-runners can capture the lion's share of coverage. But this is frequently offset by negative coverage that results from reporters' desire to inform the public of chinks in the front-runner's armor.

The losing ground storyline: When a leading candidate's public support—in primary elections or polls—sharply declines, news reflects this. Coverage becomes decidedly less favorable, as a variety of indicators—from opinions of party leaders to comments from voters—take on a negative hue.

The bandwagon narrative: When a candidate's poll ratings begin to rise sharply, news stories pick up on this, jumping on the proverbial bandwagon. News stories about the candidate become more favorable.

In each case, candidate viability—performance in primaries and election polls—is the major determinant of news favorability. There is nothing sinister in journalists employing this framework. It fits professional norms and helps reporters to make sense of a presidential campaign.

Now that we have examined the political and media logic that underlies campaigns, we can delve into presidential nomination dynamics. The road to the nominating convention starts early, a year-and-a-half before the presidential election. To paraphrase the Beatles, a group famous for their social, if not political, prognostication, this truly is "a long and winding road." It begins with the pre-primaries, the series of pivotal non-electoral events that occur in the year or two before the actual primaries begin.

PRE-PRIMARIES

The nomination season begins long before the presidential election is on the minds of American voters. Some 18 months before the 2000 election, 10 Republican candidates had declared that they were candidates for president, and a year-and-a-half before the 2004 vote, nine Democrats had announced their intention to challenge President George W. Bush. With no incumbent running in 2008, the race was wide open, and candidates were exploring a potential dash for the White House as much as two years before the November election. Ten Republicans and eight Democrats were actively campaigning by April, 2007. In 2012, a year-and-a-half before the opening gates of the Iowa caucuses were flung open, nine Republican horsemen and one Republican horsewoman, fearing an Obama apocalypse, grabbed their reins, in hopes of capturing the party's presidential nomination. By contrast, in Britain, election campaigns last about a month.

Why does the American presidential election campaign last so long? Why does it start so early? Running for president costs a lot of money, and candidates need time to raise the cash to pay for television advertisements and campaign staff. They need to develop a viable organization, with competent consultants, pollsters, speechwriters, and rank-and-file volunteers. They must build a reservoir of voter support in early caucus and primary states like Iowa and New Hampshire. To be successful, candidates must also gain national visibility through news coverage. "Visibility," Nelson Polsby and his colleagues note, "is important because news media coverage introduces candidates to the voters and shapes popular perceptions of the various contenders" (Polsby et al., 2012, p. 100). National news coverage also serves a heuristic function: It conveys key information to party leaders and fundraisers, suggesting that the candidate is a viable contender for the race. It is a strange, self-fulfilling process. A candidate gains coverage in the media because he or she is deemed a serious contender, and media attention causes the candidate to be an ever-more viable candidate for office.

The pre-primary portion of the campaign has been called the "invisible primary." The name bespeaks an appreciation that the primary—and caucus—period actually begins months before the first votes are counted, as candidates sponsor fundraisers, try to increase voter recognition, and strive to gain credibility with the news media (Polsby et al., 2012). To gain more insight into the political communication dynamics of the pre-primaries, I focus on the two most recent presidential elections.

2008

Hillary Clinton announced her candidacy for the nomination in January, 2007, forthrightly declaring on her website that "I'm in. And I'm in to win." Obama was the upstart, "a freshman senator with an exotic name, just two years out of the Illinois statehouse" (Wolffe, 2009, p. 49). But he had a gift for political oratory and had cultivated a national reputation after a riveting speech at the 2004 Democratic national convention. His message was bipartisanship, unity, and the need to find solutions outside the poll-driven brand of politics-as-usual. The message—pre-tested by Obama's pollsters—was popular with voters. Democrats wanted change, promised by Obama, more than experience, emphasized by Clinton (Heilemann & Halperin, 2010).

It came to a head on November 10, 2007 at the Jefferson–Jackson Dinner held in Des Moines, Iowa. The event, named after two iconic presidents and less a dinner than a mass political rally, was a Democratic Party ritual that attracted thousands in presidential election years. Clinton delivered a red-meat speech that emphasized that "we should be turning up the heat on the Republicans." Obama opted to take a different approach, choosing not to evoke partisan anger, but instead to emphasize the need to reject "the same old Washington textbook campaigns in favor of bringing the country together around bipartisan change in which everyone could believe." His ringing oratory bespoke an authenticity for which so many idealistic young voters hungered. His carefully prepared speech caught the tempo of the crowd and inspired the 9,000 Democrats in the auditorium to thunderous applause and ovations. The speech impressed Democratic Party leaders and produced a bonanza of pro-Obama press, giving Obama a three-point lead over Clinton in Iowa polls. The Jefferson–Jackson rally was a turning point. Obama had cleverly hit on a message of change that was ripe for voters tired of eight years of strife, war, and Republican rule. Democratic voters found themselves entranced by the twin mantras of "Change We Can Believe In" and "Yes, We Can."

At the same time, the Obama team recognized early on that it needed to pull out all the stops to win the January Iowa caucuses. If Clinton emerged victorious in Iowa, the political wind now at her back, she could develop a momentum that could easily carry her through the rest of the state contests. But if Obama could defeat her in Iowa, he could puncture a hole in the vaunted Clinton armor and alter the dynamics of the race. Harnessing social media to recruit volunteers and money, the campaign developed a formidable organization. It engaged in old-fashioned grass roots organizing, carried out by an army of volunteers that reminded older Democratic veterans of the legions that canvassed for Eugene McCarthy and Robert F. Kennedy 40 years earlier. Clinton, by contrast, seemed to be oblivious to Iowa, the eyes and ears of the campaign fixated on the national level. As a result, she failed to build a strong organization in a state that is accustomed to door-to-door retail campaigning (Balz & Johnson, 2009; Popkin, 2012; see Figure 13.2).

Figure 13.2 Hillary Clinton and Barack Obama jousted for the 2008 Democratic presidential nomination in a tight race, characterized by critical pre-primary performances, polling, and horse race-style news coverage.

Getty Images

Meanwhile, on the Republican side of the ticket, Rudy Giuliani led the GOP pack in the polls and, in the fall of 2007, picked up endorsements from prominent Republican governors and senators. The future looked bright. But strangely, the public official who had embraced the principles of relentless preparation and conveying strong beliefs throughout his career failed to develop a message suited to a national audience (Popkin, 2012). Resting on his laurels, Giuliani fell vulnerable to a Joe Biden quip: "There's only three words he mentions in a sentence: a noun, a verb, and 9/11."

Then Giuliani was hit by a spate of bad news: negative coverage that stemmed from his professional associations and marital infidelity. Bernard B. Kerrick, appointed by Giuliani to serve as New York City Police Commissioner, was indicted on 16 charges, including tax fraud and making false statements. The charges raised questions about Giuliani's professional judgment. The *coup de grâce* was the drip-drip of titillating stories of Giuliani's marital infidelities, well known in New York but not in the country as a whole. This included news detailing how he informed his second wife in a press conference that he wanted a separation; allegations that he publicly cavorted with two other women while married and mayor of New York; and reliable reports that he was on bad terms with his two children, with his daughter declaring her support for Obama, even as her father ran for president. The stories were not biased against Giuliani; he was fair game for tough coverage as a candidate for president. But the news articles undoubtedly had an impact, leading Republican voters to question some of their initial enthusiasm for the former New York City mayor. He was already unpopular with many Republicans because of his liberal positions on social issues, and the news punctured holes in Giuliani's big-city shield.

Strategically, Giuliani played his cards close to the vest. He chose to focus on big industrial states like Florida, New York, and New Jersey, where his urban appeal seemed strongest. He deemphasized early state contests in Iowa, New Hampshire, and South Carolina. But this would turn out to be a perilous strategy, one that would ultimately sink his candidacy.

2012

When an incumbent president runs for reelection, the strategic framework revolves primarily around the incumbent's record. Challengers charge that the incumbent has failed to deliver on promises made to the electorate. Presidents defend their record, while also adopting an "above the battle" posture toward the election. In 2012, the election was about Obama's performance on the economy, a theme the Republican candidates hit over and over again.

Once it became clear that conservative politicians with celebrity wattage—Sarah Palin, New Jersey Governor Chris Christie, and Indiana Governor Mitch Daniels—were not going to run, Mitt Romney became the early-on favorite to win the nomination. This meant he was the front-runner and would receive the benefits of the front-runner scenario (lots of press), but also accrue its costs, as reporters would be searching to unearth unfavorable stories about him, his political record, and his performance as head of a private equity firm. Journalists produce these stories not because they dislike the frontrunner or disagree with his or her policies, but because they see it as their job to reveal information that could cause voters to raise appropriate questions about a potential nominee or president. At the same time, the news offered a temporary boon to the candidacy of Texas Governor Rick Perry, the attractive three-term Texas governor with conservative credentials and a record of accomplishments in the Lone Star state.

News coverage helped build the candidacies of lesser-known contenders. *The New Yorker* profiled Minnesota Congresswoman Michele Bachmann, describing her personal and political characteristics (Lizza, 2011). Bachmann viewed herself as an ardent Christian conservative who had compassionately adopted 23 foster children. She staunchly opposed same-sex marriage, believing that being gay is a "personal enslavement." She called on her religious values in her quest for the Republican presidential nomination (Lizza, 2011). Bachmann garnered positive press when she won an August Iowa straw poll, an event of purely symbolic significance since it is more straw than poll, there being no scientific basis to the selection of respondents, who consist of Iowa Republicans who show up at a delightful summer festival that features a lavish supply of barbecue and entertainment, the courtesy of the presidential candidates.

In a similar fashion, news elevated the "outsider" candidacy of Herman Cain, a religiously conservative former CEO of Godfather's Pizza and restaurant association lobbyist. Ever since Watergate soured the American public on Washington, candidates from outside the conventional political milieu, such as wealthy businessman Ross Perot, who topped the polls for a time in 1992, seem refreshingly untainted by the deal-making of Washington. They hold out a certain appeal and, until their own political skeletons emerge, they hold sway with the electorate. And so it was with Cain. As he appeared more frequently on television and in TV forums, articulating an appealingly simple tax reform plan with a memorable "9-9-9" mantra (9% tax on personal income, business transactions, and federal sales), he ascended in the polls. News, advancing a bandwagon scenario, elevated his prominence. But it also led to his undoing.

During November of 2011, several women came forward, charging that Cain had sexually harassed them, one charging he ran his hand up her dress, saying "You want a job, right?" Although Cain forcefully denied the charges, his poll numbers, particularly among women, dropped. Faced with negative press and sagging poll numbers, he recognized that his campaign was unsustainable and dropped out of the race in early December.

Then came the political debates. Debates play an important role in presidential campaigns, particularly presidential debates (see Chapter 16). The number of primary debates has vastly increased in recent elections, and they have come to exert an impact on the nomination process. Debates help voters to decide how candidates perform on the big stage, wrestle with issues, and communicate complex ideas. Party leaders look to see which candidates best capture party ideology and promise to be the most viable contenders.

In 2012, the debates exerted substantial effects. Romney held his own, avoiding any mistakes or gaffes. But Rick Perry did not fare so well. Political observers and conservatives alike agreed that he had been unfocused, incoherent, and seemingly unable to put together a lucid sentence. Just as he hoped to revive his reputation, he committed a

Figure 13.3 Rick Perry, a Texas governor and one-time leading candidate for the 2012 Republican nomination, faltered and quit the race after disappointing performances in pre-primary debates.

AFP/Getty Images

deadly stumble in a November debate in Michigan. Stating that as president he would eliminate three federal agencies, he could name only two. For the life of him he could not articulate the third department he pledged to eviscerate. He counted on his fingers and ferreted through his notes. When the moderator asked if he could name the third agency, he simply and sadly said, "I can't" (Shear & Oppel, 2011). It was brain freeze in Michigan. After a painful 53 seconds of hemming and hawing, all he could offer was "Sorry, Oops." With a media outlet describing his performance with a paraphrase of the Brittany Spears song, "Oops, he did it again," and scores of negative press, Perry never regained his footing (see Figure 13.3).

Debates provide an opportunity for candidates to demonstrate political expertise. Perry's repeated failure to do this in a much-watched media forum suggested he was not ready for the rough-and-tumble prime-time stage of presidential campaigns. He experienced a drumbeat of negative coverage, consistent with the storyline of the losing ground candidate.

Complementing their efforts to perform well in debates and capture favorable news coverage, candidates strive to gain the approval of key groups and important leaders in their party. In 2012, Republican contenders wooed Tea Party conservatives, and in 2008, Clinton and Obama courted African American leaders, realizing that their endorsement carried weight with rank-and-file voters.

Lessons from the Pre-Primaries

These vignettes highlight the role that a number of factors—campaign management, news, and debates—play during the early portion of the campaign. Complementing these examples, research shows that increases in poll ratings, influential political endorsements, and media coverage during the pre-primary period significantly forecast a candidate's success in subsequent primaries (Cohen et al., 2008). Based on these examples and research, what themes emerge? What more general lessons can be gleaned from the vignettes and scholarship? Four lessons emerge:

1. *Messages matter.* A candidate with a thematic message (e.g., Barack Obama in 2008) can attract supporters hungry for a resonant appeal. A candidate who fails to articulate a compelling logic for a candidacy (Giuliani in 2008) peters out.
2. *Public speeches count.* Even during the invisible pre-primaries, partisan voters attend to what candidates say and how they say it. Obama—and Hillary Clinton too—gave compelling speeches in public forums. Republican Rick Perry performed poorly during the debates. Mediated public appearances during the pre-primaries play a pivotal role in image formation.
3. *News can make or break a candidacy.* In 2008, Obama was seen as a promising

new figure, and he garnered positive press for his oratorical skills, large crowds, and exciting, consultant-tested message (Belt, Just, & Crigler, 2012). In 2012, favorable reports lifted Bachmann and Cain for a time, but bad news killed Cain's campaign. Journalists exert an important gatekeeping function during this early phase of the campaign.

4. *Pre-primaries lay the groundwork for the stage of campaigns.* Candidates who attract a solid financial base, shore up voter support, and are regarded as serious candidates by news media in the pre-primary stage can advance during primaries and caucuses. Candidates who fail to achieve these objectives will not break out of the pack.

IOWA AND NEW HAMPSHIRE

Suppose we started from scratch and wanted to devise the best way to structure the nominations system. We might use the general election as a model and hold a national primary election for each party, giving each candidate a fair chance to gain a majority of votes. Or we might propose a series of regional primaries. There could be primary elections in the North, South, East, and West, perhaps staggered to keep political energy levels high. Alternatively, if we felt that it was important for each state to hold a primary, we might emphasize the big, representative states in each region, letting them hold their primaries (or caucuses) first. What we probably would not want to do is to pick two small, totally unrepresentative states, arrange that they hold their elections first, and then suggest that candidates who did not fare well in these state contests should withdraw from the race.

But that is exactly how the process works!

The first and pivotal electoral contests take place in Iowa and New Hampshire. Iowa and New Hampshire have lots of strengths: low crime, pleasant life-style, bucolic beauty (e.g., New Hampshire's breathtaking White Mountains and Iowa's verdant farmland; see Figure 13.4). But they hardly represent the country as a whole. The states are both more rural than urban. Iowa is in the heart of the Corn Belt; New Hampshire, called "the Granite State," is filled with quarries. Iowa has the 30th highest population and New Hampshire is ranked 42nd. They are overwhelmingly White (Iowa, 89 percent and New Hampshire, 92 percent). Their demographics, economics, climate, and some of their politics (New Hampshire's libertarian state motto is "Live Free or Die") do not mirror the rest of the country. And yet, as sure as farmers harvest Iowa corn in October and syrup lovers produce maple sugar in New Hampshire every February, the presidential campaigns expend enormous amounts of time and resources in the Corn Belt and Granite State every four years.

Figure 13.4 The Iowa (left) and New Hampshire (right) winters offer breathtaking views of snow-capped beauty. Iowa and New Hampshire are sites of the first crucial tests in the presidential nominations. Their natural beauty notwithstanding, their populace does not closely resemble the nation-as-whole, making the states odd choices for pivotal nominating events.

Getty Images/David Q. Cavagnaro and Getty Images/Larry Landolfi

Why Iowa? Why New Hampshire? There are historical reasons. New Hampshire has held the nation's first primary since 1920. Iowa has held caucuses since the mid-19th century. (There are actually several different successive Iowa caucuses—precinct, county, and state; hence the use of the plural above.) The Hawkeye State caucuses assumed importance in 1976. A little-known Georgia governor, Jimmy Carter, recognized the political import of a strong early performance in Iowa. Devoting energy and resources into the state, Carter came in first, although he garnered just 28 percent of the vote, less than the 37 percent who said they were uncommitted to any candidate. Nonetheless, the news media saw a story—or, perhaps, created one.

Iowa and New Hampshire capture the lion's share of media attention during the primary campaign period. This attention is far out of proportion to what one would expect, based on their population and the number of electoral votes the two states command. Some years back, when researchers first content-analyzed news coverage of Iowa and New Hampshire, they came across an interesting paradox. The two states—which accounted for just 3 percent of the U.S. population and 10 percent of the 270 Electoral College votes needed for presidential election—received 34 percent of the television network news coverage of the primaries (Lichter, Amundson, & Noyes, 1988). The news coverage that the two states receive dwarfs the amount given to primaries in larger states, like California, New York, and Texas (see also Buell, 2000).

It is not just the news media that focus heavily on these events. The candidates themselves devote extensive resources to winning or placing in Iowa and New Hampshire.

Party leaders closely monitor candidate performances. Fundraisers look to see which candidates are winners and therefore deserving of their support. Active, committed voters from both parties use the results to make judgments about which candidates they will support in their own state primaries. Are these two contests politically consequential because the media lavish coverage on them, or do the media lavish coverage because they are politically consequential? It is a little bit of both, as media coverage has established in the eyes of voters and political elites that winning outcomes can preordain the success of candidates in the fight for the nomination (see Mayer, 2010). "Were it not for the media," two scholars note, "the Iowa caucus and New Hampshire primary results would be about as relevant to the presidential nomination as opening-day baseball scores are to a pennant race" (Paletz & Entman, 1981, p. 36).

Frontloading

You cannot easily separate the press from politics, and these two contests are chiseled into the nomination process, key contests that shape the trajectory of presidential nominations. These early competitions—and the primaries that immediately follow New Hampshire—exert a disproportionate impact on party nominations. This is part of a process known as **frontloading**. The nominations are critically influenced by the series of contests that occur early or at the front portion of the process. As Polsby and his colleagues note:

> In practice, frontloading has mostly worked to reduce the amount of time between the beginning of the primary season and the point at which a de facto nominee emerges . . . A frontloaded primary schedule simply accelerates this process, usually producing a nominee in a matter of weeks instead of months.
>
> (2012, p. 115)

Forty years ago, primaries extended from January to June, with many delegates chosen later, in the late spring. Nowadays the process is compressed, with most of the races occurring in January through March and a sizable proportion of the pledged delegates chosen by the end of February (Polsby et al., 2012). In some cases, the presumptive nominee has emerged well before primaries and caucuses have been held in other, more populous and representative states. These states hold their elections later, and they may be of little consequence because consensus around a nominee has been reached. While the primary schedule has stabilized in recent years, possibly reducing frontloading effects, frontloading, coupled with the all-important two early contests, still influences the road to the nominating conventions.

In 2012, Michele Bachmann dropped out of the presidential race after a sixth-place showing in Iowa. Short on funds and unable to show that she could appeal to strong ideological conservatives, Bachmann lacked the financial and political moxie needed to compete in subsequent contests. Rick Perry, plagued by pre-primary problems, came in fifth in Iowa and hoped to revive his candidacy with a victory in the South Carolina primary several weeks later. But when polls suggested he would fare poorly in South Carolina, he dropped out, acknowledging that "there is no viable path forward for me."

Four years earlier, in 2008, Iowa decimated the candidacies of Democratic senators Joe Biden and Christopher Dodd. Both dropped out after poor performances in the Hawkeye State. Over on the Republican side, Rudy Giuliani had pursued an unconventional strategy: avoiding Iowa and New Hampshire, hoping that a victory in the late January Florida primary could propel him to victories in other big states. But after a disappointing third-place finish in the Sunshine State, the New York City mayor, who led the polls at the outset but fell victim to lack of message and a spate of unfavorable news, realized he was done. He withdrew and subsequently endorsed John McCain, the eventual Republican nominee.

But when candidates win Iowa and New Hampshire, they can find themselves propelled to success. Early primary victories bring a flurry of positive press, lofty expectations from influential political leaders, and an outpouring of financial donations from small donors and rich lobbyists who want to be associated with a winner. In short, they generate momentum, what George H.W. Bush termed the "Big Mo."

Effects of Iowa and New Hampshire

In the wake of victory in an early contest, media coverage coalesces, focusing on just one candidate—the winner, or a candidate who exceeds expectations. Considerations of space and time, and desire to develop a compelling storyline, push the media to focus on one or two candidates. These candidates then become celebrities, the ones who suddenly have been separated from the pack and are the star-studded foci of attention.

With just a week separating Iowa and New Hampshire, victories in both states can create an aura of inevitability and momentum. This, of course, is what campaigns hope to accomplish. Occasionally, it happens. Carter won both contests in 1976, a signature accomplishment that hurtled his campaign toward the Democratic nomination. In an earlier era, a political unknown like Carter would never have experienced such success. The media attention and surprising victories created the perception that he was a winner. More generally, as Mayer (1987) observed: "The victorious candidate is portrayed as popular, exciting, confident, in control: in short, a leader. His poll ratings are increasing; his organization is growing; his message is catching on; his crowds are large and enthusiastic. His opponents, by contrast, are dead, dying, or in disarray" (p. 14).

In 2008, Obama pulled out all the stops to defeat Hillary Clinton in Iowa. Obama won a decisive victory, with John Edwards coming in second place and Clinton placing a disappointing third. The victory was noteworthy because it showed that an African American candidate could win in a predominately White state. After delivering a thunderous acceptance speech, he sallied forth into mountainous New Hampshire, riding the wave of momentum into Manchester, and basking in a lead that suggested he could deftly defeat Clinton in a one-two Iowa–New Hampshire punch. If that happened, political experts and staffers in both campaigns acknowledged, Clinton would be through.

Now, let's pause a minute. Do you appreciate how silly this is? Iowa commands only 45 pledged convention delegates; New Hampshire has just 22. A candidate needed 2,117 delegate votes to win the Democratic nomination. These states comprised just 67 of the 2,117 delegates needed to win the nomination. As you know, both states bear little resemblance to the Democratic electorate in the host of primaries that followed. No matter. A loss in Iowa followed by a defeat in tiny New Hampshire would, the way the contemporary game is played, derail the campaign of Clinton, a luminary national candidate who had legions of supporters and voters longing to cast ballots in her behalf in their home states. Such is political reality, in which a loss in both of these early states has devastating effects on a candidate's chances to gain the nomination.

Faced with a desperate situation after Iowa, Clinton played herself and turned in what many New Hampshire voters perceived as an authentic moment of raw emotion, tearing up in a New Hampshire coffee shop when someone asked how she managed to present herself so well in the face of tough campaigning. "It's not easy. And I couldn't do it if I didn't passionately believe it was the right thing to do," she said. The widely publicized show of emotion from a famously brittle Hillary Clinton, coupled with the desire of many New Hampshire Democrats to keep Clinton in the race, resulted in a come-from-behind victory over Obama, leading to a shift in momentum and the beginning of an intense, two-candidate primary battle.

The early primary dynamics vary somewhat with the election. In some cases, candidates have won one of the early contests and failed to ride waves of momentum (Cohen et al., 2008). But, generally speaking, a candidate who loses both Iowa and New Hampshire has little chance of winning the nomination. The two contests winnow the list of viable candidates for the nomination.

Lessons from Iowa and New Hampshire

Each campaign is different, with a different slate of candidates, national problems, and political party dynamics. But certain patterns emerge:

Figure 13.5 Bill Clinton campaigned aggressively for the 1992 Democratic presidential nomination, particularly in Iowa and New Hampshire. When he came in second in New Hampshire, after news coverage of a sexual liaison threatened to derail his candidacy, he spun the runner-up outcome as a victory.

Time & Life Pictures/Getty Images

1. *The two contests exert an outsized impact on media coverage and viability percep-tions held by party elites.* Their impact is disproportionate to their size, overall representativeness, and influence in the general election.
2. *Candidates cannot succeed in these states without a good organization and lots of money.* A self-fulfilling prophecy is also at work: Early victories in Iowa and New Hampshire can strengthen organizations and attract more money.
3. *Iowa and New Hampshire exert a winnowing effect on presidential hopefuls, with losses frequently leading candidates to quit the race.* The list of active candidates drops after New Hampshire, because losses lead to perceptions that candidates can't win the nomination and drying up of fundraising dollars.
4. *Victories can sometimes lead to surges of media-created momentum that boost a candidate's poll ratings.* Momentum and surging poll ratings can exert a bandwagon effect. At the same time, candidates try to compensate for anticipated losses by "spinning," or deliberately creating low expectations for success in subsequent primaries. They then turn in a "better than expected" performance, suggesting they are viable, after all. Because reporters and political experts know what is going on, this strategy does not necessarily succeed. Still, candidates spin (see Figure 13.5).

WHAT DO YOU THINK?

What impact do the media exert on the pre-primaries and primary campaigns? Media have helped open up the process to the public and can give wings to a promising candidate. On the other hand, by concentrating coverage on winners, they can make it more difficult for innovative, non-conventional candidates to break out of the pack. How do you balance their positive and negative influences?

OTHER PRIMARIES AND THE REMAINING CAMPAIGN

The fight for the nomination does not end after New Hampshire, even though campaign-weary voters may wish it did. Other states hold their primaries and caucuses, giving voters an opportunity to make their preferences known and offering a test of the political strength of the remaining candidates.

South Carolina has emerged as a key post-New Hampshire test, still early enough in the frontloaded process to make a difference but occurring a sufficient time after the two early contests to give it a distinctive mark. It is also the first southern primary, and the state's cultural identity has emerged as a factor in the election. In 2000, Bush needed to derail McCain, after McCain decisively thumped Bush in New Hampshire. The victory gave McCain a surge of momentum. A searing underground campaign unfolded, tarnishing McCain with a series of hateful, distorted messages. An email message claimed "McCain chose to sire children without marriage," and flyers said he had a "Negro child." The information was false, derived from the fact that the McCains had lovingly adopted a dark-skinned child from Bangladesh years before. Messages falsely claimed McCain's wife was a drug addict and that McCain, who had served in Vietnam and acted courageously as a prisoner of war, had committed treason as a POW (Gooding, 2004). The attacks were never tied to Bush, though political observers suspected Bush consultant Karl Rove, who had a reputation for unleashing dark, deceptive tactics. The campaign was widely believed to have influenced South Carolina Republican voters, resulting in a big Bush win that propelled him to victories in subsequent primary states.

Eight years later, with Obama and Clinton locked in a tight race, the two candidates traded barbs in South Carolina. Bill Clinton, who had stage-managed his wife's campaign from the sidelines and was convinced that she had to fight tougher to win, launched a series of broadsides against Obama. He debunked Obama's much-heralded opposition to the Iraq War, picked at a favorable comment Obama made about former Republican President Ronald Reagan and criticized Obama for waging a negative campaign, appearing to raise the race card. The attacks backfired, offending African Americans and redounding to Obama's benefit. With a state organization formed back in 2007 and 13,000 volunteers canvassing across the state on Election Day, the Obama team was poised for victory, and win he did, trouncing Clinton by a 28 percent margin (Balz & Johnson, 2009). The South Carolina victory, along with the dramatic narrative of a hitherto-unknown African American candidate marching toward the nomination, made a good news story. Obama was the beneficiary of some good press, in keeping with the bandwagon storyline.

After South Carolina, the campaign turns primarily into a media blitz, with candidates campaigning via political advertisements and news generated through local appearances and debates. The retail, homespun approach of the early primaries gives way to a media- and technology-driven campaign.

In 2008, Clinton waged a strong campaign in the later primaries, campaigning with guts and vitality. She narrowly lost the nomination because Obama out-organized her, exploited new technology more effectively, amassed a larger, more committed volunteer base, and expended critical energy on caucuses, as well as primaries. Clinton, by contrast, overlooked the delegates that could be amassed from the relatively large number of caucuses.

There were communication-based reasons too. Obama's charisma, strategically selected message (change rather than experience), and the excitement he generated—America could actually elect an African American president—touched the souls of liberal Democrats. He had, after all, "created a kind of excitement more typical of rock stars than presidential candidates" (Cohen et al., 2008, p. 347). And although Obama's press ebbed and flowed (it plummeted when it was revealed he was linked with an incendiary Chicago preacher), he benefited from more favorable press, primarily because he was a bandwagon candidate upending a vaunted front-runner and also offered an appealing personal narrative. Critics suggested that the media subtly downgraded Clinton because she was a woman and elevated Obama because he was a cool, charismatic African American candidate (see Chapter 9). In the view of some scholars, the news media viewed Obama as an avatar of racial progress, while minimizing the degree to which Hillary Clinton served as a complementary symbol of great progress in gender equality (Lawrence & Rose, 2010).

Four years later, it was the Republicans who battled it out in key state primaries and caucuses. They clashed in South Carolina, in the large number of state contests occurring on one day, dubbed Super Tuesday, and in primaries that occurred throughout the spring. Former Pennsylvania senator Rick Santorum, who held out a strong appeal to Tea Party and White evangelical Republican voters, swept three contests—Colorado,

Minnesota, and Missouri—in one day. Santorum led Romney for a time in a national poll of Republican voters, as his conservative positions on social issues were more in sync with those of Republican voters. In the end, bankrolled by his personal fortune, Romney could easily sustain the costs required to pay for television advertisements in the final primaries and caucuses. He clinched the nomination in late April.

Lessons from the Other State Contests

1. *The candidate with the largest, wealthiest organization fares best during the later contests, as the campaign focuses primarily on media buys and political advertising.*
2. *Issues matter.* With the race winnowed to just two or three contenders, voters do consider candidates' positions on issues, particularly hot-button topics that touch on core values.

EVALUATING THE MEDIA-BASED NOMINATION SYSTEM

This discussion has shed light on the political and communication dynamics of the presidential nomination campaign. It is also important to look at normative issues. Is the current system good or bad? Does it advance democratic aims or adversely affect the body politic? This section examines two key aspects: frontloading and the media horse race coverage (see Reflections box). The intent is not to advocate one position or another, but instead to examine the nettlesome issues involved in remedies to change the nomination system and political news.

REFLECTIONS: JOCKEYING WITH THE HORSE RACE

Reporters love horse race, strategic game-based journalism. They jockey (pardon the pun!) to obtain the most prestigious political beats. Truth be told, many love the adrenalin-filled excitement that horse race stories provide and the thrills and spills of covering the biggest, grandest competition in the land. The problem is that these stories can trivialize politics and reduce ideological debates about the future of the country to superficial questions of who is ahead in the polls, and why.

It's not just the quantity of horse race stories that bothers critics. It is journalists' relentless promotion of the cynical notion that politicians are driven exclusively by winning and by nothing else. Reporters believe that virtually every candidate action—a speech, policy decision, or appeal to particular voters—is driven by winning and strategizing. For example, during the 2012 presidential campaign, Republican nominee Mitt Romney developed a plan that he hoped would help the U.S. gain energy independence, while also creating millions of jobs in oil drilling and manufacturing. The plan emphasized shifting control over the nation's energy resources from the federal government to the states. But a front-page *New York Times* article suggested, based on interviews with political, business and environmental leaders, that "Mitt Romney is making a bid for anti-Washington voters in key Western states, while dangling the promise of a big reward to major campaign supporters from the energy industry" (Lipton & Krauss, 2012, p. A1). The reporters may have been right. The plan could have been based in cynical election-year calculations. But academic critics argue that reporting like this is too cynical, ascribing the most self-interested motives to politicians. They note that public officials do articulate plans that reflect the party's platform or the needs of their constituents (Cappella & Jamieson, 1997). Candidates are not always motivated by naked self-interest, but, rather, by consistency with previous positions they have taken and a desire to serve constituents.

You would not know that from viewing press stories. Journalists frame politics negatively and through the lens of strategy. Political communication research has documented that these frames can exert strong cognitive effects. Strategically framed news strengthens recall of strategic information, while issue-oriented news bolsters recall of issues. What's more, strategy-framed news can activate cynical beliefs, for example, strengthening perceptions that "the candidates were willing to do whatever it took to win" and "nobody would talk about the hard issues, such as taxes, because that would lose voters" (Cappella & Jamieson, 1997, p. 266; see also deVreese & Elenbaas, 2008). Game-framed news can even reduce thoughtful, policy-based reasoning (Pingree, Scholl, & Quenette, 2012).

Emboldened by research, critics argue that the news overstates the extent to which politics is a strategic game. By doing so, it becomes part of the problem, producing a corrosive cynicism and distrust that discourages participation in the political system. Horse race stories that allocate space and time based on which candidate is most likely to win can also favor established candidates, perhaps to the exclusion of non-traditional political figures.

Continued

Journalists and those who defend horse race coverage do not disagree that news emphasizes the game. They argue that elections *are* horse races and candidates are adrenalin-charged, victory-obsessed, and hell-bent on winning at all costs. This is the credo of political consultants. Recall the consultant, quoted in Chapter 12, who said that "in political consulting winning is everything. As a result, no cost is too great. Survival depends on it." Reporters argue that it is incumbent upon them to present politics as it is, not as idealists would like it to be. What's more, they argue, horse race stories can stimulate interest in high-octane presidential campaigns, particularly among partisans and undecided voters (see http://www.cjr.org/campaign_desk/in_defense_of_the_right_kind_o.php?page=all for interesting pro-horse race arguments).

Critics like Cappella and Jamieson put forth a middle ground, making a useful distinction here between cynicism and skepticism. They argue that the journalists should be skeptical or wary of political campaigns, but open to information that might prove them wrong. They ought not to be cynical. Cynicism involves distrust of people, disbelief in the possibility of honesty or goodness in people's motives and the belief that naked self-interest drives everything.

One remedial idea, adopted at a variety of newspapers in the 1990s, emphasized public journalism. News organizations guided by this approach asked citizens to indicate the problems they regarded as most important, and editors organized news coverage around these issues. Another way to get around horse race coverage is to encourage the development of articles that summarize candidates' policy proposals and systematically evaluate whether the proposals are likely to work in practice.

Finally, news organizations could be rewarded for producing issue-oriented, rather than horse race, stories. Readers could click an Internet icon whenever they read an article that increased their understanding of politics. Readers' votes would be conveyed to a national journalism endowment, which could give a grant to the news outlet that produced the article (Gutmann & Thompson, 2012).

Alternatively, perhaps we should not try to meddle in political journalism, but instead recognize that the election is a first-to-the-finish-line, fiercely competitive race, and it is the job of reporters to describe it. According to this view, political campaigns are not designed to change the system, but to offer a mechanism by which candidates vie for public office. What do you think?

Frontloading and the Nominations

Let's be clear about one thing at the outset: There is broad consensus that, for all the shortcomings in the present system, it is far and away better than the old-style method, in which party leaders chose candidates in closed-door sessions. The current system happens out in the open, exposing candidate and media foibles to the sunlight of democracy. But this does not mean that the present procedures are free of problems or anywhere near ideal.

Critics point out that the nomination process is too long, beginning a year-and-a-half before the general election. First, the long campaign dispirits voters and expends hundreds of millions of dollars. Second, as noted earlier, the current procedure provides disproportionate attention to Iowa and New Hampshire. Third, frontloading shunts aside many state primaries and caucuses. In some instances, the presumptive nominee has already been chosen before voters in these later primary states vote, affording them less influence on the nominations than individuals who happen to live in states that hold their contests earlier. Fourth, the pervasive impact of an event- and narrative-driven media can distort the process, elevating the importance of dramatic but peripheral events, inducing voters to select candidates based on superficial horse race criteria, and also according arbitrary shifts of momentum unwarranted impact on political outcomes.

On the other hand, defenders remind us, the contemporary system has certain strengths. The long campaign tests candidates, weeding out those who lack the political savvy or psychological stamina to withstand the slings and arrows of a presidential nomination. It forces candidates to build a cohesive organization in a multitude of states. To the extent that these skills are required in the nation's chief executive, perhaps the current system does a pretty good job of separating out the presidential wheat from the chaff. While frontloading continues to be a problem, the past two election campaigns suggest that Iowa's and New Hampshire's effects are less pronounced than in years past. In 2008 and 2012, candidates actively contested primaries through late April, giving voters in later-primary states a greater role in the eventual outcome. Momentum effects also have dissipated (Cohen et al., 2008). Obama could not carry his Iowa victory into success in New Hampshire. Romney performed well in Iowa and won New Hampshire, but lost South Carolina.

In addition, defenders of the present system question the claim that voters base decisions on superficial candidate criteria. They argue that primary, and especially caucus, voters do make reasonable judgments about candidates' personal attributes and issue positions. Indeed, it is plausible to argue that voters are cannier than critics allege; they are not so much bowled over by horse race stores as they use this information to make rational judgments about which candidate will be the most viable party nominee. Lastly, for all the media's faults, they do enhance transparency, allowing voters to see how candidates comport themselves in public and come to grips with complex campaign issues. In this way, they offer a window into the temperament of the men and women who seek the highest office in the land.

Over the years, a number of novel remedies have been advanced, such as a national primary election, regional primaries, and shortening the length of the primary season by having primaries begin in June rather than January. Each of the remedies has problems and, in any event, the prospects for reform are non-existent because both parties are committed to maintaining the current system.

In the end, all nominating procedures have shortcomings. The question is which system is fairest, offers newcomers, as well as established candidates, an equitable shot at the nomination, maximizes the opportunities for voter preferences to influence the outcome, and does not arbitrarily advantage certain candidates or groups. Judged in this way, the present system comes off better than is commonly believed. However, in view of its varied shortcomings, there continues to be a need for improvement. One can only hope that some creative tweaking of ideas might produce a better nominating system for the two parties (see suggestions put forth at http://fixtheprimaries.com/solutions/ for more ideas).

NOMINATING CONVENTIONS

Conventions as Political Infomercials

Once upon a time, political parties held nominating conventions, and they were filled with drama. A candidate might not be nominated the first time—on the first ballot—but on a second or third ballot. (Lincoln was nominated on the third ballot in 1860.) Party leaders called the shots. Everything happened behind closed doors. The public knew nothing. Then, in the mid-20th century, conventions became somewhat more transparent, television covered them from gavel to gavel, and journalists reveled in the grandiosity of relaying history as it happened. But, of course, in those days the electorate was left out of the picture; party leaders could control what was brought to the floor, and dissident perspectives were not tolerated.

Thankfully, those days are gone. Nowadays, primary and caucus elections select the party nominees; conventions ratify the selection and promote the ticket before a national audience. Conventions function primarily as a week-long advertisement for the candidates and the party, "effectively a four-night miniseries before an audience of 20 million people or more" (Zeleny & Rutenberg, 2008). Party leaders hire media production experts who script the convention down to the wire. What looks spontaneous to a television audience has been scheduled, orchestrated, pre-planned, revised, and then readied for final production well in advance. Designed to present the party in the best possible political light, conventions are animated by theatrics, featuring a cast of thousands of delegates and emphasizing a coherent storyline that candidates can take into the fall campaign. Recognizing that the conventions are one of the few times when voters are motivated to tune in to partisan speeches, parties do their best to entice viewers, hoping the speeches, party ideology, and miscellaneous hoopla will influence opinions and behavior.

It has become an increasingly theatrical, technological show. Even as far back as 1996, conventions exploited computer technologies. Websites, then an innovation, trumpeted the accomplishments of the nominees. At the Democratic convention, President Bill Clinton addressed the convention delegates from a giant TV screen as he traveled across the Midwest. "From time to time," a columnist sarcastically observed, "he beams down at the convention . . . a loving apolitical presence who has paused along his route of march to extend a warm, electronic hug to those who await him" (Feagler, 1996).

A dozen years later, in 2008, both party conventions used theatrics—props, lighting, and special effects. Obama accepted his party's nomination at an outdoor stadium, with fireworks, video screens, and rock star entertainment. "On the 50-yard line of the football field, at a reported cost of $6 million, strategists erected a plywood Parthenon, its fake Grecian columns suggesting the White House," critic William Safire (2008) observed. Parodying Obama's book, *The audacity of hope*, Safire derided it as "the audacity of hype."

In 2012, Republican Party leaders called on producers and designers who had worked on Broadway and had built television sets for Oprah Winfrey. Their mission? To create a milieu that would change perceptions of nominee Mitt Romney, who came off stiff, formal, and not particularly warm. To do this, they constructed a $2.5 million Frank Lloyd Wright-style stage. "From its dark-wood finish to the brightly glowing high-resolution screens in the rafters that look like skylights, every aspect of the stage has been designed to convey warmth, approachability and openness," a reporter wrote (Peters, 2012a, p. 1A). They wanted it to appear not as the formal stage of a convention, but informal and folksy—like you were looking into a neighbor's living room. With broadcast networks showing only an hour of the convention in prime time in 2012, party leaders recognized that they had to capture attention and efficiently communicate just the right political image.

Contemporary nominating conventions are ceremonial rituals, designed to rally the base and activate partisan fervor. They are scripted, patriotic events, filled with feel-good moments and heart-felt spousal endorsements of the nominee, inspirational movies, and an endless supply of red, white, and blue balloons. At some basic philosophical level, a convention, as columnist Frank Bruni (2012a) observed, "is a communal lie, during which speakers and members of the audience project an excitement 10 times greater than what they really feel and a confidence about the candidate that they only wish they could muster" (p. A21).

Partisanship and Rhetoric

Inside the convention, serious business does occur. Conventions are gatherings of the party faithful, who—though they do disagree among themselves on issues, some years more than others—collectively espouse a particular philosophy of politics. Articulating and standing behind a particular ideology is one of the strengths parties offer, and conventions are opportunities to solidify and communicate these ideals. The party's ideology is summarized in its platform, a document that few voters read, but which offers a succinct statement of party positions. As political scientist Byron E. Shafer notes, "national party conventions are the major, purely partisan, formal institutions of American politics" (2010, p. 264). Political speeches play a key role in rallying the troops, particularly keynote addresses. In 2004 a young Barack Obama energized Democrats, using poise, eloquent content, and adroit turns of the phrase as he intoned that "there's not a liberal America and a conservative America; there's the United States of America."

Vice presidential candidates and presidential contenders who are relatively new to the national stage use speeches accepting the party's nomination to introduce themselves to the voting public. In 2008, Sarah Palin persuasively portrayed herself as an ordinary American, reared with good, small-town values, unimpressed by media elites, a 21st century female incarnate of Jimmy Stewart's Mr. Smith in *Mr. Smith Goes to Washington.* Four years later, the Republican vice presidential nominee, Wisconsin Congressman Paul Ryan, embellished the small-town biographical narrative, describing how he lived on the same block in Janesville, Wisconsin where he grew up and was still a member of "the same parish where I was baptized." He embraced the conservative ethos of small government, pledging to place "hard limits on the size of government," thrilling conservative convention delegates (see http://www.politico.com/news/stories/0812/80423.html).

Presidential contenders use their acceptance speeches to offer a touching biographical story and a narrative designed to propel them into the fall campaign. In an age of personalized politics, relating raw emotion sensitively—and with apparent sincerity—is a valued attribute. In 1992 Bill Clinton told his audience that he never met his father, who was killed in a car wreck, but was raised by a dedicated mother, who taught him about family values, sacrifice, and hard work.

Scripted and hokey as convention speeches can sometimes be, they can also inspire. In 1992, Mary Fisher, a mother of two who had improbably become HIV-positive, moved the Republican national convention to tears when she said, "I am one with a black infant struggling with tubes in a Philadelphia hospital. I am one with the lonely gay man sheltering a flickering candle from the cold wind of his family's rejection." In 1980, Senator Ted Kennedy, after mounting an unsuccessful challenge to President Carter, delivered a bombastic speech that concluded with this now-legendary summation: "For all those whose cares have been our concern, the work goes on, the cause endures, the hope still lives, and the dream shall never die" (see http://www.americanrhetoric.com/speeches/tedkennedy1980dnc.htm). Thus, inspirational rhetoric, a time-honored political tradition, still continues to move audiences.

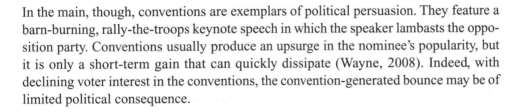

In the main, though, conventions are exemplars of political persuasion. They feature a barn-burning, rally-the-troops keynote speech in which the speaker lambasts the opposition party. Conventions usually produce an upsurge in the nominee's popularity, but it is only a short-term gain that can quickly dissipate (Wayne, 2008). Indeed, with declining voter interest in the conventions, the convention-generated bounce may be of limited political consequence.

The time-honored convention rituals—as when a convention delegate sanctimoniously intones, "Madame Chairperson, the residents of the great state of Florida, known far and wide for the quality of their oranges and the beauty of their beaches, and the non-partisan brilliance of their sun proudly nominate . . ."—are old-hat and induce fatigue after the months-long televised primaries and caucuses (Carr, 2012). Media critic David Carr suggests that conventions could gain political relevance by offering backstage, unfiltered access to behind-the-scenes conversations at conventions, showing viewers a host of unscripted scenes and telling them, reality TV show-style, what actually goes on at party conventions. Political parties, which like to tightly control the proceedings to avoid a gaffe or embarrassing mistake, might cringe, but the change might engage voters and promote conventions in an age when the very word "convention" provokes skepticism and a yawn. Carr probably made his suggestion tongue-in-cheek, but it points up the need of increasing the relevance of conventions.

WHAT DO YOU THINK?

Conventions have become three-day promotional events for the political parties. Recognizing this, many voters avoid them. Thinking about what conventions offer political parties, as well as ways of adapting them to the contemporary digital age, what suggestions can you offer to make conventions more interesting and relevant?

CONCLUSIONS

Primaries and caucuses are the arteries and veins of the presidential nomination process. They are open and relatively transparent, and media-driven. Although the process is substantially more democratic than in the 19th century, when nominees were chosen by party leaders in much-mythologized smoke-filled rooms, the contemporary system has its own set of rituals, idiosyncrasies, and problems.

There are four phases of the nominating process: (1) pre-primaries; (2) the critical Iowa and New Hampshire contests; (3) the long series of state primaries, and (4) the late summer conventions. Pre-primaries lay the groundwork. Candidates who recruit substantial funds, perform well in candidate debates, gain respectable poll numbers, and are viewed as serious contenders by news media begin the early primaries with a decided advantage. Through historical quirks, the Iowa caucuses and New Hampshire primary have assumed roles in nomination politics that are far out of proportion to their size or overall number of representatives. The nomination process is frontloaded: Early contests exert critical effects, and the bulk of the races occur in the first couple months, rather than over the course of the spring. The early primaries and caucuses winnow the contenders, with losers in Iowa and New Hampshire forced to drop out as a result of a reduced fundraising base and perceptions that their candidacies are not viable. And, given the role media play in transmitting and generating expectations, perceptions can quickly become synonymous with reality.

The news media cover the early contests, as well as the bulk of the campaign, as a horse race, a strategic game in which winning, losing, and poll numbers dominate stories. Guided by professional journalistic routines, news promotes storylines—the front-runner scenario, the losing ground storyline, and bandwagon narrative—that can influence electoral outcomes. Favorable news coverage of winners in Iowa and New Hampshire, and diminished focus on losers, can advance the victors' fortunes, while pushing losers out of the race. The nomination phase ends with conventions, highly partisan events that bring out the party faithful and are filled with ringing rhetoric that solidifies parties. In a media and Internet era, conventions function largely as choreographed infomercials, theatrical send-offs to the fall campaign.

What is the normative verdict on the nominating system and the impact of news media? Critics argue that the nomination process is far too long, gives disproportionate attention to two unrepresentative states, and assigns undue weight to peripheral increases in media momentum. What's more, frontloading shunts aside contests that occur later in the process, to some degree disenfranchising these voters from the nomination process. At the same time, critics point to shortcomings in the role news plays, noting that it trivializes politics, gives short shrift to issues, and increases voters' cynicism about the political process. There are, of course, counterarguments to these positions, advanced by political scientists and journalists. Defenders emphasize that the system lets voters know who is best able to survive a grueling test for the presidency, presents substantial news coverage of an intensely competitive race, and provides information that can be useful in evaluating the nominees during the fall campaign. It is a less-than-ideal, crazy-quilt system that manages to offer up reasonably qualified nominees. Until a better system comes along, we are stuck with this one.

14

Persuasion and Political Campaigns

You can view presidential campaigns through a variety of lenses. Campaigns are the essence of democracy, the process by which Americans grant their consent to be governed—the mechanism that confers legitimacy on democratic government. They provide venues for deliberation and opportunities to debate diverse solutions to the nation's problems. They are quadrennial rituals that pump up the nation's political circulation, energizing it with the oxygen of ideas and the adrenalin of hope. But to candidates and consultants, elections are one thing, and one thing only: exercises in persuasion. They are strategic battles to convince Americans to cast their votes in favor of a particular candidate. The weapons are arguments and appeals delivered interpersonally, on television, and in videos streamed across the Internet.

The next three chapters examine the dynamics of political campaign persuasion. The focus is the presidential election, but applications to lower-level races are also examined. This chapter, guided by psychological approaches, lays out the main concepts that drive political persuasion. Chapter 15 discusses political advertising, and Chapter 16 explores the persuasive aspects of presidential debates, while also examining debate strengths and shortcomings.

This chapter draws on persuasion approaches. **Persuasion** research examines the ways that communicator characteristics, the message, and message receivers influence attitude change. The first portion of the chapter focuses on core qualities of the political communicator and the political message, calling on examples from campaigns to illustrate the richness of the concepts. The second section focuses on the message receiver—the voter—by examining two major psychological perspectives on persuasion: the **Elaboration Likelihood Model** and **Social Judgment Theory**. Both shed light on how presidential campaigns construct messages to influence attitudes and voting behavior.

The third section looks at ways that political persuaders attempt to influence voters who harbor strong, passionate attitudes. The chapter takes a more psychological thrust than earlier chapters, necessary to help you appreciate the ways campaign messages try to get inside the heads of voters to influence their all-important vote decisions. Political candidates cannot influence voters without appreciating how they internally think about and evaluate campaign messages.

WHO SAYS IT AND WHAT THEY SAY

Communicator Qualities

The cornerstone of effective political persuasion is credibility, conveying a credible image and cultivating a favorable impression of political leadership. Credibility dates back to Aristotle, who used the term "ethos" to describe credible communicators. Decades of empirical research have documented that there is not one type of credibility, or one way to convey credibility to an audience, but several. The three key components of credibility are *expertise*, *trustworthiness*, and *good will* (McCroskey & Teven, 1999). Expertise is the knowledge, political experience, and ability ascribed to the political communicator. Trustworthiness is a communicator's integrity: honesty, character, safety, and predisposition to say what one means and mean what one says. Good will refers to perceived caring, empathy, and understanding of others' plight.

The trick, persuasion experts will tell you, is to realize that the same persuasive attribute does not operate in all elections. Instead, different aspects of credibility are relevant, depending on the particular electoral circumstance. Let's see how this works by focusing on actual elections where presidential candidates harnessed the powers of expertise, trustworthiness, and good will.

Expertise

President Richard Nixon called on expertise in the 1972 presidential election. His consultants concluded that the gruff, Machiavellian Nixon—famously nicknamed "Tricky Dick"—would not win a contest of likability, nor be seen as a candidate teeming with trust. His adviser Roger Ailes (now the president of Fox News) famously quipped that voters thought of Nixon as "a bore, a pain in the ass . . . who was forty-two years old the day he was born. They figure other kids got footballs for Christmas. Nixon got a briefcase and he loved it" (McGinniss, 1969, p. 103). However, his consultants reasoned, Nixon was respected for his intellect, experience in foreign affairs, and foreign policy accomplishments (notably, his historic 1972 peace mission to China). Nixon's ads stressed not that "you like Nixon," but "you need Nixon" (Diamond & Bates, 1992,

Figure 14.1 Credibility is a key element of political campaign persuasion. But different features of credibility matter in different electoral contexts. In 1972, President Richard M. Nixon, shown here shaking hands, was rarely viewed as a likable political figure. He emphasized his time-honored expertise in politics, resulting in a landslide victory against George McGovern, his Democratic opponent. McGovern tried to bring up Nixon's involvement in Watergate, but lacked credibility.

AFP/Getty Images

p. 180). Nixon was the anti-warm-and-fuzzy candidate, cold and steely. But his messages emphasized that he was smart, understood international issues, and knew how the political world worked. In short, he was a political expert (see Figure 14.1). Nixon thrashed his Democratic opponent, George McGovern. Throughout the campaign, McGovern tried to raise questions about Nixon's corrupt involvement in the Watergate scandal, but McGovern, new to voters and lacking credibility, could not make the case. Nixon was reelected in a landslide. Three years later, it was a different story. Nixon resigned from office, preferring resignation to all-but-certain impeachment in the wake of his complicity in the Watergate scandal. Even his time-honored expertise could not save him.

Trustworthiness

Jimmy Carter is the classic example of a candidate who put trustworthiness to work in a presidential campaign. With the nation reeling from Watergate and ex-President Nixon's jaw-dropping deceptions, Carter recognized that voters hungered for a leader who would level with them. Carter promised that he would "never tell a lie to the American people," and trustworthiness became his mantra (see Figure 14.2). He recognized that, in the wake of the Watergate scandal, trustworthiness trumped expertise in voters' eyes. With his evangelical smile and wholesome visage, Carter, the born-again Christian from sunny Georgia, struck many voters as a refreshing contrast to his opponent, President Gerald Ford. Ford had pardoned Richard Nixon—a compassionate, but controversial, act that angered many voters, and it in turn cast doubts on Ford's integrity. Carter defeated Ford by a razor-thin margin in 1976.

Figure 14.2 With the nation reeling from Watergate, the public yearned for a trustworthy presidential candidate. Jimmy Carter, shown above at the microphone, was more than happy to deliver, emphasizing his honesty and simple country boy appeal.

Getty Images

Good Will

Like trustworthiness, good will emphasizes conveying respect for the audience. But, as the name suggests, good will centers on empathy and the belief that the candidate cares about voters.

The empathy factor emerged in 2012. Mitt Romney, a man of considerable accomplishment and intelligence, came off "inauthentic." "In a confessional era,"—in which politicians are expected to personalize themselves in the media—Romney came off "stilted," like a candidate trying to "add a John Williams score to a corporate balance sheet" (Bruni, 2012a, p. A21). His "wooden monotonous" delivery, lack of variability in his tone, and forced laughs contributed to a perception that he was insincere, inauthentic, and uncaring (Alim & Smitherman, 2012, p. 5). Romney tried to emphasize his time-honored business expertise, but Obama strategists, sensing they had a winning issue, sought to prime compassion and empathy for Americans struggling with economic and unemployment woes.

Obama was able to convey likability to voters—surprising, given that he was such a private person (Dowd, 2012; see Figure 14.3). On the eve of the Democratic convention, he told Iowa voters that he knew they called his health care plan "Obamacare." That suited him fine, because "I do care," he said, emphasizing his concern with protecting the health of millions of Americans. Already struggling, Romney lost the battle for good will when a secretly recorded video revealed that he derogated the 47 percent of Americans who do not pay income taxes. When he said these Americans "believe that they are victims" and do not take "personal responsibility" for their lives, he telegraphed insensitivity to nearly half the population, as even some fellow Republicans lamented. Polls taken in the summer of 2012 showed that sizable majorities of voters in swing states perceived that Obama cared more about the needs and problems of people like them than did Romney (Zeleny & Sussman, 2012a). Although Romney made headway during the fall campaign, conveying empathy in the presidential debates, he could not overcome the good will gap.

WHAT THEY SAY: THE CAMPAIGN MESSAGE

Narrative

Announcer: (quiet symphonic music, accompanied by a video of boats pulling out of the harbor in the early morning, against a clean city skyline). It's morning again in America. Today, more men and women will go to work than ever before in our country's history . . . (video clip of newspaper boy throwing papers from his bike

Figure 14.3 In 2012, Barack Obama highlighted the third aspect of credibility: good will. Trying to contrast himself from Republican opponent Mitt Romney, Obama sought to suggest that he empathized with the economic woes of the American electorate and cared about the problems facing ordinary Americans. Romney mustered strong arguments on his behalf, but could not close the good will gap.

AFP/Getty Images

in a suburb . . .) . . . It's morning again in America (photo of a lit White House at dusk . . .) and under the leadership of President Reagan (video clip of a flag waving in the wind) our country is prouder (video of children looking upward reverently) and stronger and better.

(1984 advertisement for President Ronald Reagan, Westen, 2007, pp. 73–74)

This is political story-telling at its aesthetic best and schmaltzy worst. It exemplifies a key attribute of the political message: narrative. A **narrative** is "a cohesive and coherent story" that calls on dramatic devices, raises problems, and offers a resolution (Hinyard & Kreuter, 2007). Narratives can transport people to different psychological places, engaging them in the intuitively appealing drama of a story that promises a hopeful solution to the nation's intractable problems. A persuasive political narrative offers a clear moral message, a memorable, evocative theme with protagonists and antagonists, and rich political metaphors (Westen, 2007). Narratives can exert a strong impact on social attitudes, and candidates who offer optimistic visions of the future, relayed through stories, can gain popularity with voters (e.g., Bilandzic & Busselle, 2013).

Narratives also have moral underpinnings. Reagan's Republican Party narratives called on traditional, core American values that emphasized individualism, family, and faith. By contrast, liberal Democratic Party narrative messages have taken on a more secular hue. They have called attention to ways that social institutions have promoted inequality and require reform (Haidt, 2012). Conservatives and liberals have different social values and tend to tell different stories about the American experience. These stories take on political importance when they are placed on center stage and harnessed by strategists to persuade the mass electorate.

Candidates win election by framing issues around compelling narratives. When we say the candidate who wins election has the best story, we don't mean that he or she fabricates a fairy tale to gain votes (although that could happen!). The point is that political narratives contain dramatic devices to describe problems and offer solutions. To some degree, elections are about persuading voters to view politics through the lens of one or another party's narrative.

Other messages are also persuasive. For example, the use of a very different factor—evidence—can enhance candidates' credibility and lend cogency to their message (Reynolds & Reynolds, 2002). Candidates regularly reel off numerical facts—or those facts that bolster their side—in presidential debates. A two-sided message—one that gives the opponent's position but rebuts it—can influence attitudes (O'Keefe, 1999). Metaphors and message frames, discussed in Chapter 8, also can influence political opinions.

HOW THEY HEAR IT: VOTERS AND POLITICAL PERSUASION

The end-point of persuasion is the voter. It all boils down to what people think, how they feel about what they have heard, and for whom they vote on Election Day. How do voters process campaign messages? What causes them to change their attitudes toward a candidate? Theories and research have tackled these questions, offering insights on campaign effects.

The Role of Mental Processing and Involvement

The **Elaboration Likelihood Model of Persuasion** (ELM) stipulates that there are two routes by which people process or think about messages: the peripheral and central

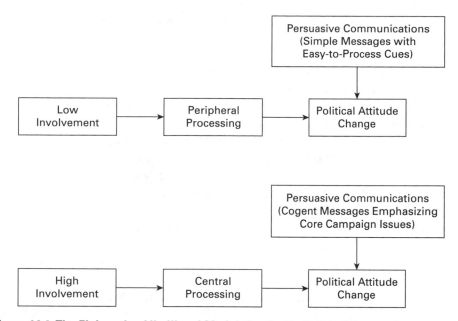

Figure 14.4 The Elaboration Likelihood Model, Applied to Political Persuasion

routes (Petty & Cacioppo, 1986). The model argues that persuaders must understand how people think about persuasive messages in order to craft compelling arguments. A key factor is political involvement, or the degree to which a campaign is perceived to be personally relevant or touches on personally consequential outcomes. Voters mentally process political information very differently under low and high involvement. In order to be in sync with how voters think, political persuaders must devise different messages for low and for highly involved individuals (see Figure 14.4).

Low Involvement

Under low involvement, voters lack interest in the campaign. Believing that the election does not bear on their own personal lives or touch on core values, they lack motivation to follow the campaign. If they plan to vote, they rely on short-circuited, simple strategies to make up their minds. The presidential campaign is no big deal to them and they don't expend much intellectual effort pondering what candidates say. They process the campaign peripherally, relying on mental shortcuts or heuristics to make their voting decision (e.g., Popkin, 1993). These cues are peripheral to the main issues in the campaign, but can be processed easily and simply. Low-involved voters rely on heuristics like political party ("I come from a family of Republicans; I'm voting for Romney, he's a good bet"); the views of influential others ("Just heard Bill Clinton gave a great speech for Obama. Clinton's terrific. I'm voting for Obama"); and easy-to-process cues ("Romney's got a business background, that qualifies him in tough economic times").

In order to persuade low-involved voters, candidates must design simple messages that do not require much mental processing. They need to match the message to voters' preference for heuristics and superficial cues. If you are a candidate appealing to voters with little interest in the campaign, you do not want to engage them in much serious thought. They will not process your message. They lack the interest or motivation to tune in. Instead, you need to produce simple messages that connect your message swiftly and persuasively with voters' low-interest political calculus. Under low involvement, candidates succeed when they emphasize appeals like these:

- endorsements, as when prominent politicians, business leaders, or celebrities support the candidate. Low-involved voters may tilt toward a candidate simply because a respected figure (Clint Eastwood for Romney, Jay-Z for Obama) speaks in the candidate's behalf;
- positive associations between the candidate and symbols like the flag and family;
- physical appeal (the candidate's speaking voice, physical attractiveness, height, and political charm, conveyed via media, may be enough to sway some low-involved voters); and
- similarity between the candidate and voters in terms of race, gender, or ethnicity. Microtargeted Facebook posts that suggest that friends "like" the candidate can carry the day among some low-involved voters.

Empirical studies document these notions. There is evidence that messages containing peripheral cues, such as those above, can be effective when voters lack involvement or are relatively uninterested in the election (Bailenson et al., 2008; Chong & Druckman, 2007b; Lenz & Lawson, 2011; Rosenberg, 1987).

Peripheral Cues in Lower-Level Elections

Peripheral message factors can be especially influential in lower-level races, such as city, state, and even Congressional elections. Every two years voters are faced with a mind-numbing series of choices. Should they choose between the judge, who snarls in his TV ads that he will lock up hardened criminals for life, or the challenger, whose common-sense, no-nonsense televised advertising appeal is designed to call up recollections of Judge Judy, the reality TV show judge? Which of the virtually unknown five candidates for county auditor is most deserving of a vote in a May primary election? Should voters give the nod to the incumbent Democrat for state senator or the challenger, who has run a compelling advertising blitz? Truth be told, most voters can scarcely remember the name of the incumbent in low-level races, let alone the challenger. And what about Congress? One candidate may have aired many memorable ads that show her talking earnestly with working-class men and women. Another candidate may boast on social media posts that she has a simple, intuitively appealing plan to cut taxes.

Faced with these choices and burdened by everyday demands of their own, people frequently rely on mental shortcuts. Even more so than in presidential races, they may choose a candidate based on whether he or she has been endorsed by well-known politicians or simply looks like a political leader. (Feminist critics have argued that the latter criterion has traditionally worked to the advantage of male politicians.) For some voters casting ballots in state elections, the appearance of a candidate's website can influence their choice. A website that has the patina of persuasion—it looks cool, feels contemporary, and has lots of appealing visuals—may carry weight with low-involved voters.

Even the repetition of a candidate's name in advertisements can exert telling effects in lower-level elections, including races for Congress. A well-respected psychological principle, **mere exposure**, asserts that repeated exposure to a neutral stimulus, product, or political candidate can enhance positive affect, leading to feelings of liking (Bornstein, 1989; Zajonc, 1968).

Mere exposure influences low-involved political decisions in the same way as it affects other choices. Which detergent should you buy? Maybe the one you saw advertised over and over again that comes quickly to mind. Why do you turn up the car radio when a rock-and-roll song ripples through the air? Perhaps because, now that you have heard it for the fifth time, the song has started to resonate and you really like its bounce and beat. Mere exposure has considerable psychological support, and there is strong evidence that it helps to explain political decision-making. A classic study by Joseph Grush and his colleagues explored whether political candidates who spent the most money on media advertising were more likely to win election than those who spent less, or had less money to spend. Focusing on low-visibility Congressional elections, Grush, McKeough, and Ahlering (1978) found that the leading spender won nearly 60 percent of the time. This far exceeded the proportion that one would expect based on chance alone.

Thus, candidates who have amassed personal fortunes or are adept fundraisers are probably more likely to win election to low-level office. Once elected, they capitalize on their reputations and the political power of incumbency. As incumbents, their names are well-known and associated with the patriotic trappings of power. Mere exposure helps to explain why incumbents win elections with such stunning frequency. Of course there are complications. Mere exposure does not work as well when voters have strong attitudes, or a particular candidate elicits negative feelings. Just repeating a candidate's name many times also will not cut it in many races for the presidency and Senate, where more citizens process information more carefully, relying on more substantive information than name recognition, affect, and positive candidate associations. But repeated, peripheral exposure to persuasive messages does help to explain why candidates can win election to lower-level offices. And advertising can be a particularly potent force in Congressional contests, where news and political debates exert less impact (West, 2014).

More generally, on a normative level, this raises the time-honored question of whether peripheral processing is a good or bad thing. Defenders argue that reliance on decision-making shortcuts makes practical sense; they argue that these shortcuts can help busy, if low-involved, voters to make reasonable choices. Basing your vote on whether a candidate seems to share your party affiliation is not an unreasonable way to make up your mind. Casting a vote for a candidate who has been endorsed by similar others is at least a rational way to decide how to vote. Critics counter that superficial political decision-making is an insult to democratic principles. The fact that candidates have the endorsement of a political party or friends does not mean that they are qualified to hold political office. Critics also worry that the system may be rigged to favor those who have the financial resources to amass money needed to win election to lower office and manipulate mere exposure to their advantage.

WHAT DO YOU THINK?

Is democracy served when voters rely on superficial, peripheral cues like appearance and reputation to decide how to cast a ballot in low-involved elections? Can you make a case that these are reasonable decision-making strategies? Do political media manipulate low-involved voters? Or do voters understand candidates' appeals and choose to make their decisions quickly and simply?

High Involvement

When voters are highly involved in the election, they think very differently about political messages. Concerned about how the electoral outcome could affect their pocketbooks, employment prospects, health care, or children's economic security, they pay considerable attention to campaign messages. The ELM says that when voters are high in involvement, they process campaign messages centrally and systematically. They consider whether presidential candidates will execute policies that advance their self-interest. They evaluate the incumbent president based on whether the chief executive has fulfilled campaign promises and improved the state of the economy (Vavreck, 2009).

Campaign messages are most likely to influence high-involved voters if they persuasively address voters' economic and social concerns, contain compelling policy arguments, and offer hopeful solutions to vexing issues of national concern (e.g., Ladd, 2007). Messages must focus on salient issues. They must resonate with voters' social values. Persuasive communications that resort to simple appeals, like mentioning the candidate's political party or associating the candidate with positive images like the flag, will not persuade these more concerned, conscientious voters. If a voter is worried about her family's economic woes, she wants more than a message that shows the candidate beaming with family members or endorsed by a credible senator. When voters are involved in electoral outcomes, candidates must persuade them by offering cogent arguments in favor of their election. The ELM says that candidates need to explain how their policies will serve voters' immediate economic needs or address core problems raised by the campaign.

In 2008, many Independent voters, who ordinarily leaned Republican, were primarily concerned with economic issues, in view of the financial crisis that befell the country. John Butler, who owned a floral shop near Youngstown, Ohio, typified these voters. Living in a part of the country hit hard by the economic downturn, Butler related that he had no choice but to lay off 25 of his 26 employees and drop his health insurance policy. "I looked at my situation and realized I couldn't afford to vote for McCain. I was as shocked as anyone," he said (Belkin, 2008, p. A5). Presumably, these involved voters, centrally processing campaign messages, were persuaded by Obama's economic recovery plan. Obama won many of these Independent voters in 2008, blaming the Republicans for the financial crisis and explaining how he could cure economic ills. Romney hoped to draw these voters back to the Republican Party in 2012, arguing that their economic plight had been made worse by Obama, and Republican policies would do more to help their pocketbooks than would those of the Democrats. During the campaign Romney attacked Obama's record, offering cogent arguments in favor of his economic plans. The Republican campaign drew more Independent voters than in 2008, but not enough to offset Obama's advantage with other groups.

Voters can also be highly involved in the election but face psychological cross-pressures. For example, some working-class women, dubbed "waitress moms," were torn. They had voted for Obama in 2008, but felt he had not fulfilled his promises to improve the economy. One New Hampshire woman, Emmakate Paris, said she was worried about insurance, taxes, "the price of gas, everything." Based on the ELM, Romney tried to persuade voters like Ms. Paris by framing the election around Obama's economic policies, arguing that his own business background and economic plan would better serve her economic self-interest. The problem for Romney was that voters like Ms. Paris were troubled by Romney's conservative policies toward birth control and abortion (Seelye, 2012). Obama's strategists devised social issues appeals to women such as Ms. Paris, arguing that the president's positions on abortion and birth control were more in sync with the needs of working women. Exit polls showed that women favored Obama over Romney by a double-digit margin.

When People Have Strong Political Passions: Barriers to Persuasion

The discussion so far has emphasized that political persuaders can influence voters' attitudes by selecting an appropriate communicator characteristic, designing a compelling message, or tailoring the communication to fit voters' involvement in the election. But in some cases, these appeals fall on deaf ears because people have strong political attitudes and party attachments.

Attitudes on such issues as affirmative action, abortion, and gun control can be fiercely held. Voters can also display fervent loyalty to the Republican or Democratic Party. Animated by a well-developed ideological world-view, voters evaluate candidates through the lens of their political viewpoints. Strong attitudes are characterized by symbolic attachments, linkage to core social values, and certainty (people are convinced that their attitude is correct; see Krosnick & Petty, 1995). Strong attitudes are a blessing and a curse: They embolden people to become involved in politics and work for change, but they also can blind individuals to alternative positions on the issue. When people have a strong position on an issue, they invariably see everything related to the topic through the lens of the attitude. Armed with a strong attitude, people are hardly objective, but deeply subjective and frequently unwilling to consider alternative points of view. What's more, strong partisans can be fiercely loyal to their political party, to the point of putting aside their intellectual beliefs and giving credence to the position advocated by their cherished group (Cohen, 2003).

This illustrates **selective perception**, the psychological tendency to perceive and interpret messages so that they are consistent with a strong preexisting set of beliefs, attitudes, or partisan attachments. Political messages—blogs, speeches, debate performances, and ads—run up against these. Voters with strong partisan sentiments quickly reject positions that are at odds with their attitudes. They also gravitate to news outlets that sing the praises of their political group and mock the refrains of the other side (see Reflections box). These ideas may call to mind the limited effects model described in Chapter 3. The limited effects approach, refined to reflect the current era (Bennett & Iyengar, 2008) and broadened to accommodate a host of media effects, sheds some light on contemporary campaign persuasion.

REFLECTIONS: SELECTIVE EXPOSURE AND POLITICAL MEDIA

Is persuasion dead?

A political writer, Matt Miller, using the term persuasion rather informally, asked this question some years back. He raised these provocative arguments:

> Ninety percent of political conversation amounts to dueling "talking points." Best-selling books reinforce what folks thought when they bought them. Talk radio and opinion journals preach to the converted. Let's face it: the purpose of most political speech is not to persuade but to win, be it power, ratings, celebrity or even cash. By contrast, marshaling a case to persuade those who start from a different position is a lost art. Honoring what's right in the other side's argument seems a superfluous thing that can only cause trouble, like an appendix. Politicos huddle with like-minded souls in opinion cocoons that seem impervious to facts.
>
> (Miller, 2005)

Thus, Democrats denied for years that Reagan had helped to defeat the Soviet Union during the Cold War, despite considerable consensus this was the case. Republicans refused to give Clinton credit for improving the economy in the 1990s, in spite of widespread agreement that he had. Scores of prejudiced individuals continued to believe that Obama is a Muslim, although this too is contradicted by the facts.

We live in social worlds peopled by individuals like us. Americans tend to live near and talk to others who share their points of view (Bishop, 2008). Voters are more inclined to communicate with people who share their political attitudes than with those who disagree (Mutz, 2006). We get email attachments and Facebook posts from friends who share our political ideology. We click the "like" button and send the post that happily reinforces our political attitude to another friend, enjoying the bubble of similarity and the cocoon of political friendship that suggests our view is shared universally. If you are a conservative Republican, you probably talk more with conservatives than with liberals. If you are a liberal Democrat, chances are you exchange YouTube posts, including those that make fun of Republican pratfalls, with like-minded others. In either case, you probably

Continued

don't correspond too much with followers of alternative political parties, like the Green, Libertarian or . . . Florida Whig Party!

Media choices are highly selective. People tend to tune in to and prefer news outlets that trumpet their political perspective. This is known as **selective exposure**. Selective exposure is a well-researched phenomenon. It is interesting and complicated (Garrett, 2009; Holbert, Garrett, & Gleason, 2010; Knobloch-Westerwick, 2012). There are times when people, curious about opposing positions, will seek out information that challenges their point of view. But there is evidence that political partisans prefer news and information outlets that support their attitudes. Consider the illustrative findings from an experiment by Iyengar and Hahn (2009). In their study, a series of identical news stories were attributed to Fox News, CNN, National Public Radio (NPR), or the BBC. Research participants read a series of headlines that were attributed to one of the four news outlets. Individuals were asked to indicate which of the four news reports they would like to read. As selective exposure predicted, conservatives and Republicans preferred news reports from Fox. They avoided stories from the more liberal NPR and CNN. Liberals and conservatives opted to read stories from CNN and NPR. They avoided Fox.

Thus, it is easy today for voters to find information that reinforces their worldview: Fox for Republicans, MSNBC for Democrats, and alternative party websites for voters who disdain the two major parties (Bennett & Iyengar, 2008). Perched before their computer screens and soaking in partisan information, viewers may find that that their beliefs about the political world are hardened by what they see and hear, an "echo chamber" effect, as Iyengar and Hahn (2009), and Jamieson and Cappella (2008), put it. And this is exactly what happens. Viewing these talk shows and opinion programs reinforces partisan biases and increases political polarization (Stroud, 2010, 2011). So, Fox causes conservative Republican viewers to become more conservative, and MSNBC leads liberal Democrats to become more liberal. This is disturbing. Americans are divided on social issues; some experts believe the country is becoming more fragmented and polarized. When opinion-molders like conservative Rush Limbaugh, employ ridicule and name-calling to sustain their cause and disparage the opposition, they can undermine political consensus and efforts to forge a common ground (Jamieson & Cappella, 2008). And vice versa for arrogant liberal talk show hosts.

Is it all bad? Are there no positive features in contemporary political communication? Actually, there is a silver lining. Tuning in to media outlets that reinforce your point of view has positive effects. It energizes you, strengthens your core beliefs, and propels you to get involved in political campaigns. In an engaging analysis, Natalie Jomini Stroud (2011) found that conservatives and Republicans who use conservative media genres, and liberals and Democrats who rely on liberal news programs, are particularly likely to participate in politics. "Partisan media have a place in a democracy. They can unite likeminded individuals, help them to organize their political thinking, and motivate them to participate," she helpfully notes (p. 183).

This is complicated stuff. Participating in politics requires a commitment that can be strengthened by watching programs that promote a partisan political perspective. Yet democracy, particularly the deliberative type, requires an open-minded exploration of different perspectives through communication. Ideally, this involves a give-and-take persuasion, in which individuals listen to different points of view. This kind of persuasion—which honors what is right in the other side's arguments, as Miller noted—is what eludes us. We have fierce partisan persuasion, which lambasts the other side and celebrates our own; these messages unleash the activists, admirably motivating them to participate in politics. But messages that seek a middle ground or attempt to bring out the best in different political points of view are sorely absent, perhaps reflecting and contributing to the polarization in American politics that collectively impedes the ability of people of different perspectives to locate compromises that serve the greater good.

What is your view? Do you think most political persuasion pushes the electorate into two camps? Or is it doing what it should, seeking to activate those with strong partisan attitudes, with partisan media serving a host of democracy-enhancing functions?

So, how do you persuade people with strong passions? How do you influence voters who have already formed opinions about the candidates? How do candidates try to move voters with strong partisan attachments? The answer: Very carefully.

Persuasion theorists emphasize that the best way to influence a strongly held attitude is to appreciate its dynamics and its underlying structure. Nearly half a century ago, the psychologists Muzafer and Carolyn Sherif (1967) developed a social judgment theory approach to study persuasion and social attitudes. **Social judgment theory** emphasizes that people do not objectively evaluate a communication based on the merits of the arguments. Instead, they compare the advocated position with their own viewpoint, calling on their own social judgments. If the communicator is generally in sync with what they believe, they accept the message and may even feel stronger about the issue.

If the speaker takes a position that seems to diverge from their opinion, they distance or contrast the speaker's position from their own and reject the communicator's arguments. The lesson for political candidates is clear: Don't try to change voters' attitude about an issue, particularly a hot-button topic like abortion or guns. Instead, try to convince voters that you share their attitude on the topic. Be careful what you say, lest voters interpret your statements as indicating that you disagree with their position, leading them to reject your candidacy.

To be sure, candidates do articulate ideological positions on issues. Republican and Democratic candidates embrace different visions of the future. As a general rule, presidential candidates do stand for certain principles. But they must be scrupulously careful when they address hot-button issues, or they will not get elected.

Obama had to walk a particularly delicate line on these issues, as the first African American president. If he was perceived as emphasizing (even occasionally) the concerns of Black Americans, still struggling with vestiges of racism, he would earn the ire of those White voters who reluctantly voted for him in 2008. But when he seemed oblivious to the needs of the Black community, passionate activists like Cornel West, a university professor, and Tavis Smiley, a radio host, called him out, charging he was insufficiently sensitive to the problems that African Americans faced. Obama struggled with this throughout his first term. He expressed empathy with the parents of Trayvon Martin, when their son was tragically killed in Florida for reasons that some assumed were rooted in racial prejudice. "If I had a son, he'd look like Trayvon," Obama said, with much compassion. But, acting on the advice of media staffers, he declined to appear on Black Entertainment Television during his first six months of office. "I'm not the president of Black America. I'm the president of the United States of America," he emphasized (Kantor, 2012).

In these ways, Obama followed the precepts of social judgment theory, which stresses the importance of sculpting a message so it fits audience members' attitudes and falls within their range of acceptable positions. Romney did the same; during the Republican primaries, he emphasized income tax cuts and repeal of Obama's health care plan, two positions with which Republicans staunchly agreed. During the general election campaign, he tempered his positions, trying to cultivate support from more moderate voters.

Politicians strive mightily to avoid positions that are or seem to be at odds with what voters believe on core issues. Thus, in July, 2012, even after the terrible shooting spree in a Colorado movie theater that killed 12 people, Obama said nothing about gun control, a position that Democrats have traditionally endorsed. His refusal was strategic, because polling at that juncture showed that a majority of Americans opposed a ban on handguns and assault rifles (Kristof, 2012). This highlights a paradox of politics. Candidates must display moral principles to get elected. But if the principles they exhibit while in office contradict the values of key constituents, they will not be reelected.

MOBILIZATION: GETTING OUT THE BASE

As the Reflections box suggested, not all campaign communication is classic persuasion. Not all political messages try to change or modify attitudes. Some messages try to strengthen political beliefs. Remember: Partisan attitudes are strongly held, and many people have their minds made up long before the fall campaign. As a result, political persuaders also attempt to reinforce attitudes, bringing them to the fore, and making sure that people act on what they believe. They try to mobilize voters. This is popularly known as "getting out the base": activating the party's core cadre of supporters to make sure they cast votes on Election Day (see Figure 14.5).

Mobilizing supporters is especially important in campaigns for Congress. Congressional races typically elicit less interest from the bulk of voters than do presidential contests. Candidates marshal a host of messages, some emphasizing their similarity with voters. In other cases, they bring up "wedge" or hot-button issues, like abortion, immigration, or (for many years) gay marriage (Hillygus & Shields, 2008). By deliberating and even

Figure 14.5 Voter mobilization plays an important role in presidential campaigns. A strong get-out-the-vote effort can win elections. By activating partisan commitments, through microtargeting and old-fashioned interpersonal contact, campaigns can bring out the base, helping to turn a close election into an electoral victory. As shown above, Obama supporters worked the phones the day before the November 6, 2012 election, while Romney backers canvassed voters with classic political signage.

Bloomberg via Getty Images and Getty Images

dishonestly raising the specter that a divisive proposal on, say, immigration, abortion, or the minimum wage will become policy, political strategists can energize their base and sometimes even push conflicted voters to cast a vote on behalf of their candidate.

Employing a variety of techniques to mobilize core supporters—such as advertising, computerized lists of likely voters, and a cadre of dedicated volunteers working the phones on Election Day—can greatly increase candidates' chances of winning elections. High-tech tools play an important role in voter mobilization efforts.

Technology and Campaign Mobilization

Chicago, October, 2012: Obama's young staffers worked insanely long hours, eyes focused on computer screens, as a digital clock marked the seconds, minutes, hours, and days until the November election. With the help of a large data base, they worked to increase registration among favorable voting blocs in swing states and to locate voters who had told campaign workers they would vote for Obama, but needed some gentle nudging to get them to actually cast their vote on Election Day (Rutenberg, 2012a). They had it down to a science. Applying political persuasion strategies, Obama's campaign specialists assigned battleground state voters four numbers, a first number indicating the probability they would back Obama, a second quantifying the likelihood they would actually cast a vote, a third number signifying the probability an inconsistent voter who backed Obama could be goaded to vote, and a fourth metric evaluating the likelihood that a voter could be persuaded by a conversation on a specific issue (Tufekci, 2012). What's more, their sophisticated, well-financed technology allowed them to evade one of the stumbling blocks of political phone-calling: the recipient's caller ID identifying the phone call as a junk call or one coming from a dreaded political party headquarters. When Obama operatives made the calls, their personal phone numbers appeared on the recipient's caller ID.

The Democrats had adapted a technique perfected by Republican super-strategist Karl Rove, who believed that victory in 2004 was less a matter of persuading voters than one of mobilizing the already converted. Focusing on registering Republican voters and increasing voter turnout, Rove and his minions deployed a systematic plan to contact voters. He went so far as to send an 18-wheel vehicle called Reggie the Registration Rig to NASCAR races and country-music performances to register sympathetic Republicans. Thanks to these efforts, the Republicans registered some three million new voters prior to the 2004 election, and Bush captured a larger share of the Hispanic vote in 2004 than he did in 2000 (Lizza, 2012). The lesson: Voter mobilization wins elections.

Communication plays an important part in voter mobilization. One method is micro-targeting (see Chapter 11). Persuaders use high-tech tools to locate voters who are sympathetic to their message and then direct communications via electronic and social media to these individuals. Campaign strategists might plant cookies on targeted voters' computers, helping them to discover if voters clicked onto particular websites. A voter who regularly visited evangelical Christian and Republican Party websites might receive tailored messages to encourage her to translate conservative attitudes into a vote for a Republican candidate. Similarly, research shows that certain programs, like *Dancing with the Stars* and *Grey's Anatomy*, have attracted more Republicans, while programs like *Late Show with David Letterman* and *Sixty Minutes* capture more Democratic voters. Persuaders would try to mobilize Republicans by placing ads on the first two programs, while they would target Democrats by advertising on the second shows (see http://campaignstops.blogs.nytimes.com/2012/04/15/let-the-nanotargeting-begin/). The ELM suggests that issue-oriented messages microtargeted to particular voter segments could encourage central processing and strengthen political attitudes.

Face-to-Face Mobilization Efforts

A second way to mobilize voters is interpersonal: "contact from an enthusiastic human being" (Lizza, 2012, p. 66). For example, Romney's Ohio canvassing campaign called on the 60-something Henry and Donna Peters. They knocked on doors in a Cincinnati suburb, holding a clipboard containing Romney leaflets, gently making their appeals while carefully avoiding walking on the lawns of the home-owners they spoke with (Davey & Wines, 2012).

Research shows that voters who have been interpersonally contacted by campaign volunteers are often more likely to vote than those who have not been contacted. Re-contacting people who have indicated an intention to vote increases the likelihood they will turn out at the polls (Green & Gerber, 2008). By reminding voters of their commitment to vote for a particular candidate, campaigns can put the idea at the top of their consciousness, activate democratic values, and help people to translate attitude into action. This is good for democracy. From the perspective of campaigns, it tells us that media are not the only variable in campaigns. Good old-fashioned door-to-door canvassing matters. And it matters because a number of voters have strong attitudes and are not easily influenced by the opposition's messages. But energetic human communication can nudge them into translating attitudes into action at the polls.

WHAT DO YOU THINK?

Is high-tech microtargeting manipulative, exploiting voters' personal preferences for candidates' political gain? Or is it a legitimate way to use persuasion to win elections?

CONCLUSIONS

Presidential campaigns are full-throated efforts to persuade voters. Candidates want to get elected, and they harness persuasive communications to make their case. This is a good thing. Persuasion is not coercive. It is a civilizing force that embraces logic, verbal arguments, evidence, and emotional appeals. It becomes problematic when candidates use persuasive techniques that distort and deceive, an issue taken up in the next chapter.

Persuasion theories offer a roadmap to understand campaigns. Candidates harness the three pillars of credibility—expertise, trustworthiness, and good will. Political persuaders also employ narrative messages that tell stories by weaving together symbolic themes.

Voters' own motivations and attitudes play important roles in political persuasion. As the Elaboration Likelihood Model states, candidates attempt to tailor messages to fit voters' involvement levels and processing strategies. Under low involvement, voters process messages peripherally, and simple appeals, such as endorsements and party-based appeals, are effective. When voters are involved in an election, they care about the outcome and think carefully about the issues. Appeals to voters' self-interest and carefully framed economic arguments can carry the day. Campaign messages can change the attitudes and voting behavior of undecided voters who are open to persuasion.

Yet we should not underestimate the role that voters' own strongly held opinions play in elections. Voters are not blank slates. As social judgment theory emphasizes, they selectively perceive information in accord with their biases. Candidates must tread carefully. If candidates make blunt statements about social issues—or even say something that one segment of voters finds objectionable—they can be perceived as opposing voters' heart-felt positions. Some voters may reject the candidate on these grounds. Voters are not always entirely rational or fair.

The current media environment, with toxic cable opinion shows and intensely-opinionated websites, can exacerbate these trends. When addressing issues that arouse voters' passions, candidates face ethical and political dilemmas. If they take a principled position, they may be true to their ideals, but may alienate key voting blocs. But by opting not to advocate for what they believe, they forfeit a claim to be acting out of principle. Such is politics. Politicians must choose their causes wisely.

Sometimes candidates deliberately opt to raise divisive issues, trying to influence persuadable voters. A Republican candidate might try to woo undecided Democratic voters who oppose same-sex marriage by suggesting that the Democratic candidate supports gay marriage. A Democratic candidate could appeal to undecided Republican voters who favor stem-cell research by suggesting that the Republican candidate opposes stem-cell research. They relay these negative appeals using high-tech techniques like microtargeting. As two political scientists aptly note, "candidates continually look for strategies to gain the slightest edge over their competition, and technological innovations are one way that candidates look for an electoral advantage" (Hillygus & Shields, 2008, p. 198). This reminds us that just because a strategy is cool and high-tech does not mean it advances democratic aims.

But you know that campaigns are not exercises in moral philosophy. Persuasion is not synonymous with truth. Candidates stretch positions to appeal to diverse voting blocs. They frame issues differently with different constituents. In the final analysis, presidential campaigns are not designed to get the public thinking about complex policy problems or to help voters appreciate that solving the nation's political conundrums requires an appreciation of diverse points of view. This raises an interesting, important question: Does a system that places a premium on persuasion, while minimizing deliberation, build a strong democracy? If so, our system is doing just fine. But if not, how can we reconcile these two rather different philosophical objectives?

CHAPTER 15

Political Advertising

The political advertisement begins as Joe Soptic, balding, with hollow circles beneath his eyes, sadly explains that he was a steelworker for 30 years. He still displays pride as he slips on a hard hat. "We had a reputation for quality products," he says. "It was something that was American-made." As he talks, the screen lights up with images of a steel plant. Fire rains down from the melting of steel, and a driver carts raw materials from one part of the plant to another. "We weren't rich, but I was able to put my daughter through college," Soptic explains.

John Wiseman, a big-shouldered man with a moustache, who worked for the steel company for 28 years, now appears on the screen. He speaks in a deep, sonorous voice. "Having a good paying job that you can support and raise a family on is hugely important." Soptic intones: "That stopped with the sale of the plant to Bain Capital." The video shifts to a depiction of Mitt Romney. Romney is shown gesturing enthusiastically, knowingly telling a group that "I know how business works. I know why jobs come and why they go."

Here comes Soptic, who appears on the screen again. He says that Romney's private equity firm, Bain Capital, "made as much money off it [the steel plant] as they could, and they closed it down, and they filed for bankruptcy, without any concern for the families of the communities."

His view is echoed by two older guys, Andy Cruz and Jack Cobb, who each worked for the steel plant for more than a quarter of a century. Sitting outside a house, they put it starkly: "It was like a vampire. They came in and sucked the life out of us," Cobbs says. Joe Soptic closes out the ad, with haunting comments: "I was devastated. Makes me angry. Those guys were all rich. They all had more money than they'll ever spend. Yet they didn't have the money to take care of the very people that made the money for them" (see "Steel"—YouTube at www.youtube.com/watch?v=sWiSFwZJXwE).

This brutally negative commercial, sponsored by the Obama campaign and aired in the spring of 2012, was one of many attack ads the candidates and super-political action committees ran during the presidential campaign. Advertising—particularly negative advertising—is a key element in political campaigns. Ads are the principal modality by which candidates communicate to voters in presidential elections, and they play an increasing role in elections across the world (see Box 15.1). Negative spots are discussed endlessly in the news and are planned strategically by consultants.

Most of us have opinions about political ads. We admire their artistry or dislike their manipulation of cherished symbols. We fear their impact on vulnerable Americans, while dismissing their impact on us, convinced they have little effect on our own attitudes. We frequently lament that there are so many of them, experiencing them as eye-sores and believing that they hinder democracy. Scholars have also pondered political advertising, offering concepts and research-based analyses to explain its effects. This chapter unpacks these issues, examining the impact and conundrums of political ads. The first section describes the main attributes of contemporary campaign ads and promotional strategies. The next section examines the influences of political ads on voters, illustrating concepts with real-life examples. The final portion of the chapter offers a critical perspective, examining virtues and drawbacks of negative ads, and ways that media can correct misperceptions.

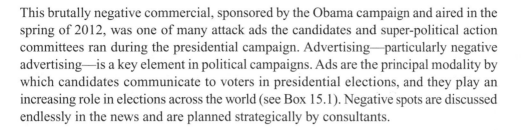

BOX 15.1 POLITICAL ADVERTISING AND MARKETING WORLD-WIDE

A television commercial stoked fears of economic calamities to convince Greeks to vote for the New Democratic Party. An older, British political video hyped the Labour Party's accomplishments, featuring a member of the classic British pop group, the Spice Girls. In Israel, where personalized politics and political ads have emerged with increasing frequency, observers routinely refer to the "carnivaliza-tion" of Israeli politics (Caspi & Leshem, 2006; Shaefer, Weimann, & Tsfati, 2008). And in Italy, they talk about the "Berlusconi factor," referring to the many ways that Italian prime minister Silvio Berlusconi, the billionaire, scandal-prone media mogul, lavished his resources on political media campaigns known for their

Continued

pageantry in a country with a time-honored reputation for both aesthetics and excess (Mazzoleni, 2006).

The common denominator is **political marketing**, the application of commercial marketing strategies to political media campaigns. Politics is now marketed in electoral campaigns across the world in what scholars call global political marketing (Lees-Marshment, 2010). Candidates utilize campaign techniques pioneered in the United States and sometimes hire big-time American consultants to develop campaign strategies.

Marketing is a broad concept that describes the processes by which a society communicates and distributes products and services of value to consumers. In commercial marketing, a seller exchanges a particular product for money from consumers. In political marketing, the candidate delivers a series of promises in exchange for votes from the electorate. As marketing scholar Bruce I. Newman (1994) explains: "The candidate is in reality a service provider and offers a service to his consumers, the voters, much in the same way that an insurance agent offers a service to his consumers . . . Candidates operate in a dynamic environment, fast, changing, and full of obstacles that present marketing challenges that require flexibility" (p. 9). Scholars have developed models of the political marketing process, adapting commercial marketing concepts to politics (e.g., Cwalina, Falkowski, & Newman, 2011; Henneberg & O'Shaughnessy, 2007; Kotler & Kotler, 1999; Newman, 1999).

It is not just the United States where polls and consultant-driven political ads prevail. The American model—for better or worse—has come to dominate political marketing world-wide. Even in European countries, where elections have long revolved around political parties, campaigns have become increasingly candidate-centered, as the media promote or lampoon the exploits of colorful candidates. The British media focused on the personality of Tony Blair, who was parodied as "George Bush's poodle" for his stalwart support of the Iraq War. Berlusconi, Italy's colorful former prime minister, personalized Italian politics and transformed himself into a distinctive brand that initially centered on his self-made success, enviable wealth, and sexual prowess, but turned tawdry with stories about seedy parties at his homes with countless women and even a prostitute memorably known as Ruby Heartstealer (Donadio & Povoledo, 2011, p. 10).

Political marketing is so pervasive that it operates on the level of the nation-state. Countries market themselves, using contemporary branding principles. As researcher Jonathan Rose noted, some years back Jordan's King Abdullah chaired the "Jordan First" organization, which sought to "implant Jordan in the hearts of Jordanians." The Belgian prime minister, concerned about the country's image in the wake of pornography and corruption scandals, actually hired a firm to try to market a new national image, complete with a new logo and an Internet suffix ".be" as a cultural symbol (Rose, 2010, p. 256).

Does political marketing serve democracy? Defenders argue that marketing, with its emphasis on polling and understanding voter needs, helps put candidates in touch with voters. If conducted honestly and openly, political marketing can advance democratic aims, accurately transmitting citizens' concerns to public officials and helping duly elected leaders to develop programs that serve voters' needs.

Others disagree. Critics point out that voters are not consumers who receive services from political providers. Instead, voters are citizens, the fundamental constituents of a democratic society, whose ideas and objectives elected leaders must represent and channel into public policy. Bennett and Manheim (2001) note that "the very transformation of publics into exclusive target audiences is a blow to the democratic ideal of publics as inclusive deliberative bodies" (p. 280).

We're not going to solve this problem here. It reflects different views about just what is realistic in a mass society in which media and advertising have come to occupy much of the public space. Liberal and libertarian philosophers, who embrace the rights of individuals and the private market, are supportive of political marketing, while proponents of the deliberative democratic approach spotlight its shortcomings.

CHARACTERISTICS OF PRESIDENTIAL CAMPAIGN ADS

Political advertising has played a colorful role in presidential campaigns for more than half a century. The first prominent televised political advertisements were broadcast in the 1952 presidential campaign, more than 60 years ago. Presidential campaign advertising has evolved and changed in several ways since that time.

First, political advertising is increasingly funded by outside political groups. Large numbers of presidential campaign ads are purchased by super-political action committees (PACs), which have greatly expanded since the Supreme Court's Citizens United decision (see Chapter 12). Super-PACs now pay for numerous political ads that are bankrolled by corporations, unions, lobbying groups, or billionaires, who gave over $61 million in 2012 (Blow, 2012). Super-PACs, operating secretly and independently of campaigns, can underwrite nasty attack ads. Because they are technically not political organizations, these PACs are not legally required to reveal the names of their donors to the Federal Election Commission (McIntire & Confessore, 2012). It's a game: Candidates can condemn the attack spots, saying they are shocked at how negative the ads have become. At the same time, they benefit from PAC-sponsored attacks on their opponents.

Second, more money is shelled out on political advertising now than ever before. The 2012 election was the most expensive presidential election in U.S. history. Approximately $6 billion was spent, with an estimated $3.3 billion expended on political advertising, easily exceeding the $2.5 billion spent in 2008 (Peters, 2012b). By way of comparison, a mere $600 million was spent on political ads in 1996 (Perloff, 1998).

However, the 2010 Citizens United Supreme Court decision opened the floodgates, and the 2012 election set new records (see Chapter 12). The city of Las Vegas marked a record in 2012, with more than 73,000 political ads, making the "city of excess" the place with the greatest number of TV campaign ads in one year (Peters, 2012b, p. A1). Across the country, some local TV stations were forced to cut minutes from their evening news programs to fit in all the spots.

A third characteristic of political advertising is its negativity. There are many types of political ads, including: (a) talking heads, where candidates speak directly into the camera; (b) testimonials, in which credible individuals speak for or against the political candidate; and (c) issue ads, where candidates explain what they will do, if elected, or have accomplished during their terms. Ads such as these can also be positive or negative, and there are a variety of specific negative ad appeals, such as those that offer comparisons between the candidates, and others that feature a direct attack on the opponent's character. The big news is that negative ads have increased dramatically since the 1950s.

In 1952, 25 percent of political ads were negative. In 1960, when John F. Kennedy faced Richard Nixon, only 12 percent of major political ads were negative. Then came President Lyndon Johnson's iconic "Daisy ad" in 1964, where a girl picked petals off a daisy as the mushroom cloud of a nuclear bomb exploded, the ad not-so-subtly suggesting what Johnson's opponent might do if elected president. In 1964, 50 percent of major ads were negative. Influenced by the apparent success of the "Daisy" spot and responding to the turbulence of the late 1960s, both candidates expanded the use of attack ads in 1968 (West, 2010; see Figure 15.1).

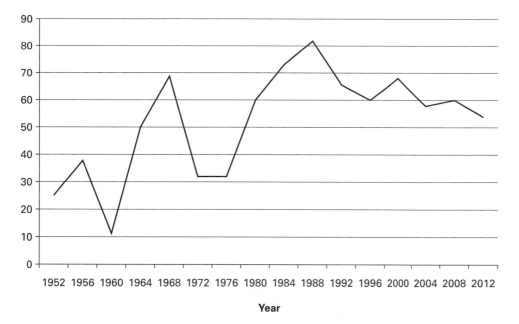

Figure 15.1 Negative Advertising as a Proportion of Total Ads in Presidential Elections.

(1952–2008 data from West [2010]; 2012 data [June 1 through first 3 weeks of October] from Wesleyan Media Project [Common Dreams, 2012].)

Numbers on vertical axis denote proportion of negative to total ads

Negative ads declined in the 1970s, in the wake of the national soul-searching that occurred after the end of the Vietnam War and Watergate. But they increased dramatically over the course of the 1980s. The 1988 election remains the most negative on record, with the incendiary attacks on Democrat Michael Dukakis, including ads that controversially suggested that Dukakis's policies had led to a brutal Black-on-White crime. Negative ads continued apace, ebbing and flowing over time, but still accounting for a majority of prominent political ads in the general election (West, 2010). In a similar fashion, a study of Congressional campaigns in 2002, 2004, and 2006 found that negativity increased on websites and in television advertising (Druckman, Kifer, & Parkin, 2010).

Fourth, ads are typically of high production value, using evocative images, music, and compelling cinematography to create moods. Reagan's classic "Morning in America" ad, described in Chapter 14, linked feel-good music and iconic images of American culture with President Ronald Reagan. A famous negative spot, a George H.W. Bush 1988 attack on his opponent's record on crime, used menacing music while the camera panned on prisoners moving endlessly through a revolving prison door. A controversial 2012 Obama ad pointed fingers at Mitt Romney's Bain Capital firm, intimating (incorrectly) that Bain Capital was responsible for the death of the wife of a Bain-owned steel plant worker by failing to provide health insurance. It is all a far cry from hokey 1952 "Eisenhower Answers America" ads, in which the celebrated Republican presidential candidate stared into a camera, offering stilted statements in response to pre-recorded questions from viewers he never met. (To view actual presidential campaign ads from 1952 through 2012, see http://www.livingroomcandidate.org/.)

Political advertising has changed in one additional way over the past 50 years, leading to the fifth characteristic of contemporary ads. *The purchase and timing of ads have become more strategic, with a strong emphasis on both conventional and interactive technologies.*

Nowadays, rather than spending money on advertising purchases in all 50 states, contemporary consultants argue that they get a bigger bang for the buck by focusing on swing states. Contending that it is not cost-effective to spend money in states that are locked up by a candidate, strategists prefer purchases that target states where the outcome is in doubt. In 2008 and 2012, battleground states widely viewed as critical to the electoral outcome received the lion's share of ads. Voters in Nevada, Virginia, Florida, and Ohio received large numbers of ads. In Nevada, where ads blanketed the evening news, the general manager of a Las Vegas television station said, "We have a joke around here. Pretty soon, we're going to have such long commercial breaks that people are going to tune in and all they'll hear is: 'Hello, welcome to News 3. And good-bye'" (Peters, 2012b, p. A16). Focusing on battleground states makes sense strategically, but it is like frontloading: It concentrates a disproportionate attention on certain states, while neglecting others.

Presidential nominees also advertise earlier in the campaign than they did in years past. Rather than running ad blitzes only in the fall, strategists begin the onslaught earlier, hoping to persuade and lock in key voting blocs. In March 2004, shortly after John Kerry had clinched the Democratic nomination, the Bush campaign began broadcasting $60 million in negative spots in 19 key states (West, 2014). Then, in late summer the notorious "Swift Boat" spots were aired that savaged Kerry's Vietnam War record as the commander of a naval Swift Boat, making questionable claims that Kerry had distorted his military accomplishments (Zernike & Rutenberg, 2004). Eight years later, the Obama campaign and liberal PACs borrowed a chapter from the Swift Boat book by launching negative broadsides at Romney well before the fall campaign (see Peters, 2011).

An additional feature of strategic political advertising is the preeminent role played by the Internet and social media. The game is no longer waged only on television. Increasingly, ads are placed on YouTube and via a host of social networking sites like

Twitter. Microtargeting techniques help to position ads so that they reach particular voter segments. Strategists also email ads to reporters, hoping that they will describe attack ads in news stories. Candidates respond to an opponent's negative spots immediately, concerned that if they let an attack stand, the arguments will begin to seep in and register with the public. Importantly, campaigns strive to gain a presence in the conversation on social media which is edgier, quirkier, and more youthful than one-way TV advertising (see Box 15.2).

BOX 15.2 STUMPING WITH SOCIAL MEDIA: TWITTER AND TUMBLR AS WEAPONS OF POLITICAL PERSUASION

Time was that when candidates tried to reach young voters, they looked to the stars.

Politicians gazed toward the Hollywood hills. Their consultants dialed up the private numbers of Barbra Streisand, Clint Eastwood, and Arnold Schwarzenegger, hoping to convince the princesses and princes of entertainment to lend their glitter to a campaign event. Campaign strategists might look east, as when they asked New Jersey's gravelly voiced Bruce Springsteen to belt out his passionate elegies of American dreams turned sour at Democratic rallies. Or they might adapt a popular song to convey a thematic message, as Bill Clinton did in 1992 with Fleetwood Mac's "Don't stop thinking about tomorrow."

How quaint these strategies seem! How utterly 20th century!

Nowadays, strategists do not attend exclusively to entertainment celebrities, songs, or even TV spots, but to cyberspace, particularly social media. They are especially likely to direct advertisements and promotional messages to social networking sites when trying to reach young adults. Given the ubiquity of cell phones and popularity of hand-held mobile technologies among young people, politicians recognize that they can communicate directly with these voters, instantly and anywhere. More than 80 percent of 18- to 29-year-olds are wireless Internet users, and 72 percent of the online 18- to 29-year-old group use social networking sites (Brenner, 2013; Lenhart et al., 2010). Young voters may not watch television and therefore may never see conventional TV ads. But they are

Continued

rarely without their cell phones or laptops and they spend considerable time on social media. As a result, reporter Jenna Wortham (2012) observes:

> Campaigns want to inject themselves into the conversation on services like Tumblr, where political dialogue often takes the form of remixed photos and quirky videos . . . They are taking to fields of online battle that might seem obscure to the non-Internet-obsessed—sharing song playlists on Spotify, adding frosted pumpkin bread recipes to Pinterest and posting the candidates [*sic*] moments at home with the children on Instagram.

Sure, consultants still line up big stars for rallies, but they are more consumed with interjecting candidates into the spicier conversation of social media. If Willy Sutton, as he famously said, robbed banks because that's where the money is, candidates promote themselves on the social web because that's where young voters are.

In 2012, Mitt Romney innovatively purchased a promotional tweet, a tweet that surfaces on timelines of campaign followers or pops up on the user's screen when particular search terms are punched in. Not to be outdone, the morning after Romney announced in a presidential debate that he would cut funding for the Public Broadcasting System, the Obama Tumblr posted a picture of *Sesame Street*'s Big Bird with the caption, "Mitt Romney's Plan to Cut the Deficit: Fire This Guy" (Wortham, 2012).

Candidates for Congress also use Twitter in campaigns. They harness other interactive tools, such as iPhone apps, to broadly transmit campaign messages and photos, as well as requests for supporters to volunteer for the Congressional campaign (Johnson, 2011).

What impact do these promotional messages exert on voters? Do they influence attitudes or voting behavior? No one knows for sure. As you know, we cannot assume that a message has an effect simply because it appears on a media site. Posts like those above may have preached only to the choir, never reaching politically uninterested voters or individuals who lack the economic resources to regularly tap into the social web (Edgerly et al., 2013). Individuals also filter messages—and that includes tweets and Facebook posts—through their attitudes. Many of those who are exposed to these posts are probably already committed to one candidate or the other. The message may reinforce attitudes or propel someone to send in a small donation, both of which are bona fide political media effects. It is also possible that the message can sway voters with weak partisan loyalty. Research shows that a politician's personalized Twitter message can enhance evaluations and perceived intimacy, but only among individuals with weak party identification (Lee & Oh, 2012).

"What's the return on putting your pants on in the morning? We don't know," said an executive at Socialbakers, a company that offers social media analytic tools. "But we just know it's bad if you don't do it" (Wortham, 2012). That is not a particularly persuasive reason—either practically or normatively—to devote precious resources to social media. But, as was the case with television advertising years ago, consultants fear that if they don't promote their candidates on social media, the other side will, and they will be left in the lurch. Alas, social media has now joined the ranks of big-time promotional political persuasion, for better or for worse.

WHAT DO YOU THINK?

What effects do candidates' promotional messages, transmitted via social media, exert? Do they influence attitudes toward candidates? Do they simply preach to the choir? How can voters use social media to change the dynamics of a campaign?

NEGATIVE ADVERTISING

They are the Darth Vader, the Voldemort of contemporary politics, "the electronic equivalent of the plague" (West, p. 70; see Figure 15.2). Few aspects of modern politics generate as much criticism as negative political commercials. Make no mistake: Candidates have traded insults and brutal barbs since the earliest American elections. Thomas Jefferson's allies accused President John Adams of plotting to create a dynasty with his sons. Jefferson's enemies charged that Jefferson had a sexual relationship with a slave (true, according to recent historical accounts). Andrew Jackson's political opponents pulled out all stops, calling Jackson's mother a prostitute and his wife an adulteress. By these standards, today's advertisements are pretty tame. But negative ads reach more people than did the attacks of two centuries ago, and they are dressed up in the garb of contemporary media technologies, embellished by cinematic production techniques and amplified by the tools of dramatic narrative. No consultant worth his or her salt would advise against the use of negative ads.

Figure 15.2 Negative advertising plays a central role in political campaigns. The majority of presidential campaign political commercials are negative, offering issue- or image-based criticisms of the opposing candidate.

Time & Life Pictures/Getty Images

How can this be, you ask? Don't people hate negative ads? They say they do. As Jill Buckley, a Democratic consultant, explained, "People say they hate negative advertising, but it works. They hate it and remember it at the same time" (Johnson-Cartee & Copeland, 1991, p. 15). Social science research helps to explain why information contained in negative ads can be so memorable.

There is empirical evidence that people remember negative ads better than positive spots and recognize negative ads more quickly than positive ads (Newhagen & Reeves, 1991; Shapiro & Rieger, 1992). There are several reasons for this. We attach more weight psychologically to negative than to positive information. Negative events capture our attention, exerting a stronger impact on impressions and evaluations. Negative information elicits stronger and faster responses than positive information (O'Keefe, 2012). Perhaps because people hope or expect that events will be positive, they are captivated by the negative. You go to a party. Four friends say kind, sweet things about your outfit, your sense of humor, the quality of your work, even your pet cat. One friend makes a brief, sarcastic comment about the words you used in a Facebook post. Which comment do you remember? Which one causes you to ruminate on your drive home? Research suggests it is the sarcastic crack. In the same fashion, negative political information can be more memorable than positive statements. What's more, negative ads can be hard to refute, as a denial invites the perception that the attacked candidate has something to hide.

Although political advertising effects are complex, political consultants believe negative spots can influence poll numbers (Devlin, 1995). Consultants fear that if they don't run negative spots, the opponents will. Thus, a self-fulfilling prophecy—an arms race of negative information—ensues.

The press covers negative ads, offering consultants another incentive to develop and run them. They get a double whammy: possible payoff from the negative ad and then a freebie when media cover the negative spot. Spooky negative ads make for good television. And while journalists may criticize a negative spot—and report on factual inaccuracies—campaign strategists figure that voters will not tune in to the news reports that correct the misinformation. Consultants assume that if voters do attend to the corrective information, they will remember the dramatic advertising storylines better than the more complicated factual correctives.

NEGATIVE AD IMPACT

Limits

All this suggests that negative ads have powerful, hypodermic effects. Theories and research discussed in previous chapters make it clear that their impact is limited by a host of social and psychological factors. There are two conditions under which negative spots are particularly unlikely to influence attitudes. First, they will not succeed in changing the minds of partisans. Strong attitudes are notoriously difficult to change, as noted in Chapter 14. People who strongly support a candidate will not alter their opinion after watching a series of negative ads.

Second, negative ads will not work if the hit (Mafia language is sometimes used to describe negative campaigning) is too strong, below the belt, unbelievable, socially inappropriate, or factually untrue.

In one graphic example, a Democratic candidate strayed over the line, attacking Republican opposition to abortion even in cases of rape or incest. In an emotional ad, a young woman called her father on the phone. "Daddy? It's Mary Ellen," the female voice said. "Daddy . . . something terrible . . . Daddy." A male voice interrupted. "Mr.

Sawyer? This is Lieutenant Kennan at police headquarters. Your daughter has been raped. Now she's not been harmed, but if you and Mrs. Sawyer and . . ." (voice faded). Focus groups were moved. "Respondents put their heads down, they avoided eye contact with the moderators," the advertising consultant said (Kern, 1989, p. 124). The respondents were so shaken that the consultant recommended dropping the spot. It had gone too far, launching an attack that seemed to shock and appall rather than change attitudes.

In 2008, Republican presidential nominee John McCain chose not to engage in a series of attacks that focused on a controversial Chicago reverend who served as the spiritual leader of a church to which Obama had belonged for 20 years. Reverend Jeremiah Wright was a charismatic, beloved preacher, but one who also had strayed over the line by seeming to suggest that the U.S. had brought on the September 11 attacks through its militaristic foreign policies. Perhaps because the ads might have been seen as touching on racial issues, suggesting that he was race-baiting, McCain chose not to bring Reverend Wright into his 2008 advertising campaign. His decision, probably a wise one, underscores the risky nature of negative ads and the recognition that they can backfire. (See http://www.press.uchicago.edu/Misc/Chicago/284996.html for classic negative spots that raise some of these issues.)

Advertising Effects

So, what influences do political ads exert? Research documents that presidential campaign advertising can influence voters' beliefs and attitudes toward candidates. The concepts of agenda-setting, priming, and framing, discussed earlier, are particularly helpful in shedding light on political advertising effects.

Learning

First, some good news—or news that may surprise you. People learn from political advertisements. They acquire knowledge about candidates' issue positions and their personal qualities (Freedman, Franz, & Goldstein, 2004; Kaid, 2004, 2006). This can be a good thing, inasmuch as it provides candidates with a way to convey their backgrounds and perspectives to voters, without the filter of news.

Reinforcement

Political advertisements can also bolster partisan attitudes. Advertising effects are heightened when themes resonate with voters' social concerns and political beliefs (Ansolabehere & Iyengar, 1995). Ads can reinforce beliefs, activate sentiments, and bring out the base in close elections.

Agenda-Setting and Priming

Candidates develop ads to set the agenda and prime voters. They want voters to focus on the issues they believe to be most important—those that play to their strengths. In agenda-setting terms, candidates devise commercials to convince voters that their (the candidate's) issues should be the ones voters call to mind.

They also hope to prime voters. As discussed in Chapter 6, voters use a variety of criteria to evaluate presidential candidates. They consider personal attributes, such as experience and compassion, or they may take into account the candidate's positions on the economy or foreign affairs. Candidates try to prime the agendas that they believe are most consequential. They want voters to pay heed to their campaign issues when deciding for whom to vote. The candidate who emphasizes the ailing economy in agenda-setting ads would like voters to regard economic problems, and the candidate's expertise in fixing them, as the most important factors to consider when casting a ballot.

Research on the 1992 election illustrates how candidate Bill Clinton harnessed agenda-setting and priming to his advantage. With the nation's economy sagging and middle-class families feeling the brunt of a recession, economic issues and unemployment were overwhelmingly viewed as the nation's top problems. Democratic consultant James Carville famously brandished a sign, "The Economy, Stupid," in the Little Rock, Arkansas headquarters to underscore the point, lest anyone forget. His blunt statement became the mantra of the Clinton campaign. Clinton reinforced this message, building an agenda around the economy, asking voters to recall how the incumbent president, George H.W. Bush, had promised in 1988 that they would be better off four years from now. Reminding voters that family health care costs had risen nearly $2,000 in four years, the advertising voiceover asked, "Well, it's four years later. How're you doing?"

Clinton's ads helped set an economic agenda. They primed voters by suggesting that a candidate's ability to improve the economy was the most important factor to consider when making the vote choice. Voters with high exposure to advertising were more likely than those with low exposure to base their vote decision at least in part on the economy. They were also more inclined to believe that Clinton possessed the ability to improve the economy (West, 2010).

Sixteen years later, in 2008, candidates, media, and voters again converged on the economy in the wake of the financial crisis, the collapse of a major securities company, and the largest single-day drop in the Dow Industrial average since September 11, 2001. Most voters regarded the economy as the most important issue facing the country and cited it as the key factor influencing their vote decision. With the agenda set, the stage was set for priming. The Democrats seized the opportunity, recognizing that the public blamed the party in power (the Republicans) for economic woes and typically regarded Democrats as more capable than Republicans of resolving economic problems (Kinder, 2003). Obama sought to prime economic issues, encouraging voters to regard a candidate's performance in the economic sphere as the most important factor in their voting choice.

He argued that his policies would do more than McCain's to restore economic solvency. Criticizing McCain for stating that "the fundamentals of the economy are sound," Obama contended that his opponent was ill-suited to managing America's financial problems. One Obama ad employed this priming strategy:

> *Announcer:* Maybe you're struggling just to pay the mortgage on your home. But recently John McCain said, "The fundamentals of our economy are strong." Hmmm. Then again, that same day, when asked how many houses he owns . . . McCain lost track. He couldn't remember. Well, it's seven. Seven houses. And here's one house America can't afford to let John McCain move into.

Obama's strategy worked. Voters expressed their confidence in his ability to make the right decisions on the economy (Toner and Nagourney, 2008). Sixty percent of voters said the economy was the most important issue facing the country, and most of them voted for Obama (Calmes & Thee, 2008).

This informal evidence for priming is backed up by empirical research. A large-scale field experimental study of televised campaign advertising found that TV ads exerted a strong, short-term impact on voter preferences (Gerber et al., 2011). The researchers argued that the ads influenced voters by priming or bringing to mind key political evaluations.

Framing

"Campaigns," Kinder (2003) observed, "are not so much debates over a common set of issues as they are struggles to define what the election is about" (p. 365). How true this statement is! Candidates who can convince voters to adopt their framework for viewing the issues can win the White House. Think of it this way: There is consensus in difficult economic times that economic conditions are the most important problems ailing the country. Framing emphasizes that the salience of economic issues is not the only factor that influences voting. Rather, what also matters is how candidates frame the economy—how they talk about it and what they choose to emphasize.

In 2012, Republican candidate Mitt Romney framed the election around Obama's inability to improve the economy. His messages emphasized job losses and the "crushing"

Figure 15.3 In 2012, Republican presidential nominee Mitt Romney framed campaign ads around Obama's handling of the economy, emphasizing high unemployment and job losses attributed to Obama's leadership.

Getty Images

debt; he hammered on the facts that more than 23 million Americans were out of work and close to 1 in 6 Americans were living in poverty (see Figure 15.3). One of his ads, modeled after a 2008 Obama commercial, flashed facts on the screen, such as evidence of 40 straight months of over 8 percent unemployment and millions of home-owners still underwater on mortgages. Dramatic music accompanied the factual claims. Then, quoting an ill-advised statement Obama had made that "the private sector is doing fine," the ad used those six words against him: "The private sector is doing fine? How can President Obama fix our economy if he doesn't understand it's broken?"

The Obama campaign counter-framed. Recognizing that "in a weak economy, hope and change would not work," his advisers spent one-fifth of the campaign budget on attack ads that ran in the summer of 2012 (Lizza, 2012, p. 62). They sought to define Romney before the Republican nominee could position himself. Obama's strategists framed the election as a contest between Obama, who (they argued) had championed programs that benefited the middle class, and Romney, a "richer-than-rich" capitalist who favored tax cuts for the rich and did not have the middle class's collective back. The Obama campaign developed the Joe Soptic ad described at the outset of the chapter, as well as a spot, which recruited more than 2 million YouTube hits, that showed an audio clip of a crooning Romney warbling "America the Beautiful." As Romney sang, words scrolled across the screen, informing voters that "Mitt Romney's firms shipped jobs to Mexico and China" and "had millions in a Swiss bank account." The ad underlined the contrast between Romney's patriotic words and his purportedly un-American behavior.

Framing may have made a difference. Given the tepid economic recovery, Romney should have been successful at making the election a referendum on Obama's steward-ship of the economy. Yet nearly 6 in 10 voters who thought their family's situation was about the same as it was in 2008 voted for Obama (Calmes & Thee-Brenan, 2012). Obama's attack ads, alleging that Romney's Bain Capital firm had plundered companies and cost workers their jobs, which were shown in the spring, may have had some impact on the opinions of undecided voters in battleground states (Rutenberg & Zeleny, 2012b). Like the Swift Boat ads unleashed against John Kerry in 2004 and the attacks on Dukakis in 1988, these ads seemed to have had an impact because they were broadcast before voters had formed strong opinions toward the candidate.

In sum, political advertising can impart information, strengthen attitudes, shape the agenda, and influence the ways voters frame candidates. The operative word is "can." Political ads are not speeding bullets that inject political messages into voters' brains. Research discussed in the previous chapter and highlighted by the classic limited effects model underscores the limits of persuasive political ads. What's more, it is difficult to tease out advertising effects from the host of other influences simultaneously occurring in campaigns. Political advertising remains as much an art as a science. The best we can say is that political ads can influence the attitudes of low-involved voters by stimulating peripheral processes. Ads can set the agenda and frame issues when voters are higher in involvement. They have the potential to exert strong short-term effects (Gerber et al, 2011), and they can mobilize voters, helping them to translate political attitudes into voting behavior. In close elections, candidates assume that negative ads make a difference, and they spend lots of money trying to attack and demonize oppo-nents, calling on subtle techniques of psychological persuasion.

NEGATIVE ADS: THE GOOD, THE BAD, AND THE UGLY

Now let's turn to values and the normative issues that surround negative advertisements. Are negative ads good or bad? Well, that depends on what you mean by those terms, right? With an eye toward normative effects of negative ads, let's review the pros, cons, and misleading facets of negative advertising.

In Defense of Negative Ads

Critics argue that negative campaign ads turn off voters, causing them to stay home when they might have shown up at the polls. But there is little evidence that negative campaigns uniformly depress voter turnout (Arceneaux & Nickerson, 2010; Krupnikov, 2011; Lau & Pomper, 2004; Lau, Sigelman, & Rovner, 2007). In fact, negative ads have a variety of positive features.

First, negative ads focus more on issues than do positive spots (Geer, 2006). A positive ad may not trash the opponent, but it can contain lots of puffed-up Pollyannish descriptions of the candidate. Negative ads frequently criticize the opponent's position on an economic, health, social, or foreign policy issue. The ad may put the opponent down, but it bases its criticism on something more substantial than puff. It offers a policy-based criticism or evidence, and these represent cogent arguments for or against voting for a candidate.

Second, negative ads get people thinking, arguing, and actively processing politics. They engage voters' minds in a way that blander, positive ads do not (see Brader, 2006; Kam, 2006). Think about Romney's ad that attacked Obama's economic record or Obama's spots that offered a harsh portrait of Romney's private equity firm. You may have agreed or disagreed with them, but they made you think about the economy under Obama and the effects that a corporate buy-out exerts on workers. Messages that stimulate thinking encourage the kind of deliberation on which strong democracy depends.

Third, negative campaign messages can promote political interest, encouraging activists to work harder for their candidate and knock on more doors, with arguments against the opposing candidate at the ready (Brooks & Geer, 2007.) After all, it is the partisans, not the ambivalent, who participate in electoral causes (Mutz, 2006). They are the ones who sit in campaign offices making phone calls for up to 15 hours a day. Partisans are the foot soldiers of democracy. If negative ads activate and persuade them to go out and work harder for their side, that can't be an entirely bad thing. It may even be good for politics.

Fourth, negative advertising provides a check on the system. As critic Bradley Smith points out, "Without attention-grabbing, cogent, memorable, negative campaigning, almost no challenger can hope to win unless an incumbent has just been found guilty of a heinous crime" (1996, p. A22). Negative ads offer challengers ways to lay out shortcomings in incumbents' records. As political scientist John C. Geer notes, "If the public wants to have accountability, someone has to do the accounting and that accounting is not done through positive feel-good appeals, but through harsh political attack where voters are made aware of the problems of the incumbent" (2006, p. 110).

Absent negative commercials, Ronald Reagan might not have convinced the electorate to unseat Jimmy Carter, who presided over a sagging economy with double-digit inflation. Without negative ads, Bill Clinton could not have called out George H.W. Bush for his lackluster stewardship of the economy.

Criticisms of Negative Ads

The above arguments present a forceful defense of negative advertising. However, there is another side, one that points to problems with negative spots.

First, negative ads clutter the airwaves with uncivil attacks on people who aspire to represent and lead the citizenry. Negative ads can dispirit voters and reduce trust in government (Ansolabehere & Iyengar, 1995; Lau & Pomper, 2004; Lau, Sigelman, & Rovner, 2007). We want people to feel that they can influence government and change bad policies. Negative advertising can depress feelings of efficacy.

Second, negative ads reward opposition research, a tawdry type of political consulting in which strategists dig for dirt and try to uncover skeletons in the opponent's closet. Advertising specialists then take these juicy, occasionally seamy, tidbits and place them front-and-center in negative spots. This is a mean-spirited way to knock off a candidate who may otherwise have a fine record of public service. It can lift a candidate's statements out of context and imply that one misstatement, inept policy decision, or foolish personal behavior accurately represents the candidate's personality or time-honored record of attainments. Negative advertising abuses persuasion, exploiting story-telling to present a narrative that ridicules another human being for one unctuous purpose: Unseating the candidate and yanking away his or her power.

Third, negative ads trifle with truth. To be sure, negative spots do offer issue-based criticisms of incumbents' records and raise reasonable questions about the opponent's positions on policy questions or qualifications for office. But here is the rub: Ads have famously distorted or falsified the opponent's record with misleading statements. It is instructive to review three examples, two from 2012 and a classic from 1988, the campaign that had the most negative spots ever (West, 2010).

Deceptive Negative Ads in 2012

A pro-Obama PAC developed a frequently promoted ad that starred Joe Soptic, the steelworker described earlier. Soptic talked matter-of-factly about how he and his family lost their health care when Mitt Romney and Bain Capital closed his steel plant in Kansas. He explained that his wife became ill shortly after he lost his health care policy. She had Stage 4 cancer and there was nothing anyone could do to save her. Soptic

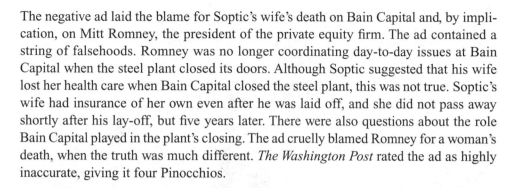

concluded, with biting understatement, "I do not think Mitt Romney realizes what he's done to anyone. And, furthermore, I do not think Mitt Romney is concerned" (see "Understands"—YouTube at www.youtube.com/watch?v=Nj70XqOxptU).

The negative ad laid the blame for Soptic's wife's death on Bain Capital and, by implication, on Mitt Romney, the president of the private equity firm. The ad contained a string of falsehoods. Romney was no longer coordinating day-to-day issues at Bain Capital when the steel plant closed its doors. Although Soptic suggested that his wife lost her health care when Bain Capital closed the steel plant, this was not true. Soptic's wife had insurance of her own even after he was laid off, and she did not pass away shortly after his lay-off, but five years later. There were also questions about the role Bain Capital played in the plant's closing. The ad cruelly blamed Romney for a woman's death, when the truth was much different. *The Washington Post* rated the ad as highly inaccurate, giving it four Pinocchios.

Late in the campaign, Romney aired a whopper of his own. His ads were targeted at voters in Ohio, the ever-important swing state that was widely believed to play a pivotal role in the outcome of the election. Romney sought to undermine Obama's argument that government bailout of the automobile industry, battered by the financial crisis, had saved many auto-related Ohio jobs. His ad stated that Chrysler, which was the recipient of federal bailout funds, planned to produce Jeeps in China. The ad suggested that the jobs would come at the expense of jobs in Ohio. "What happened to the promises made to autoworkers in Toledo and throughout Ohio?" the ad asked.

In truth, the company was considering increasing production in China for sales that took place only in China. It was not transplanting jobs from Ohio to China. The fact-checking service PolitiFact gave it a "Pants on Fire" (as in "Liar, liar, pants on fire") designation, later rating it as the 2012 Lie of the Year (Holan, 2012; Rutenberg & Peters, 2012).

Crime in 1988

In 1988 Vice President George H.W. Bush faced Democratic nominee Michael Dukakis, a former governor of Massachusetts (see Figure 15.4). In the summer, Dukakis led George H.W. Bush by 17 points. Bush's consultants figured that if they wanted to win they could not just emphasize Bush's experience as vice president or economic growth in the Reagan–Bush 1980s. They had to go negative.

Focus group participants said they were uncomfortable with Dukakis's support of a Massachusetts prison furlough program that permitted prisoners to receive weekend passes from jail. The intent of furloughs is to reintegrate prisoners into society in an

Figure 15.4 In 1988 Republicans directed a heavy barrage of negative advertising against Democratic nominee Michael Dukakis (shown here), portraying him as out of step with "mainstream" American values. The 1988 ads were controversial, and the 1988 campaign had the highest proportion of negative ads in contemporary times.

Time & Life Pictures/Getty Images

effort to help rehabilitate them. However, Massachusetts allowed one prisoner, Willie Horton, to receive as many as 10 weekend passes from jail. Horton was significant in several respects. He was a convicted murderer. On one of his prison leaves, he fled to Maryland, where he kidnapped a young couple and repeatedly raped the woman. Horton was also Black. The woman was White.

A series of infamous ads was developed, televised, and repeatedly shown. Ads were devised by a PAC that was independent of the Bush campaign. In this way, Bush could benefit from the attacks, but profess that he had no role in the development of the nasty spots.

The centerpiece was the "Revolving Door" segment. This spot exploited the symbol of a revolving door to highlight Dukakis's policy of permitting prisoners to go in and out of prison, presumably forever. In the ad, the announcer stated that: "As governor,

Michael Dukakis vetoed mandatory sentences for drug dealers. He vetoed the death penalty. His revolving door prison policy gave weekend furloughs to first-degree murderers not eligible for parole." The visual track reinforced the message by showing a revolving door, composed of bars, that rotates as a long line of men in prison garb walk in and then out the door.

The words "*268 escaped*" were then superimposed on the screen, cueing the announcer to dramatically intone: "While out, many committed other crimes, like kidnapping and rape." The ad invited the incorrect inference that 268 first-degree murderers had jumped furlough to rape and kidnap innocent people (Jamieson, 1992). But of the 268 prisoners who skipped furlough during Dukakis's first two terms as governor, only four were first-degree murderers not eligible for parole, and only one of these went on to kidnap and rape. That man was Willie Horton. Obviously, if four prisoners jump furlough, it is bad, and if one kidnaps and rapes, it is terrible. But the ad implied more, and the implication strayed from the truth.

There was another, more serious problem with the anti-Dukakis advertising campaign. Another ad running at the same time starkly portrayed Horton as "a scowling Black man with a disheveled Afro" (Mayer, 2012b, p. 42). While on furlough, the ad said, he raped a White woman and stabbed her fiancé. The ads—*268 escaped* and the Horton spots—worked together, encouraging voters to see a Black man—a murderer and rapist—as the personification of Dukakis's revolving door prison policy. The ads deliberately invoked a racist archetype and linked it with Dukakis, priming voters and perhaps triggering fears and hostility among some Whites (Mendelberg, 2001). The man who developed the ads, Larry McCarthy, defended them, noting that people take crime seriously, that it was "every suburban mother's greatest fear," and he just wanted to find a way to move voters (Mayer, 2012b).

In sum, the balance sheet on negative advertising is complex and multifaceted. Negative ads provide challengers with a legitimate way to contest established incumbents, they promote accountability, and can increase voters' awareness of shortcomings in the opponent's campaign. The downsides are that negative ads can trifle with the truth and mislead voters. Candidates can steer clear of responsibility for attacks sponsored by sympathetic, independent political groups.

It is difficult to make a simple statement as to whether negative advertising is more good than bad or more bad than good. Certainly, the ads offer benefits, more than is ordinarily assumed. But do they represent the optimal method to wage a high-stakes campaign about important public issues (see Reflections box)?

REFLECTIONS: USING NEGATIVE ADS CONSTRUCTIVELY

Contrary to popular opinion, negative campaigning can have positive effects. As the chapter noted, negative ads prominently discuss issues, typically more than positive spots, catalyze active voter processing of politics, and stimulate interest and enthusiastic partisan participation. The rub is that negative ads can be nasty, mean-spirited, and downright deceptive.

There is nothing that says negative campaign messages must include nasty attacks on the opponent. Communicating the drawbacks of a policy or shortcomings of an opponent can advance democratic aims. To help appreciate this, you might think about an issue you feel strongly about or an elected official with whom you disagree. Write a short political persuasive message that criticizes the policy or position of the candidate. Be critical, but polite. Use arguments, not aggression. Write a two-sided message that gives your position and the viewpoint of the other side or candidate. Then thoughtfully refute the alternative point of view.

CORRECTING MISPERCEPTIONS

Even defenders of negative campaign ads acknowledge that it is important that false claims are rebutted and truthful information is circulated. How can misleading ads be controlled, countered, or checked? Don't look to the Federal Election Commission (FEC) or the Federal Communications Commission (FCC). The FEC enforces U.S. campaign finance laws, and the FCC regulates broadcast, wire, and satellite communications. There is little they can to do regulate campaign advertising because the courts have ruled that political campaign speech is protected by the First Amendment. That's good in many ways, but it also leaves open the possibility of mischief: abuses by campaign consultants who push the envelope on truth.

The news media and fact-checking groups provide additional ways to check and refute inaccurate claims. FactCheck.org and PolitiFact.com offer non-partisan checks on deceptive ads. Non-partisan fact-checkers scrutinize candidate ads, comparing claims that candidates make about opponents with verifiable facts, and looking to see if the claims are factually accurate. Journalists frequently turn to these groups when preparing articles that discuss negative ads. They develop lengthy reports called ad watches or fact checks, which describe a negative ad and assess its truth value. Ad-watching news stories are excellent educational tools that can lead viewers to regard the targeted ad as less fair and less important (Cappella & Jamieson, 1994). Unfortunately, they have shortcomings.

First, fact-checking news reports run the risk of magnifying the effects of the misleading spot (Ansolabehere & Iyengar, 1995). In their zeal to describe the juicy, misleading tidbits of a particular ad, journalists rebroadcast, or in websites attach, the ad, giving it free publicity and a double whammy of promotion. News viewers may see or hear the deceptive ad and ignore the journalistic criticism, much to the delight of the strategists who developed the spot.

Second, technical problems can minimize fact-check effects. The printed information that identifies the sponsor of the ad—or corrects the misinformation—may not be on the screen long enough to allow viewers to process and remember the information (West, 2010).

The third problem is viewer selectivity. In an era of niche media, people can tune into cable news programs, blogs, and posts that reinforce their view of the political world, while blissfully ignoring programming with which they disagree. As a result of partisan biases, viewers may never even see fact checks that correct false claims advanced by their candidate. Fox viewers may not learn about FactCheck.org's criticism of a Romney spot because Fox chose not to air it. MSNBC viewers may never see a factual critique of an Obama ad because MSNBC opted not to show the ad or describe its factual errors. Partisans live in media worlds which pleasantly reinforce their political viewpoints. This means that they may never tune into media outlets that question their side's political spots. Yet democracy is enhanced when people make thoughtful judgments and consider perspectives other than their own.

Making matters worse, campaign consultants play to these trends. They sometimes derogate the fact-checkers, adopting a self-serving, strangely postmodern critique. After PolitiFact gave one prominent Romney ad a "Pants on Fire" rating, the Romney campaign chose to dig in its heels. Rather than acknowledging the inaccuracy and trying to correct it, a Romney aide maligned fact-checking services, claiming that "fact checkers come to this with their own sets of thoughts and beliefs, and we're not going to let our campaign be dictated by fact-checkers." At different points of the 2012 presidential campaign, both sides repeated claims that were false (Cooper, 2012).

This is troubling because it indicates that campaigns may be so determined to win at any cost that they choose to ignore the facts. By trying to suggest that "hey, it's all relative, and fact-checkers are biased too," Romney's pollster derogated fact-checking services that work hard to adopt non-partisan criteria of evaluating claims. Fact-checking sites regularly point out inaccuracies in ads developed by parties and PACs across the political spectrum. They provide an important service by calling attention to inaccurate or deceptive commercials. Research suggests that fact-checking reports are particularly likely to correct misperceptions if they clearly state that viewers are watching portions of a misleading commercial and call attention to the erroneous claims (Perloff, 1998).

The good news is that fact-checks can register with voters. In Ohio, Romney's misleading ad that suggested Chrysler was moving automobile jobs from Ohio to China failed to achieve its stated objective. Widely publicized fact checks pointing to false statements in the ad seem to have left an imprint on voters (Nagourney et al., 2012). Thanks in part to these corrective communications, the ad backfired.

WHAT DO YOU THINK?

How can media and other political communications most effectively correct misleading ads? How can they encourage a more transparent system of political persuasion?

CONCLUSIONS

Political advertising is a centerpiece of presidential campaigns. Ads are the primary modality by which candidates communicate with voters in a mediated political age. Several billion dollars were spent on political advertising during the 2012 election, with a disturbing number of ads funded by outside PACs that are not accountable to voters. Campaigns spend substantial time, effort, and money developing visually compelling ads, placing them strategically in key markets in swing states, and swiftly posting answers to opponents' negative ads online. Negative ads predominate in presidential elections because they are memorable, garner news coverage, and are widely believed by consultants to move poll numbers. However, negative ads do not always work. If they run up against strong preexisting attitudes or are perceived to be unfair, they can fizzle or boomerang.

Political ads can influence the agenda, prime issues, and persuasively frame problems or candidate attributes. Presidential candidates have used ads to prime economic issues and to frame the election around the shortcomings of the opposing candidate, sometimes developing visceral appeals that lambast the opposing candidate in ways that voters dislike, but frequently remember. Although they are roundly condemned, negative advertisements offer benefits to voters and the larger political system. They can contain considerable issue information, stimulate political thinking, activate partisans, and offer challengers a viable way to unseat incumbents. But negative ads have shortcomings: They can dispirit voters and reward dirt-digging that deliberately invites false inferences. Negative advertising, as Schudson (1986) would acknowledge, is a complex, multi faceted, and "uneasy" type of persuasive communication.

In the end, presidential elections are about persuasion, and persuasion is not equivalent to truth. As Geer (2006, p. 158) notes, "politics is about disagreement," and disagreement is bound to lead its protagonists to cannily frame, slant, and even distort. Lau and Pomper (2004) emphasize that "elections are about choices, not courtesy" (p. 93). In the end, we cannot depend on candidates to offer entirely truthful statements. This is why the nation needs a vigilant press that holds political leaders' feet to the fire and challenges them when they trifle with truth.

16 Presidential Debates

Debates have a long history in American politics. "The American political system grew up with debate," Kathleen Hall Jamieson and David S. Birdsell (1988) remind us. "Colonial assemblies debated revolution, the Constitutional Convention debated the Constitution, and Congress debated the law" (p. 17).

The most famous debates—the ones that leap to mind when political debates are discussed—were the Lincoln–Douglas debates of 1858. Abraham Lincoln, who had served in Congress and acquired a reputation as a spell-binding orator, ran against Stephen Douglas, the incumbent, for a U.S. Senate seat in Illinois. They debated seven times in as many Illinois cities. The debates were rhetorical tours de force that harnessed legal argumentation, historical appeals to the Founding Fathers, and stirring moral oratory. The issue was slavery. Douglas embraced popular sovereignty. He adopted the relativist position that questions of morality must be decided by the people themselves. Thus, each state had the right to decide to continue slavery, or abolish the institution (Burt, 2013). Lincoln adopted an absolutist natural rights perspective, forcefully arguing that slavery was morally wrong (Zarefsky, 1990; see also interesting websites, such as http://www.ushistory.org/us/32b.asp and Lincoln–Douglas Debates—Angry Town Halls of 1858 on http://www.youtube.com/watch?v=AKfNMel5dug).

The Lincoln–Douglas debates have been justly celebrated as masterful exemplars of political rhetoric. Let's not mythologize them.

First, they took place in a senatorial—not, as often assumed, presidential—campaign. Arguments may have been lofty, but they were also weapons of electoral persuasion. Both debaters crafted arguments to appeal to voters. Douglas won the election, in part because his debate and campaign arguments persuaded the undecided, swing voters of Illinois that Lincoln was a radical abolitionist.

Second, contrary to legend, audiences probably were not enraptured and mesmerized by the debaters' eloquence. Many of the thousands who did attend the debates were picnicking, their attention focused on the food, not the candidates; others attended not to hear the arguments, but to partake in the drama of the moment (Zarefsky, 1990). In this way, audience members were not unlike today's political junkies who tune in to CNN or Fox to follow the horse race.

Thirdly and importantly, the premise of the debate—that slavery should be debated—nowadays strikes us as preposterous, offensive to our moral sensibilities. It seems so patently obvious that slavery has no defense that any formal debate on the topic seems inappropriate, and certainly unworthy of celebration. At the time, sadly, the topic was a matter of debate, reminding us that political communication is a function of a particular time and place.

This brings us to today. With presidential debates a central part of the presidential campaign landscape, it is important to understand debate content and effects, as well as the larger policy complexities. The chapter focuses on presidential debates because they have stimulated the most scholarly research. However, the issues and conclusions have implications for the variety of political debates that occur in state and Congressional election campaigns.

The chapter examines debates from a variety of vantage points. The first portion of the chapter sets the stage by discussing major functions of debates and defining a presidential debate. The second section reviews fundamental political features and formats of debates. The third section examines the strategic influences of debates, drawing on major presidential debates of the past half-century, as well as social science research. Subsequent sections examine cognitive effects of debates on voters and the role debates play in the political system.

The final portion of the chapter, bringing together the chapters in this part of the book, offers a broad postscript on the 2012 election.

DEBATE FUNCTIONS AND DEFINITION

Presidential debates serve three different functions for the political communication system.

For candidates, they are, first and foremost *political* events. From the perspective of presidential candidates, debates offer key opportunities "to win over undecided voters, to reinforce voters who have already made a decision concerning whom to vote for," and to change the minds of more open-minded voters (Hinck, 1993, p. 2). Candidates do not want to educate the electorate. They want to exploit debates to achieve concrete political objectives (Kraus, 1988).

Debates play a different role for voters. They help voters to decide which candidate best serves their interest, who shares their values, and how the candidates might perform as president. For partisan activists, debates are key opportunities to shore up the base and articulate strategies to appeal to swing voters. For politically interested voters, debates stimulate conversation, sometimes funny and edgy conversations on social media and via Twitter. For less involved voters, they are like stock car races, where you cheer for your driver and secretly hope an exciting minor accident will occur, in the form of a gaffe or goof committed by the opposing candidate.

Presidential debates also perform symbolic functions for the larger political system. They represent the only live, real-time forum in which candidates stand side by side, discussing policy issues. They put potential leaders before citizens in a relatively unmediated forum. Unlike in political commercials or microtargeted Internet messages, arguments are not packaged by consultants. Unlike the news, debates are not screened and edited by journalistic gatekeepers. They are exercises in civic education that help citizens to acquire new information, approach issues more complexly, and consider new perspectives on vexing problems. At least that is the hope.

These three functions can conflict. A debate that advances a candidate's political needs may not serve voters if it evades the issues. A debate that crystallizes issues can enhance voter knowledge. But if candidates end up making statements that turn off swing voters, they lose. A debate that thoughtfully articulates divergent dimensions of policy problems can advance civic goals. But if the discussion is couched in policy-wonks' abstractions, it can go over the heads of less educated voters.

Definition

Presidential debates are not authentic debates. A debate, J.J. Auer correctly (1962) points out, is: "(1) a confrontation, (2) in equal and adequate time, (3) of matched contestants, (4) on a stated proposition, (5) to gain an audience decision" (p. 146). Any of you who debated in high school or college knows this very well. Debaters research a topic, present detailed arguments, and prepare persuasive rebuttals on a specific issue. One side defends the proposition and the other refutes it. A judge determines who wins, based on carefully honed criteria. A well-respected genre of debate, derived from the classic 1858 debates, is called Lincoln–Douglas.

Although candidates in the presidential debates compete for the most powerful job on the planet, they do not debate in the true sense of the word. They do not debate a stated proposition, like "Taxes on people who earn more than a $1 million should be increased to reduce the deficit," or "There should be an immediate ban on assault rifles," or "The U.S. should do whatever is necessary to prevent Iran from getting a nuclear weapon." Instead, their debates revolve around generic domestic policies or foreign affairs. Questions can focus on image, such as a candidate's likability or experience. Debaters are not forced to address specific issues or rebut opponents. They can elide issues and ignore opponents' arguments. A judge does not adjudicate the decision, based on a reasoned analysis of arguments and rebuttals. A poll is taken after the debate, and Americans use a host of criteria, including the candidate's non-verbal skills and demeanor, to decide who won.

Better to view a debate as a joint appearance or face-to-face encounter. A **presidential debate** is defined here as "the joint appearance by two or more opposing candidates, who expound on their positions, with explicit and equitable provisions for refutation without interruption" (Martel, 1983, p. 2).

Debates can feature considerable clash on the issues (McKinney & Carlin, 2004). Candidates formulate arguments on policy matters, proclaiming accomplishments, attacking the opponent, and offering spirited defenses of their own positions (Benoit & Harthcock, 1999). When questions require candidates to take stands that can alienate key constituents, presidential debaters frequently equivocate or offer vague platitudes. For good or for ill, debates are political encounters.

DEBATE POLITICS AND FORMATS

Modern presidential debates began in 1960, with the Kennedy–Nixon debates. The 1960 debates were the first televised debates between presidential candidates. After a 16-year hiatus, which probably occurred because of the aftershocks of the Kennedy assassination, 1960s protests, and Watergate, debates began in earnest in 1976. Debates have been held in every presidential election since then. They are now ritualized, institutionalized features of the American presidential election. Debates are sponsored by the Commission on Presidential Debates, a non-profit organization that chooses the locations, dates, and debate moderators, working in concert with the two major political parties.

Long before the actual debates occur, candidates' consultants engage in a series of strategic debates. Issues under discussion include the length of time candidates should get to answer questions, whether candidates should sit or stand, if candidates should be able to take notes with pencil and paper, and even the proper height of the podium. Candidates pay attention to these things. So do their consultants. They realize that format and contextual cues can influence audience impressions.

Consider the height factor. Consultants do not want their candidate to be at a disadvantage. In 1976, Jimmy Carter, who was shorter than President Gerald Ford, reportedly inserted lifts in his shoes and wore them during the debates (Jamieson & Birdsell, 1988). Prior to the 1984 vice presidential debate, Democratic consultants did not want their candidate—the 5'4" Geraldine Ferraro—to be looking up at the more than 6-foot tall Republican candidate, George H.W. Bush. Overruling Republicans' objections, they constructed a ramp that resembled the floor covering so Ferraro could be closer to Bush's height without having to visibly step up on any object.

Candidates leave nothing to chance. They recognize that voters judge debates, based on televised cues. A faulty appearance can diminish candidate evaluations. Even subtle cues, shown in split-screen shots, can influence perceptions. A candidate who forgets he or she is being televised when the opponent is speaking, and displays displeasure or irritation, can elicit unfavorable reactions from partisan viewers, reports communication researcher Dietram Scheufele (cf. Peters, 2012c).

Political adviser Myles Martel noted aptly that "it would be no exaggeration to compare the . . . presidential debate process with an advanced game of chess. Nearly every move regarding the decisions to debate, formats, strategies and tactics, and the execution of the debates themselves, was fraught with political implications" (quoted in Kraus, 1988, p. 33).

There are typically three presidential debates, usually lasting 90 minutes. Debates are high-water marks of the fall campaign, national media events that generate immense buzz (Dayan & Katz, 1992). Candidates extensively prepare, trying to rebut anticipated arguments from the opponent. They stage mock debates, with fellow politicians role-playing their opponent. In 2012, Senator John Kerry, the Democratic nominee in 2004, played Mitt Romney, and Ohio Senator Rob Portman, an experienced presidential debate role-player, played Obama. He was so good at parroting likely Obama attacks he actually got under Romney's skin.

Strategists also play the expectations game, tamping down expectations for their candidate. As the 1996 Clinton–Dole debate approached, Dole's campaign managers deliberately poor-mouthed their candidate. "Surely everybody in America knows Bill Clinton is the greatest debater since Benjamin Disraeli," a Dole aide said, comparing Clinton to the storied British prime minister in an effort to reduce expectations for Dole. Sixteen years later, in 2012, a senior Romney adviser engaged in an even bigger hype, saying that Obama "is widely regarded as one of the most talented political communicators in modern history" (Bruni, 2012b, p. 27). Obama, for his part, pooh-poohed his debating skill, saying "Governor Romney, he's a good debater. I'm just O.K."

Formats

There are three debate formats: (1) press conference, where a group of pre-selected reporters ask candidates questions; (2) single moderator, where the moderator, typically a television anchor or political correspondent, asks questions and serves as umpire; and (3) town hall meeting, featuring questions from the audience, frequently undecided voters, typically moderated by a well-known journalist.

The structure of the debate varies, depending on the format and negotiations between rival candidates in a particular election. The amount of time candidates get to respond to questions, number of minutes allocated for rebuttals, and whether there is time for general discussion of debate questions depends on the particular debate (Tuman, 2008). Opening and closing statements are standard features of presidential debates.

Each format has strengths and weaknesses. The press conference, which consists of news reporters, ensures that panelists are experienced and will ask knowledgeable questions. Its weakness is that reporters can ask complicated questions or pose queries designed to trap candidates rather than engage in a policy dialogue (Hellweg, Pfau, & Brydon, 1992). Reporters can also be removed from the everyday world in which ordinary voters reside. Although the press conference format has been employed in other debate settings, like primary debates, it has been used less prominently in presidential debates in recent elections.

The single moderator format reduces the chaos of having a team of journalists hurl questions at candidates. Much depends on the skill of the moderator in making sure candidates stick by the rules. In 1992, a single moderator debate turned into a virtual free-for-all, as the moderator lost control. In 2012, moderator Jim Lehrer was both complimented and criticized. He earned plaudits for letting Romney and Obama converse on a topic for 15-minute intervals, offering the public an opportunity to judge the candidates without journalistic gatekeeping. But others criticized Lehrer for letting the candidates talk beyond their allotted limits and not pressing them when they made misleading statements.

The main benefit of town hall meeting debates is that they bring ordinary people into the electoral process, allowing voters to question candidates directly. By giving citizens the opportunity to communicate directly with candidates for the highest office in the land, the town hall meeting privileges democratic values. Candidates adopt a more voter-centered style, focusing on issues that are on voters' minds (McKinney, 2005). People can zero in on issues that elude the elite media, but are on voters' radar screens. In 2012, a woman asked the candidates to explain their positions on gun control, in the wake of a recent school shooting. She seemed to catch the candidates off guard. Town hall debates can also bring people into the process, stimulating millions of tweets about candidate performance and gaffes. On the other hand, the town hall format has shortcomings. Sometimes voters don't ask good questions. Town hall meetings also do not always provide opportunities for follow-up questions that can push candidates to articulate ideas or clarify misleading remarks.

STRATEGIC DEBATE EFFECTS

What strategic effects do debates exert on voters? How do they influence the campaign? Reporters speculate about these questions, but scholars try to offer answers. By drawing on historical and social science research, I present some general conclusions about debate effects on the campaign (see http://www.youtube.com/watch?v=4Y8SZDH3B_4 for clips of some classic presidential debate moments).

Visuals Matter

If there is one debate that defined the institution of presidential debates of the 20th century, it was this one. If you had to select the debate that generated the most famous empirical study, it would be this one. If scholars were asked to name the debate that exerted the largest impact on the election—or was that widely *perceived* to have had the greatest effect on the election—it would be this one too. It was the first debate between John F. Kennedy and Richard M. Nixon during the heat of the fall 1960 presidential election (see Figure 16.1). Here is a description of the debate, along with the way candidates appeared:

> "The candidates need no introduction," moderator Howard K. Smith announced to 80 million Americans. Richard Nixon, for his part, looked like an ill-at-ease, unshaven, middle-aged fellow recovering from a serious illness. Jack Kennedy, by contrast, was elegant in a dark, well-tailored suit that set off his healthy tan. Kennedy sat poised, his legs crossed, his hands folded on his lap; Nixon had his legs awkwardly side by side, his hands dangling from the chair arms.
>
> (Matthews, 1996, p. 150)

So began the first presidential debate of the 1960 campaign. Kennedy immediately took the offensive, using his opening statement to lay out a vision (the need to get America moving again) and to create a favorable image of himself as a bold, energetic leader. As the debate wore on, Nixon regained his stride, developing compelling arguments. But even when he articulated credible arguments, Nixon looked fatigued and ill, "his eyes exaggerated hollows of blackness, his jaws, jowls, and face drooping with strain" (White, 1962, p. 289). In fact, Nixon was recovering from a knee injury sustained a

Figure 16.1 The iconic Kennedy–Nixon debate of 1960. During the first presidential debate, Kennedy's personal appearance—his elegance and handsome features—contrasted sharply with Nixon's unseemly jowls and five o'clock shadow. The debate produced a sea-change in attitudes toward political media, leading observers to conclude that on TV the visual dwarfs the verbal.

month before. He refused to use TV makeup, his light skin did not project well before the camera, and his notorious "five o'clock shadow" coarsened his face. Nixon's appearance seemed to take a toll. The next day a now-famous research study was conducted. The survey found that people who watched the debate on television believed Kennedy had won. But those who listened to the debate on radio came to the opposite conclusion: They thought Nixon won (Kraus, 1996).

The study has been endlessly discussed, the findings ceaselessly dissected. Did candidate looks trump what they said? Did the television medium favor appearance over verbal substance? Alternatively, did Kennedy's nasal New England twang sound worse over radio, reducing his credibility with radio listeners? We don't know the answers to these questions. The best scholarship on the subject suggests that appearance did count for a great deal in the first debate, and Kennedy's visual presence, coupled with Nixon's unseemly appearance, probably led TV viewers to pronounce him the winner (Druckman, 2003; Kraus, 1996).

The debate produced a sea-change in attitudes toward political media. A generation of consultants and candidates concluded that on television the visual dwarfs the verbal, and physical appearance trumps substantive issues. Nixon ruefully concluded that "what hurt me the most in the first debate was not the substance of the encounter between Kennedy and me, but the disadvantageous contrast in our physical appearances . . . The fact remains one bad camera angle on television can have far more effect on the election outcome than a major mistake in writing a speech" (Kraus, pp. 83–84). Resonating to Nixon's message and the received wisdom on this issue, presidential candidates in the years that followed 1960 paid close attention to the role visual image could play in debates, maintaining eye contact with the camera, and smiling at appropriate moments to convey likability.

But the popular consensus simplifies political reality. On the one hand, visual impressions do play a critical role in presidential debates. Appearance does count. But Kennedy complemented his attractive image with persuasive arguments and compelling words. Most voters pay careful attention to at least some of presidential debates and will not be bowled over by a pretty face that mouths platitudes or offers poor arguments. (Physically attractive candidates like Dan Quayle and Sarah Palin did not score victories in their vice presidential debates.) Second, the first 1960 debate enhanced Kennedy's image and probably contributed to his razor-thin victory (White, 1962). But, contrary to myth, it was not the sole reason he defeated Nixon. Kennedy also benefited from making a heart-felt, but politically strategic, phone call to Rev. Martin Luther King, Jr.'s wife, expressing sympathy upon learning that her husband faced a six-month jail term for courageously protesting segregation in Atlanta. The phone call may have won him the support of many Black voters.

In sum, several lessons emerged from the first 1960 presidential debate. The most consequential is that the medium matters. Physical appearances count on television. Visual cues can influence candidate perceptions.

Narrative and Argumentation Count

When Ronald Reagan debated President Jimmy Carter in 1980, there were conflicting expectations about Reagan's performance. He was an experienced political figure, a former California governor, and movie actor whose communication skills were well respected. But some voters worried that he was a political extremist and perhaps, when it came to military interventions, a little "trigger-happy." To counteract these fears and reinforce positive impressions, he needed to turn in a strong debate performance.

Reagan articulated a persuasive vision, brimming with ideas and optimism. In his closing statement, speaking confidently and looking intently into the camera, he invited voters to consider a series of now-famous questions:

> I think when you make that [voting] decision, it might be well if you would ask yourself, are you better off than you were four years ago? Is it easier for you to go and buy things in the stores than it was four years ago? Is there more or less unemployment in the country than there was four years ago? Is America as respected throughout the world as it was? Do you feel that our security is as safe, that we're as strong as we were four years ago? And if you answer all of those questions "yes," why then, I think your choice is very obvious as to whom you will vote for. If you don't agree, if you don't think that this course that we've been on for the last four years is what you would like to see us follow for the next four, then I could suggest another choice that you have.
> (E.g., see http://www.debates.org/index.php?page=october-28-1980-debate-transcript)

In all likelihood, these lines had been scripted long in advance. No matter. They were delivered with dramatic force, humor, and an understatement that bolstered their impact. They also hit home with Americans who were frustrated by a poor economy, double-digit inflation, and Carter's apparent inability to change economic course. They resonated with a public angered by the Carter administration's apparent helplessness in the face of the Iranian government's seizure of American hostages in Tehran.

There was more to Reagan's debate performance than the famous one-liners. He presented an optimistic message, bolstered by strong arguments, and steeped in a narrative infused with American values that paid homage to the aspirations of the electorate (Ritter & Henry, 1994). He promised to lead a crusade "to take government off the backs of the great people of this country and turn you loose again to do those things that I know you can do so well."

Argumentation plays an important part in debates. Candidates who advance coherent arguments, harness evidence, forcefully rebut the opponent's claims, connect ideas with time-honored symbols, and embed their statements in a compelling narrative win debates (see Figure 16.2).

Credibility Matters

In a media age, credibility and the ability to project a credible image on television counts for a lot.

Figure 16.2 Ronald Reagan overcame the doubts of skeptics in a 1980 presidential debate. In a performance peppered with humorous one-liners and unified by an optimistic narrative, he outperformed his opponent, President Jimmy Carter. The debate showed that narrative and cogent argumentation, especially when delivered by an experienced TV hand, can be pivotal in presidential debates.

NBCU Photo Bank via Getty Images

In a 1992 presidential debate, Bill Clinton showcased one of the core components of credibility: good will. With voters concerned that President George H.W. Bush had lost touch with ordinary Americans, Clinton decided to play the empathy card in a town hall debate. A woman, Marissa Hall, boldly came up to ask, "How has the national debt personally affected each of your lives?" It was a strange question because the debt is a macro entity that has indirect and very complex effects on individuals, but Ms. Hall wanted to see how the candidates related to the economic plight of ordinary people. Bush, taking the question literally, understandably stumbled, even asking her to rephrase the question. "I'm not sure I get it. Help me with the question and I'll try to answer it," he said. Clinton, recognizing that an intellectual answer was less important than conveying empathy, turned, Oprah-style, to Ms. Hall, and asked her ever-so-gently to explain "how it affected you again. You know people who lost their jobs and lost their homes?" He conveyed good will, explaining that in his state when people lost their jobs, "there's a good chance I'll know them by their names." He went on to articulate the economic problems that ailed the country and he laid the blame squarely on the policies of Republican Presidents Reagan and Bush (see Figure 16.3).

Clinton's ability to calibrate his answers to the format of the debate—warm-and-fuzzy, folksy, and interpersonal—bolstered his image. His debate performance, strengthened by policy knowledge, enhanced his momentum, helping him defeat Bush in the 1992 election.

Figure 16.3 Bill Clinton displayed canny television-age credibility in a key 1992 presidential debate featuring Clinton, President George H.W. Bush, and independent candidate Ross Perot. Clinton showed that he was comfortable in the more intimate town hall debate arena as he conveyed verbal and non-verbal empathy with the concerns of a citizen posing a question.

Time & Life Pictures/Getty Images

Non-Verbal Communication Can Be Consequential

Non-verbal and subtle verbal cues matter in debates. For some voters they are simple cues, decision-making heuristics that help them cut through complicated, incomprehensible policy statements. For others they constitute a legitimate way to evaluate candidates in an electronic and interactive media age.

During the first 2012 presidential debate between Obama and Romney, Obama seemed listless and detached, and occasionally disdainful during the debate, eyeing his notes, looking down or gulping when Romney pointed to the president's inability to lift the ailing economy. Romney was lithe, alert, looking intently at the camera during his closing remarks, which Obama neglected to do. Romney was full of energy, the boxer always on his feet, jabbing the opponent with punch after punch, hardly the wooden figure of months before. He seemed to exude confidence, whereas Obama appeared tentative at times (see Figure 16.4). Polls showed Romney won the debate, in no small part because of his sensitivity to communicator cues and TV optics.

Even Obama acknowledged that his non-verbal and other communicative behavior worked to his disadvantage. "I guess the consensus is that we didn't have a very good night," he told his senior campaign strategist. "That is the consensus," the strategist readily agreed (Nagourney et al., 2012, P14).

With television networks offering a split screen presentation of the debate, viewers get to see how candidates emote and communicate non-verbally. When Obama looked down

Figure 16.4 Non-verbal communication, the language of political television, played a key role in the first debate of 2012, as a listless President Obama seemed ill-prepared, in comparison to the more buoyant Mitt Romney. Scholars have debated whether television unduly elevates the role played by non-verbal cues in presidential debates.

AFP/Getty Images

at his notes in the first 2012 debate, tens of millions of viewers took notice. When Vice President Joe Biden laughed when opponent Paul Ryan spoke in the 2012 vice presidential debate, viewers either approved, enjoying his non-verbal put-downs, or disapproved, perceiving his behavior unbecoming of a vice president. In either case, non-verbal cues exerted an impact on perceptions.

Television networks regularly show reaction shots in presidential debates, displaying the non-verbal responses of the non-speaking debater. This can call attention to seemingly peripheral reactions—looking at one's notes or evincing a small, but perceptible, grimace—that distract viewers from the substance of a candidate's comments. These reactions can influence audience perceptions of candidate likability (Seiter et al., 2009).

WHAT DO YOU THINK?

Are political debates authentic debates, or just candidates posturing before the camera? Debates do show candidate clashes on the issues, sometimes offering more issue discussion than the news does. But answers can be scripted. Candidates posture to present themselves as warm, fuzzy, and likable. Do debates help to advance voters' deliberation about election issues?

News Media Can Alter Campaign Dynamics

Debates take place in the context of a voracious press. The news media do not just cover the event live, but they endlessly analyze the optics in post-debate commentary. Television replays key snippets. They are shared on YouTube and tweeted about endlessly. Tracking polls look to see if a particular candidate got a bounce. Voters, lacking knowledge of all the complex issues discussed in debates, can turn to journalists for guidance. News media verdicts on who won the debates can function as heuristics, influencing voters' evaluations. In short, news coverage of debates itself exerts an impact (Fridkin et al., 2008; Lemert et al., 1991).

1976: Ford vs. Carter

The classic example of news media effects occurred in the wake of the second debate between President Gerald Ford and his Democratic challenger, Jimmy Carter (see Figure 16.5). A panelist asked Ford a question about United States–Soviet relations, suggesting that the Soviet Union might be getting the better of the U.S. in foreign affairs. After initially arguing that his administration had been pursuing negotiations with the Soviet Union from the vantage point of strength, Ford seemed to accept the premise of the

Figure 16.5 President Gerald Ford faced off against Democratic challenger Jimmy Carter in the second 1976 presidential debate. Ford misspoke on Soviet domination of Eastern Europe, a gaffe that went unnoticed until the media discussed and replayed the mistake over and over again. News media verdicts on presidential debates can occasionally exert strong effects on public opinion.

NBCU Photo Bank via Getty Images

question, responding defensively in a devastating blunder. "There is no Soviet domination of Eastern Europe, and there never will be under a Ford administration," he said, failing to appreciate the obvious fact that in 1976 the Soviet Union dominated and even occupied many Eastern European countries.

The gaffe was not immediately apparent to most Americans. Polls conducted after the debate revealed a razor-thin outcome, with 44 percent saying Ford won, 43 percent giving the nod to Carter, and the rest undecided. As the networks played and replayed Ford's remark, and comments that he had blundered, voters took notice. Polls conducted between 5 p.m. and midnight the day after the debate showed how much difference a day can make in politics. The verdict now? Sixty-two percent thought Carter won, 17 percent called Ford the winner (see also Berquist, 1994; Lemert et al., 1991; Patterson, 1980).

Although Ford's statement was inaccurate and misleading, it was not the profound error of judgment that journalists suggested at the time. When you go back and read the debate transcript, you discover that what Ford meant when he said that "there is no Soviet domination of Eastern Europe" was that *the people* of the Eastern European countries—Poland, Rumania, and Yugoslavia—did not regard themselves as dominated by the Soviet Union, and that each nation had its own autonomy, freedom, and pride. Clearly, Ford knew that the countries in Eastern Europe were under Soviet control. What happened was that Ford got carried away by his own rhetoric and made a statement that was factually incorrect (Perloff, 1998).

And he got hammered for it. You can argue that when someone is running for president, or is president, he or she should be held to a higher standard. If candidates make a mistake in a high-profile presidential debate, then they have to expect that news media coverage will hold them accountable. Or you can argue that the news blew this story totally out of proportion, getting stuck in a feeding frenzy of contemporary journalism. In any case, the news coverage—along with Ford's subsequent ineptness in stubbornly sticking to his statement—caused opinions of Ford's debate performance to plummet. Ford lost ground at a key moment in the campaign, Carter gained momentum, and public perceptions shifted in Carter's favor. The news media verdict on the second Ford–Carter debate may have played a small part in Carter's victory.

2000: Gore vs. Bush

During the heated 2000 presidential campaign, journalists subtly, and sometimes humorously, advanced different narratives of candidates Al Gore and George W. Bush. Bush was viewed as not especially bright and a mediocre student—in short, an "inexperienced dolt" (Jamieson & Waldman, 2003, p. 60). News features described Gore as prone to embellish the truth and hype his professional biography—a "serial exaggerator." (Gore famously said that he "took the initiative in creating the Internet." Gore seemed to have been suggesting that he deserved credit because, as a senator, he had taken a leadership role in providing the funding that transformed a small computer network into a computerized global system. However, the claim seemed farfetched.)

The journalistic narrative took on importance in the wake of the first presidential debate. During the debate, in an effort to emphasize his leadership experience, Gore claimed that he had accompanied the director of the Federal Emergency Management Agency to visit the site of forest fires in Texas. It turned out that, although Gore had toured disaster sites as vice president, he had not accompanied the director to the Texas forest fires. Gore also slightly misspoke about Florida school overcrowding, although the substance of his remarks was accurate (Jamieson & Waldman, 2003). Post-debate press coverage emphasized the inaccurate and "suspect" nature of Gore's statements. You can interpret this as legitimate focus on a candidate's tendency to misstate facts, or over-coverage of a trivial matter. What is noteworthy is that post-debate news coverage influenced voters' perceptions of the debate. Opinions of Gore's honesty declined over the course of the following week. A survey found that as each day passed, more respondents believed Bush won the debate (Jamieson & Waldman, 2003).

Do Debates Influence Election Outcomes?

This is the big question. Candidates, consultants, and pundits frequently pose it. They sometimes debate it. You need to appreciate that it is hard to assess the effects of debates on the electoral outcome. It is empirically difficult to tease out debate effects from other media events occurring at the same time during the campaign. Just because opinions of candidates change after a debate does not mean the debate *caused* the impact. Effects could be results from the debate, news commentary about the debate, a combination of the debate and news commentaries, social media comments, or from unrelated messages, like negative ads that replay candidate debate gaffes. It is also hard to quantify the contribution that debate exposure has on the outcome of the election. Measurements can be unreliable. Nonetheless, social scientists, using refined statistical techniques, have tried to determine the impact of presidential debates on electoral outcomes. Their research has offered insights.

The consensus is that presidential debates can change the outcome of a presidential election—but rarely do. By the time that debates occur, late in the fall campaign, most voters have their minds made up (Holbrook, 1996). Despite the media hoopla, debates are more likely to attract partisans, who have already decided which candidate to support and view the debates to primarily cheer on their candidate (Stimson, 2004). Other voters have already developed perceptions of candidates that are not easy to shake with a debate performance, even if a candidate seems less than likable. Some low-involvement voters who are still undecided may not tune in to the debate. Thus, a debate victory by a come-from-behind candidate may not influence judgments. In most cases, debates simply solidify the position of the front-runner.

In a handful of cases, debates seem to have influenced the electoral outcome. The first Kennedy–Nixon debate of 1960 elevated Kennedy's image, and Kennedy's poll ratings increased from neck-and-neck with Nixon to a four percentage point lead after the last debate (Harwood, 2012). Reagan's stunning defeat of Carter in the 1980 debate helped to turn the tide in Reagan's favor. Egged on by a feeding frenzy of news coverage, the key 1976 Carter–Ford debate and the 2000 Bush–Gore debates may have contributed to Carter's and Bush's victories (Hillygus & Jackman, 2003). When the candidates are neck-and-neck around the time of the debates, debates can make a difference, though it is hard to know exactly how much. But when one candidate leads by a wide margin, debates are not likely to turn the tide.

Even if they don't change the electoral outcome, debates do exert effects. Challengers typically gain stature by holding their own and keeping their cool when appearing in the same public forum as the president (Polsby et al., 2012). Debates, both presidential and vice presidential, drive news coverage and influence online buzz (see Box 16.1).

BOX 16.1 VICE PRESIDENTIAL DEBATES: FIRST DO NO HARM

Ever since the 1976 debate between Republican Bob Dole and Democrat Walter Mondale, vice presidential debates have emerged as ritualized features of presidential campaigns. The vice presidential debate serves several functions for the political system (Hinck, 1993). First, it provides voters with an opportunity to evaluate the individuals who could take the reins of power in the event of tragedy. Second, it offers people the opportunity to assess the judgments of the presidential candidates. The choice of a vice president is the most consequential decision that a presidential candidate makes over the course of the campaign. Third, the debate can influence campaign dynamics. Freer to engage in attacks than the presidential candidates, who must project an unflappable, above-the-battle persona, vice presidential debaters try to jab at vulnerabilities in the opposition candidate. The unwritten rule for vice presidential contenders is not to diminish the image of the individual at the top of the ticket. The guiding strategic principle: First do no harm.

The 1984 debate between Vice President George H.W. Bush and Congresswoman Geraldine Ferraro was historic because it represented the first time that a female candidate participated in a vice presidential debate. At one point, Bush seemed to adopt a condescending attitude toward Ferraro, volunteering to help her understand the difference between Iran and the Embassy in Lebanon. The comment smacked of sexism and Ferraro called him on his "patronizing attitude." Ferraro's performance boosted the Democratic ticket. It also showcased the ability of a woman candidate to stand her ground in a debate with the vice president, advancing the cause of women in politics. Politically, like most vice presidential

Continued

encounters, the debate exerted little impact on the outcome of the election. The Republican ticket—Reagan–Bush—won in a landslide.

In a classic 1988 debate, Democratic vice presidential candidate Lloyd Bentsen displayed credibility, coming off as a self-confident, experienced political leader (Decker, 1994, p. 178). He also used pauses for maximum effect, as seen in this now-classic interchange between Bentsen and his Republican opponent, a youthful Dan Quayle. When Quayle favorably compared himself to John F. Kennedy, Bentsen replied slowly and with apparent sobriety, his words gaining momentum as they were spoken:

> Senator, I served with Jack Kennedy. (pause). I knew Jack Kennedy. (pause). Jack Kennedy was a friend of mine. (longer pause.) Senator, you're no Jack Kennedy.
>
> (Decker, 1994, p. 179)

Bentsen's attack sent the room into gales of laughter and was played over and over again on network television news. It was an incredible sound bite, and the news media squeezed as much as they could from it. Bentsen, an experienced politician, undoubtedly knew the impact his one-liner would achieve, and chose it for this reason. However, his debate victory did not alter the campaign trajectory. The Republicans—Bush and Quayle—won the election handily.

Twenty years later, in 2008, the nation was treated to a much-talked-about debate between Joe Biden and Sarah Palin (see Figure 16.6). The news media framed the debate around whether Palin would come off competent or embarrass herself. The candidates had different tasks. Palin needed to display expertise in order to convince skeptical voters she was up to the job. Biden could not come off as aggressive, lest he be perceived as bullying a woman. "Do whatever you need to do—take four Percocet, deploy Zen breathing techniques—to prevent yourself from attacking this woman," a reporter humorously advised. "And do just as much not to pay attention to her. Even if she pulls out her breast pump during commercials, keep your eyes glazed over on the middle distance!" (Lithwick, 2008).

In the end, both candidates performed well, enhancing ratings of their image and issue expertise (McKinney, Rill, & Watson, 2011). Biden seemed to have won on debating points, answering the moderator's questions and rebutting Palin's arguments more effectively. Palin, for her part, displayed issue knowledge and

Figure 16.6 Vice presidential debates give voters the opportunity to evaluate the qualifications of the candidates who could assume the reins of power in the event of tragedy. The 2008 debate between Republican nominee Sarah Palin and Democrat Joe Biden offered no surprises, with both candidates performing up to snuff and Palin exceeding expectations of doubtful naysayers. The debate famously spawned a Saturday Night Live skit, starring Tina Fey as Palin, exerting a short-term impact on attitudes in what researchers dubbed "the Fey effect."

Getty Images

projected confidence. Her colloquial litany included "Joe Six-Pack," "you betcha," "doggone it," and lots of dropped "gs". She smiled, winked, and conveyed enormous vitality. A number of Republicans felt energized, their doubts about her competence reduced, if not totally eliminated. Her performance seemed to have solidified the base.

A funny *Saturday Night Live* (SNL) skit lampooned both candidates, showing Biden pontificating and Palin playing the flute like she was a beauty pageant

Continued

contestant. (The skit was viewed more than five million times on YouTube.) The skit seems to have influenced voters' attitudes. Baumgartner, Morris, and Walth (2012) explored what they called "the Fey effect." They discovered that young adults who watched the SNL spoof of Palin's debate performance were especially likely to disapprove of John McCain's selection of Palin as his vice presidential running mate. However, the researchers did not believe that the debate influenced the election outcome, noting that the vice presidential candidate typically does not change most people's vote decision. By the time of the vice presidential debate, Obama had amassed a solid lead over McCain. But the debate exerted other effects: It attracted a huge audience, demonstrated anew that a female politician could hold her own with a male candidate, and convinced many viewers that Tiny Fey could do Sarah Palin better than Palin herself!

DEBATE EFFECTS ON VOTERS

Besides influencing campaign dynamics, presidential debates exert specific effects on voters and the larger political system.

Debates Attract Huge National Audiences

People tune in for a number of reasons: vote-guidance, seeking out of supportive information, intellectual curiosity, entertainment, and even the possibility that a candidate will deliver a zinger or commit a gaffe. The humorist Molly Ivins joked, with tongue not entirely in cheek, that "political debates are sort of like stock-car races—no one really cares who wins, they just want to see the crashes" (Hahn, 1994, p. 208). In 2008, presidential debates garnered an average of 57 million viewers (Kenski & Jamieson, 2011). Four years later, more than 70 million Americans watched the first Obama–Romney debate on television and the Internet, a large, impressive audience in an era of specialized and fragmented media.

Millions watch debates, which is a good thing. But it's not like viewers are glued to the TV or computer screen, taking in every word or policy position. Attention is sporadic. Few individuals watch a debate from start to finish, and only political junkies view presidential and vice presidential debates in their entirety (Sears & Chaffee, 1979). What's more, watching a debate does not mean that people buy in to everything that candidates say. Exposure does not equal effects.

Debates Reinforce Candidate Attitudes

As Klapper noted more than a half-century ago and psychological research has since confirmed, viewers are selective. They filter debates through preexisting biases. Even when the opponent outperforms their preferred candidate, partisans do not change their view of the competitor. In 2004 Democrat John Kerry bested Bush in the debates, but no matter. Republican viewers did not change their opinion of Bush or develop a favorable image of Kerry (Cho & Ha, 2012).

Partisan viewers also point fingers, emphasizing the misstatements and "lies" told by the other side, while glossing over mistakes committed by their candidate. Even though independent fact checks found that both candidates misstated facts during the first 2012 presidential debate, the liberal website Moveon.org charged that Romney had lied and distorted Obama's record. Although the moderator of the 2012 vice presidential debate received much praise for trying to draw out both candidates, conservatives charged that she was biased because she pushed the Republican vice presidential candidate, Paul Ryan, to lay out specific economic plans.

During the second presidential debate, Romney offered an impassioned defense of his commitment to equality in the workplace, explaining that as governor of Massachusetts he made a "concerted effort" to find women who had the qualifications to become members of his Cabinet. But when he mentioned that women's groups (whom he approached to help him) brought back "whole binders full of women," the unusual phrase created a feeding frenzy on the Internet, stimulating a Facebook fan page called "Binders Full of Women," which recruited numerous satirical likes. Liberals read in Romney's phrase an insincere support for women's rights, conveniently ignoring his statements that he sought to bring qualified women into his Cabinet and a willingness to offer flexible working hours. In these ways, viewers selectively perceive debates, leading to strengthening of preexisting attitudes.

Presidential Debates Exert a Host of Democracy-Enhancing Effects

One of the broader, civic purposes of debates is to offer a forum that engages citizens, expanding their understanding of issues and encouraging deliberation. Research shows that debates fulfill these functions. Voters become better informed about candidates' issue positions from viewing presidential debates (Benoit, Hansen, & Verser, 2003; Carlin & McKinney, 1994; Holbrook, 1999; Miller & MacKuen, 1979). Debate viewing also expands the number of campaign issues that voters use to assess candidates (Benoit et al., 2003).

Presidential debates also encourage viewers to talk about the campaign interpersonally and on social networking sites, which can light up after a debate. Comments are predictably critical. After the second 2012 presidential election debate turned feisty, one man tweeted: "Is there anything more awkward than putting two guys on stools 10 feet apart on a huge stage and asking them to look natural for 90 minutes?" Responding to Romney's statement that he had received "binders full of women," one woman sarcastically posted on Amazon.com that "Being a very curvy lady, I really need more of a plus-sized binder to fit into. Will one be made available soon? . . . I'll keep my eyes peeled and my fingers crossed that a larger version will soon hit the market!" (Krumboltz, 2012).

Showcasing interest in the debates, millions of people live-tweeted during the presidential debates. Twitter and social media offer creative opportunities for citizens to interpret debates in their own terms, rather than those offered by debaters or the mainstream media. They also can make politics entertaining. For example, a number of Americans followed celebrities' tweets about the debates. While celebrity tweets were not particularly impressive, from a political philosophy perspective, they were fun to read. For example:

Nina Dobrev (Canadian actress and model): "I love that OBAMA is wearing a breast cancer wrist band during the debate! Way to support it!!!"

Elizabeth Hasselbeck: "Um . . . Mr. President . . . Your plan clearly stinks. Record debt. Record unemployment. ½ of college grads will have no job."

Kathy Griffin: "I wish they would address the Armenian threat: the Kardashians."

Lady Gaga (calling on one of her famous songs): "Thought the president was passionate and knowledgeable and modern. Felt almost like he kept poker face last 2 debates and then came like Rocky."

(see http://www.tvguide.com/News/Final-
Presidential-Debate-Tweets-1054983.aspx)

DEBATE BALANCE SHEET

With the previous discussion in mind, I invite you to examine the pros and cons, and normative issues, surrounding presidential debates.

Style versus Substance

Critics argue that candidates' non-verbal behaviors swamp the content of what they say. Candidates are evaluated on their television communication skills rather than on the arguments they speak. A sneer or discomfited look can speak louder than a carefully honed rhetorical argument. For example, in the first 2012 debate, Obama offered a cogent defense of his health care policy and lamented the lack of specificity in Romney's plans. But he was widely criticized because he looked down at his notes, grimaced, and seemed less animated than Romney. Does style overwhelm substance in debates? What is meant by style and substance?

These questions have long generated controversy. You can find inklings of it in ancient Greece, when Plato criticized the Sophists, teachers who traveled from city to city, offering courses on oratory and speaking style. To Plato, truth was the highest value. He lamented that the Sophists sacrificed painstaking arguments for stylish pseudo-arguments that won the approval of the people, but actually contained underlying flaws.

The issue has come up in American politics and in the presidential debates of 1988, when Democrat Michael Dukakis gave a direct and logical argument to a question on the death penalty, but was savaged for his lack of emotion (see Box 16.2).

The issue is complex. It is true that television debates do place visual, non-verbal, and TV communication skills front-and-center. But, as we have discussed, it is not clear this is a bad or unreasonable thing. You can argue that it is eminently reasonable to focus on a candidate's personal qualities when making up one's mind on how to cast a vote. Leadership in a media age consists of manipulating images. You can argue that part of the substance of a debate is the style in which candidates present their answers.

Although critics contend that packaging candidates for debates is a crass, manipulative approach, debate defenders adopt a different perspective. Myles Martel (1983) notes:

> To put this issue in perspective, it might be helpful to ask this question: When a person seeking a job wears his best suit for the interview, attends more meticulously than usual to grooming needs, and demonstrates more poise, better listening habits and closer attention to what he says than usual, is he being unduly manipulative? Of course not. Job interviews are imbued with image-oriented rituals rooted in the applicant's needs for survival and success. Campaign debates, too, are forms of job interviews imbued with image-oriented rituals which we need to understand before passing judgment.
>
> (p. 3)

BOX 16.2 TRICKERY OR TRUTH IN A CLASSIC DEBATE

A classic moment in the 1988 presidential campaign came early in the second presidential debate. The Democratic nominee, former Massachusetts governor Michael Dukakis, faced Republican vice president George H.W. Bush. It had been a hard-fought campaign, with Republicans pummeling Dukakis for his "icy" demeanor and lack of emotion. Commentators hoped that Dukakis would show some affect, the sort of thing that plays well on television.

Hoping to elicit an emotional response, CNN anchor Bernard Shaw asked Democratic nominee Michael Dukakis a freighted question: "Governor, if Kitty Dukakis were raped and murdered, would you favor an irrevocable death penalty for the killer?"

Dukakis answered without hesitating. "No, I don't Bernard," he replied. "And I think you know that I've opposed the death penalty during all of my life" (Simon, 1990, p. 291).

Post-debate reaction to Dukakis's reply was swift and harsh. He had shown no emotion, critics said. Couldn't he have at least showed some raw affect when asked what he would do if his own wife had been raped and killed? He had flubbed the "warm and fuzzy test," pundits declared. However, journalist Roger Simon offered a different perspective:

> People across the country would express outrage over Dukakis' calm and cool answer. Yet was Dukakis' position that outrageous? . . . Dukakis believed that people of principle make principled decisions. And they stick to them. That is what integrity is about. O.K., the critics said, but even if Dukakis didn't favor the death penalty, couldn't he have shown a little emotion in answering the question?

> After all, Dukakis' handlers had said before the debate that they were preparing him for a "Willie Horton type" question. And they had written an "emotional" answer for Dukakis. It was one in which he talked about his father, a doctor for fifty-two years, who at age seventy-seven, had been beaten, bound and gagged by an intruder looking for drugs. And then he would talk about his elder brother, Stelian, who had been killed by a hit-and-run driver in 1973. It was an answer in which Dukakis said he knew what it was like to be a victim of crime.

> But when the time came to give the answer, Dukakis did not. Instead, he told the truth. Dispassionately, he expressed his true feelings. And he was savaged for it. He was savaged for giving a sincere and unemotional answer instead of giving an insincere and emotional one.
>
> But if he had given the prepared answer, would that really have made him any more warm? Or would it have just made him a better performer, a better actor? If he had given his prepared response, the people, press included, would have praised him. He would have been congratulated for delivering his lines as written, just as George Bush did.
>
> By the final presidential debate, we were demanding the road show. Fool us, we were saying. Trick us. Fake a little sincerity for us.
>
> (Simon, 1990, pp. 292–293)

Discussing or Skirting Issues

When they discuss policy issues, candidates are not entirely truthful. They inflate their records and distort the facts of their opponents' positions. Thanks to FactCheck.org and other evidence-based news services, we know that during the 2012 debates, both candidates exaggerated their records and made false statements about their opponent. During the first presidential debate, Obama charged that Romney proposed a $5 trillion tax cut, but this was not true. In the second debate, Romney claimed that, as a result of the bad economy, 580,000 women lost jobs during Obama's administration. The actual number was about 93,000 (FactCheck.org, 2012b).

Critics note that presidential debates steer clear of big issues facing the country. The 1988 debates did not provide a compelling discussion of an issue on the horizon: how the U.S. should posture itself in a post-Cold War world. The 1996 debates did not offer an honest discussion of how to cut Social Security or Medicare. The 2000 debates did not touch on the problem posed by terrorism that was just around the corner.

In 2012, debates sometimes focused on small-scale differences between candidates on tax cuts and the budget deficit. Conspicuously absent were the big issues: how the nation could grow a 21st century economy, which could no longer depend on manufacturing, in which the twin forces of globalization and new technologies have made traditional jobs obsolete. Global warming and gun control received scant attention.

Presidential debates are not without weaknesses. But they have salutary effects. They force candidates to discuss policy issues, standing or sitting side-by-side in a public forum. Debates also perform a teaching function, educating young people about politics, helping them to appreciate norms of political discourse (Friedenberg, 1994). On a broader level, debates exert a civilizing impact on aggressive, bitter, and even dirty presidential campaigns. They force candidates to smile and shake hands before the cameras. They require them to talk with each other and employ lofty language and cogent arguments. As Edward Hinck (1993) observes, "candidates fight for office rhetorically, by arguing in full view of audiences that expect their leaders to symbolize their most precious democratic value: choice through rational dialogue" (p. 7; see Reflections box).

Even so, there are ways to improve debates, and scholars have advanced a number of suggestions (e.g., Jamieson & Birdsell, 1988). You might mull these over, asking yourself if you think these ideas could elevate the discourse in debates and whether you have any other ideas. Prescriptions include:

1. Focus each debate on one topic, such as Medicare, how to expand economic opportunities for young people, climate control, or gun violence.
2. Center the debate on a specific proposition (Jamieson & Birdsell, 1988). These could include: Should Medicare be replaced with a private insurance subsidy? Should the U.S. impose a tax on carbon to address global warming? Should assault weapons be banned?
3. Give candidates more time to develop and answer questions.
4. Consider innovative formats, such as a standard 45-minute candidate debate, followed by a British Parliament-style debate, with Congressional leaders asking tough questions of the opposition candidate.
5. Feature a national contest, in which young people compete to ask the most non-standard, but thoughtful questions. Winners would get the opportunity to ask their questions, along with a follow-up.

REFLECTIONS: DEBATING THIRD PARTIES AND DEBATES

One issue that frequently surfaces when critics examine debates is whether alternative or third party candidates should participate. One reason they typically do not is that the two major parties exert substantial control over debate formats. The Presidential Debates Commission stipulates that third party candidates must garner an average of 15 percent of support in five major opinion polls to qualify for debates. This occurred in 1992, when businessman Ross Perot, an Independent, cleared the threshold. Republican Congressman John Anderson, who also garnered 15 percent poll support and ran as an Independent, participated in a two-person debate with Ronald Reagan in 1980. Excluding third parties gives the debates a status quo, Establishment focus. More radical issues and controversies that the two parties would rather not handle are left out of debates.

In 2012, in line with suggestions advanced by leading debate scholars (Carlin et al., 2009), television relayed a debate among presidential candidates from four major alternative parties, including the Green and Libertarian Parties. The debate, hosted by Larry King, did not get major billing. It was shown on C-Span. But it was broadcast, and a number of interesting proposals were discussed. These included the ethics of U.S. wiretapping, extension of the Patriot Act, benefits of legalizing marijuana, and requiring a balanced federal budget. Some of the ideas, of course, sound good, but once you start trying to implement them in real-world situations, you realize how impractical they are. Still, it would have been interesting to have heard the two major political party nominees discuss these issues.

On the other hand, there is a reason for limiting debates to the major two parties and insisting that third parties have 15 percent public support before they can partake. Do you know how many alternative political parties and groups there are in the U.S.? Some raise important issues, others have zany ideas. Where would you draw the line? Defenders of the present structure argue that by opening the floodgates, debate planners would render debates absurd or meaningless, and seriously reduce their political significance. By at least insisting on a 15 percent threshold, the Debates Commission guarantees that a third party candidate has tapped into the views held by a sizable number of Americans. But this perpetuates a status quo orientation. What do you think? How can we reconcile these different values? Should we?

WHAT DO YOU THINK?

How can we improve political debates? How can formats be changed to encourage more thoughtful give-and-take? Or is this an impractical exercise, because debates occur in a highly charged political context and are fundamentally political encounters? What is your assessment?

CONCLUSIONS

Presidential debates are media events that bestride the fall campaign like a colossus. They serve different functions for candidates, voters, and the political system. For candidates, they are first and foremost political encounters, designed to shore up support among key voting blocs. Undecided voters turn to the debates to help them make up their minds. Partisans watch debates to cheer on their candidate. For the larger political system, debates are exercises in civic education that help the nation come to grips with complex, contested issues, while also exerting a civilizing effect on a contentious election. Although presidential debates are not debates in the classic sense of the term, they do offer a joint appearance of two or more candidates discussing issues, and rebutting one another's claims, without interference from the press.

Debates represent high-stakes encounters for presidential candidates. They prepare extensively and focus endlessly on optics and appearances. Their consultants play the expectations game, trying to lower expectations for the candidate so that a less-than-stellar performance can be declared a success. It is all part of strategic spin. The three major debate formats are press conference, single moderator, and town hall meeting. Candidates adapt their strategy to fit the particular format.

A half-century of research on debates has yielded a host of conclusions. Visual appearances matter. Affect is also important: Likability, credibility, and effective use of non-verbal cues can improve candidate evaluations. But debates involve more than non-verbal cues and affect. Candidates who articulate cogent arguments, employ evidence, persuasively rebut the opponent's claims, and embed their statements in a coherent narrative win debates.

In addition, given that debates are media events, it should not surprise us that news media verdicts of who won can influence audience perceptions. Although debates rarely change the outcome of an election, they can be consequential, influencing momentum and critically swaying undecided voters when the race is particularly close.

What is the balance sheet on debates? Are they good for democracy? Or do they prize entertaining style over political substance? Presidential debates offer exposure to candidates' issue positions and the clash of divergent ideas. They give voters an opportunity to hear candidates offer cogent, ideologically based answers, even if they are presented in a compressed time period. They also can allow citizens to participate, if vicariously, through social media formats.

Debates are imperfect institutions: Candidates duck questions, play to the cameras, and avoid discussion of big issues that could advance the polity, for fear their answers could alienate swing voters. They have a status quo orientation in that they include only the nominees of the two established parties. And yet they have virtues: debates help to civilize hard-fought campaigns, advancing one of democracy's core values: choice through discussion. They offer voters a glimpse of how a candidate might lead by communicating in a media age. We should not be surprised that debates involve so many tradeoffs. They are political events that take place in a polarized, politicized environment. Yet, given their potential, it behooves scholars to dream up ways to improve debate formats so that they can be as effective in educating as they are in electioneering, and as helpful in offering novel solutions as they are in trotting out the tried-and-true.

POSTSCRIPT

Al was relieved. The 2012 election had ended, and negative advertising that ceaselessly cascaded across his television set had disappeared. Al, a certified public accountant from suburban Cleveland, follows politics and attack ads closely. In several conversations during the campaign, he lamented the frequency and vitriol of negative ads. Can't stand those negative ads, he said; they're cluttering up the TV airwaves, and what earthly purpose do they serve? Negative ads dispirit him and make him more cynical about politics. It was music to his ears, he suggested, when he no longer was greeted by a negative spot and the candidate's words "I approve this message." So, when the 18-month ordeal came to a close, he felt relieved.

Obama must have been relieved too. He had slipped during the first debate, only to get back on his game in the following two debates, crisscrossing the county with some of the same energy and charisma that he harnessed in 2008. But it was not the same election, and Obama wasn't the same candidate. He was "no longer the abstract embodiment of intertwined notions of Hope and Change. He [was] the president, with a record to defend" (Winter, 2012, p. A1). He could no longer promise to change Washington. He *was* Washington. He could no longer run on promises to get the economy rolling again. He had improved the economy in certain ways, missed other opportunities, and in any case was held accountable for his record of achievements and failures. He looked older and wearier, if wiser. Crowds still flocked to see, hear, even touch him, but they no longer were locked in a dream-like trance, but focused more seriously and concretely on down-to-earth issues, like jobs and taxes.

Obama had harnessed the tools of incumbency and political persuasion to pull off a broad, convincing electoral victory. He argued that the economy improved under his watch, and about 4 in 10 voters who agreed with this assessment voted for him. Framing the election around his steadfast commitment to advancing the interests of the middle class, consistently outscoring a capable opponent in good will and empathy, and successfully (if sometimes inaccurately) depicting Romney as a rich capitalist out of touch with the needs of middle-class Americans, he pulled off victories in swing states. He even benefited from an October surprise: Hurricane Sandy. Nearly two-thirds of voters, some probably undecided, said his handling of the crisis was a factor in their vote decision (Calmes & Thee-Brenan, 2012).

But if his supporters were euphoric, cheering and yelling and crying at Chicago's McCormick Place the night of the election and in the wee hours of the morning after, political communication observers remarked on problems, pointing to shortcomings in the larger system.

The first is the nomination system. The process is unbearably long. It lasts not for several weeks or months, as it does in other western democracies, but for more than a year: 18 months to be exact. The election crowds out other stories and consumes journalistic resources that could be more usefully expended in dozens of other areas, ranging from a collective exploration of community problems to deeper explanations of the country's financial crisis.

A second nomination-related problem is frontloading. The bunching up of primaries and contests at the beginning of the race elevates the importance of money, fundraising, and peripheral factors like momentum. The continued emphasis on two lovely, but unrepresentative, states makes little sense. It frequently shunts aside a variety of other state contests, in effect disenfranchising these voters. The news media horse race and incessant polling can turn a serious process into a circus, encouraging lampooning rather than respect.

Third, there is the devilish problem caused by money itself. Some $6 billion were spent on the presidential election in 2012, with about half of that spent on political ads. Some of these ads were misleading and uninformative. A great deal of the money was raised by a handful of wealthy individuals or, alternatively, by political action committees working secretively, with no accountability to voters or the larger political process. Republicans and Democrats both benefited from big money. Indeed, despite his lofty campaign promises to change politics-as-usual, in 2008 Obama became the first major presidential candidate to reject public campaign funding. By doing this, he avoided federal spending limits and could spend unlimited amounts of money on his campaign. In 2012, campaign spending broke all previous records, with more than $3 billion spent on political advertising alone.

Think of the many ways these dollars could have been spent—on schools, infrastructure, social problems, alternative parties with new ideas, or jump-starting bipartisan groups that could collaborate on innovative proposals for social change.

Fourth, for all the hoopla about gaping differences between the candidates, supposedly serious discussions of contemporary problems during presidential debates, and the bromide that "this is a campaign about issues," the truth is that preciously little dialogue about societal problems transpires during presidential campaigns. True, advertisements present candidates' stands on issues, and candidates do take sharply different positions during presidential debates, in part to appeal to different political constituencies. But there is preciously little serious discussion that delves deeper, to the multiple roots of social problems. When candidates offer proposals, they are small in scale and carefully poll-tested to make certain they do not alienate key constituencies. Parties do not use the campaigns to introduce new policy proposals, jump-start a discussion, and build political support. This is not the purpose of campaigns. They are waged to get a candidate elected and give a party control of one or both of the houses of Congress. That's politics.

But think about the big issues out there that weren't discussed. For example, as critic Paul Krugman observed:

> The sad truth about this year's economic debate is that the biggest issue facing the federal government—the issue that should be uppermost in our minds—is not being discussed at all. Most of what happens in our economy is beyond the reach of government policy. . . . There is one thing, however, the Government can and must control: its own budget. And it is heading inexorably toward fiscal disaster, as the baby boomers in the tens of millions march steadily toward the age at which they can claim Social Security and Medicare. . . . [We] expect responsible adults to start preparing for their retirement decisions in advance; why shouldn't we ask the same of our Government? Unfortunately, everything that a responsible government should be doing now—raising taxes, raising the retirement age, scaling back benefits for those who can manage without them (that means for the affluent, not the poor) is political poison.

> (1996, p. A15)

Are you ready for this? The column was written long before the 2012 election—16 years before to be exact, during the heat of the 1996 presidential campaign. Just as these issues were not broached in 1996, they were not discussed in depth in 2012 either. Neither Romney nor Obama presented blueprints on how to slow spending on entitlements, while offering protection to society's most vulnerable. Neither campaign addressed long-term deficit reform by, for example, advancing "a credible bipartisan, multiyear deficit-reduction plan . . . that matches the scale of our problem—one with substantial tax reform and revenue increases, a gasoline tax, deep defense cuts and cutbacks to both Social Security and Medicare" (Friedman, 2011, p. A27).

Neither candidate discussed ways to give Americans access to the kind of education that could set them up for jobs of tomorrow, while also jump-starting the economy. This is imperative because the manufacturing industries that employed many working-class Americans in the 20th century are gone, outsourced, victims of the global economy, and never to return to these shores. Sadly, globalization and advances in technology that have replaced jobs in manufacturing take a larger toll on lower-class Americans, increasing inequality. Inequality, which impedes economic growth and reinforces poverty (a fifth of American children live in impoverished circumstances) received little attention during the campaign (Stiglitz, 2013). Even as Hurricane Sandy invited discussion of the devastating effects of global warming, neither candidate advanced ideas on how the U.S. should devise sane policies to cope with climate change.

"Has there ever been a campaign with so few major plans on the table?" political columnist David Brooks (2012) asked rhetorically. Well, actually, yes. All campaigns steadfastly avoid new ideas, out of fear that broaching them will alienate key groups or be used against candidates in spooky negative ads. This is understandable politically and flows from a liberal democratic notion of campaigns. But it is lamentable from a deliberative democratic perspective that emphasizes that campaigns should engage the electorate in policy dialogues that bring us closer to thinking through and solving core problems.

And yet. Rays of hope glimmered. The 2012 campaign sparked interest across the land. People tweeted, posted, emailed, and i-chatted about candidates, gaffes, and issues. The press covered the campaign thoroughly and critically. Seventy million people watched presidential debates. More than 117 million Americans voted. It was not a record turnout and tens of millions chose not to show up at the polls. But in an age of skepticism about politics and cynicism about politicians, the turnout announced that many voters still cared.

In New York City, hobbled by the after-effects of Hurricane Sandy, poll workers ran out of affidavit ballots for individuals displaced by the hurricane. Ballot scanners were broken or jammed. Still, people waited in line for more than three hours to vote.

Partisans committed to Obama–Biden and Romney–Ryan worked at a feverish pitch for months, mobilizing voters, canvassing, calling undecided voters, phoning committed voters, making sure people had rides to the polls, knocking on doors, in some cases driving long distances to campaign for a cause that stirred political passions.

At its best, the national clatter of voices opened up the political pores and stimulated partisan sensibilities. It might not have produced a new perspective on the problems that ailed the nation, but it did get people talking and pushed them to think about political issues. In a nation of some 300 million individuals driven by their own ambitions and pursuing their own diverse dreams, this is no small accomplishment. It suggests that, for all its problems, the more than two-century-old American experiment in democracy is still vital, throbbing with life (Perloff, 2012).

America's democratic star seemed to gleam brighter on Inauguration Day, 2013, when Obama spoke of extending human rights before a diverse crowd comprising "elegant African-American women in full length mink coats and matching hats," "high school mariachi performers from Texas—including some who took their first plane ride to get here" (and) "musicians in new purple uniforms who traveled from places like Des Moines and Montgomery, Alabama , to march with a gay and lesbian band." They were, as reporter Sheryl Stolberg noted, "the faces of those left behind by the political process in decades and centuries past" (2013, p. A11).

An outmoded nomination process, big money, and a media consumed by sound bites and celebrity chatter continue to plague the American electoral system. But the dedication shown by political activists, combined with Obama's clarion call for collective political action in his second Inaugural, and the majestic attendance at his Inaugural Address by so many individuals who had been left behind, suggested that American politics still has some life left in it and may yet be capable of zestful rejuvenation.

Glossary

Agenda-building: the process through which policy agendas, or the political priorities of political elites, develop and are influenced by factors such as the media agenda and public opinion.

Agenda-setting: the process through which mass media communicate the importance or salience of issues to the public, influencing public perceptions of the most important issues facing the nation or a community.

Cascading activation: a model arguing that political frames flow downward from the White House, through other key elites, the media, and to the public, with each actor in the process influencing political communication, as well as being influenced by it.

Caucus: a local public gathering where party members publicly deliberate about candidates, decide which presidential candidate they will support and choose delegates to the nominating convention.

Citizens United: 2010 Supreme Court decision that ruled that the government cannot prohibit spending by corporations and unions in elections. The decision expanded free speech but also allowed unprecedented corporate money to potentially influence the political process.

Classical Greek direct democracy: as expounded in ancient Athens, this philosophical approach emphasizes direct citizen participation in politics, equality in theory (though not in practice), and citizens' obligation to contribute to the common good of the community. It also emphasizes the role played by rhetorical debate and the formulation of reasoned arguments about justice.

Constructionism: an approach to political media effects, combining psychological and mass communication approaches, that examines how people actively construct meaning from media messages.

Content analysis: a systematic method to quantitatively examine the characteristics, themes, and symbols in a communication.

Delegate: an individual who attends the nominating convention and formally casts a vote for a candidate. Most delegates are chosen through the primaries and caucuses; elite superdelegates are elected officials and influential members of parties.

Deliberative democracy: a contemporary perspective on democratic theory that emphasizes the importance of organized community deliberation on issues; citizens' articulation of cogent arguments that can be publicly justified and exert an impact on policy; and communications that promote deliberation and collective dialogue on politics.

Democracy: a form of government that, in its bare-bones form, emphasizes rule of the people. Numerous, more complex perspectives on democracy have been formulated over the years. They stipulate, in the main, that democracy mandates: the right of all citizens to vote, free and fair elections that involve competition between more than one political party, freedom of expression, including freedom for those who oppose the party in power, and a civil society characterized by the right to form civic associations.

Elaboration Likelihood Model: social psychological model of persuasion that emphasizes cognitive processes. Applied to politics, the model suggests that political persuasion strategies flow from the ways voters process messages.

Elite democratic theory: a perspective asserting that democracy involves a competition among elite groups or influential political parties. Elite democracy emphasizes that citizens can fulfill their democratic function simply by exercising their opportunity to vote for or against different elites.

Elites: leaders; influential individuals who wield power, as a function of income, status, or political connections.

Experiment: a controlled study that provides evidence of causation through random assignment of individuals to a treatment or control group.

Family communication patterns: ways in which parents communicate politics to children, primarily by emphasizing harmony or encouraging concept exploration.

Framing: selecting particular aspects of an issue and making connections in ways that emphasize a particular definition, evaluation, and remedy.

Frontloading: characteristic of contemporary nominating system, where primaries and caucuses have been increasingly pushed up to the "front" or ever-earlier portion of the nominations. Nominations are critically influenced by contests that occur early on, like Iowa and New Hampshire.

Gatekeeping: the process by which editors, reporters, and news executives, as well as contemporary online bloggers, commentators, and news aggregators like Google News, decide which information will enter society's "gates," through a process that includes exclusion, selection, and framing.

Hegemony: a loosely organized, controversial notion stipulating that a nation's news media follows and transmits the perspectives of the power structure, propping up the ruling political and economic elite.

Heuristic: mental shortcut used to help an individual make a decision. In politics, examples include recommendations of interpersonal and media opinion leaders and political party affiliation.

Horse race news: press coverage that emphasizes who is ahead, polls, and the strategic game, in the manner of a classic horse race.

Hypothesis: a specific prediction, ideally derived from a theory, that can be tested through evidence.

Indexing: the idea that political media index news so that it closely reflects the range of voices expressed by political elites.

Intermedia agenda-setting: the impact that news coverage from particular media outlets exerts on coverage by the mainstream media in a community, state, or country.

Irony: a complex comedic device that uses language to suggest an incongruity between the surface and deeper meanings of an event.

Knowledge gap: a philosophically problematic situation in which media exacerbate existing differences in knowledge between the "haves," or individuals high in socio-economic status, and the "have-nots," or those lower in education and status.

Liberal democracy: the classical libertarian approach that emphasizes the importance of preserving individual liberties; representation guaranteed through elections; politics as a marketplace of ideas, in which truth emerges through its collision with falsehood (as John Stuart Mill put it); and a feisty no-holds-barred press that challenges government.

Limited effects model: a model of mass communication effects that says media have minimal impact; a primary influence lies in reinforcement of existing attitudes. Media are believed to work in conjunction with other social forces to influence the public.

Macro level: the public, institutional, or policy domain—the political communication arena that focuses on broad media effects on public opinion, political institutions, or public policy.

Media: technologies that intercede between the communicator and message recipient, filtering the message through selection of words, images, and formats.

Media routines: normal, routinized procedures, including news values, deadlines, and dependence on official sources, that journalists employ to do their jobs.

Mere exposure: repeated exposure to a neutral or little-known political candidate can increase liking.

Micro level: the individual level—the political communication arena that examines media effects on individuals' thoughts, feelings, or behaviors.

Microtargeting: a contemporary media persuasion strategy, whereby campaigns tailor political messages to match a target audience's characteristics, frequently by harnessing online and social media.

Narrative: a coherent, compelling story that calls on dramatic devices, raises problems, and offers a resolution.

News bias: a consistent media pattern in presentation of an issue, in a way that reliably favors one side, or minimizes the opposing side, in a context where it can reasonably be argued that there are other perspectives on the issue that are also deserving of coverage.

Normative models: perspectives on what should or ought to be. These prescribe or develop idealized models rather than describing what is.

Normative theory: a theory that prescribes or suggests how life ought to be lived; in the present case, a guiding political philosophy.

Opinion leader: influence agent that can shape audience attitudes.

Persuasion: a symbolic process by which communicators try to induce individuals to freely change their own attitudes through transmission of a message.

Political communication: the process by which language and symbols, employed by leaders, media, or citizens, exert intended or unintended effects on the political cognitions, attitudes, or behavior of individuals or on outcomes that bear on the public policy of a nation, state, or community.

Political marketing: application of marketing principles, such as segmentation, positioning, and mass exchange of products and services of value, to politics.

Political socialization: the manner in which a society transmits knowledge, norms, attitudes, and values from generation to generation, preserving continuity and ideally permitting change.

Politics: the science of deciding who gets what, when, and why; the process by which a group of citizens who have a range of viewpoints on an issue arrive at collective agreement on decisions that are viewed as binding on the group as a whole.

Poll: a sample survey of the electorate that offers quick, immediate information about opinions and preferences.

Presidential debate: the joint appearance by at least two competing presidential candidates, who articulate their positions, with formal rules for refutation of opposing arguments.

Presidential primary: a state-wide election that gives voters, using a secret ballot, the opportunity to select the party's presidential nominee.

Priming: the impact of the media agenda on the criteria voters employ to evaluate candidates for public office.

Propaganda: a form of communication in which the leaders of government have near or total control over the transmission of information, typically relying on mass media deception to influence masses of people.

Public journalism: an approach to journalism that tries to engage citizens and community residents in public dialogues; citizens, not journalists, drive the agenda.

Push poll: unethical telemarketing strategy or pseudo-poll, in which respondents are fed false or misleading information about a candidate or his/her opponent in an effort to influence the voter's attitude prior to the election.

Republic: representative democracy; a democratic form of government that derives its legitimacy from citizens' election of other citizens to represent them in policymaking decisions.

Satire: a form of humor that employs ridicule to expose people's foibles.

Schema: a mental structure that includes systematic knowledge about situations and people that has been extracted from previous experiences.

Selective perception: psychological tendency to perceive political messages in the light of existing beliefs, so that one judges communications as supporting what one already believes.

Separation of powers: power is constitutionally shared by three branches of government: the executive (e.g., president), legislature (Congress) and judiciary (Supreme Court). This involves a series of checks and balances among the three branches.

Social Judgment Theory: classic psychological theory of attitudes and persuasion that emphasizes the role that preexisting attitudes play in judgments of persuasive messages. Messages are persuasive to the degree that they are perceived as congenial with the existing attitude, and are ineffective to the extent they are seen as contradicting a core attitude.

Social science: a scientific approach to understanding human cognition and behavior that tests hypotheses derived from theories, using different research methods, to build a body of knowledge.

Source: individual who relays information to a reporter. Official government sources can uphold the status quo, but sources who want to blow the whistle on government abuse can play a key role in journalistic exposés.

Survey: a questionnaire or interview-based study that seeks to document a correlation or relationship between two or more variables in a real-world setting, identifying factors that can best predict a particular outcome.

Theory: a large, sweeping conceptualization that offers a wide-ranging explanation of a phenomenon and generates concrete hypotheses about when and why specific events will occur.

Two-step flow: classic model of communication effects that says media influence opinion leaders, who in turn influence the mass public. It stimulated much research and is one of a variety of perspectives on the diffusion or flow of information in society.

References

Aalberg, T., & Curran, J. (Eds.) (2012). *How media inform democracy: A comparative approach.* New York: Routledge.

Aalberg, T., van Aelst, P., & Curran, J. (2012). Media systems and the political information environment: A cross-national comparison. In T. Aalberg & J. Curran (Eds.), *How media inform democracy: A comparative approach* (pp. 33–49). New York: Routledge.

AAPOR. (2008). *Report of the AAPOR Ad Hoc Committee on the 2008 presidential primary polling.* Online: http://www.aapor.org/Report_of_the_AAPOR_Ad_Hoc_Committee_on_the_Presidential_Primary_Polling1.htm. (Accessed: July 4, 2012.)

AAPOR Cell Phone Task Force (2010). *New considerations for survey researchers when planning and conducting RDD telephone surveys in the U.S. with respondents reached via cell phone numbers.* Presented for AAPOR Council by the Cell Phone Task Force (P.J. Lavrakas, Chair).

Achter, P. (2009). Racing Jesse Jackson: Leadership, masculinity, and the Black presidency. In J.L. Edwards (Ed.), *Gender and political communication in America: Rhetoric, representation, and display* (pp. 107–127). Lanham, MD: Lexington Books.

Ackerman, B., & Ayres, I. (2002). *Voting with dollars: A new paradigm for campaign finance.* New Haven: Yale University Press.

Adatto, K. (2008). *Picture perfect: Life in the age of the photo op.* Princeton, NJ: Princeton University Press.

Aday, S. (2010). Chasing the bad news: An analysis of 2005 Iraq and Afghanistan war coverage on NBC and Fox News Channel. *Journal of Communication, 60,* 144–164.

Alford, J., Funk, C., & Hibbing, J. (2005). Are political orientations genetically transmitted? *American Political Science Review, 99,* 153–167.

Alim, H.S., & Smitherman, G. (2012, September 9). Obama's English. *The New York Times* (Sunday Review), 5.

Alterman, E. (2003). *What liberal media? The truth about bias and the news.* New York: Basic Books.

Althaus, S.L., & Kim, Y.M. (2006). Priming effects in complex information environments: Reassessing the impact of news discourse on presidential approval. *Journal of Politics, 68,* 960–976.

An., S., & Jin, H.S. (2004). Interlocking of newspaper companies with financial institutions and leading advertisers. *Journalism & Mass Communication Quarterly, 81*, 578–600.

Anderson, K.V. (2011). "Rhymes with blunt": Pornification and U.S. political culture. *Rhetoric & Public Affairs, 14*, 327–368.

Ansolabehere, S., & Iyengar, S. (1995). *Going negative: How attack ads shrink and polarize the electorate.* New York: Free Press.

Arceneaux, K. (2010). The benefits of experimental methods for the study of campaign effects. *Political Communication, 27*, 199–215.

Arceneaux, K., & Nickerson, D.W. (2010). Comparing negative and positive campaign messages: Evidence from two field experiments. *American Politics Research, 38*, 54–83.

Armoudian, M., & Crigler, A.N. (2010). Constructing the vote: Media effects in a constructionist model. In J.E. Leighley (Ed.), *The Oxford handbook of American elections and political behavior* (pp. 300–325). New York: Oxford University Press.

Asher, H. (2007). *Polling and the public: What every citizen should know (7th ed.).* Washington, D.C.: CQ Press.

Asher, H. (2012). *Polling and the public: What every citizen should know (8th ed.).* Washington, D.C.: CQ Press.

Auer, J.J. (1962). The counterfeit debates. In S. Kraus (Ed.), *The great debates: Kennedy vs. Nixon, 1960* (pp. 142–150). Bloomington, IN: Indiana University Press.

Babbie, E. (2004). *The practice of social research (10th ed.).* Belmont, CA: Thomson/Wadsworth.

Bachen, C., Raphael, C., Lynn, K.-M., McKee, K., & Philippi, J. (2008). Civic engagement, pedagogy, and information technology on web sites for youth. *Political Communication, 25*, 290–310.

Bagdikian, B.H. (2004). *The new media monopoly.* Boston: Beacon Press.

Bai, M. (2012, July 22). How did political money get this loud? *The New York Times Magazine*, 14, 16, 18.

Bailenson, J.N., Iyengar, S., Yee, N., & Collins, N.A. (2008). Facial similarity between voters and candidates causes influence. *Public Opinion Quarterly, 72*, 935–961.

Baker, P., & Shear, M.D. (2013, January 17). Obama vows broad campaign to fight gun violence. *The New York Times*, A1, A16.

Ball, T. (2011). Manipulation: As old as democracy itself (and sometimes dangerous). In W. Le Cheminant & J.M. Parrish (Eds.), *Manipulating democracy: Democratic theory, political psychology, and mass media* (pp. 41–58). New York: Routledge.

Balmas, M., & Sheafer, T. (2010). Candidate image in election campaigns: Attribute agenda setting, affective priming, and voting intentions. *International Journal of Public Opinion Research, 22*, 204–229.

Balz, D., & Johnson, H. (2009). *The battle for America 2008: The story of an extraordinary election.* New York: Viking.

Banaji, M.R., & Heiphetz, L. (2010). Attitudes. In S.T. Fiske, D.T. Gilbert, & G. Lindzey (Eds.), *Handbook of social psychology* (5th ed., Vol. 1, pp. 353–393). New York: Wiley.

Bandura, A. (1971). Analysis of modeling processes. In A. Bandura (Ed.), *Psychological modeling: Conflicting theories* (pp. 1–62). Chicago: Aldine-Atherton.

Bantz, C.R., McCorkle, S., & Baade, R.C. (1981). The news factory. In G.C. Wilhoit & H. deBock (Eds.), *Mass communication review yearbook* (Vol. 2., pp. 366–389). Beverly Hills, CA: Sage.

Barabas, J., & Jerit, J. (2009). Estimating the causal effects of media coverage on policy-specific knowledge. *American Journal of Political Science, 53*, 73–89.

Barber, B. (1984). *Strong democracy: Participatory politics for a new age.* Berkeley: University of California Press.

Barry, D. (2011, September 11). What we kept. *The New York Times* (Special section, The reckoning: America and the world a decade after 9/11), 17.

Barry, E. (2011a, August 17). Before voting, Russian leaders go to the polls. *The New York Times*, A1, A8.

Barry, E. (2011b, December 11). Tens of thousands protest against Putin in Moscow. *The New York Times*, 1, 18.

Baughman, J.L. (1987). *Henry R. Luce and the rise of the American news media.* Boston: Twayne Publishers.

Baum, M.A. (2002). Sex, lies, and war: How soft news brings foreign policy to the inattentive public. *American Political Science Review, 96*, 91–109.

Baum, M.A. (2003). *Soft news goes to war: Public opinion and American foreign policy in the new media age.* Princeton, NJ: Princeton University Press.

Baum, M. (2012). Media, public opinion, and presidential leadership. In A.J. Berinsky (Ed.), *New directions in public opinion* (pp. 258–270). New York: Routledge.

Baumgartner, F.R., Linn, S., & Boydstun, A.E. (2010). The decline of the death penalty: How media framing changed capital punishment in America. In B.F. Schaffner & P.J. Sellers (Eds.), *Winning with words: The origins and impact of political framing* (pp. 159–184). New York: Routledge.

Baumgartner, J., & Morris, J.S. (2006). *The Daily Show* effect: Candidate evaluations, efficacy, and American youth. *American Politics Research, 34*, 341–367.

Baumgartner, J.C., Morris, J.S., & Walth, N.L. (2012). The Fey effect: Young adults, political humor, and perceptions of Sarah Palin in the 2008 presidential election campaign. *Public Opinion Quarterly, 76*, 95–104.

Baym, G. (2005). *The Daily Show*: Discursive integration and the reinvention of political journalism. *Political Communication, 22*, 259–276.

Baym, G. (2009). Stephen Colbert's parody of the postmodern. In J. Gray, J.P. Jones, & E. Thompson (Eds.), *Satire TV: Politics and comedy in the post-network era* (pp. 124–144). New York: New York University Press.

Baym, G. (2010). *From Cronkite to Colbert: The evolution of broadcast news.* Boulder, CO: Paradigm Publishers.

Beail, L., & Longworth, R. Kinney (2013). *Framing Sarah Palin: Pit bulls, Puritans, and politics.* New York: Routledge.

Becker, L.B., McCombs, M.E., & McLeod, J.M. (1975). The development of political cognitions. In S.H. Chaffee (Ed.), *Political communication: Strategies for research* (pp. 21–63). Newbury Park, CA: Sage.

Becker, L.B., & Whitney, D.C. (1980). Effects of media dependencies. *Communication Research, 7*, 95–120.

Belkin, D. (2008, November 1). In Ohio, downturn upends old loyalties. *The Wall Street Journal*, A5.

Bell, C.V., & Entman, R.M. (2011). The media's role in America's exceptional politics of inequality: Framing the Bush tax cuts of 2001 and 2003. *International Journal of Press/ Politics, 16*, 548–572.

Belt, T.L., Just, M.R., & Crigler, A.N. (2012). The 2008 media primary: Handicapping the candidates in newspapers, on TV, cable, and the Internet. *The International Journal of Press/Politics, 17*, 341–369.

Bennett, W.L. (1994). The news about foreign policy. In W.L. Bennett & D.L. Paletz (Eds.), *Taken by storm: The media, public opinion, and U.S. foreign policy in the Gulf War* (pp. 12–40). Chicago: University of Chicago Press.

Bennett, W.L. (1996). *News: The politics of illusion (3rd ed.)*. White Plains, NY: Longman.

Bennett, W.L., & Iyengar, S. (2008). A new era of minimal effects? The changing foundations of political communication. *Journal of Communication, 58*, 707–731.

Bennett, W.L., Lawrence, R.G., & Livingston, S. (2006). None dare call it torture: Indexing and the limits of press independence in the Abu Ghraib scandal. *Journal of Communication, 56*, 467–485.

Bennett, W.L., Lawrence, R.G., & Livingston, S. (2007). *When the press fails: Political power and the news media from Iraq to Katrina*. Chicago: University of Chicago Press.

Bennett, W.L., & Manheim, J.B. (2001). The big spin: Strategic communication and the transformation of pluralist democracy. In W.L. Bennett & R.M. Entman (Eds.), *Mediated politics: Communication in the future of democracy* (pp. 279–298). Cambridge: Cambridge University Press.

Bennett, W.L., & Manheim, J.B. (2006). The one-step flow of communication. *Annals of the American Association of Political and Social Science, 608*, 213–232.

Bennett, W.L., Wells, C., & Freelon, D. (2011). Communicating civic engagement: Contrasting models of citizenship in the youth web sphere. *Journal of Communication, 61*, 835–856.

Benoit, W.L. (2011). Content analysis in political communication. In E.P. Bucy & R.L. Holbert (Eds.), *The sourcebook for political communication research: Methods, measures, and analytical techniques* (pp. 268–279). New York: Routledge.

Benoit, W.L., & Harthcock, A. (1999). Functions of the great debates: Acclaims, attacks, and defenses in the 1960 presidential debates. *Communication Monographs, 66*, 341–357.

Benoit, W.L., Hansen, G.J., & Verser, R.M. (2003). A meta-analysis of the effects of viewing U.S. presidential debates. *Communication Monographs, 70*, 335–350.

Benson, R., & Neveu, E. (Eds.) (2005a). *Bourdieu and the journalistic field*. Malden, MA: Polity.

Benson, R., & Neveu, E. (2005b). Introduction: Field theory as a work in progress. In R. Benson & E. Neveu (Eds.), *Bourdieu and the journalistic field* (pp. 1–25). Malden, MA: Polity.

Berelson, B., Lazarsfeld, P.F., & McPhee, W.N. (1954). *Voting: A study of opinion formation in a presidential campaign*. Chicago: University of Chicago Press.

Berkowitz, D. (1997). Non-routine news and newswork: Exploring a What-a-Story. In D. Berkowitz (Ed.), *Social meanings of news: A text-reader* (pp. 362–375). Thousand Oaks, CA: Sage.

Berquist, G. (1994). The 1976 Carter–Ford presidential debates. In R.V. Friedenberg (Ed.),

Rhetorical studies of national political debates, 1960–1992 (2nd ed., pp. 29–44). Westport, CT: Praeger.

Bilandzic, H., & Busselle, R. (2013). Narrative persuasion. In J.P. Dillard & L. Shen (Eds.), *The Sage handbook of persuasion: Developments in theory and practice* (2nd ed., pp. 200–219). Thousand Oaks, CA: Sage.

Bineham, J.L. (1988). A historical account of the hypodermic model in mass communication. *Communication Monographs, 55*, 230–246.

Bishop, B. (with R.G. Cushing) (2008). *The big sort: Why the clustering of like minded America is tearing us apart.* Boston: Houghton-Mifflin.

Black, L.W., Burkhalter, S., Gastil, J., & Stromer-Galley, J. (2011). Methods for analyzing and measuring group deliberation. In E.P. Bucy & R.L. Holbert (Eds.), *The sourcebook for political communication research: Methods, measures, and analytical techniques* (pp. 323–345). New York: Routledge.

Bleske, G.L. (1991). Ms. Gates takes over: An updated version of a 1949 case study. *Newspaper Research Journal, 12*, 88–97.

Blow, C.M. (2012, July 28). Where's the outrage? *The New York Times*, A17.

Blow, C.M. (2013, January 12). Revolutionary language. *The New York Times*, A17.

Blumberg, S.J., & Luke, J.V. (2007). Coverage bias in traditional telephone surveys of low-income and young adults. *Public Opinion Quarterly, 71*, 734–749.

Blumenthal, S. (2012, October 22). Lincoln plays to win. *Newsweek*, 32–38.

Boehlert, E. (2006). *Lapdogs: How the press rolled over for Bush.* New York: Free Press.

Boller, P.F., Jr. (2004). *Presidential campaigns: From George Washington to George W. Bush.* New York: Oxford University Press.

Boorstin, D.J. (1961). *The image: A guide to pseudo-events in America.* New York: Harper & Row.

Bornstein, R.F. (1989). Exposure and affect: Overview and meta-analysis of research, 1968–1987. *Psychological Bulletin, 106*, 265–289.

Boulianne, S. (2009). Does Internet use affect engagement? A meta-analysis of research. *Political Communication, 26*, 193–211.

Bourdieu, P. (2005). The political field, the social science field, and the journalistic field. In R. Benson & E. Neveu (Eds.), *Bourdieu and the journalistic field* (pp. 29–47). Malden, MA: Polity.

Boyle, M.P., Schmierbach, M., Armstrong, C.L., Cho, J., McCluskey, M., McLeod, D.M., & Shah, D.V. (2006). Expressive responses to news stories about extremist groups: A framing experiment. *Journal of Communication, 56*, 271–288.

Braden, M. (1996). *Women politicians and the media.* Lexington, KY: University Press of Kentucky.

Brader, T. (2006). *Campaigning for hearts and minds: How emotional appeals in political ads work.* Chicago: University of Chicago Press.

Bradley, A.M., & Wicks, R.H. (2011). A gendered blogosphere? Portrayal of Sarah Palin on political blogs during the 2008 presidential campaign. *Journalism & Mass Communication Quarterly, 88*, 807–820.

Bradsher, K., & Duhigg, C. (2012, December 27). Signs of changes taking hold in electronics factories in China. *The New York Times*, A1, A10–11.

Breed, W. (1955/1997). Social control in the newsroom: A functional analysis. *Social Forces, 33,* 326–355. Reprinted in D. Berkowitz (Ed.), *Social meanings of news: A text-reader* (pp. 107–122). Thousand Oaks, CA: Sage.

Brenner, J. (2013). *Pew Internet: Mobile. Pew Internet & American Life Project.* Pew Research Center. Online: http://pewinternet.org/Commentary/2012/ February/Pew-Internet-Mobile. aspx. (Accessed: March 8, 2013.)

Brewer, M.D. (2010). The evolution and alteration of American party coalitions. In L.S. Maisel & J.M. Berry (Eds.), *The Oxford handbook of American political parties and interest groups* (pp. 121–142). New York: Oxford University Press.

Brewer, P.R. (2001). Value words and lizard brains: Do citizens deliberate about appeals to their core values? *Political Psychology, 22,* 45–64.

Breyer, S. (2010). *Making our democracy work: A judge's view.* New York: Knopf.

Brock, D., Rabin-Havt, A., & Media Matters for America (2012). *The Fox effect: How Roger Ailes turned a network into a propaganda machine.* New York: Anchor Books.

Brooks, D. (2012, July 31). Dullest campaign ever. *The New York Times,* A19.

Brooks, D.J., & Geer, J.G. (2007). Beyond negativity: The effects of incivility on the electorate. *American Journal of Political Science, 51,* 1–16.

Brundidge, J., & Rice, R.E. (2009). Political engagement online: Do the information rich get richer and the like-minded more similar? In A. Chadwick & P.N. Howard (Eds.), *Routledge handbook of Internet politics* (pp. 144–156). New York: Routledge.

Bruni, F. (2012a, August 28). Huggability and helium. *The New York Times,* A21.

Bruni, F. (2012b, October 2). Trembling before Mitt. *The New York Times,* A27.

Bucy, E.P., & Bradley, S.D. (2011). What the body can tell us about politics: The use of psychophysiological measures in political communication research. In E.P. Bucy & R.L. Holbert (Eds.), *The sourcebook for political communication research: Methods, measures, and analytical techniques* (pp. 525–540). New York: Routledge.

Bucy, E.P., & Grabe, M.E. (2007). Taking television seriously: A sound and image bite analysis of presidential campaign coverage, 1992–2004. *Journal of Communication, 57,* 652–675.

Buell, E.H., Jr. (2000). The changing face of the New Hampshire primary. In W. Mayer (Ed.), *In pursuit of the White House 2000: How we choose our presidential nominees* (pp. 87–144). Chatham, NJ: Chatham House.

Burns, E. (2006). *Infamous scribblers: The Founding Fathers and the rowdy beginnings of American journalism.* New York: PublicAffairs.

Burt, J. (2013). *Lincoln's tragic pragmatism: Lincoln, Douglas, and moral conflict.* Cambridge, MA: Belknap Press of Harvard University Press.

Busch, A.E. (2012). Political movements, presidential nominations, and the Tea Party. In W.G. Mayer & J. Bernstein (Eds.), *The making of the presidential candidates 2012* (pp. 59–92). Lanham, MD: Rowman & Littlefield.

Bystrom, D.G., Banwart, M.C., Kaid, L.L., & Robertson T.A. (2004). *Gender and candidate communication: VideoStyle, WebStyle, NewsStyle.* NewYork: Routledge.

Bystrom, D.G., & Brown, N.J. (2011). Videostyle 2008: A comparison of female vs. male political candidate television ads. In M.S. McKinney & M.C. Banwart (Eds.), *Communication in the 2008 U.S. election: Digital natives elect a president* (pp. 211–240). New York: Peter Lang.

Calmes, J. (2012, June 8). How do you like Bill Clinton in your corner? *The New York Times*, A17.

Calmes, J., & Thee, M. (2008, November 5). Polls find Obama built broader base than past nominees. *The New York Times*, P1, P10.

Calmes, J., & Thee-Brenan, M. (2012, November 7). Electorate reverts to a familiar partisan divide. *The New York Times*, A1, P5.

Campbell, K.K., & Jamieson, K.H. (2008). *Presidents creating the presidency: Deeds done in words*. Chicago: University of Chicago Press.

Cantril, H., Gaudet, H., & Herzog, H. (1940). *The invasion from Mars: A study in the psychology of panic*. Princeton, NJ: Princeton University Press.

Cappella, J.N., & Jamieson, K.H. (1994). Broadcast adwatch effects: A field experiment. *Communication Research, 21*, 342–365.

Cappella, J.N., & Jamieson, K.H. (1997). *Spiral of cynicism: The press and the public good*. New York: Oxford University Press.

Carlin, D.B., & McKinney, M.S. (1994). *The 1992 presidential debates in focus*. Westport, CT: Praeger.

Carlin, D.B., Vigil, T., Buehler, S., & McDonald, K. (2009). *The third agenda in U.S. presidential debates: DebateWatch and Viewer Reactions, 1996–2004*. Westport, CT: Praeger.

Caro, R.A. (2012). *The passage of power: The years of Lyndon Johnson*. New York: Knopf.

Carr, D. (2012, May 28). A doomed romance with a paper. *The New York Times*, B1, B2.

Caspi, D., & Leshem, B. (2006). From electoral propaganda to political advertising in Israel. In L.L. Kaid & C. Holtz-Bacha (Eds.), *The Sage handbook of political advertising* (pp. 109–127). Thousand Oaks, CA: Sage.

Cassidy, J. (2012, March 8). Memo to Mitt: Let Romney be Romney. *The New Yorker*. Online: http://www.newyorker.com/online/blogs/johncassidy/2012/03/memo-to-mitt-let-romney-be-romney.html. (Accessed: June 30, 2013.)

Chaffee, S.H. (Ed.) (1975). *Political communication: Issues and strategies for research*. Beverly Hills, CA: Sage.

Chaffee, S.H., & Hochheimer, J.L. (1985). The beginnings of political communication research in the United States: Origins of the "limited effects" model. In M. Gurevitch & M.R. Levy (Eds.), *Mass communication review yearbook* (Vol. 5, pp. 75–104). Newbury Park, CA: Sage.

Chaffee, S.H., McLeod, J.M., & Wackman, D. (1973). Family communication patterns and adolescent political participation. In J. Dennis (Ed.), *Socialization to politics: A reader* (pp. 349–364). New York: Wiley.

Chaffee, S.H., Ward, S., & Tipton, L.P. (1970). Mass communication and political socialization. *Journalism Quarterly, 47*, 647–659, 666.

Chaffee, S.H., & Yang, S.-M. (1990). Communication and political socialization. In O. Ichilov (Ed.), *Political socialization, citizenship education, and democracy* (pp. 137–157). New York: Teachers College Press.

Cho, J., & Ha, Y. (2012). On the communicative underpinnings of campaign effects: Presidential debates, citizen communication, and polarization in evaluations of candidates. *Political Communication, 29*, 184–204.

Chong, D., & Druckman, J.N. (2007a). A theory of framing and opinion formation in competitive elite environments. *Journal of Communication, 57*, 99–118.

Chong, D., & Druckman, J.N. (2007b). Framing public opinion in competitive democracies. *American Political Science Review, 101*, 637–655.

Christians, C.G., Glasser, T.L., McQuail, D., Nordenstreng, K., & White, R.A. (2009). *Normative theories of the media: Journalism in democratic societies.* Urbana: University of Illinois Press.

Cohen, B.C. (1963). *The press and foreign policy.* Princeton, NJ: Princeton University Press.

Cohen, G.L. (2003). Party over policy: The dominating impact of group influence on political beliefs. *Journal of Personality and Social Psychology, 85*, 808–822.

Cohen, J. (1998). Democracy and liberty. In J. Elster (Ed.), *Deliberative democracy* (pp. 185–231). Cambridge: Cambridge University Press.

Cohen, M., Karol, D., Noel, H., & Zaller, J. (2008). *The party decides: Presidential nominations before and after reform.* Chicago: University of Chicago Press.

Cohen, N. (2011, June 13). Shedding hazy light on a legend. *The New York Times*, B1, B9.

Cohen, N. (2012, November 22). Fighting with weapons, and postings on Twitter. *The New York Times*, A18.

Cole, D. (2013, January 2). Who pays for the right to bear arms? *The New York Times*, A19.

Coleman, S., & Blumler, J.G. (2009). *The Internet and democratic citizenship: Theory, practice and policy.* New York: Cambridge University Press.

Common Dreams (2012, October 25). A low-down, dirty, rotten and expensive 2012 presidential election. Online: https://www.commondreams.org/headline/2012/10/25. (Accessed: February 27, 2013.)

Confessore, N. (2012a, April 13). Campaigns plan maximum push to raise money. *The New York Times*, A1, A15.

Confessore, N. (2012b, May 8). Liberal donors will spend big on grass roots. *The New York Times*, A1, A16.

Confessore, N., & Luo, M. (2012, February 2). Secrecy shrouds "Super PAC" funds in latest filings. *The New York Times*, A1, A16.

Confessore, N., & Rutenberg, J. (2011, December 31). PAC ads rip at Gingrich as Romney stands clear. *The New York Times*, A1, A12.

Cooper, M. (2012, September 1). Fact-checkers howl, but both sides seem attached to dishonest ads. *The New York Times*, A12.

Cooper, M., & Sussman, D. (2013, January 18). Massacre at school sways public in way earlier shootings didn't. *The New York Times*, A1, A14.

Coulter, A. (2008). *Guilty: Liberal "victims" and their assault on America.* New York: Crown Forum.

Cramer, R.B. (1992). *What it takes: The way to the White House.* New York: Random House.

Cranberg, G., Bezanson, R., & Soloski, J. (2001). *Taking stock: Journalism and the publicly traded newspaper company.* Ames, IA: Iowa State University Press.

Cwalina, W., Falkowski, A., & Newman, B.I. (2011). *Political marketing: Theoretical and strategic foundations.* Armonk, NY: M.E. Sharpe.

Dahl, R.A. (1989). *Democracy and its critics.* New Haven: Yale University Press.

Dahlgren, P. (2000). The Internet and the democratization of civic culture. *Political Communication, 17*, 335–340.

D'Alessio, D., & Allen, M. (2000). Media bias in presidential elections: A meta-analysis. *Journal of Communication, 50*, 133–156.

D'Angelo, P., & Kuypers, J.A. (Eds.) (2010). *Doing news framing analysis: Empirical and theoretical perspectives.* New York: Routledge.

Davey, M. (2013, January 3). A soaring homicide rate, a divide in Chicago. *The New York Times*, A1, A12.

Davey, M., & Wines, M. (2012, November 4). In Ohio, a study in contrasts as 2 campaigns get out vote. *The New York Times*, 1, 20, 21.

Davis, R., Baumgartner, J.C., Francia, P.L., & Morris, J.S. (2009). The internet in U.S. election campaigns. In A. Chadwick & P.N. Howard (Eds.), *Routledge handbook of Internet politics* (pp. 13–24). New York: Routledge.

Davis, R., & Owen, D. (1998). *New media and American politics.* New York: Oxford University Press.

Dayan, D., & Katz, E. (1992). *Media events: The live broadcasting of history.* Cambridge, MA: Harvard University Press.

Dearing, J.W., & Rogers, E.M. (1996). *Agenda-setting.* Thousand Oaks, CA: Sage.

Decker, W.D. (1994). The 1988 Quayle–Bentsen vice presidential debate. In R.V. Friedenberg (Ed.), *Rhetorical studies of national political debates, 1960–1992* (2nd ed., pp. 167–185). Westport, CT: Praeger.

Delli Carpini, M.X., & Keeter, S. (1996). *What Americans know about politics and why it matters.* New Haven: Yale University Press.

Denton, R.E., Jr., & Kuypers, J.A. (2008). *Politics and communication in America: Campaigns, media, and governing in the 21st century.* Long Grove, IL: Waveland Press.

Devlin, L.P. (1995). Political commercials in American presidential elections. In L.L. Kaid & C. Holtz-Bacha (Eds.), *Political advertising in western democracies: Parties and candidates on television* (pp. 186–205). Thousand Oaks, CA: Sage.

deVreese, C.H., & Elenbaas, M. (2008). Media in the game of politics: Effects of strategic metacoverage on political cynicism. *Press/Politics, 13*, 285–309.

Diamond, E., & Bates, S. (1992). *The spot: The rise of political advertising on television* (*3rd ed.*). Cambridge, MA: MIT Press.

Dinkin, R.J. (1989). *Campaigning in America: A history of election practices.* New York: Greenwood Press.

Dominick, J.R. (2009). *The dynamics of mass communication: Media in the digital age* (*10th ed.*). New York: McGraw-Hill.

Domke, D. (2001). Racial cues and political ideology: An examination of associative priming. *Communication Research, 28*, 772–801.

Donadio, R., & Povoledo, E. (2011, November 13). Magnetic and divisive, a man whose politics were always personal. *The New York Times*, 10.

Dorman, W.A., & Livingston, S. (1994). News and historical content: The establishing phase of the Persian Gulf policy debate. In W.L. Bennett & D.L. Paletz (Eds.), *Taken by storm: The media, public opinion, and U.S. foreign policy in the Gulf War* (pp. 63–81). Chicago: University of Chicago Press.

Douglas, S.J. (2010). *The rise of enlightened sexism: How pop culture took us from girl power to girls gone wild.* New York: St. Martin's Griffin.

Dowd, M. (2012, August 12). Likability index. *The New York Times* (Sunday Review), 13.

Dowd, M. (2013, April 7). Can we get Hillary without the foolery? *The New York Times* (Sunday Review), 1, 11.

Downs, A. (1972). Up and down with ecology: The "issue-attention cycle." *The Public Interest, 28,* 38–50.

Draper, R. (2010, November 17). The rogue room. *The New York Times Magazine,* 42–49, 56, 60, 62.

Draper, R. (2012, July 8). The price of power. *The New York Times Magazine,* 20–25, 38.

Druckman, J.N. (2001). On the limits of framing effects: Who can frame? *Journal of Politics,* 63, 1041–1066.

Druckman, J.N. (2003). The power of television images: The first Kennedy–Nixon debate revisited. *Journal of Politics, 65,* 559–571.

Druckman, J.N., Kifer, M.J., & Parkin, M. (2010). Timeless strategy meets new medium: Going negative on Congressional campaign Web sites, 2002–2006. *Political Communication, 27,* 88–103.

Duhigg, C. (2012, October 14). Campaigns mine personal lives to get out vote. *The New York Times,* 1, 14.

Dulio, D.A. (2004). *For better or worse? How political consultants are changing elections in the United States.* Albany, NY: State University of New York Press.

Easton, D., & Dennis, J. (1965). The child's image of government. *The Annals of The American Academy of Political and Social Science, 361,* 40–57.

Easton, D., & Dennis, J. (1973). The child's image of government. In J. Dennis (Ed.), *Socialization to politics: A reader* (pp. 59–81). New York: Wiley.

Edgerly, S., Bode, L., Kim, Y.M., & Shah, D.V. (2013). Campaigns go social: Are Facebook, YouTube and Twitter changing elections? In T.N. Ridout (Ed.), *New directions in media and politics* (pp. 82–99). New York: Routledge.

Edwards, J.L. (Ed.) (2009). *Gender and political communication in America: Rhetoric, representation, and display.* Lanham, MD: Lexington Books.

Edy, J.A., & Meirick, P.C. (2007). Wanted, dead or alive: Media frames, frame adoption, and support for the war in Afghanistan. *Journal of Communication, 57,* 119–141.

Eligon, J. (2013, March 9). A state backs guns in class for teachers. *The New York Times,* A1, A13.

Elliott, J. (2010b, August 3). Michael Bloomberg delivers stirring defense of mosque. *Salon.* Online: http://www.salon.com/2010/08/03/mayor_bloomberg_on_mosque/. (Accessed: January 14, 2012.)

Emery, M., & Emery, E. (1992). *The press and America: An interpretive history of the mass media (7th ed).* Englewood Cliffs, NJ: Prentice Hall.

Enda, J. (2011, October–November). Campaign coverage in the time of Twitter. *American Journalism Review.* Online: http://www.ajr.org/article.asp?id=5134. (Accessed: March 9, 2013.)

Entman, R.M. (1989). *Democracy without citizens: Media and the decay of American politics.* New York: Oxford University Press.

Entman, R.M. (2004). *Projections of power: Framing news, public opinion, and U.S. foreign policy.* Chicago: University of Chicago Press.

Entman, R.M. (2010). Framing media power. In P. D'Angelo & J.A. Kuypers (Eds.), *Doing news framing analysis: Empirical and theoretical perspectives* (pp. 331–355). New York: Routledge.

Entman, R.M. (2012). *Scandal and silence: Media responses to presidential misconduct.* Cambridge: Polity Press.

Entman, R.M., & Page, B.I. (1994). The news before the storm: The Iraq war debate and the limits to media independence. In W.L. Bennett & D.L. Paletz (Eds.), *Taken by storm: The media, public opinion, and U.S. foreign policy in the Gulf War* (pp. 82–101). Chicago: University of Chicago Press.

Epstein, E.J. (1973). *News from nowhere.* New York: Random House.

Ettema, J.S., & Glasser, T.L. (1998). *Custodians of conscience: Investigative journalism and public virtue.* New York: Columbia University Press.

Eveland, W.P., & Hively, M.H. (2009). Political discussion frequency, network size, and "heterogeneity" of discussion as predictors of political knowledge and participation. *Journal of Communication, 59*, 205–224.

Eveland, W.P., Jr., & Morey, A.C. (2011). Challenges and opportunities of panel designs. In E.P. Bucy & R.L. Holbert (Eds.), *The sourcebook for political communication research: Methods, measures, and analytical techniques* (pp. 19–33). New York: Routledge.

Eveland, W.P., Jr., & Scheufele, D.A. (2000). Connecting news media use with gaps in knowledge and participation. *Political Communication, 17*, 215–237.

Eveland, W.P., Jr., & Seo, M. (2007). News and politics. In D.R. Roskos-Ewoldsen & J.L. Monahan (Eds.), *Communication and social cognition: Theories and methods* (pp. 293–318). Mahwah, NJ: Erlbaum Associates.

Ewen, S. (1996). *PR! A social history of spin.* New York: Basic Books.

FactCheck.org (2012a, December 20). Gun rhetoric vs. gun facts. Online: http://factcheck.org /2012/12/gun-rhetoric-vs-gun-facts/. (Accessed: January 10, 2013.)

FactCheck.org (2012b, October 17). FactChecking the Hofstra debate. Online: http://factcheck. org/2012//10/factchecking-the-hofstra-debate/. (Accessed: October 18, 2012.)

Fahim, K., & El Sheikh, M. (2013, March 31). Egypt orders arrest of satirist over skits on Islam and Morsi. *The New York Times*, 10.

Falk, E. (2010). *Women for president: Media bias in nine campaigns (2nd ed.).* Urbana, IL: University of Illinois Press.

Farnsworth, S.J., & Lichter, S.R. (2011). *The nightly news nightmare: Media coverage of U.S. presidential elections, 1988–2008 (3rd ed.).* Lanham, MD: Rowman & Littlefield.

Farnsworth, S.J., & Lichter, S.R. (2012). How television covers the presidential nomination process. In W.G. Mayer & J. Bernstein (Eds.), *The making of the presidential candidates 2012* (pp. 133–158). Lanham, MD: Rowman & Littlefield.

Feagler, D. (1996, August 28). Act one: Night of miracles raises curtain on big show. *The Plain Dealer*, 2A.

Feldman, L. (2011). Partisan differences in opinionated news perceptions: A test of the hostile media effect. *Political Behavior, 33*, 407–432.

Feldman, L., & Young, D.G. (2008). Late-night comedy as a gateway to traditional news: An analysis of time trends in news attention among late-night comedy viewers during the 2004 presidential primaries. *Political Communication, 25*, 401–422.

Finley, M.I. (1973). *Democracy ancient and modern*. New Brunswick, NJ: Rutgers University Press.

Finley, M.I. (1983). *Politics in the ancient world*. Cambridge: Cambridge University Press.

Fischer, D. Hackett (1965). *The revolution of American conservatism: The Federalist Party in the era of Jeffersonian democracy*. New York: Harper & Row.

Fischer, D. Hackett (1994). *Paul Revere's ride*. New York: Oxford University Press.

Fishman, M. (1997). News and nonevents: Making the visible invisible. In D. Berkowitz (Ed.), *Social meaning of news: A text-reader* (pp. 210–229). Thousand Oaks, CA: Sage.

Fowler, J.H., Loewen, P.J., Settle, J., & Dawes, C.T. (2011). Genes, games, and political participation. In P.K. Hatemi & R. McDermott (Eds.), *Man is by nature a political animal: Evolution, biology, and politics* (pp. 207–223). Chicago: University of Chicago Press.

Fraile, M. (2011). Widening or reducing the knowledge gap? Testing the media effects on political knowledge in Spain (2004–2006). *International Journal of Press/Politics, 16*, 163–184.

Frantzich, S.E. (2009). E-politics and the 2008 presidential campaign: Has the Internet "arrived?" In W.J. Crotty (Ed.), *Winning the presidency 2008* (pp. 135–151). Boulder, CO: Paradigm Publishers.

Freedman, P., Franz, M., & Goldstein, K. (2004). Campaign advertising and democratic citizenship. *American Journal of Political Science, 48*, 723–741.

Fridkin, K.L., Kenney, P.J., Gershon, S.A., & Woodall, G.S. (2008). Spinning debates: The impact of the news media's coverage of the final 2004 presidential debate. *Press/Politics, 13*, 29–51.

Friedenberg, R.V. (1994). Patterns and trends in national political debates: 1960–1992. In R.V. Friedenberg (Ed.), *Rhetorical studies of national political debates, 1960–1992* (2nd ed., pp. 235–259). Westport, CT: Praeger.

Friedman, M.P. (2009). Simulacrobama: The mediated election of 2008. *Journal of American Studies, 43(2)*, 341–356.

Friedman, T.L. (2011, November 23). Go big, Mr. Obama. *The New York Times*, A27.

Galston, W.A. (2011, November 6). Telling Americans to vote, or else. *The New York Times* (Week in Review), 9.

Galtung, J., & Ruge, M.H. (1965). The structure of foreign news. *Journal of Peace Research, 2*, 64–90.

Gamson, W.A., & Modigliani, A. (1987). The changing culture of affirmative action. In R.A. Braumgart (Ed.), *Research in political sociology* (Vol. 3, pp. 137–177). Greenwich, CT: JAI.

Gans, H.J. (1979). *Deciding what's news*. New York: Pantheon.

Garrett, R.K. (2009). Politically motivated reinforcement seeking: Reframing the selective exposure debate. *Journal of Communication, 59*, 676–699.

Gastil, J. (2008). *Political communication and deliberation*. Thousand Oaks, CA: Sage.

Gaziano, C. (1997). Forecast 2000: Widening knowledge gaps. *Journalism & Mass Communication Quarterly, 74*, 237–264.

Geer, J.G. (2006). *In defense of negativity: Attack ads in presidential campaigns*. Chicago: University of Chicago Press.

Geller, P. (2010, May 6). Monster mosques pushes ahead in shadow of World Trade Center Islamic death and destruction. *Atlas Shrugs*. Online: http://atlasshrugs2000.typepad.com/atlas_shrugs/ 2010/05/monster-mo– (Accessed: January 13, 2012.)

Gerber, A.S., Gimpel, J.G., Green, D.P., & Shaw, D.R. (2011). How large and long-lasting are the persuasive effects of televised campaign ads? Results from a randomized field experiment. *American Political Science Review, 105*, 135–150.

Gitlin, T. (1978). Media sociology: The dominant paradigm. *Theory and Society, 6*, 205–253.

Gladwell, M. (2000). *The tipping point: How little things can make a big difference.* Boston: Little, Brown.

Goldberg, B. (2002). *Bias: A CBS insider exposes how the media distort the news.* Washington, D.C.: Regnery.

Gonzenbach, W.J. (1996). *The media, the president, and public opinion: A longitudinal analysis of the drug issue, 1984–1991.* Mahwah, NJ: Erlbaum Associates.

Gooding, R. (2004, November). The trashing of John McCain. *Vanity Fair.* Online: http://www.vanityfair.com/politics/features/2004/11/mccain200411. (Accessed: August 18, 2012.)

Gottlieb, R., & Wolt, I. (1977). *Thinking big: The story of the Los Angeles Times, its publishers, and their influence on southern California.* New York: G.P. Putnam's Sons.

Grabe, M.E., & Bucy, E.P. (2011). Image bite analysis of political visuals: Understanding the visual framing process in election news. In E.P. Bucy & R.L. Holbert (Eds.), *The sourcebook for political communication research: Methods, measures, and analytical techniques* (pp. 209–237). New York: Routledge.

Graber, D.A. (1988). *Processing the news: How people tame the information tide (2nd ed.).* New York: Longman.

Graber, D.A. (2001). *Processing politics: Learning from television in the Internet age.* Chicago: University of Chicago Press.

Gray, J., Jones, J.P., & Thompson, E. (2009). The state of satire, the satire of state. In J. Gray, J.P. Jones, & E. Thompson (Eds.), *Satire TV: Politics and comedy in the post-network era* (pp. 3–36). New York: New York University Press.

Green, D., Palmquist, B., & Schickler, E. (2002). *Partisan hearts and minds: Political parties and the social identities of voters.* New Haven: Yale University Press.

Green, D.P., & Gerber, A.S. (2008). *Get out the vote. How to increase voter turnout (2nd ed.).* Washington, D.C.: Brookings Institution Press.

Green, J. (2011). The tragedy of Sarah Palin. *The Atlantic.* Online: http://www. theatlantic.com/magazine/archive/2011/06/the-tragedy-of-sarah-palin/8492/. (Accessed: July 1, 2011.)

Greenberg, S.B. (2011, July 31). Why voters tune out Democrats. *The New York Times* (Sunday Review), 1, 6.

Groseclose, T. (2011). *Left turn: How liberal media bias distorts the American mind.* New York: St. Martin's Press.

Grush, J.E., McKeough, K.L., & Ahlering, R.F. (1978). Extrapolating laboratory exposure research to actual political elections. *Journal of Personality and Social Psychology, 36*, 257–270.

Guggenheim, L., Kwak, N., & Campbell, S.W. (2011). Nontraditional news negativity: The relationship of entertaining political news use to political cynicism and mistrust. *International Journal of Public Opinion Research, 23*, 287–314.

Gutmann, A., & Thompson, D. (2012). *The spirit of compromise: Why governing demands it and campaigning undermines it.* Princeton, NJ: Princeton University Press.

Haberman, C. (2012, September 30). Publisher who transformed The Times for new era. *The New York Times,* Online: http://www.nytimes.com/2012/09/30/nyregion/arthur-o-sulzberger-publisher-who-transformed-times-dies-at-86.html?pagewanted=all&_r=0. (Accessed: September 22, 2013)

Habermas, J. (1996). *Between facts and norms: Contributions to a discourse theory of law and democracy*. Cambridge, MA: MIT Press.

Hahn, D.F. (1994). The 1992 Clinton–Bush–Perot presidential debates. In R.V. Friedenberg (Ed.), *Rhetorical studies of national political debates, 1960–1992* (2nd ed., pp. 187–210). Westport, CT: Praeger.

Haidt, J. (2012). *The righteous mind: Why good people are divided by politics and religion*. New York: Pantheon Books.

Hallin, D.C. (1986). *The "uncensored war": The media and Vietnam*. New York: Oxford University Press.

Hallin, D.C. (1992). Sound bite news: Television coverage of elections, 1968–1988. *Journal of Communication, 42(2)*, 5–24.

Hallin, D.C., & Gitlin, T. (1994). The Gulf War as popular culture and television drama. In W.L. Bennett & D.L. Paletz (Eds.), *Taken by storm: The media, public opinion, and U.S. foreign policy in the Gulf War* (pp. 149–163). Chicago: University of Chicago Press.

Hallin, D.C., & Mancini, P. (2004). *Comparing media systems: Three models of media and politics*. New York: Cambridge University Press.

Hart, R.P. (1994). *Seducing America: How television charms the modern voter*. New York: Oxford University Press.

Hart, R.P. (2013). Politics in the digital age: A scary prospect? In T.N. Ridout (Ed.), *New directions in media and politics* (pp. 210–225). New York: Routledge.

Hart, R.P., & Hartelius, E.J. (2007). The political sins of Jon Stewart. *Critical Studies of Mass Communication, 24*, 263–272.

Harwood, J. (2012, October 1). Using debates to turn electoral tide is difficult but not impossible. *The New York Times*, A12.

Hatemi, P.K., & McDermott, R. (Eds.) (2011). *Man is by nature a political animal: Evolution, biology, and politics*. Chicago: University of Chicago Press.

Hayes, A.F., Preacher, K.J., & Myers, T.A. (2011). Mediation and the estimation of indirect effects in political communication research. In E.P. Bucy & R.L. Holbert (Eds.), *The sourcebook for political communication research: Methods, measures, and analytical techniques* (pp. 434–465). New York: Routledge.

Hayes, D., & Guardino, M. (2010). Whose views made the news? Media coverage and the march to war in Iraq. *Political Communication, 27*, 59–87.

Heilemann, J., & Halperin, M. (2010). *Game change: Obama and the Clintons, McCain and Palin, and the race of a lifetime*. New York: Harper.

Held, D. (2006). *Models of democracy (3rd ed.)*. Stanford, CA: Stanford University Press.

Hellweg, S.A., Pfau, M., & Brydon, S.R. (1992). *Televised presidential debates: Advocacy in contemporary America*. New York: Praeger.

Henneberg, S.C., & O'Shaughnessy, N.J. (2007). Theory and concept development in political marketing: Issues and an agenda. *Journal of Political Marketing, 6*, 5–31.

Herman, E.S., & Chomsky, N. (2002). *Manufacturing consent: The political economy of the mass media*. New York: Pantheon.

Hertog, J.K., & McLeod, D.M. (2001). A multiperspectival approach to framing analysis: A field guide. In S.D. Reese, O.H. Gandy, Jr., & A.E. Grant (Eds.), *Framing public life: Perspectives on media and our understanding of the social world* (pp. 139–161). Mahwah, NJ: Erlbaum Associates.

Hertsgaard, M. (1988). *On bended knee: The press and the Reagan presidency*. New York: Farrar Straus Giroux.

Hertzberg, H. (2013, April 8). Senses of entitlement. (The talk of the town). *The New Yorker*, 23–24.

Hetherington, M. (2012). Partisanship and polarization. In A.J. Berinsky (Eds.), *New directions in public opinion* (pp. 101–118). New York: Routledge.

Hillygus, D.S. (2011). The evolution of election polling in the United States. *Public Opinion Quarterly, 75*, 962–981.

Hillygus, D.S., & Jackman, S. (2003). Voter decision making in Elec⸍ ɔn 2000: Campaign effects, partisan activation, and the Clinton legacy. *American Jour ɹl of Political Science, 47*, 583–596.

Hillygus, D.S., & Shields, T.G. (2008). *The persuadable voter: Wedge issues in presidential campaigns*. Princeton, NJ: Princeton University Press.

Hinck, E.A. (1993). *Enacting the presidency: Political argument, presidential debates, and presidential character*. Westport, CT: Praeger.

Hinyard, L.J., & Kreuter, M.W. (2007). Using narrative communication as a tool for health behavior change: A conceptual, theoretical, and empirical overview. *Health Education & Behavior, 34*, 777–792.

Hively, M.H., & Eveland, W.P., Jr. (2009). Contextual antecedents and political consequences of adolescent political discussion, discussion elaboration, and network diversity. *Political Communication, 26*, 30–47.

Hmielowski, J.D., Holbert, R.L., & Lee, J. (2011). Predicting the consumption of political TV satire: Affinity for political humor, *The Daily Show*, and *The Colbert Report. Communication Monographs, 78*, 96–114.

Hoffman, L.H., & Thomson, T.L. (2009). The effect of television viewing on adolescents' civic participation: Political efficacy as a mediating mechanism. *Journal of Broadcasting & Electronic Media, 53*, 3–21.

Hoffman, L.H., & Young, D.G. (2011a). Political communication survey research: Challenges, trends, and opportunities. In E.P. Bucy & R.L. Holbert (Eds.), *The sourcebook for political communication research: Methods, measures, and analytical techniques* (pp. 55–77). New York: Routledge.

Hoffman, L.H., & Young, D.G. (2011b). Satire, punch lines, and the nightly news: Untangling media effects on political participation. *Communication Research Reports, 28*, 159–168.

Hofstetter, C.R. (1976). *Bias in the news: Network television coverage of the 1972 presidential campaign*. Columbus: Ohio State University Press.

Hogan, J.M. (2013). Persuasion in the rhetorical tradition. In J.P. Dillard & L. Shen (Eds.), *The Sage handbook of persuasion: Developments in theory and practice* (2nd ed., pp. 2–19). Thousand Oaks, CA: Sage.

Holan, A.D. (2012, December 13). Claim on Jeep jobs is "Lie of the Year." *The Plain Dealer*, A1, A8.

Holbert, R.L., & Bucy, E.P. (2011). Advancing methods and measurement: Supporting theory and keeping pace with the modern political communication environment. In E.P. Bucy & R.L. Holbert (Eds.), *The sourcebook for political communication research: Methods, measures, and analytical techniques* (pp. 3–15). New York: Routledge.

Holbert, R.L., Garrett, R.K., & Gleason, L.S. (2010). A new era of minimal effects? A response to Bennett and Iyengar. *Journal of Communication, 60*, 15–34.

Holbert, R.L., & Hmielowski, J.D. (2011). Secondary analysis in political communication viewed as a creative act. In E.P. Bucy & R.L. Holbert (Eds.), *The sourcebook for political communication research: Methods, measures, and analytical techniques* (pp. 81–95). New York: Routledge.

Holbrook, T.M. (1996). *Do campaigns matter?* Thousand Oaks, CA: Sage.

Holbrook, T.M. (1999). Political learning from presidential debates. *Political Behavior, 21*, 67–89.

Hollihan, T.A. (2009). *Uncivil wars: Political campaigns in a media age (2nd ed.)*. Boston: Bedford/St. Martin's.

Hornik, R. (2006). *Personal Influence* and the effects of the national youth anti-drug media campaign. *Annals of the American Association of Political and Social Science, 608*, 282–300.

Huckfeldt, R., & Sprague, J. (1995). *Citizens, politics, and social communication: Information and influence in an election campaign.* New York: Cambridge University Press.

Hurley, P.A., & Hill, K.Q. (2010). In search of representation theory. In J.E. Leighley (Ed.), *The Oxford handbook of American elections and political behavior* (pp. 716–740). New York: Oxford University Press.

Ichilov, O. (1990). Introduction. In O. Ichilov (Ed.), *Political socialization, citizenship education, and democracy* (pp. 1–8). New York: Teachers College Press.

Iyengar, S. (1991). *Is anyone responsible? How television frames political issues.* Chicago: University of Chicago Press.

Iyengar, S. (2004). Engineering consent: The renaissance of mass communications research in politics. In J.T. Jost, M.R. Banaji, & D.A. Prentice (Eds.), *Perspectivism in social psychology: The yin and yang of scientific progress* (pp. 247–257). Washington, D.C.: American Psychological Association.

Iyengar, S. (2011). Experimental designs for political communication research: Using new technology and online participant pools to overcome the problem of generalizability. In E.P. Bucy & R.L. Holbert (Eds.), *The sourcebook for political communication research: Methods, measures, and analytical techniques* (pp. 129–148). New York: Routledge.

Iyengar, S., & Hahn, K.S. (2009). Red media, blue media: Evidence of ideological sensitivity in media use. *Journal of Communication, 59*, 19–39.

Iyengar, S., & Hahn, K.S. (2011). The political economy of mass media: Implications for informed citizenship. In W. Le Cheminant & J.M. Parrish (Eds.), *Manipulating democracy: Democratic theory, political psychology, and mass media* (pp. 209–228). New York: Routledge.

Iyengar, S., & Kinder, D.R. (1987). *News that matters: Television and American opinion.* Chicago: University of Chicago Press.

Iyengar, S., & Kinder, D.R. (2010). *News that matters: Television and American opinion (Updated ed.).* Chicago: University of Chicago Press.

Jackson, B. (2008). *Cell phones and political polls*. Online: http://www.factcheck. org/2008/02/ cell-phones-and-political-polls. (Accessed: June 24, 2012.)

Jackson, D.J. (2002). *Entertainment & politics: The influence of pop culture on young adult political socialization*. New York: Peter Lang.

Jacoby, J. (2010, June 6). A mosque at ground zero? *The Boston Globe*. Online: http://www. boston.com/bostonglobe/editorial_opinion/oped/articles– (Accessed: January 13, 2012.)

Jakubowicz, K. (1996). Television and elections in post-1989 Poland: How powerful is the medium? In D.L. Swanson & P. Mancini (Eds.), *Politics, media, and modern democracy: An international study of innovations in electoral campaigning and their consequences* (pp. 129–154). Westport, CT: Praeger.

Jamieson, K.H. (1984). *Packaging the presidency: A history and criticism of presidential campaign advertising*. New York: Oxford University Press.

Jamieson, K.H. (1986). The evolution of political advertising in America. In L.L. Kaid, D. Nimmo, & K.R. Sanders (Eds.), *New perspectives on political advertising* (pp. 1–20). Carbondale, IL: Southern Illinois Press.

Jamieson, K.H. (1992). *Dirty politics: Deception, distraction, and democracy*. New York: Oxford University Press.

Jamieson, K.H. (1995). *Beyond the double bind: Women and leadership*. New York: Oxford University Press.

Jamieson, K.H., & Birdsell, D.S. (1988). *Presidential debates: The challenge of creating an informed electorate*. New York: Oxford University Press.

Jamieson, K.H., & Cappella, J.N. (2008). *Echo chamber: Rush Limbaugh and the conservative media establishment*. New York: Oxford University Press.

Jamieson, K.H., & Dunn, J. (2008). The "B" word in traditional news and on the web: Entering "Hillary"and "Bitch" we found more than five hundred YouTube videos. *Nieman Reports, 62*, 31–33.

Jamieson, K.H., & Waldman, P. (2003). *The press effect: Politicians, journalists, and the stories that shape the political world*. New York: Oxford University Press.

Jarvis, S.E. (2011). The use of focus groups in political communication research. In E.P. Bucy & R.L. Holbert (Eds.), *The sourcebook for political communication research: Methods, measures, and analytical techniques* (pp. 283–299). New York: Routledge.

Jennings, M.K., & Niemi, R.G. (1968). The transmission of political values from parent to child. *American Political Science Review, 62*, 169–183.

Jerit, J., & Barabas, J. (2006). Bankrupt rhetoric: How misleading information affects knowledge about Social Security. *Public Opinion Quarterly, 70*, 278–303.

Johnson, D.W. (2000). The business of political consulting. In J.A. Thurber & C.J. Nelson (Eds.), *Campaign warriors: The role of political consultants in elections* (pp. 37–52). Washington, D.C.: Brookings Institution Press.

Johnson, D.W. (2007). *No place for amateurs: How political consultants are reshaping American democracy (2nd ed.)*. New York: Routledge.

Johnson, D.W. (2011). *Campaigning in the twenty-first century: A whole new ballgame?* New York: Routledge.

Johnson, D.W. (2012). Formative years of political consulting in America, 1934–2000. *Journal of Political Marketing, 11*, 54–74.

Johnson, K. (2011, August 26). Unfiltered images, turning perceptions upside down. *The New York Times*, C22.

Johnson, T.J. (Ed.) (2014). *Agenda setting in a 2.0 world: New agendas in communication.* New York: Routledge.

Johnson, T.J., & Wanta, W. (with Byrd, J.T., & Lee, C.) (1995). Exploring FDR's relationship with the press: A historical agenda-setting study. *Political Communication, 12*, 157–172.

Johnson-Cartee, K.S., & Copeland, G.A. (1991). *Negative political advertising: Coming of age.* Hillsdale, NJ: Lawrence Erlbaum Associates.

Jones, C.A. (2011). Political advertising, digital fundraising and campaign finance in the 2008 election: A First Amendment normative analysis. In M.S. McKinney & M.C. Banwart (Eds.), *Communication in the 2008 U.S. election: Digital natives elect a president* (pp. 89–104). New York: Peter Lang.

Jones, J.P. (2010). *Entertaining politics: Satiric television and political engagement (2nd ed.).* Lanham, MD: Rowman & Littlefield.

Kahl, M.L., & Edwards, J.L. (2009). An epistolary epilogue: Learning from Sarah Palin's vice presidential campaign. In J.L. Edwards (Ed.), *Gender and political communication in America: Rhetoric, representation, and display* (pp. 267–277). Lanham, MD: Lexington Books.

Kahn, K. Fridkin (1994). The distorted mirror: Press coverage of women candidates for statewide office. *Journal of Politics, 56*, 154–173.

Kahn, K. Fridkin (1996). *The political consequences of being a woman: How stereotypes influence the conduct and consequences of political campaigns.* New York: Columbia University Press.

Kahneman, D. (2011). *Thinking, fast and slow.* New York: Farrar, Straus and Giroux.

Kaid, L.L. (2004). Political advertising. In L.L. Kaid (Ed.), *Handbook of political communication research* (pp. 155–202). Mahwah, NJ: Lawrence Erlbaum Associates.

Kaid, L.L. (2006). Political advertising. In S.C. Craig (Ed.), *The electoral challenge: Theory meets practice* (pp. 79–96). Washington, D.C.: CQ Press.

Kam, C.D. (2006). Political campaigns and open-minded thinking. *Journal of Politics, 68*, 931–945.

Kang, J.C. (2013, July 28). Crowd-sourcing a smear. *The New York Times Magazine*, 36–42, 50–51.

Kaniss, P. (1991). *Making local news.* Chicago: University of Chicago Press.

Kantor, J. (2012, October 21). For president, a complex calculus of race and politics. *The New York Times*, 1, 22.

Katz, E., & Lazarsfeld, P.F. (1955). *Personal Influence: The part played by people in the flow of mass communication.* Glencoe, IL: Free Press of Glencoe.

Katz, R.S. (1997). *Democracy and elections.* New York: Oxford University Press.

Kaye, B.K., & Johnson, T.J. (2011). *The shot heard around the World Wide Web: Who heard what where about Osama bin Laden's death.* Paper presented to annual convention of Midwest Association for Public Opinion Research, Chicago.

Keep guns out of criminal hands. (2013, March 23). *The New York Times*, A18.

Kenski, K., Gottfried, J.A., & Jamieson, K.H. (2011). The rolling cross-section: Design and utility for political research. In E.P. Bucy & R.L. Holbert (Eds.), *The sourcebook for political communication research: Methods, measures, and analytical techniques* (pp. 34–54). New York: Routledge.

Kenski, K., & Jamieson, K.H. (2011). Presidential and vice presidential debates in 2008: A profile of audience composition. *American Behavioral Scientist, 55*, 307–324.

Kern, M. (1989). *30-second politics: Political advertising in the eighties*. New York: Praeger.

Kerr, P. (1986, November 17). Anatomy of an issue: Drugs, the evidence, the reaction. *The New York Times*, 1, 12.

Keum, H., Hillback, E.D., Rojas, Gil de Zuniga, H., Shah, D.V., & McLeod, D.M. (2005). Personifying the radical: How news framing polarizes security concerns and tolerance judgments. *Human Communication Research, 31*, 337–364.

Kim, S.-H., Han, M., & Scheufele, D.A. (2010). Think about him this way: Priming, news media, and South Koreans' evaluation of the president. *International Journal of Public Opinion Research, 22*, 299–319.

Kim, Y.M. (2005). Use and disuse of contextual primes in dynamic news environments. *Journal of Communication, 55*, 737–755.

Kinder, D.R. (2003). Communication and politics in the age of information. In D.O. Sears, L. Huddy, & R. Jervis (Eds.), *Oxford handbook of political psychology* (pp. 357–393). New York: Oxford University Press.

Kinder, D.R. (2007). Curmudgeonly advice. *Journal of Communication, 57*, 155–162.

Kinsella, J. (1988). *Covering the plague: AIDS and the American media*. New Brunswick, NJ: Rutgers University Press.

Kirkpatrick, D.D., & Sanger, D.E. (2011, February 14). A Tunisian–Egyptian link that shook Arab history. *The New York Times*, A1, A9–A10.

Klapper, J.T. (1960). *The effects of mass communication*. New York: Free Press.

Klein, J. (2006). *Politics lost: How American democracy was trivialized by people who think you're stupid*. New York: Doubleday.

Knobloch-Westerwick, S. (2012). Selective exposure and reinforcement of attitudes and partisanship before a presidential election. *Journal of Communication, 62*, 628–642.

Koff, S. (2012, July 8). Retail chain's failure stokes a contentious election issue. *The Plain Dealer*, A1, A8.

Kosicki, G.M. (1993). Problems and opportunities in agenda-setting research. *Journal of Communication, 43*, 100–127.

Kosicki, G.M., McLeod, D.M., & McLeod, J.M. (2011). Looking back and looking forward: Observations on the role of research methods in the rapidly evolving field of political communication. In E.P. Bucy & R.L. Holbert (Eds.), *The sourcebook for political communication research: Methods, measures, and analytical techniques* (pp. 543–569). New York: Routledge.

Kotler, P., & Kotler, N. (1999). Political marketing: Generating effective candidates, campaigns, and causes. In B.I. Newman (Ed.), *Handbook of political marketing* (pp. 3–18). Thousand Oaks, CA: Sage.

Kovach, B., & Rosenstiel, T. (2007). *The elements of journalism: What newspeople should know and the public should expect (revised edition)*. New York: Three Rivers Press.

Kraus, S. (1988). *Televised presidential debates and public policy*. Hillsdale, NJ: Lawrence Erlbaum Associates.

Kraus, S. (1996). Winners of the first 1960 televised presidential debate between Kennedy and Nixon. *Journal of Communication, 46(4)*, 78–96.

Kristof, N.D. (2012, July 26). Safe from fire, but not from guns. *The New York Times*, A23.

Krosnick, J.A., & Kinder, D.R. (1990). Altering the foundations of support for the president through priming. *American Political Science Review, 84*, 497–512.

Krosnick, J.A., & Petty, R.E. (1995). Attitude strength: An overview. In R.E. Petty & J.A. Krosnick (Eds.), *Attitude strength: Antecedents and consequences* (pp. 1–24). Hillsdale, NJ: Lawrence Erlbaum Associates.

Krugman, P.R. (1996, September 4). First, do no harm. *The New York Times*, A15.

Krumboltz, M. (2012). Sarcastic binder reviews a hit on Amazon. *Yahoo! News.* Online: http://news.yahoo.com/blogs/ticket/sarcastic-binder-reviews-hit-amaz... (Accessed: October 18, 2012.)

Krupnikov, Y. (2011). When does negativity demobilize? Tracing the conditional effect of negative campaigning on voter turnout. *American Journal of Political Science, 55*, 796–812.

Kühne, R., Schemer, C., Matthes, J., & Wirth, W. (2011). Affective priming in political campaigns: How campaign-induced emotions prime political opinions. *International Journal of Public Opinion Research, 23*, 485–507.

Kuypers, J. (2002). *Press bias and politics: How the media frame controversial issues.* New York: Praeger.

Kuypers, J.A. (2006). *Bush's war: Media bias and justifications for war in a terrorist age.* Lanham, MD: Rowman & Littlefield.

Ladd, J.M. (2007). Predispositions and public support for the president during the war on terrorism. *Public Opinion Quarterly, 71*, 511–538.

Ladd, J.M. (2012). *Why Americans hate the media and how it matters.* Princeton, NJ: Princeton University Press.

Lakoff, G. (2004). *Don't think of an elephant! Know your values and frame the debate.* White River Junction, VT: Chelsea Green Publishing.

Lang, G.E., & Lang, K. (1983). *The battle for public opinion: The president, the press, and the polls during Watergate.* New York: Columbia University Press.

Lang, K. (2011, September 2). Personal communication to Richard M. Perloff.

Lang, K., & Lang, G.E. (2006). *Personal Influence* and the new paradigm: Some inadvertent consequences. *Annals of the American Association of Political and Social Science, 608*, 157–178.

Larmer, B. (2011, October 30). Where an Internet joke is not just a joke. *The New York Times Magazine*, 34–39.

Lasswell, H. (1927). *Propaganda technique in the world war.* New York: Knopf.

Lasswell, H. (1936). *Politics: Who gets what, when, how.* New York: McGraw-Hill.

Lau, R.R., & Pomper, G.M. (2004). *Negative campaigning: An analysis of U.S. Senate elections.* New York: Rowman & Littlefield.

Lau, R.R., Sigelman, L., & Rovner, I.B. (2007). The effects of negative political campaigns: A meta-analytic reassessment. *Journal of Politics, 69*, 1176–1209.

Lavrakas, P.J., & Bauman, S.L. (1995). Page One use of presidential pre-election polls: 1980–1992. In P.J. Lavrakas, M.W. Traugott, & P.V. Miller (Eds.), *Presidential polls and the news media* (pp. 35–49). Boulder, CO: Westview Press.

Lawrence, R.G. (2010). Researching political news framing: Established ground and new horizons. In P. D'Angelo & J.A. Kuypers (Eds.), *Doing news framing analysis: Empirical and theoretical perspectives* (pp. 265–285). New York: Routledge.

Lawrence, R.G., & Rose, M. (2010). *Hillary Clinton's race for the White House: Gender politics and the media on the campaign trail.* Boulder, CO: Lynne Rienner Publishers.

Lazarsfeld, P.F., Berelson, B., & Gaudet, H. (1944). *The people's choice: How the voter makes up his mind in a presidential campaign.* New York: Columbia University Press.

Le Bon, G. (1896). *The crowd: A study of the popular mind.* London: Ernest Benn.

Le Cheminant, W., & Parrish, J.M. (2011). Introduction: Manipulating democracy: A reappraisal. In W. Le Cheminant & J.M. Parrish (Eds.), *Manipulating democracy: Democratic theory, political psychology, and mass media* (pp. 1–24). New York: Routledge.

Lee, E.-J., & Oh, S.Y. (2012). To personalize or depersonalize: When and how politicians' personalized tweets affect the public's reactions. *Journal of Communication, 62,* 932–949.

Lees-Marshment, J. (2010). Global political marketing. In J. Lees-Marshment, J. Strömbäck & C. Rudd (Eds.), *Global political marketing* (pp. 1–15). New York: Routledge.

Leff, L. (2005). *Buried by the Times: The Holocaust and America's most important newspaper.* New York: Cambridge University Press.

Leibovich, M. (2010, October 3). Being Glenn Beck. *The New York Times Magazine,* 35–41, 53–54, 57.

Lemert, J.B., Elliott, W.R., Bernstein, J.M., Rosenberg, W.L., & Nestvold, K.J. (1991). *News verdicts, the debates, and presidential campaigns.* New York: Praeger.

Lenhart, A., Purcell, K., Smith, A., & Zickuhr, K. (2010). *Social media and young adults—Pew Internet and Life Project.* Pew Research Center. Online: http://www.pewinternet.org/Reports/2010/Social-media-and-young-adults. (Accessed: September 22, 2013.)

Lenz, G.S., & Lawson, C. (2011). Looking the part: Television leads less informed citizens to vote based on candidates' appearance. *American Journal of Political Science, 55,* 574–589.

Lessig, L. (2011a). *Republic, lost: How money corrupts Congress—and a plan to stop it.* New York: Twelve.

Lessig, L. (2011b, November 16). More money can beat big money. *The New York Times.* Online: http://www.nytimes.com/2011/11/17/opinion/in-campaign-financing-more-money-can-beat-big-money.html. (Accessed: June 30, 2013.)

Lichter, S.R., Amundson, D., & Noyes, R. (1988). *The video campaign: Network coverage of the 1988 primaries.* Washington, D.C.: American Enterprise Institute for Public Policy Research.

Lichter, S.R., Rothman, S., & Lichter, L.S. (1986). *The media elite.* Bethesda, MD: Adler & Adler.

Lippmann, W. (1922). *Public opinion.* New York: Free Press.

Lipstadt, D.E. (1986). *Beyond belief: The American press and the coming of the Holocaust 1933–1945.* New York: Free Press.

Lipton, E., & Krauss, C. (2012, August 23). Giving reins to the states over drilling. *The New York Times.* Online: http://www.nytimes.com/2012/08/24/us/romney-would-give-reins-to-states-on-drilling-on-federal-lands.html?page wanted=all&_r=0. (Accessed: July 2, 2013.)

Lithwick, D. (2008, September 8). How to debate a girl, and win. *Slate.* Online: http://www.slate.com/articles/news_and_politics/2008/09/how_to_debate_a_girl_and_win.html. (Accessed: March 29, 2013.)

Lizza, R. (2011, August 15). Leap of faith: The making of a Republican front-runner. *The New Yorker.* Online: http://www.newyorker.com/reporting/2011/08/15/110815fa_fact_lizza. (Accessed: September 22, 2013.)

Lizza, R. (2012, October 29 & November 5). The final push: The Obama team's high-risk strategy. *The New Yorker*, 62–63, 66–69.

Lowry, D.T., & Shidler, J.A. (1998). The sound bites, the biters, and the bitten: A two-campaign test of the anti-incumbent bias hypothesis in network TV news. *Journalism & Mass Communication Quarterly, 75,* 719–729.

Lubken, D. (2008). Remembering the straw man: The travels and adventures of *hypodermic*. In D.W. Park & J. Pooley (Eds.), *The history of media and communication research: Contested memories* (pp. 19–42). New York: Peter Lang.

Madhani, A. (2012, December 27). Tighter gun laws favored in poll. *USA Today*, A1.

Mancini, P., & Swanson, D.L. (1996). Politics, media, and modern democracy: Introduction. In D.L. Swanson & P. Mancini (Eds.), *Politics, media, and modern democracy: An international study of innovations in electoral campaigning and their consequences* (pp. 1–26). Westport, CT: Praeger.

Mandelbaum, M. (2007). *Democracy's good name: The rise and risks of the world's most popular form of government.* New York: PublicAffairs.

Manheim, J.B. (2011). *Strategy in information and influence campaigns: How policy advocates, social movements, insurgent groups, corporations, governments, and others get what they want.* New York: Routledge.

Martel, M. (1983). *Political campaign debates: Images, strategies, and tactics.* New York: Longman.

Martinez, M.D. (2010). Why is American turnout so low, and why should we care? In J.E. Leighley (Ed.), *The Oxford handbook of American elections and political behavior* (pp. 107–124). New York: Oxford University Press.

Matthes, J. (2006). The need for orientation towards news media: Revising and validating a classic concept. *International Journal of Public Opinion Research, 18,* 422–444.

Matthews, C. (1996). *Kennedy & Nixon: The rivalry that shaped postwar America.* New York: Simon & Schuster.

Mayer, J. (2012b, February 13 & 20). Attack dog. *The New Yorker*, 40–44, 47–49.

Mayer, W.G. (1987). The New Hampshire primary: A historical overview. In G.R. Orren & N.W. Polsby (Eds.), *Media and momentum: The New Hampshire primary and nomination politics* (pp. 9–41). Chatham, NJ: Chatham House.

Mayer, W.G. (2010). How parties nominate presidents. In L.S. Maisel & J.M Berry (Eds.), *The Oxford handbook of American political parties and interest groups* (pp. 185–203). New York: Oxford University Press.

Mazzoleni, G. (2006). TV political advertising in Italy: When politicians are afraid. In L.L. Kaid & C. Holtz-Bacha (Eds.), *The Sage handbook of political advertising* (pp. 241–257). Thousand Oaks, CA: Sage.

Mazzoleni, G., & Schulz, W. (1999). "Mediatization"of politics: A challenge for democracy? *Political Communication, 16,* 247–262.

McChesney, R.W. (2004). *The problem of the media: U.S. communication politics in the twenty-first century.* New York: Monthly Review Press.

McCombs, M. (2004). *Setting the agenda: The mass media and public opinion.* Cambridge: Polity Press.

McCombs, M., & Reynolds, A. (2009). How the news shapes our civic agenda. In J. Bryant &

M.B. Oliver (Eds.), *Media effects: Advances in theory and research* (3rd ed., pp. 1–16). New York: Routledge.

McCombs, M.E., & Shaw, D.L. (1972). The agenda-setting function of mass media. *Public Opinion Quarterly, 36*, 176–187.

McConnell, M.W. (2012, June 24). You can't say that. *The New York Times Book Review*, 14.

McCroskey, J.C., & Teven, J.J. (1999). Goodwill: A reexamination of the construct and its measurement. *Communication Monographs, 66*, 90–103.

McDevitt, M. (2006). The partisan child: Developmental provocation as a model of political socialization. *International Journal of Public Opinion Research, 18*, 67–88.

McDevitt, M., & Chaffee, S. (2002). From top-down to trickle-up influence: Revisiting assumptions about the family in political socialization. *Political Communication, 19*, 281–301.

McDevitt, M., & Ostrowski, A. (2009). The adolescent unbound: Unintentional influence of curricula and ideological conflict seeking. *Political Communication, 26*, 11–29.

McDonald, D.G. (2004). Twentieth-century media effects research. In J.D.H. Downing, D. McQuail, P. Schlesinger, & E. Wartella (Eds.), *The Sage handbook of media studies* (pp. 183–200). Thousand Oaks, CA: Sage.

McGerr, M. (1986). *The decline of popular politics: The American North, 1865–1928*. New York: Oxford University Press.

McGinniss, J. (1969). *The selling of the president*. New York: Penguin.

McGraw, K.M., & Ling, C. (2003). Media priming of presidential and group evaluations. *Political Communication, 20*, 23–40.

McIntire, M., & Confessore, N. (2012, July 8). Groups shield political gifts of businesses. *The New York Times*, 1, 15.

McIntire, M., & Luo, M. (2012, February 26). Fine line between "Super PACs" and campaigns. *The New York Times*, 1, 14.

McKinney, M.S. (2005). Engaging citizens through presidential debates: Does the format matter? In M.S. McKinney, L.L. Kaid, D.G. Bystrom, & D.B. Carlin (Eds.), *Communicating politics: Engaging the public in democratic life* (pp. 209–221). New York: Peter Lang.

McKinney, M.S., & Banwart, M.C. (2011). The election of a lifetime. In M.S. McKinney & M.C. Banwart (Eds.), *Communication in the 2008 U.S. election: Digital natives elect a president* (pp. 1–9). New York: Peter Lang.

McKinney, M.S., & Carlin, D.B. (2004). Political campaign debates. In L.L. Kaid (Ed.), *Handbook of political communication research* (pp. 203–234). Mahwah, NJ: Lawrence Erlbaum Associates.

McKinney, M.S., Rill, L.A., & Watson, R.G. (2011). Who framed Sarah Palin? Viewer reactions to the 2008 vice presidential debate. *American Behavioral Scientist, 55*, 212–231.

McLeod, J.M., Becker, L.B., & Byrnes, J.E. (1974). Another look at the agenda-setting function of the press. *Communication Research, 1*, 131–165.

McLeod, J.M., & Shah, D.V. (2009). Communication and political socialization: Challenges and opportunities for research. *Political Communication, 26*, 1–10.

McNair, B. (1995). *An introduction to political communication*. London: Routledge.

Mendelberg, T. (2001). *The race card: Campaign strategy, implicit messages, and the norm of equality*. Princeton, NJ: Princeton University Press.

Metzger, M.J. (2009). The study of media effects in the era of Internet communication. In R.L. Nabi & M.B. Oliver (Eds.), *The Sage handbook of media processes and effects* (pp. 561–576). Thousand Oaks, CA: Sage.

Meyrowitz, J. (1986). *No sense of place: The impact of electronic media on social behavior.* New York: Oxford University Press.

Meyrowitz, J. (2009). Medium theory: An alternative to the dominant paradigm of media effects. In R.L. Nabi & M.B. Oliver (Eds.), *The Sage handbook of media processes and effects* (pp. 517–530). Thousand Oaks, CA: Sage.

Mill, J.S. (1859/2009). *On liberty and other essays.* New York: Kaplan Publishing.

Miller, A.H., & MacKuen, M. (1979). Informing the electorate: A national study. In S. Kraus (Ed.), *The great debates: Carter vs. Ford, 1976* (pp. 269–297). Bloomington, IN: Indiana University Press.

Miller, D. (Ed.) (1987). *The Blackwell encyclopedia of political thought* (p. 390). New York: Blackwell.

Miller, J.M., & Krosnick, J.A. (2000). News media impact on the ingredients of presidential evaluations: Politically knowledgeable citizens are guided by a trusted source. *American Journal of Political Science, 44*, 295–309.

Miller, M. (2005, June 4). Is persuasion dead? *The New York Times.* Online: http://www.nytimes.com/2005/06/04/opinion/04miller_oped.html. (Accessed: September 16, 2012.)

Miller, M.M., & Denham, B. (1994). Horserace, issue coverage in prestige newspapers during 1988, 1992 elections. *Newspaper Research Journal, 15*, 20–28.

Mindich, D.T.Z. (2005). *Tuned out: Why Americans under 40 don't follow the news.* New York: Oxford University Press.

Morin, R. (1996, February 5–11). Tuned out, turned off. *The Washington Post National Weekly Edition,* 6–8.

Morozov, E. (2011). *The Net delusion: The dark side of Internet freedom.* New York: PublicAffairs.

Morreale, J. (2009). Jon Stewart and *The Daily Show*: I thought you were going to be funny! In J. Gray, J.P. Jones, & E. Thompson (Eds.), *Satire TV: Politics and comedy in the post-network era* (pp. 104–123). New York: New York University Press.

Morrison, D.E. (2006). The influences influencing *Personal Influence:* Scholarship and entrepreneurship. *Annals of the American Association of Political and Social Science, 608*, 51–75.

Moy, P., Xenos, M.A., & Hess, V.K. (2005). Priming effects of late-night comedy. *International Journal of Public Opinion Research, 18*, 198–210.

Murray, C. (2012). *Coming apart: The state of White America 1960–2010.* New York: Crown Forum.

Mutz, D.C. (2006). *Hearing the other side: Deliberative versus participatory democracy.* Cambridge: Cambridge University Press.

Nadeau, R., Nevitte, N., Gidengil, E., & Blais, A. (2008). Elections campaigns as information campaigns: Who learns what and does it matter? *Political Communication, 25*, 229–248.

Nagourney, A., Parker, A., Rutenberg, J., & Zeleny, J. (2012, November 8). How a race in the balance went to Obama. *The New York Times,* P1, P14.

Napoli, P.M. (2003). *Audience economics: Media institutions and the audience marketplace.* New York: Columbia University Press.

Nelson, T.E., & Oxley, Z.M. (1999). Issue framing effects on belief importance and opinion. *Journal of Politics, 61*, 1040–1067.

Neuman, W.R. (1986). *The paradox of mass politics: Knowledge and opinion in the American electorate*. Cambridge: Harvard University Press.

Neuman, W.R., Just, M.R., & Crigler, A.N. (1992). *Common knowledge: News and the construction of political meaning*. Chicago: University of Chicago Press.

Newhagen, J.E., & Reeves, B. (1991). Emotion and memory responses for negative political advertising: A study of television commercials used in the 1988 presidential election. In F. Biocca (Ed.), *Television and political advertising, Volume 1: Psychological processes* (pp. 197–220). Hillsdale, NJ: Lawrence Erlbaum Associates.

Newman, B.I. (1994). *The marketing of the president: Political marketing as campaign strategy*. Thousand Oaks, CA: Sage.

Newman, B.I. (1999). *The mass marketing of politics: Democracy in an age of manufactured images*. Thousand Oaks, CA: Sage.

Niemi, R.G., & Junn, J. (1998). *Civic education: What makes students learn*. New Haven: Yale University Press.

Nimmo, D. (1975). Images and voters' decision-making processes. In M.J. Schlinger (Ed.), *Advances in Consumer Research, 2*, 771–781.

Nisbet, M.C. (2010). Knowledge into action: Framing the debates over climate change and poverty. In P. D'Angelo & J.A. Kuypers (Eds.), *Doing news framing analysis: Empirical and theoretical perspectives* (pp. 43–83). New York: Routledge.

Norris, P. (Ed.) (1997). *Women, media, and politics*. New York: Oxford University Press.

Offe, C., & Preuss, U.K. (1991). Democratic institutions and moral resources. In D. Held (Ed.), *Political theory today* (pp. 143–171). Stanford, CA: Stanford University Press.

O'Keefe, D.J. (1999). How to handle opposing arguments in persuasive messages: A meta-analytic review of the effects of one-sided and two-sided messages. In M.E. Roloff (Ed.), *Communication yearbook 22*, 209–249.

O'Keefe, D.J. (2012). From psychological theory to message design: Lessons from the story of gain-framed and loss-framed persuasive messages. In H. Cho (Ed.), *Health communication message design: Theory and practice* (pp. 3–20). Thousand Oaks, CA: Sage.

Orwell, G. (1946). *Animal farm*. New York: Harcourt, Brace.

Owen, D. (2006). The Internet and youth civic engagement in the United States. In S. Oates, D. Owen, R.K. Gibson (Eds.), *The Internet and politics: Citizens, voters and activists* (pp. 20–38). London: Routledge.

Paletz, D.L., & Entman, R.M. (1981). *Media. Power. Politics*. New York: Free Press.

Pan, Z., & Kosicki, G.M. (1997). Priming and media impact on the evaluations of the president's performance. *Communication Research, 24*, 3–30.

Parenti, M. (2011). *Democracy for the few (9th ed.)*. Boston: Wadsworth.

Pariser, E. (2011). *The filter bubble: What the Internet is hiding from you*. New York: Penguin Press.

Parker, A. (2012, November 2). Romney advance team works every angle in pursuit of visual perfection. *The New York Times*, A14.

Partnoy, F. (2012, July 8). Beyond the blink. *The New York Times* (Sunday Review), 5.

Pasek, J., Kenski, K., Romer, D., & Jamieson, K.H. (2006). America's youth and community engagement: How use of mass media is related to civic activity and political awareness in 14- to 22-year-olds. *Communication Research, 33*, 115–135.

Patterson, T.E. (1980). *The mass media election: How Americans choose their president.* New York: Praeger.

Patterson, T.E. (1993). *Out of order.* New York: Knopf.

Patterson, T.E., & McClure, R.D. (1976). *The unseeing eye: The myth of television power in national elections.* New York: G.P. Putman.

Pavlik, J. (2000). The impact of technology on journalism. *Journalism Studies, 1*, 229–237.

Perlmutter, D.D. (2008). *Blogwars.* New York: Oxford University Press.

Perloff, R.M. (1998). *Political communication: Politics, press, and public in America.* Mahwah, NJ: Lawrence Erlbaum Associates.

Perloff, R.M. (1999). Elite, popular, and merchandised politics: Historical origins of presidential campaign marketing. In B.I. Newman (Ed.), *Handbook of political marketing* (pp. 19–40). Thousand Oaks, CA: Sage.

Perloff, R.M. (2000). The press and lynchings of African Americans. *Journal of Black Studies, 30*, 315–330.

Perloff, R.M. (2009). Mass media, social perception, and the third-person effect. In J. Bryant & M.B. Oliver (Eds.), *Media effects: Advances in theory and research* (3rd ed., pp. 252–268). New York: Taylor & Francis.

Perloff, R.M. (2012, November 13). *The sound of political silence descends on Ohio.* Commentary, WKSU Radio.

Pessen, E. (1985). *Jacksonian America: Society, personality, and politics (Rev. ed.).* Urbana, IL: University of Illinois Press.

Peter, J. (2003). Country characteristics as contingent conditions of agenda setting: The moderating influence of polarized elite opinion. *Communication Research, 30*, 683–712.

Peters, J.W. (2011, November 27). TV attack ads aim at Obama early and often. *The New York Times*, 1, 4.

Peters, J.W. (2012a, August 20). A careful effort seeks to reveal a real Romney. *The New York Times*, A1, A12.

Peters, J.W. (2012b, October 16). 73,000 political ads test even a city of excess. *The New York Times*, A1, A16.

Peters, J.W. (2012c, October 10). Networks like split-screens in debates, even if the candidates don't. *The New York Times*, A11.

Peters, J.W. (2012d, November 6). Dueling bitterness on cable news. *The New York Times*, A10, A11.

Petty, R.E., & Cacioppo, J.T. (1986). The Elaboration Likelihood Model of persuasion. In L. Berkowitz (Ed.), *Advances in experimental social psychology* (Vol. 19, pp. 123–205). New York: Academic Press.

Pew Research Center for the People and the Press (2010). Cell phones and election polls: An update. Online: http://pewresearch.org/pubs/1761/cell-phones-and-election-polls-201... (Accessed: June 25, 2012.)

Pew Research Center for the People and the Press (2011a). *Internet gains on television as public's main news source.* Online: http://www.people-press. org/2011/01/04/internet-gains-on-television. (Accessed: October 21, 2011.)

Pew Research Center for the People and the Press (2011b). *Press widely criticized, but trusted more than other information sources: Views of the news media, 1985–2011*. Online: http://www.people-press.org/2011/09/22/presswidely-criticized-but... (Accessed: April 10, 2012.)

Pew Research Center for the People and the Press (2012a). *What voters know about Campaign 2012*. Online: http://www.people-press.org/2012/08/10/what-voters-know-about-ca... (Accessed: January 13, 2013.)

Pew Research Center for the People and the Press (2012b). *What the public knows about the political parties*. Online: http://www.people-press.org/2012/04/11/what-the-public-knows-about– (Accessed: January 13, 2013.)

Pew Research Center for the People and the Press (2012c). *Trends in news consumption: 1991–2012. In changing news landscape, even television is vulnerable*. Online: http://www.people-press.org/files/legacy-pdf/2012 News Consumpti– (Accessed: March 16, 2013.)

Pew Research Center's Project for Excellence in Journalism (2011). *The tablet revolution: How people use tablets and what it means for the future of news*. Online: http://www.journalism. org/analysis_report/tablet. (Accessed: November 12, 2011.)

Pilkington, E., & Michel, A. (2012, June 14). Mitt Romney's campaign closing gap on Obama in digital election race. *The Guardian*. Online: http://www.guardian. co.uk/world/2012/jun/ 14/romney-campaign-digital-data-obama. (Accessed: June 26, 2012.)

Pingree, R.J., Scholl, R.M., & Quenette, A.M. (2012). Effects of postdebate coverage on spontaneous policy reasoning. *Journal of Communication, 62*, 643–658.

Polsby, N.W., Wildavsky, A. Schier, S.E., & Hopkins, D.A. (2012). *Presidential Elections: Strategies and structures of American politics (13th ed.)*. Lanham, MD: Rowman & Littlefield.

Popkin, S.L. (1993). Information shortcuts and the reasoning voter. In B. Grofman (Ed.), *Information, participation, and choice: An economic theory of democracy in perspective* (pp. 17–36). Ann Arbor, MI: University of Michigan Press.

Popkin, S.L. (2012). *The candidate: What it takes to win—and hold—the White House*. New York: Oxford University Press.

Price, V., & Tewksbury, D. (1997). News values and public opinion: A theoretical account of media priming and framing. In G.A. Barnett & F.J. Boster (Eds.), *Progress in communication sciences: Advances in persuasion* (Vol. 13, pp. 173–212). Greenwich, CT: Ablex.

Prior, M. (2002). Political knowledge after September 11. *PS: Political Science and Politics, 35*, 523–529.

Prior, M. (2005). News vs. entertainment: How increasing media choice widens gaps in political knowledge and turnout. *American Journal of Political Science, 49*, 577–592.

Prior, M. (2007). *Post-broadcast democracy: How media choice increases inequality in political involvement and polarizes elections*. New York: Cambridge University Press.

Project for Excellence in Journalism (2012a, April 9). *Campaign 2012 in the media: Romney's coverage is mixed, his rivals do worse*. Online: http://www.journalism.org/commentary backgrounder/pejs_election_r– (Accessed: April 28, 2012.)

Project for Excellence in Journalism (2012b, April 23). *How the media covered the 2012 primary campaign.* Online: http://www.journalism.org/analysis_report/frames_campaign_coverage (Accessed: August 12, 2012.)

Protess, D.L., Cook, F.L., Doppelt, J.C., Ettema, J.S., Gordon, M.T., Leff, D.R., & Miller, P. (1991). *The journalism of outrage: Investigative reporting and agenda-building in America.* New York: Guilford Press.

Rainie, L., Smith, A., Schlozman, K.L., Brady, H., & Verba, S. (2012). *Social media and political engagement.* Pew Internet & American Life Project. Online: http://pewinternet.org/Reports/2012/Political-Engagement.aspx. (Accessed: September 22, 2013)

Reese, S.D. (2007). The framing project: A bridging model for media research revisited. *Journal of Communication, 57*, 148–154.

Reese, S.D. (2010). Finding frames in a web of culture: The case of the war on terror. In P. D'Angelo & J.A. Kuypers (Eds.), *Doing news framing analysis: Empirical and theoretical perspectives* (pp. 17–42). New York: Routledge.

Reese, S.D., & Danielian, L.H. (1989). Intermedia influence and the drug issue: Converging on cocaine. In P.J. Shoemaker (Ed.), *Communication campaigns about drugs: Government, media, and the public* (pp. 29–45). Hillsdale, NJ: Erlbaum Associates.

Reynolds, R.A., & Reynolds, J.L. (2002). Evidence. In J.E. Dillard & M. Pfau (Eds.), *The persuasion handbook: Developments in theory and practi*ce (pp. 427–444). Thousand Oaks, CA: Sage.

Rich, F. (2006). *The greatest story ever sold: The decline and fall of truth from 9/11 to Katrina.* New York: Penguin Press.

Rivers, W. (1962, Spring). The correspondents after 25 years. *Columbia Journalism Review, 1*, 5.

Ritter, K., & Henry, D. (1994). The 1980 Reagan–Carter presidential debate. In R.V. Friedenberg (ed.), *Rhetorical studies of national political debates, 1960–1992* (2nd ed., pp. 69–93). Westport, CT: Praeger.

Robinson, J.P., & Levy, M.R. (1986). *The main source: Learning from television news.* Beverly Hills, CA: Sage.

Robinson, M.J., & Sheehan, M.A. (1983). *Over the wire and on TV: CBS and UPI in Campaign '80.* New York: Russell Sage Foundation.

Rogers, E.M., & Dearing, J.W. (1988). Agenda-setting research: Where has it been? Where is it going? In J. Anderson (Ed.), *Communication yearbook 11* (pp. 555–594). Newbury Park, CA: Sage.

Rose, J. (2010). The branding of states: The uneasy marriage of marketing to politics. *Journal of Political Marketing, 9*, 254–275.

Rosen, J., & Merritt, D., Jr. (1994). *Public journalism: Theory and practice.* Dayton, OH: Kettering Foundation.

Rosenberg, S.W., with McAfferty, P. (1987). The image and the vote: Manipulating voters' preferences. *Public Opinion Quarterly, 57*, 31–47.

Roskos-Ewoldsen, D.R., Roskos-Ewoldsen, B., & Dillman Carpentier, F. (2009). Media priming: An updated synthesis. In J. Bryant & M.B. Oliver (Eds.), *Media effects: Advances in theory and research* (3rd ed., pp. 74–93). New York: Routledge.

Rubin, D.M., & Sachs, D.P. (1973). *Mass media and the environment: Water resources, land use and atomic energy in California.* New York: Praeger.

Runkel, D.R. (Ed.) (1989). *Campaign for president: The managers look at '88*. Dover, MA: Auburn House.

Rutenberg, J. (2012, October 26). To Obama workers, winning takes grunt work and math. *The New York Times*, A1, A19.

Rutenberg, J. (2013, February 24). A conservative provocateur, using a blowtorch as his pen. *The New York Times*, 1, 4.

Rutenberg, J., & Peters, J.W. (2012, October 30). G.O.P. turns fire on Obama pillar, the auto bailout. *The New York Times*, A1, A12.

Rutenberg, J., & Zeleny, J. (2012a, March 8). Obama mines for voters with high-tech tools. *The New York Times*, A1, A17.

Rutenberg, J., & Zeleny, J. (2012b, July 1). Bain attacks make inroads for president. *The New York Times*, 1, 17.

Sabato, L.J. (1981). *The rise of political consultants*. New York: Basic Books.

Sabato, L.J. (1991). *Feeding frenzy: How attack journalism has transformed American politics*. New York: Free Press.

Sabato, L.J., & Simpson, G.R. (1996). *Dirty little secrets: The persistence of corruption in American politics*. New York: Times Books.

Safire, W. (2008, August 31). The audacity of hype. *The New York Times*. Online: http://www.nytimes.com/2008/08/31/opinion/31safire.html. (Accessed: August 29, 2012.)

Schaffner, B.F., & Sellers, P.J. (2010). Introduction. In B.F. Schaffner & P.J. Sellers (Eds.), *Winning with words: The origins and impact of political framing* (pp. 1–7). New York: Routledge.

Schattschneider, E.E. (1960). *The semisovereign people: A realist's view of democracy in America*. New York: Holt, Rinehart & Winston.

Scheufele, B.T., & Scheufele, D.A. (2010). Of spreading activation, applicability, and schemas: Conceptual distinctions and their operational implications for measuring frames and framing effects. In P. D'Angelo & J.A. Kuypers (Eds.), *Doing news framing analysis: Empirical and theoretical perspectives* (pp. 110–134). New York: Routledge.

Scheufele, D.A. (1999). Framing as a theory of media effects. *Journal of Communication, 49*, 103–122.

Scheufele, D.A. (2000). Agenda-setting, priming, and framing revisited: Another look at cognitive effects of political communication. *Mass Communication & Society, 3*, 297–316.

Scheufele, D.A., & Iyengar, S. (in press). The state of framing research: A call for new directions. In K. Kenski & K.H. Jamieson (Eds.), *The Oxford handbook of political communication theories*. New York: Oxford University Press.

Scheufele, D.A., & Tewskbury, D. (2007). Framing, agenda-setting, and priming: The evolution of three media effects models. *Journal of Communication, 57*, 9–20.

Schlozman, K.L., Verba, S., & Brady, H.E. (2012, November 11). Sunday dialogue: Giving all citizens a voice. *The New York Times* (Sunday Review), 2.

Schmidt, M.S. (2012, April 1). For Occupy Movement, a challenge to recapture momentum. *The New York Times*, 19.

Schneider, S.M., & Foot, K.A. (2006). Web campaigning by U.S. presidential primary candidates in 2000 and 2004. In A.P. Williams & J.C. Tedesco (Eds.), *The Internet election: Perspectives on the Web in Campaign 2004* (pp. 21–36). Lanham, MD: Rowman & Littlefield.

Schudson, M. (1986). *Advertising, the uneasy persuasion*. New York: Basic Books.

Schudson, M. (1995). *The power of news*. Cambridge, MA: Harvard University Press.

Schudson, M. (1998). *The good citizen: A history of American civic life*. New York: Martin Kessler Books.

Schudson, M., & Tifft, S.E. (2005). American journalism in historical perspective. In G. Overholser & K.H. Jamieson (Eds.), *The press* (pp. 17–47). New York: Oxford University Press.

Schuman, H., & Corning, A. (2012). Generational memory and the critical period: Evidence for national and world events. *Public Opinion Quarterly, 76*, 1–31.

Schumpeter, J. (1976). *Capitalism, socialism and democracy*. London: Allen and Unwin.

Sears, D.O. (1990). Whither political socialization research? The question of persistence. In O. Ichilov (Ed.), *Political socialization, citizenship education, and democracy* (pp. 69–97). New York: Teachers College Press.

Sears, D.O., & Chaffee, S.H. (1979). Uses and effects of the 1976 debates: An overview of empirical studies. In S. Kraus (Ed.), *The great debates: Carter vs. Ford, 1976* (pp. 223–261). Bloomington, IN: Indiana University Press.

Sears, D.O., & Funk, C.L. (1999). Evidence of the long-term persistence of adults' political predispositions. *Journal of Politics, 61*, 1–28.

Seelye, K.Q. (2012, October 25). Crucial subset: Female voters still deciding. *The New York Times*, A1, A15.

Seiter, J.S., Weger, Jr., H., Kinzer, H.J., & Jensen, A.S. (2009). Impression management in televised debates: The effect of background nonverbal behavior on audience perceptions of debaters' likeability. *Communication Research Reports, 26*, 1–11.

Semetko, H.A., & Mandelli, A. (1997). Setting the agenda for cross-national research: Bringing values into the concept. In M. McCombs, D.L. Shaw & D. Weaver (Eds.), *Communication and democracy: Exploring the intellectual frontiers in agenda-setting theory* (pp. 195–207). Mahwah, NJ: Erlbaum.

Sen, A. (1981). *Poverty and famines: An essay on entitlement and deprivation*. Oxford: Oxford University Press.

Settle, J.E., Dawes, C.T., & Fowler, J.H. (2009). The heritability of partisan attachment. *Political Research Quarterly, 62*, 601–613.

Shaefer, T., Weimann, G., & Tsfati, Y. (2008). Campaigns in the holy land: The content and effects of election news coverage in Israel. In J. Strömbäck & L.L. Kaid (Eds.), *The handbook of election news coverage around the world* (pp. 209–225). New York: Routledge.

Shafer, B.E. (2010). The pure partisan institution: National party conventions as research sites. In L.S. Maisel & J.M. Berry (Eds.), *The Oxford handbook of American political parties and interest groups* (pp. 264–284). New York: Oxford University Press.

Shah, D.V., Cho, J., Eveland, W.P., Jr., & Kwak, N. (2005). Information and expression in a digital age: Modeling Internet effects on civic participation. *Communication Research, 32*, 531–565.

Shah, D.V., McLeod, D.M., Gotlieb, M.R., & Lee, N.-J. (2009). Framing and agenda-setting. In R.L. Nabi & M.B. Oliver (Eds.), *The Sage handbook of media processes and effects* (pp. 83–98). Thousand Oaks, CA: Sage.

Shah, D.V., McLeod, J.M., & Lee, N.-J. (2009). Communication competence as a foundation for civic competence: Processes of socialization into citizenship. *Political Communication, 26*, 102–117.

Shapiro, M.A., & Rieger, R.H. (1992). Comparing positive and negative political advertising on radio. *Journalism Quarterly, 69*, 135–145.

Sheafer, T. (2007). How to evaluate it: The role of story-evaluative tone in agenda-setting and priming. *Journal of Communication, 57*, 21–39.

Shear, M.D. (2012, January 30). If Twitter is any clue, Axelrod thinks a lot about Romney. *The New York Times*. Online: http://the caucus.blogs.nytimes.com/2012/01/30/if-twitter-is-any-clue-a– (Accessed: July 6, 2012.)

Shear, M.D., & Oppel, R.A., Jr. (2011, November 9). For Perry, a cringe-worthy gaffe. *The New York Times*. Online: http://thecaucus.blogs.newyorktimes.com/2011/11/09/for-perry-a-cringe-worthy-gaffe/? (Accessed: March 7, 2013.)

Shear, M.D., & Zeleny, J. (2011, October 6). After summer of speculation, Palin says she won't join the 2012 race. *The New York Times*, A18.

Shehata, A., & Strömbäck, J. (2013). Not (yet) a new era of minimal effects: A study of agenda setting at the aggregate and individual levels. *International Journal of Press/Politics, 18*, 234–255.

Shen, F., & Edwards, H.H. (2005). Economic individualism, humanitarianism, and welfare reform: A value-based account of framing effects. *Journal of Communication, 55*, 795–809.

Shenkman, R. (2008). *Just how stupid are we? Facing the truth about the American voter*. New York: Basic Books.

Sherif, M., & Sherif, C.W. (1967). Attitude as the individual's own categories: The social judgment–involvement approach to attitude and attitude change. In C.W. Sherif & M. Sherif (Eds.), *Attitude, ego-involvement, and change* (pp. 105–139). New York: Wiley.

Shoemaker, P.J. (1991). *Gatekeeping*. Thousand Oaks, CA: Sage.

Shoemaker, P.J., & Cohen, A.A. (Eds.) (2006). *News around the world: Content, practitioners, and the public*. New York: Routledge.

Shoemaker, P.J., Eichholz, M., Kim, E., & Wrigley, B. (2001). Individual and routine forces in gatekeeping. *Journalism & Mass Communication Quarterly, 78*, 233–246.

Shoemaker, P.J., & Reese, S.D. (1991). *Mediating the message: Theories of influences on mass media content*. White Plains, NY: Longman.

Shoemaker, P.J., & Reese, S.D. (1996). *Mediating the message: Theories of influences on mass media content (2nd ed.)*. White Plains, NY: Longman.

Shoemaker, P.J., & Vos, T.P. (2009). *Gatekeeping theory*. New York: Routledge.

Shoemaker, P.J., Wanta, W., & Leggett, D. (1989). Drug coverage and public opinion, 1972–1986. In P.J. Shoemaker (Ed.), *Communication campaigns about drugs: Government, media, and the public* (pp. 67–80). Hillsdale, NJ: Erlbaum Associates.

Siebert, F.S., Peterson, T., & Schramm, W.L. (1973). *Four theories of the press: The authoritarian, libertarian, social responsibility, and Soviet communist concepts of what the press should be and do*. Freeport, NY: Books for Libraries Press.

Sigal, L. (1986). Who: Sources make the news. In R.K. Manoff & M. Schudson (Eds.), *Reading the news* (pp. 9–37). New York: Pantheon.

Sigelman, L., & Bullock, D. (1991). Candidates, issues, horse races, and hoopla: Presidential campaign coverage, 1888–1988. *American Politics Quarterly, 19*, 5–32.

Simon, R. (1990). *Road show*. New York: Farrar, Straus, Giroux.

Simonson, P. (2006). Introduction. *Annals of the American Association of Political and Social Science, 608*, 6–24.

Singer, N. (2011, September 11). On campus, it's one big commercial. *The New York Times* (Sunday Business), 1, 4.

Sloan, W.D., & Williams, J.H. (1994). *The early American press, 1690–1783*. Westport, CT: Greenwood Press.

Smith, B.A. (1996, October 8). Time to go negative. *The Wall Street Journal*, A22.

Smith, C.A. (1990). *Political communication*. San Diego, CA: Harcourt Brace Jovanovich.

Sniderman, P.M., Brody, R.A., & Tetlock, P.E. (1991). *Reasoning and choice: Explorations in political psychology*. New York: Cambridge University Press.

Sobieraj, S., & Berry, J.M. (2011). From incivility to outrage: Political discourse in blogs, talk radio, and cable news. *Political Communication, 28*, 19–41.

Society of Professional Journalists (1996). *SPJ Code of Ethics*. Online: http://www.spj.org/ethicscode.asp. (Accessed: November 21, 2012.)

Spiker, J.A. (2011). Motherhood, God and country: Sarah Palin's 68 days in 2008. In M.S. McKinney & M.C. Banwart (Eds.), *Communication in the 2008 U.S. election: Digital natives elect a president* (pp. 241–254). New York: Peter Lang.

Steel, R. (1999). *Walter Lippmann and the American century*. New Brunswick, NJ: Transaction Publishers.

Steinhauer, J. (2013a, February 19). Pro-gun voices in Congress are open to bullet capacity limits. *The New York Times*, A1, A3.

Steinhauer, J., & Savage, C. (2012, December 18). Pro-gun Democrats signaling openness to limits; Town starts the mournful task of saying goodbye. *The New York Times*, A1, A26.

Stelter, B. (2011, December 1). Camps are cleared, but "99 percent" still occupies the lexicon. *The New York Times*, A1, A22.

Stelter, B. (2012). You can change the channel, but local news is the same. *The New York Times*, A1, A3.

Stephens, M. (2007). *A history of news*. New York: Oxford University Press.

Stiglitz, J. (2013). Inequality is holding back the recovery. *The New York Times* (Sunday Review), 1, 8–9.

Stimson, J.A. (2004). *Tides of consent: How public opinion shapes American politics*. Cambridge: Cambridge University Press.

Stolberg, S.G. (2013, January 22). A day of celebration for a diverse crowd savoring a moment in history. *The New York Times*, A11, A15.

Stone, W.J. (2010). Activists, influence, and representation in American elections. In L.S. Maisel & J.M. Berry (Eds.), *The Oxford handbook of American political parties and interest groups* (pp. 285–302). New York: Oxford University Press.

Streitmatter, R. (2008). *Mightier than the sword: How the news media have shaped American history (2nd ed.)*. Boulder, CO: Westview.

Strömbäck, J., & Kaid, L.L. (2008). A framework for comparing election news coverage around the world. In J. Strömbäck & L.L. Kaid (Eds.), *The handbook of election news coverage around the world* (pp. 1–18). New York: Routledge.

Stromer-Galley, J., & Baker, A.B. (2006). Joy and sorrow of interactivity on the campaign trail: Blogs in the primary campaign of Howard Dean. In A.P. Williams & J.C. Tedesco (Eds.), *The Internet election: Perspectives on the Web in Campaign 2004* (pp. 111–131). Lanham, MD: Rowman & Littlefield.

Strother, R.D. (2003). *Falling up: How a redneck helped invent political consulting.* Baton Rouge, LA: Louisiana State University Press.

Stroud, N.J. (2010). Polarization and partisan selective exposure. *Journal of Communication, 60,* 556–576.

Stroud, N.J. (2011). *Niche news: The politics of news choice.* New York: Oxford University Press.

Stroud, N.J. (2013). The American media system today: Is the public fragmenting? In T.N. Ridout (Ed.), *New directions in media and politics* (pp. 6–23). New York: Routledge.

Sundar, S.S., & Bellur, S. (2011). Concept explication in the Internet age: The case of political interactivity. In E.P. Bucy & R.L. Holbert (Eds.), *The sourcebook for political communication research: Methods, measures, and analytical techniques* (pp. 485–504). New York: Routledge.

Sunstein, C. (2001). *Republic.com.* Princeton, NJ: Princeton University Press.

Swanson, D.L., & Mancini, P. (1996). Patterns of modern electoral campaigning and their consequences. In D.L. Swanson & P. Mancini (Eds.), *Politics, media, and modern democracy: An international study of innovations in electoral campaigning and their consequences* (pp. 247–276). Westport, CT: Praeger.

Takeshita, T. (2006). Current critical problems in agenda-setting research. *International Journal of Public Opinion Research, 18,* 275–296.

Tavernise, S. (2012, January 12). Survey finds rising strain between rich and the poor. *The New York Times,* A11.

Tavernise, S., & Gebeloff, R. (2013, March 10). Share of homes with guns shows 4-decade decline. *The New York Times,* 1, 22.

Tedesco, J.C. (2011). The complex Web: Young adults' opinions about online campaign messages. In M.S. McKinney & M.C. Banwart (Eds.), *Communication in the 2008 U.S. election: Digital natives elect a president* (pp. 13–31). New York: Peter Lang.

Tewksbury, D., & Scheufele, D.A. (2009). News framing theory and research. In J. Bryant & M.B. Oliver (Eds.), *Media effects: Advances in theory and research* (3rd ed., pp. 17–33). New York: Routledge.

The Economist (2011, July 9). The news industry, Special report in *The Economist,* 3–16.

Thurber, J.A. (2000). Introduction to the study of campaign consultants. In J.A. Thurber & C.J. Nelson (Eds.), *Campaign warriors: The role of political consultants in elections* (pp. 1–9). Washington, D.C.: Brookings Institution Press.

Tichenor, P.J., Donohue, G.A., & Olien, C.N. (1970). Mass media flow and differential growth in knowledge. *Public Opinion Quarterly, 34,* 159–170.

Tichenor, P.J., Donohue, G.A., & Olien, C.N. (1980). *Community conflict and the press.* Thousand Oaks, CA: Sage.

Toobin, J. (2012, May 21). Money unlimited. *The New Yorker,* 36–47.

Toner, R., & Nagourney, A. (2008, September 18). McCain seen as less likely to bring change, poll finds. *The New York Times*, A1, A22.

Towner, T.L., & Dulio, D.A. (2011). An experiment of campaign effects during the YouTube election. *New Media & Society, 13*, 626–644.

Tracy, K. (2010). *Challenges of ordinary democracy: A case study in deliberation and dissent.* University Park, PA: Pennsylvania State University Press.

Traugott, M.W. (2005). The accuracy of the national pre-election polls in the 2004 presidential election. *Public Opinion Quarterly, 65*, 642–654.

Traugott, M.W., & Lavrakas, P.J. (2008). *The voter's guide to election polls (4th ed.).* Lanham, MD: Rowman & Littlefield.

Trent, J.S., Friedenberg, R.V., & Denton, R.E., Jr. (2011). *Political campaign communication: Principles and practices (7th ed.).* Lanham, MD: Rowman & Littlefield.

Trent, J.S., Short-Thompson, C., Mongeau, P.A., Metzler, M.S., Erickson, A.K., & Trent, J.D. (2010). Cracked and shattered ceilings: Gender, race, religion, age, and the ideal candidate. *American Behavioral Scientist, 54*, 163–183.

Troy, G. (1996). *See how they ran: The changing role of the presidential candidate (Rev. ed.).* Cambridge, MA: Harvard University Press.

Tuchman, B. (1962). *The guns of August.* New York: Macmillan.

Tufekci, Z. (2012, November 17). Beware the smart campaign. *The New York Times*, A23.

Tuman, J.S. (2008). *Political communication in American campaigns.* Thousand Oaks, CA: Sage.

Turow, J. (1997). *Breaking up America: Advertisers and the new media world.* Chicago: University of Chicago Press.

Valentino, R.A. (1999). Crime news and the priming of racial attitudes during evaluations of the president. *Public Opinion Quarterly, 63*, 293–300.

Vavreck, L. (2009). *The message matters: The economy and presidential campaigns.* Princeton, NJ: Princeton University Press.

Vega, T. (2012, February 21). Online data helping campaigns customize ads. *The New York Times*, A1, A13.

Wanta, W., & Ghanem, S. (2007). Effects of agenda-setting. In R.W. Preiss, B.M. Gayle, N. Burrell, M. Allen, & J. Bryant (Eds.), *Mass media effects research: Advances through meta-analysis* (pp. 37–51). Mahwah, NJ: Erlbaum.

Wartella, E. (1996). The history reconsidered. In E.E. Dennis & E. Wartella (Eds.), *American communication research – The remembered history* (pp. 169–180). Mahwah, NJ: Lawrence Erlbaum Associates.

Wartella, E., & Reeves, B. (1985). Historical trends in research on children and the media: 1900–1960. *Journal of Communication, 35*, 118–135.

Wartella, E.A., & Stout, P.A. (2002). The evolution of mass media and health persuasion models. In W.D. Crano & M. Burgoon (Eds.), *Mass media and drug prevention: Classic and contemporary theories and research* (pp. 19–34). Mahwah, NJ: Lawrence Erlbaum Associates.

Wayne, S.J. (2008). *The road to the White House 2008: The politics of presidential elections (8th ed.).* Boston: Thomson Wadsworth.

Weaver, D.H. (1984). Media agenda-setting and public opinion: Is there a link? In R.N. Bostrom (Ed.), *Communication yearbook 8* (pp. 680–691). Beverly Hills, CA: Sage.

Weaver, D.H., Beam, R.A., Brownlee, B.J., Voakes, P.S., & Wilhoit, G.C. (2007). *The American journalist in the 21st century: U.S. news people at the dawn of a new millennium.* Mahwah, NJ: Erlbaum Associates.

Weimann, G. (1994). *The influentials: People who influence people.* Albany: State University of New York Press.

Wertheimer, F. (2012, June 14). Citizens United: Watergate redux. *Politico.* Online: http://www.politico.com/news/stories/0612/77436.html. (Accessed: July 24, 2012.)

West, D.M. (2010). *Air wars: Television advertising in election campaigns, 1952–2008 (5th ed.).* Washington, D.C.: CQ Press.

West, D.M. (2014). *Air wars: Television advertising and social media in election campaigns 1952–2012 (6th ed.).* Washington, D.C.: CQ Press.

Westen, D. (2007). *The political brain: The role of emotion in deciding the fate of the nation.* New York: Public Affairs.

Wexler, B.E., Adwan, S., & Bar-Tal, D. (2013, March 7). Trying to bridge the Mideast divide. *The New York Times* (Letter to the Editor), A22.

White, D.M. (1950). The "Gate Keeper": A case study in the selection of news. *Journalism Quarterly,* 27, 383–390.

White, T.H. (1962). *The making of the president 1960.* New York: Atheneum.

White, T.H. (1973). *The making of the president, 1972.* New York: Bantam.

Wilson, J.Q., & DiIulio, J.J., Jr. (2001). *American government: Institutions and policies (8th ed.).* Boston: Houghton Mifflin.

Winter, D. (2012, October 31). A face more careworn, a crowd less joyful. *The New York Times.* http://www.nytimes.com/interactive/2012/10/31/us/politics/damon-winter-obama-election-photos.html. (Accessed: July 3, 2013.)

Winter, J., & Eyal, C. (1981). Agenda-setting for the civil rights issue. *Public Opinion Quarterly,* 45, 376–383.

Wolffe, R. (2009). *Renegade: The making of a president.* New York: Crown Publishers.

Wolfsfeld, G. (2011). *Making sense of media and politics: Five principles in political communication.* New York: Routledge.

Wolfsfeld, G., Segev, E., & Sheafer, T. (2013). Social media and the Arab Spring: Politics comes first. *International Journal of Press/Politics, 18,* 115–137.

Wortham, J. (2012, October 7). Campaigns use social media to lure younger voters. *The New York Times.* Online: http://www.nytimes.com/2012/10/08/technology/campaigns-use-soci. . . (Accessed: September 22, 2013)

Wright, R. (2011). *Rock the casbah: Rage and rebellion across the Islamic world.* New York: Simon & Schuster.

Xenos, M.A., & Becker, A.B. (2009). Moments of Zen: Effects of *The Daily Show* on information seeking and political learning. *Political Communication, 26,* 317–332.

Xenos, M., & Foot, K. (2008). Not your father's Internet: The generation gap in online politics. In W.L. Bennett (Ed.), *Civic life online: Learning how digital media can engage youth* (pp. 51–70). Cambridge, MA: MIT Press.

Yaffa, J. (2012, February 26). The Kremlin's not laughing now. *The New York Times* (Sunday Review), 4.

Young, D.G., & Tisinger, R.M. (2006). Dispelling late-night myths: News consumption among late-night comedy viewers and the predictors of exposure to various late-night shows. *Press/Politics, 11,* 113–134.

Zajonc, R.B. (1968). Attitudinal effects of mere exposure. *Journal of Personality and Social Psychology Monographs Supplement, 9* (2, Pt. 2), 1–27.

Zaller, J. (2003). A new standard of news quality: Burglar alarms for the monitorial citizen. *Political Communication, 20*, 109–130.

Zarefsky, D. (1990). *Lincoln Douglas and slavery: In the crucible of public debate.* Chicago: University of Chicago Press.

Zeleny, J. (2012, August 11). Romney renews push to connect with voters and close empathy gap. *The New York Times*, A8.

Zeleny, J., & Rutenberg, J. (2008, August 17). For convention, Obama's image is all-American. *The New York Times.* Online: http://www.nytimes.com/2008/08/ 18/us/politics/18convention. html. (Accessed: September 22, 2013)

Zeleny, J., & Sussman, D. (2012a, August 1). New polls show Obama has edge in 3 large states. *The New York Times*, A1, A12.

Zernike, K. (2010). *Boiling mad: Inside Tea Party America.* New York: Times Books.

Zernike, K., & Rutenberg, J. (2004, August 20). Friendly fire: The birth of an anti-Kerry ad. *The New York Times.* Online: http://www.newyorktimes.com/2004/ 08/20/politics/ campaign/20swift.html. (Accessed: September 22, 2013)

Zukin, C., Keeter, S., Andolina, M., Jenkins, K., & Delli Carpini, M.X. (2006). *A new engagement? Political participation, civic life, and the changing American citizen.* New York: Oxford University Press.

Subject Index

Author Index

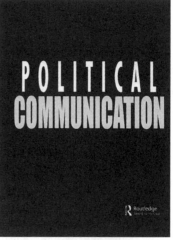

Making Sense of Media and Politics
Five Principles in Political Communication

Gadi Wolfsfeld

Politics is above all a contest, and the news media are the central arena for viewing that competition. One of the central concerns of political communication has to do with the myriad ways in which politics has an impact on the news media and the equally diverse ways in which the media influences politics. Both of these aspects in turn weigh heavily on the effects such political communication has on mass citizens.

In *Making Sense of Media and Politics*, Gadi Wolfsfeld introduces readers to the most important concepts that serve as a framework for examining the interrelationship of media and politics:

- political power can usually be translated into power over the news media
- when authorities lose control over the political environment they also lose control over the news
- there is no such thing as objective journalism (nor can there be)
- the media are dedicated more than anything else to telling a good story
- the most important effects of the news media on citizens tend to be unintentional and unnoticed.

By identifying these five key principles of political communication, the author examines those who package and send political messages, those who transform political messages into news, and the effect all this has on citizens. The result is a brief, engaging guide to help make sense of the wider world of media and politics and an essential companion to more in-depths studies of the field.

Hardback: 978-0-415-88522-5
Paperback: 978-0-415-88523-2
eBook: 978-0-203-83987-4

For ordering and further information please visit:

www.routledge.com

An Introduction to Political Communication, 5th Edition

Brian McNair

An Introduction to Political Communication introduces students to the complex relationship between politics, the media and democracy in the United Kingdom, United States and other contemporary societies. Brian McNair examines how politicians, trade unions, pressure groups, NGOs and terrorist organizations make use of the media.

Individual chapters look at political media and their effects, the work of political advertising, marketing and public relations, and the communicative practices of organizations at all levels, from grass-root campaigning through to governments and international bodies.

This fifth edition has been revised and updated to include:

- the 2008 US presidential election, and the early years of Barack Obama's term
- the MPs' expenses scandal in Britain, and the 2010 UK election campaign
- the growing role of bloggers and online pundits such as Guido Fawkes in the political agenda setting process
- the emergence of social media platforms such as Twitter, YouTube and Facebook, and their destabilizing impact on the management of political crises all over the world, including the Iranian pro-reform protests of July 2009 and the Israeli attack on the anti-blockade flotilla of May 2010
- the growing power of Wikileaks and other online information sources to challenge state control of classified information.

Hardback: 978-0-415-59643-5
Paperback: 978-0-415-59644-2
eBook: 978-0-203-82869-4

For ordering and further information please visit:

www.routledge.com

The Dynamics of Persuasion, 5th Edition
Communication and Attitudes in the 21st Century

Richard M. Perloff

With substantial revisions reflecting new research and changes in society, the fifth
edition of *The Dynamics of Persuasion* introduces students to major theories of
persuasion and attitudes, using theory as the key to unlock the mysteries of contemporary social influence. Organized in terms of major concepts, issues, and persuasion
contexts, the book offers a lucid introduction to the body of scholarly knowledge on
persuasion, up-to-date examples of persuasion in real life, and a thorough discussion
of the ethics of persuasion in contemporary society.

**This package includes a free one-year subscription to an enhanced Interactive
eTextbook**, complete with author-narrated chapter synopses, videos, exercises, flashcards, and more resources for instructors and students.

Key features of the interactive e-textbook:

- Anytime, anywhere access via VitalSource's Bookshelf; the most used eTextbook
  platform in the world
- End-of-chapter interactive exercises; multiple-choice exercises to encourage students
  to test their understanding of the key concepts
- Audio chapter introductions from the author
- Note taking and sharing functionalities
- Clickable definitions for key terms
- Hyperlinked further reading with links to key websites selected by the author
- A full color version of the text.

Pack – Book & Online: 978-0-415-50742-4

For ordering and further information please visit:

www.routledge.com

Campaigning for President 2012, 2nd Edition
Strategy and Tactics

Edited by Dennis W. Johnson

In this important and timely volume, Dennis W. Johnson has assembled an outstanding team of political scientists and political professionals to examine one of the fiercest and most closely fought presidential elections of our time.

Like its predecessor on the 2008 race, *Campaigning for President 2012: Strategy and Tactics* focuses on political management. It is written by both campaigns and elections scholars and practitioners, who highlight the role of political consultants and campaigns while also emphasizing the strategy and tactics employed by the candidates, the national political parties, and outside interests.

The contributors explore the general mood of the electorate in the 2012 election, the challenges Obama faced after his first term, the primaries, money, communication, the important issues of the election, and finally the election itself. This is the most comprehensive and broad treatment of the 2012 presidential election available.

Hardback: 978-0-415-84299-0
Paperback: 978-0-415-84300-3
eBook: 978-0-203-75814-4

For ordering and further information please visit:

www.routledge.com